ADVENTURES IN SHONDALAND

ADVENTURES IN SHONDALAND

Identity Politics and the Power of Representation

EDITED BY

RACHEL ALICIA GRIFFIN
AND MICHAELA D. E. MEYER

RUTGERS UNIVERSITY PRESS
New Brunswick, Camden, and Newark, New Jersey, and London

Library of Congress Cataloging-in-Publication Data

Names: Griffin, Rachel Alicia, editor. | Meyer, Michaela D.E., editor.
Title: Adventures in Shondaland : identity politics and the power of representation /
    edited by Rachel Alicia Griffin, Michaela D.E. Meyer.
Description: New Brunswick : Rutgers University Press, 2018.
Identifiers: LCCN 2018004645| ISBN 9780813596327 (hardback) |
    ISBN 9780813596310 (paperback)
Subjects: LCSH: Rhimes, Shonda—Criticism and interpretation. | ShondaLand
    (Firm)—History. | Women television producers and directors—United States. |
    African American television producers and directors. | African American women
    screenwriters. | Television broadcasting—Social aspects—United States. |
    BISAC: PERFORMING ARTS / Television / History & Criticism.
Classification: LCC PN1992.4.R515 A38 2018 | DDC 791.4502/32—dc23
LC record available at https://lccn.loc.gov/2018004645

A British Cataloging-in-Publication record for this book is available
from the British Library.

www.rutgersuniversitypress.org

Manufactured in the United States of America

To each of the loves in my life; I am grateful, grateful, grateful.

—Rachel

Cristina Yang was the voice I'd been waiting for: "If you want crappy things to stop happening to you, then stop accepting crap and demand something more." Shonda Rhimes notes—"By spending a full hour with Cristina once a week, you were likely spending more time with her than you spent with most people in your life. That relationship was real." I am eternally grateful for that relationship and the courage it provided. She inspired me to make substantial changes that enriched my life more than I can say. I am living, instead of dreaming, my dreams.

—Michaela

Last, but certainly not least, we dedicate this collection to John T. Warren. Before his death, John suggested to each of us separately that we should meet and be brilliant in each other's company. Soon after he passed away, we took John's advice and had dinner together. Needless to say, he was right. Our collaboration is just one example of the many works in Communication that simply would not exist without John's infinite efforts to mentor and inspire.

—Rachel & Michaela

CONTENTS

Introduction: Riding Shondaland's Rollercoasters:
Critical Cultural Television Studies in the 21st Century   1
MICHAELA D. E. MEYER AND RACHEL ALICIA GRIFFIN

PART I: QUALITY TELEVISION'S CULTURAL DOMINANCE:
THE AUTEUR COMES TO TELEVISION STUDIES

1   Trauma, Spin, and Murder: The Carnival Spectacle
in Shondaland   23
RICHARD G. JONES JR. AND EMILY VAJJALA

2   Wounded Detachments, Differential Alliances:
Beyond Identity and Telos in Shondaland's Heterotopia   42
JOAN FABER MCALISTER

3   Abortion in Shondaland: Daring Departures from
Oppressive Industry Conventions   60
JESSICA L. FURGERSON

4   Soundtracking Shondaland: Televisual Identity Mapped
through Music   79
JENNIFER BILLINSON AND MICHAELA D. E. MEYER

PART II: SHONDALAND'S PARADOXICAL IDENTITY
POLITICS AND THE FANTASTICAL "POST"

5   Race (Lost and Found) in Shondaland: The Rise of
Multiculturalism in Prime-Time Network Television   101
JADE PETERMON

6   Emb(Race)ing Visibility: Callie Torres's (Im)Perfect
Operation of Bisexuality on *Grey's Anatomy*   120
SHADEE ABDI AND BERNADETTE MARIE CALAFELL

7   The Problematics of Postracial Colorblindness: Exploring
Cristina Yang's Asianness in *Grey's Anatomy*   138
STEPHANIE L. YOUNG AND VINCENT PHAM

8   Interracial Intimacies: From Shondaland to the Postracial
Promised Land   156
MYRA WASHINGTON AND TINA M. HARRIS

PART III: CONSUMPTION, ETHICS, AND MORALITY:
SHONDALAND FANDOM AS CULTURAL MEANING MAKING

9   #BlackLivesMatter on *Scandal*: Analyzing Divergent Fan
     Reactions to "The Lawn Chair" Episode   179
     MARK P. ORBE

10   Blurring Production Boundaries with Fan Empowerment:
     Scandal as Social Television   197
     MARY INGRAM-WATERS AND LESLIE BALDERAS

11   Media Criticism and Morality Policing on Twitter:
     Fan Responses to *How to Get Away with Murder*   214
     MELISSA AMES

12   Dying for the Next Episode: Living and Working within
     Shondaland's Medical Universe   235
     SEAN SWENSON

     Notes on Contributors   253
     Index   259

ADVENTURES IN SHONDALAND

INTRODUCTION

Riding Shondaland's Rollercoasters: Critical Cultural Television Studies in the 21st Century

MICHAELA D. E. MEYER AND
RACHEL ALICIA GRIFFIN

Shonda Rhimes is one of the most powerful industry players in contemporary U.S. network television. For over a decade, she dominated the American Broadcasting Company's (ABC) Thursday night lineup. Branded "Thank God It's Thursday" (TGIT), a play on ABC's marketing for TGIF in the 1990s, Rhimes's programs can draw same-day audiences of thirty-seven million viewers.[1] Globally acclaimed as creator and showrunner of *Grey's Anatomy* (ABC 2005–present), *Private Practice* (ABC 2007–2013), and *Scandal* (ABC 2012–2018), Rhimes's production company—Shondaland—is also responsible for *Off The Map* (ABC 2011), *How to Get Away with Murder* (ABC 2014–present), *The Catch* (ABC 2015–2017), *Still Star-Crossed* (ABC 2017–present), *For the People* (ABC 2018–present), and *Station 19* (ABC 2018–present).[2] Holding firmly at fourth place in television broadcast network rankings, ABC's success with scripted series rather than "inflated averages from sports coverage" is almost single-handedly attributed to Rhimes's televisual artistry.[3] Complimenting her success on "the most lucrative night of programming on TV," network entertainment president Paul Lee says Rhimes "has managed to maintain an intimacy with her audience—a genuine connection at a mass scale."[4] Operating under an exclusive, mutually beneficial contract between ABC and Shondaland, Rhimes has been described as "Disney's Primetime Savior," an "indispensable creator," and an "uberproducer."[5] It is common knowledge in the television industry that "there are few sure bets in television unless you're talking about Shonda Rhimes."[6] This "sure thing" will come to an end for ABC soon, as Rhimes recently announced signing an exclusive deal with Netflix following the conclusion of her exclusive contract with ABC in 2018. Commenting on the shift, Rhimes says that her move to Netflix is "based on my vision for myself as a storyteller and for the evolution of my company," and offers "the opportunity to build a vibrant new storytelling home for writers with the unique creative freedom and instantaneous global reach provided by Netflix's singular sense of innovation."[7]

The inspiration for *Adventures in Shondaland: Identity Politics and the Power of Representation* rests in the complex cultural moment characterized by Rhimes's meteoric rise to stardom, her reign (or cultural appointment) as television's diversity queen, and Shondaland's almost universally lauded melodramatic narratives. In essence, Rhimes and Shondaland present a compelling case study for illuminating key issues in critical/cultural studies and television/media studies. From a critical/cultural perspective, Shondaland is a particularly provocative site for analyses that are attentive to identity politics, postidentity politics, power, and representation because Rhimes and her team exercise their creative license to address innumerable societal issues such as: adoption, parenthood, abortion, infidelity, organ donation, infertility, bereavement and death, beauty and body politics, mental and physical health, sexual violence, mass violence, natural disasters, and war. That Rhimes leads the charge in doing so with intentionally diverse characters and storylines that center, for example, on interracial friendships and relationships, LGBTIQ (lesbian, gay, bisexual, transgender, intersex, queer) relationships and parenting, the impact of disability on familial and work dynamics, and complex representations of womanhood sets her distinctly apart from her peers, most of whom overwhelmingly identify as white and male. Indicative of the television industry's norm since the advent of quality television, of the forty-two showrunners for new 2017–2018 programming on the Big Five networks (ABC, FOX, CBS, NBC, and The CW), 90 percent were white and 71 percent were male.[8]

Describing her marginalized positionality as a black woman in an overwhelmingly white and male industry in *Year of Yes: How to Dance It Out, Stand in the Sun, and Be Your Own Person*, Rhimes says, "I am what I have come to call an F.O.D.—a First. Only. Different. . . . We all have that same weary look in our eyes. The one that wishes people would stop thinking it remarkable that we can be great at what we do while black, while Asian, while a woman, while Latino, while gay, while a paraplegic, while deaf . . . when you are a F.O.D., you are saddled with that extra burden of responsibility—whether you want it or not."[9] Rhimes's explicit politicization of her positionality in conjunction with her willingness to align herself with marginalized subgroups she doesn't identify with provides a rich site for scholars to more holistically and complexly theorize how identity politics currently operates in U.S. televisual landscapes. Academic scholarship that situates micro and macro manifestations of intersectionality as central to critical/cultural media analysis remains emergent in the communication discipline, and Shondaland's work provides opportunities to explore what is currently at stake in power-laden landscapes controversially deemed postracial, postfeminist, and postidentity politics.[10] Thus, a key purpose of this collection is to address the ways Rhimes's positionality and Shondaland's creative work exists within a particular cultural moment in which the significance and signification of identity politics is being fiercely debated. Taken together, theorizations of television representation and intersectional identity politics expand traditional definitions of what critical/cultural scholarship looks like and does.

Beyond identity politics, Shondaland's work also exists in a particular cultural moment in media studies. In the past forty years, critical/cultural media scholars have firmly entrenched an academic standoff between text-centered and audience-oriented approaches to media content.[11] Although the debate continues, academic critiques of television still tend to privilege rhetorical and textual approaches, particularly in the communication discipline. These approaches often overlook that "economically advantaged, and highly professionalized" traditional media conglomerates control the production process and that these industries are driven by capitalist ideologies.[12] Moreover, audience-oriented approaches often fall short of addressing contemporary neoliberal discourses of audience sovereignty—whereby "enlightened" cultural subjects select and consume "quality" media products, thereby producing profit for large media corporations.[13] Instead, fan studies that valorize "engagement" and "cultural resistance" are far more common academic contributions to television criticism. Currently, television studies research is gradually shifting toward more synergized analyses that offer complex interrogations of the multifaceted interrelationship between producers, texts, and consumers. In his seminal work on encoding and decoding, Stuart Hall turned critical scholarship toward interrogating media as a process of text, audience, and production. Instead of viewing these as separate points of entry into popular discourse, he argued that mediated "discourse must then be translated—transformed again—into social practice if the circuit is to be both completed and effective. If no 'meaning' is taken, there can be no 'consumption' . . . the event must become a 'story' before it can become a *communicative* event."[14] Although Hall is frequently referenced in television scholarship, we rarely see academic work that theorizes and positions televisual content across and among these dimensions. From a television studies perspective, this collection theorizes the contemporary complexity of issues such as quality discourses; increased audience access to producers, actors, and production decisions; and the rise of audience sovereignty through digital and social media.

To appeal to scholars working in critical/cultural and media studies, this book is organized in three distinct sections, each representing key theorizations of Shondaland shows as case studies in both academic circles. First, as editors and authors, we address the traditional "production" element of media studies through the rise of quality television and the television auteur. This section complicates how we understand production in academic contexts, encouraging scholars to embrace television producers as auteurs who are part of interpretive communities with specific norms, ideals, and visions of quality. Second, we engage intersecting identity politics through the numerous colorblind, postracial, and, more broadly, postidentity strategies that permeate contemporary media discourses to discipline diversity. In doing so, we expose a myriad of pedagogical messages and meanings represented by Shondaland's televisual texts. Finally, we expand scholarship on audiences by moving away from singular arguments of resistance and fandom toward intricate interrogations of layered audience meaning making. This section specifically highlights how audience consumption is framed by technology and how the meaning audiences create from television images is contested cultural space. Taken together, these sections illuminate the synergistic shifts between producing, representing, and consuming media. Blurring the traditional boundaries between production, text, and audience, the chapters in each section thematically cut across foci, mechanisms, and dynamics that shape and shade the landscape of television in its entirety. We expand on each of these sections below by outlining key aspects of the academic argument each section addresses as well as the contributions each chapter offers individually.

QUALITY TELEVISION'S CULTURAL DOMINANCE: THE AUTEUR COMES TO TELEVISION STUDIES

Our first section interrogates the rise of the television auteur during an era of quality television. Historically, the academic study of film and television has occurred along specific and divisive lines based on available media technologies. Early on in television scholarship, academics argued that television's small screen, lower resolution, lack of technological access, and the embedded nature of advertising rendered television substantially and significantly different than film.[15] As a result, television developed its own specific visual and aesthetic style to suit these limitations of the medium. However, as technology improved, particularly with advances such as digitization, "the living room gradually transformed into a home cinema and a 'cinematic' visual quality became ever more important in television production and the discourses surrounding and validating the medium."[16] Additionally, changes in broadcast delivery, new systems of production and distribution, and widespread economic restructuring based on branding and market segmentation significantly transformed the way television producers and directors approach, disseminate, and fund their art.[17]

Since the turn of the twenty-first century, industry interest in "quality television"—most commonly associated with long-form, scripted television drama—has expanded. The rise of "quality" dramas that twist or combine genre conventions indicate that genres operate as cultural, discursive categories across television industries, audiences, public policy, critics, and historical contexts.[18] As a result, televised narratives that were once firmly entrenched in a particular genre or narrative form are taking on more postmodern, hybridized qualities. Simultaneously, the rise of subscription television services (such as HBO, Showtime, and more recently, Netflix, Hulu, and Amazon) diversified the market for scripted television alongside technological advances in live-streaming making content more readily available to viewers. Currently, cultural calls to "cut the cable TV cord" and "ditch cable" are commonplace, and audiences can more easily customize their viewing experience by tailoring it to specific networks or types of networks.[19] Thus, cultural studies of television have increasingly moved away from the more traditional political economy arguments concerning ownership of media outlets and conglomerates toward arguments concerning producers of televisual content. Due to these changes, contemporary television producers (such as Dick Wolf, Chuck Lorre, Greg Berlanti, and now Shonda Rhimes) are more visibly and audibly recognizable to their respective audiences than ever before in the history of television.

The cultural dynamics articulated above have resulted in a dramatic transformation of the day-to-day logistics of the television industry. The surge of scripted original TV shows in the United States alone was well over four hundred by the end of 2016, indicating that "L.A. may have more showrunners than taco trucks."[20] Showrunning is now television's counterpart to the film auteur. Film auteurs are typically regarded as individuals whose influence and artistic control is so profound that they give a film its personal and unique stamp. Auteur theory centers predominantly on the technical competence of the director, a director's distinguishable personality and signature, and the interior range of meanings produced by the director's work.[21] In television, the role of showrunner—"a position once so rarefied and coveted that you'd have been hard pressed to name 50 people who held it"—has become a staple of producing quality, scripted television series.[22] Describing the industry uptick, Rhimes says, "Now that the television industry has exploded and there are 300 percent more television shows than there were, looking for writers, looking for everything else, it's hard out here."[23]

For Rhimes and Shondaland, the shift from television's analog form to its new era of digitization and the proliferation of opportunities for auteurs is incredibly important. Her renowned stature as a showrunner is undisputed in the industry, yet scholarship examining Rhimes's work is limited almost exclusively to critiques of her "color-blind casting" policies and their significance to theorizations of race in critical television studies.[24] While Rhimes's endorsement of colorblindness is an important aspect of her auteurist practice to examine, this focus, often narrowly predicated upon the black/white racial binary, is limiting. Cognizant of this tendency, *Adventures in Shondaland* authors theorize Rhimes's role as an auteur by broadening the scope of critical/cultural television research. The four chapters in this section deconstruct Rhimes's signature showrunning style and interrogate the implications of "Shondafication" in the television industry and, more broadly, U.S. American society. Since television showrunners are now comparable to film auteurs, these chapters respond to the need for critical/cultural scholarship to account for showrunners' specific, stylized creative visions.

Richard G. Jones Jr. and Emily Vajjala open this section by analyzing Rhimes as an auteur through a Bakhtinian lens. They find that Rhimes's signature style across three shows (*Grey's Anatomy, Scandal,* and *How to Get Away with Murder*) reflects Bakhtin's conceptualization of the carnival through ritual spectacle, excess, and grotesque realism which, in turn, enacts repetitive cycles of degeneration and regeneration. Anchored by Rhimes's Disney-inspired production company name "Shondaland," signaling an amusement park, they thoroughly expose Shondaland's "carnivalesque" storytelling visually encapsulated by the production company's fiery rollercoaster logo. For Jones and Vajjala, the art of Shondaland is a carnival, similar to those in the Middle Ages, that provides respite from hierarchical domination and normativity through highly stylized and exaggerated narratives. As the carnival master, Rhimes directs attention to cultural issues via "rollercoaster" rides (i.e., Shondaland shows) replete with excitement, awe, and panic. More somberly, Joan Faber McAlister argues that *How to Get Away with Murder* (also referred to as *HTGAWM*) constructs a Foucauldian heterotopia for viewers. She argues that the show produces "shocking storylines" in which wounded and flawed characters elicit empathy and forgiveness from fans—this too is another key element of Rhimes's signature style. Theorizing the complex aftermath of audience identification with villainous characters targeted by misogyny and bigotry, McAlister argues that *HTGAWM* offers an opportunity for "radical reflexivity" when "conventions such as rule and exception, normality and deviance, center and margin, good and evil" are overturned in favor of a world so complex that yearning for justice in response to unjust intersecting oppressions is too simplistic.

The two remaining chapters in this section hone in on specific facets of Rhimes's signature style that challenge contemporary television industry norms. Jessica L. Furgerson examines representations of abortion, contending that Shondaland's narrative foregrounding of abortion in several shows (*Grey's Anatomy, Private Practice,* and *Scandal*) illustrates women's diverse responses to unplanned pregnancy. From an industry perspective, Furgerson argues that narratives of abortion have been historically taboo on television unless addressed through a lens largely confined to patriarchal logics. Conversely, Shondaland's frequent and complicated abortion narratives "daringly depart from previous portrayals in terms of style and substance." More specifically, Rhimes's work exposes the ideological constraints on televised representations of reproductive choices and expands cultural discourse about these life experiences. While Furgerson's chapter is specific to pregnancy discourses, it also showcases how Rhimes uses narrative form to spotlight an urgent cultural issue—particularly in the wake of recent political efforts to defund Planned Parenthood and diminish women's access to birth control and abortion services. On a different cultural note, Jennifer Billinson and Michaela

D. E. Meyer examine Shondaland through the lens of popular music and soundtracking. The proliferation of technology over the past two decades exposed the infrastructure of popular music production and distribution as unsustainable in the present-day age of digitization. Billinson and Meyer unravel how Shondaland's innovative use of popular music within televisual narrative produces a key element of her signature style: using music to heighten emotionality, foster melodramatic complexity, and empower fringe recording artists. Through an examination of how storylines are soundtracked in three different series (*Grey's Anatomy*, *Scandal*, and *How to Get Away with Murder*), Billinson and Meyer identify how the productive synergies between television and popular music blur understandings of context and medium.

SHONDALAND'S PARADOXICAL IDENTITY POLITICS AND THE FANTASTICAL "POST"

This section catechizes the role Shonda Rhimes and Shondaland narratives play in conversations about intersectional identity politics and the critical/cultural impetus to challenge assertions that the U.S. and global world are "post" the need for meaningful considerations of identities, power dynamics, and systemic oppressions (i.e., "post" erroneously conveys that society is beyond and/or has transcended concerns of years past). Alongside being exasperated by the reductive attention paid to her positionality as an African American woman and declaring "I really hate the word *diversity*," as a self-proclaimed F.O.D. role model Rhimes consistently expresses frustration with the lack of diversity in the television industry which, in turn, necessitates F.O.D. role models and refutes postracialism.[25] Aligning with her frustration, we contend that her positionality as a black woman in Hollywood is monumentally important—both in her presence at the showrunning table and in representational politics within Shondaland's narratives. According to the *Hollywood Diversity Report*, racial and ethnic minorities comprise only 4.2 percent of show creators of broadcast comedies and dramas; additionally, mirroring the severe lack of diversity among showrunners even as opportunities for television production skyrocket, the vast majority of television writing staffs have 10 percent or fewer racial and ethnic minorities.[26] Utilizing race as an example to underscore ineffectual homogeneity, the domination of media by white industry professionals creates a lack of representation in both the creation of television content and character performance in television narratives. Describing the interdependent relationship between the two when asked how to more productively diversify the industry in accordance with the real world, Rhimes says, "It's who is telling the stories . . . because the people telling the stories are the people deciding who you see onscreen, they're the people who are deciding who are in the writer's rooms, they're the people deciding on the crew."[27] Quite simply, yet provocatively, Rhimes describes her own showrunning approach as normalizing rather than diversifying; she says, "I am making TV look like the world looks. . . . I am NORMALIZING television."[28]

Specific to the intersections of race and gender, Tara-Lynne Pixley argues, "In its more than 60 years of national and global reach, television's stereotypical images of blackness and womanhood have been both pervasive and unrelenting."[29] Highlighting Rhimes's determined acumen to address diversity and representation, Moffitt, Puff, and Jackson situate *Scandal* as an emblem of Shondaland's venture to set a progressive example and catalyze industry change.[30] In fact, before the Kerry Washington–led *Scandal*, a black woman had not headlined a network television series since *Get Christie Love* in 1974.[31] By coupling the creation of roles and opportunities with the intention to diversify (i.e., normalize) the industry, Rhimes's success has inspired a television market largely driven by economic copycatting. Competing networks and Rhimes's showrunning peers, upon witnessing the success of Shondaland shows, began launching series with lead characters of color, for example, *Jane the Virgin* (CW 2014–present), *Empire* (FOX 2015–present), and *Extant* (CBS 2014–2015). ABC's *Quantico* (2015–present) created by Joshua Safran, for instance, is described in the *New York Times* as "*Homeland* meets the Shonda Rhimes ouevre, with the ensemble casting and sexual tension of *Grey's Anatomy* plus the flashbacks and mentor-mentee dynamic of *How to Get Away With Murder* and the Olivia Pope-like family baggage of *Scandal*," ultimately perceived as "a Shonda Rhimesian terrorism drama that Ms. Rhimes didn't make."[32] While ABC and its parent conglomerate, the Walt Disney Company, have astutely heralded Rhimes's creative vision to generate profitable representational equality and opportunities for people of color working in Hollywood, other networks have lagged far behind. Exemplary of this stark contrast, leading network CBS (Columbia Broadcast System) debuted six new scripted television shows starring six white male lead protagonists in 2016.[33]

Scholars interrogating Rhimes's creative work and Shondaland production practices from a critical/cultural perspective, however, have not been nearly as celebratory as popular media commentary on Rhimes's influential representational politics. Maryann Erigha explains that Rhimes's success is preconditioned on the same path of success suggested for most black creative workers in Hollywood—"Be black but not too black."[34] Amy Long is even more critical, claiming Rhimes simultaneously works "to erase the specificity and the multiple, intersecting power relations that produce people of color's varied experiences of marginalization and to reproduce racist and sexist assumptions embedded in many, less 'socially aware' popular culture forms."[35] Kristen Warner takes it up another notch by leveling a critique not only at Rhimes's creative work, but the means by which she utilizes normative industry logics to garner Shondaland's success: "Rhimes's blindcasting works to acknowledge difference in ways that will cause the least amount of discomfort to white audiences while providing an illusion that under liberal individualism, the marketplace will do right by historically marginalized individuals. This is a post-racial network world indeed."[36] While well-grounded in critical/cultural theory and most certainly offering well-founded readings of Rhimes's work and Shondaland, these critiques do not dig deeply into intersectional identity politics, particularly in theorizing the overlap between context (entertainment industry), intersecting marginalized identities (black femininity), and creative product (television narratives).

Perhaps the most complex academic reading of Rhimes to date comes from Ralina Joseph, who argues that Rhimes is unique in that she utilizes strategic ambiguity to redefine black respectability politics. Joseph argues, "Strategic ambiguity is not silence or evasion; it's a choice to take on a certain amount of risk, to play with fire, to appropriate something that is used *against* you and make it work *for* you."[37] Strategic ambiguity is especially essential to scrutinizing Rhimes because her intersecting marginalized identities as black and female converge with her esteemed status in Hollywood, wealth, and tokenized hypervisibility in the public sphere. Joseph explains that black men (such as *Grey's Anatomy*'s Jesse Williams) are granted discursive space in popular culture to "speak truth to power" in ways that black women are not (very often) allowed to occupy.[38] In this context, wherein hooks' articulation of "imperialist white-supremacist capitalist patriarchal culture" remains potent as "an expression of 21st century Black respectability politics" even for black women at the top of their professions, "strategic ambiguity functions as a sometimes conflated, sometimes confounding, always post-racial Black feminist resistance."[39] In the case of Rhimes and other black celebrity women (e.g., Michelle Obama, Tyra Banks, Oprah Winfrey, Beyoncé Knowles, Janelle Monáe, Laverne Cox, Serena Williams, Lupita Nyong'o, Kerry Washington, Viola Davis), strategic ambiguity productively "knits together the contradictions of resistance in the post-racial-meets-#BlackLivesMatter moment by featuring two sometimes contradictory elements—colorblindness, and race-womanhood (or "wokeness")—with an exceptionally feminist grace."[40] In other words, identities, politics, and identity politics meaningfully coexist in ambivalent cultural contexts in which positionalities, values, and actions appear adversarial but, in actuality, fluidly function in service of progressive ideals.

Understanding Rhimes as an auteur who deliberately produces narratives that address marginalization is fundamental to theorizing the cultural impact she has leveraged via Shondaland. Although criticisms of her work tend to focus on the representation of black women, the range and depth of Rhimes's creative representations warrants more comprehensive critical scrutiny. As such, the chapters in this section build upon existing scholarship to widen our scholarly focus in a postidentity politics landscape. Anchoring this section, Jade Petermon provides crucial historical and political grounding for understanding the rise of postidentity politics in contemporary U.S. American society. Her careful mapping of how the television industry attends to race in tandem with presidential discourses and political trends illustrates just how entwined television is with cultural sensibilities.

To theorize the rise of Rhimes and Shondaland, Petermon confronts the ideological alignment between neoliberalism and "multicultural colorblind television" to craft a cautionary tale addressing the United States' longstanding failure to sustain systemic change in favor of equality.

While Petermon's opening analysis approaches the creation of television text from a metatheoretical perspective, the other three chapters in this section attend to specific representations of (post)identity politics or positionality within Shondaland shows. Given Rhimes's work as creator, showrunner, and writer of *Grey's Anatomy*, coupled with its impressive fourteen-year run, *Grey's* offers a variety of characters that make key statements about postidentity politics. Shadee Abdi and Bernadette Marie Calafell offer an intersectional analysis of *Grey's* character Calliope Iphegenia "Callie" Torres, exposing how the show tempers Callie's Latina positionality with her bisexuality to appease normative audiences. Through a careful analysis of Callie's storylines, Abdi and Calafell expose how Callie, being paired with only white romantic partners, renders her bisexuality more normatively palatable at the intersections of race, ethnicity, religion, gender, and sexuality. The authors persuasively argue that Callie's close proximity to whiteness gives Shondaland leeway to pursue storylines that complicate representational queer politics at the expense of progressive representational racial politics and to the benefit of whiteness. Ultimately, they argue that "Callie's narrative is less about the empowerment of bisexual women of color and more about normalizing discourses of white (patriarchal) queerness."

Stephanie L. Young and Vincent Pham continue a critique of *Grey's Anatomy* by analyzing Cristina Yang's character. Similar to Abdi and Calafell's intersectional approach, Young and Pham anchor their critique of Cristina's representation through her positionality as a Korean American Jewish woman. Yet, the authors resist the dominant cultural impulse to simply regard Sandra Oh's character as one of the most striking representations of Asian American womanhood on prime-time television, an outlook amplified by Rhimes herself who regards Cristina as "the walking validation of my dreams."[41] Instead, they position Cristina as an "honorary white" character stereotypically portrayed in accordance with model minority and Dragon Lady tropes. They also question the appropriative convenience of Cristina's Korean American Jewishness being taken for granted in the series until she is called upon to "triangulate whiteness and blackness with Asianness caught in the middle." Young and Pham caution that when characters of color are consumed by whiteness' commitment to postracial colorblindness, there is a "missed opportunity to re-envision and further complicate" contemporary identity politics. Myra Washington and Tina M. Harris extend these observations to Shondaland's newer shows *Scandal* and *How to Get Away with Murder*, both featuring a lead African American woman. While public commentary has focused almost exclusively on these representations as positive gains for black women, Washington and Harris critically examine how each protagonist is represented in romantic interracial relationships with white men (Olivia Pope and Fitzgerald Grant and Olivia and Jake Ballard on *Scandal,* and Annalise Keating and Sam Keating on *How to Get Away with Murder*). Compellingly, the authors couple these interracial intimacies with Rhimes's interviews and speeches for insight into Shondaland's casting, representation, and production processes. "Taken altogether, these elements form a transdiscursive body of work that provides signs, tropes, character and narrative archetypes, norms, and structures for other showrunners to replicate Shondaland's highly successful signature formula." Herein lies the problem Washington and Harris expose: what appear to be subversive representations of interracial romance ultimately function to "make audiences feel good about society" through colorblind and postracial logics that are masked as progressive and therefore are mistakenly celebrated and formulaically reproduced in the industry.

CONSUMPTION, ETHICS, AND MORALITY: SHONDALAND FANDOM AS CULTURAL MEANING MAKING

The third and final section expands and critically interrogates the positionality of audiences in contemporary television criticism. Although the terms *audience* and *fan* are not always used interchangeably in academic work, when examining cultural discourse surrounding Shondaland's shows, it is clear that audiences are largely comprised of loyal fans. Thus, considering the role that audience dynamics plays is necessary for theorizing Shondaland's cultural footprint as a production company. In early television scholarship, there was a distinction between film as a "high" form of media art whereas television was deemed a "low" form of mass consumer culture. As a result, historically, studies of television fans were often linked to theorizations of resistance—television viewers were eschewed as evading the cultural lure of "high" entertainment and painted as those who enjoyed the simpler pleasures a "low" medium had to offer. John Fiske conceptualized fans as those individuals "associated with the cultural tastes of subordinated formations of the people, particularly those disempowered by any combination of gender, age, class and race."[42] In this vein, as a leading fan studies scholar, Henry Jenkins championed fans as useful interpretive communities that cocreate "collective intelligence" as a means of cultivating collective strategies of resistance.[43] Thus, academic studies of fandom often argue that fans produce "a purposeful political intervention" allowing them to evade "dominant ideologies," and leverage the tools needed to "rigorously defend fan communities against their ridicule in the mass media and by non-fans."[44]

    With the rise of the internet and digital technologies, the focus on studying fans as cohesive audiences shifted away from this resistant, optimistic, and liberated positionality. Instead of positioning fandom as an utterly emancipatory cultural practice, several scholars began arguing that fan communities are far more likely to recreate cultural distinctions and social hierarchies within their communities than to imagine a world unfettered by hegemonic constraints.[45] This shift—one from audiences as politically motivated, savvy social-activists to individuals still trapped within cultural hierarchies—ultimately opened a third, more nuanced space for audience studies. Several critical/cultural theorists have noted a rise in neoliberalist logics that insist "individuals can and should be responsible for themselves," and that the freedoms of embracing this responsibility are concretely linked to discourses that favor individual agency and private acts of consumption within a capitalist economy.[46] When mapped onto contemporary television production practices, this shift manifests as a rhetoric of "audience sovereignty" whereby audiences have incredible amounts of power to shape and control production decisions through the collective and consumptive power of supporting profitable television ventures.[47] As a result of this unparalleled lifeline to producers of media largely generated by digitization and social media, television content is not merely a textual artifact. Ergo, television production is not simply about the creation of televisual texts alone, but a webbed process of creating and sharing meaning among audience stakeholders.[48] In other words, the synergy between media producers, their audiences, and the impact that relationship has on shaping the content and meaning of television texts is substantially enhanced in the age of digital media under neoliberalist logic.

Within this audience context, Rhimes's interactions with fans, along with fan interactions with a multitude of Shondaland creators, producers, actors, and other fans, strongly contributes to the success of the shows. In broadcast television, the shows most watched by women tend to be the most watched overall, and media companies often implicitly (and sometimes explicitly) privilege audiences who are affluent, highly educated, socially liberal, urban, and mostly white.[49] *Grey's Anatomy*, *Scandal*, and *How to Get Away with Murder*, in particular, draw large audiences with high degrees of crossover into these desirable advertising demographics. Indicative of Shondaland's appeal and success, in 2017, a 30-second advertisement on the long-running *Grey's Anatomy* cost $184,273; on *Scandal* it cost $151,177; and on *How to Get Away with Murder*, $145,772.[50] Moreover, the fact that Rhimes's work is melodramatic in construction adds complexity to the role audience response plays because "melodramatic TV is part and parcel of a never-ending cycle of consumerism within an eternal postmodern present."[51] Shondaland's melodramas offer viewers the opportunity to consume multiple, manifold narratives saturated with potent insights into ethics and morality set in the powerful social institutions of medicine, law, and politics. Subsequently, it is imperative that an examination of audience interpretations and reactions to Shondaland shows view television culture as a "historically specific set of institutionally embedded relations of government in which forms of thought and conduct of extended populations are targeted for transformation—partly via the extension through the social body of forms, techniques and regimens of aesthetic and intellectual culture in relation to discourses of moral regulation."[52]

To date, while scholarship analyzing Shondaland's narratives from a textual perspective has appeared steadily, fan studies are almost nonexistent. Providing an important foray into the positionality of audiences in relation to Shondaland shows, Apryl Williams and Vanessa Gonlin offer an analysis of fans' Twitter use surrounding *How to Get Away with Murder*. They avoid highly theoretical interpretations of fan behavior in favor of articulating "second screening" through Twitter use as a space where fans "demand a more multifaceted depiction of Black women in media."[53] Building upon this important early observation, the chapters in this section push the boundaries of fan studies by interrogating fandom as a site of interpretive labor that may or may not attend to issues of social justice and injustice.

This section begins with two essays questioning the role of audience sovereignty in contemporary fan studies. Mark P. Orbe's carefully crafted analysis of *Scandal's* polemic "The Lawn Chair" episode exposes how a televisual representation aired during the height of the Black Lives Matter movement provided a key "fictional" site for audiences to negotiate historical transgressions, contemporary tensions, and identity politics. By analyzing responses posted on *Scandal's* official Facebook page through the lens of standpoints and social locations, Orbe maps how audiences link the episode's portrayal of racialized police brutality and protest on television to real world discourses and experiences. Ironically, many fans were upset that a show about politics had "political views" about race. This frustration, often directed at Rhimes personally, illustrates significant challenges regarding audience sovereignty in that some viewers welcome "getting political" while others want their media consumption to remain fiction. Orbe concludes that "fans' Facebook comments reflect how one episode is capable of signifying multiple meanings for different individuals," and calls for *Scandal* to embrace "radical polysemy" rather than the show's current approach of sporadically politicizing race amid its overarching commitment to colorblindness.

Mary Ingram-Waters and Leslie Balderas extend Orbe's thread by examining *Scandal* fans on a different platform—Twitter. In recent years, Twitter has become an essential component of real-time television viewing, with producers and creators establishing official hashtags for following conversations about television episodes, storylines, and series. Ingram-Waters and Balderas explain that this new era of "social television" connects fans in more immediate and tangible ways, and offers fans the ability to directly interact with industry professionals including writers, directors, and actors. Rhimes and her *Scandal* team innovatively live-tweeting to engage fans during broadcast episodes elevated ABC's TGIT lineup to become "the gold standard" for social television via Twitter.[54] Ingram-Waters and Balderas illustrate how Twitter functions as a contested space where viewers negotiate meaning and advocate for creative changes in the series' storylines. As an exemplar of their argument, they examine a particular instance where the producers generated "#SaveJake?" to gauge viewers' reactions to *Scandal*'s season 5 finale. Viewers hoping for Jake's exit were critical of the ideological preference revealed in the hashtag and responded with a competing tag, "#DieJakeDie." This type of "talking back" to industry players has become elemental to social television, yet Ingram-Waters and Balderas caution that despite the promise of shared influence between industry actors and fans, social television "does not deliver a democratization of creative inputs." In other words, media industries will allow audiences to *feel* important and reap the benefits of Twitter fans' "valuable unpaid labor," but creative decisions rest conclusively within the industry.

The final two chapters in our collection examine discourses of morality and ethics in relation to audiences specifically and television viewing more generally. Melissa Ames examines the highly successful *How to Get Away with Murder*. Similar to Ingram-Waters and Balderas, Ames is concerned with viewers' "second-screening," or multiple viewing practices in conjunction with consumption of television narratives. Ames argues that the emergence of Twitter use while watching television coincides with fear-mongering warnings "about the negative impact technology has on cultural ethics." Instead of taking this melancholic stance, Ames examines how viewers interpret episodes that parallel real world ethical and moral dilemmas ranging from murder to justice to equality. Signaling a diminution in fan interest in social justice, her findings are less liberatory than more traditional fan scholars might like. When analyzing fan responses, Ames found that "the number of tweets devoted to melodramatic commentary versus social commentary suggests that Twitter users were more preoccupied by the fictional bad behavior than the real world bad behavior they were scripted to highlight." This finding questions the usefulness of scripted television to make poignant cultural commentary and gives rise to a fundamental question: if fans are not engaging with deeper cultural meanings beyond fictive representations, does the narrative change our cultural perceptions of morality and ethics?

Utilizing an entirely different method to engage consumption, ethics, and morality, Sean Swenson examines his own positionality as both a *Grey's Anatomy* and *Private Practice* fan and a hospital transporter. Guided by autoethnography's commitment to reflexive cultural commentary, Swenson struggles in/with/through the consumption of medical melodramas that trade in life and death for the sake of entertainment and profitable popularity. Offering a narrative inquiry into the social institutions of media and medicine, the author interrogates what Mbembe terms *necropolitics* in reference to the capacity of the nation-state or those in power "to dictate who may live and who must die."[55] In tandem with heated contemporary debates over health care, Swenson conveys that his professional experience "dealing with hospital deaths substantiate the invisible reliance upon death that permeates Shondaland's healthcare centers." The invisibility of death in a business reliant upon death is theorized as an ironic representation mirrored in the real world that undercuts patient autonomy, ethics, and agency to privilege physicians as doctor-heroes. Swenson rebukes this practice by responding to essential questions at the crossroads of medical melodramas and necropolitics: "What place is given to life, death, and the human body? . . . How are they inscribed in the order of power?"[56]

INTELLECTUAL PLAY IN SHONDALAND'S AMUSEMENT PARK

In *Year of Yes*, Shonda Rhimes declares that "telling stories. Smooth stories. Funny stories. Epic stories" is her superpower; as the editors of this intellectually rigorous collection, we unequivocally agree. This collection was not fashioned to throw shade on Rhimes's hard-earned prosperity as one of the most successful showrunners in the history of television or to discredit the admirable media empire she built out of her imagination.[57] Nor do we cave to the cultural pressures to simplistically romanticize Rhimes, celebrate her F.O.D status in Hollywood, or curtail Shondaland shows as "only" entertainment. Rather, each of the twelve chapters in *Adventures in Shondaland* offers heuristic critical analysis of television to compel cultural engagement because media consumption is U.S. American society's favorite pastime. "TV is still the preferred choice for overall viewing" and adults spend on average thirty-five hours and twenty-six minutes per week watching television.[58] For better and for worse—therein lies the profound pedagogical capacity of Shondaland.

Acknowledging her influence as a showrunner during an International Emmy Founders Award acceptance speech in November 2016, Rhimes describes television as the "most powerful source of communication in the world."[59] Mindful of Donald Trump's recent election to the U.S. presidency and the confluence between representation, politics, and identity politics, she continues with: "A lot of people right now are scared, nervous or worried: people of color, any woman who values her body and her choices, LGBTQ people, immigrants, Muslims, people with disabilities. . . . They're afraid their voices will no longer be heard, or they believe they're going to be silenced. . . . My pen has power—I'm thinking about that." Ultimately, those of us riding Shondaland's vibrant rollercoasters should embrace the opportunity to capitalize upon Rhimes's vocal visibility and Shondaland's mass popularity to expand and amplify scholarly inquiry—our pens too have power. Honoring this labor among those who, like us, are loyal Shondaland fans—we can absolutely critique what we love and love what we critique.

NOTES

1. Lacy Rose, "Hollywood's Most Powerful Black Female Showrunner," *Hollywood Reporter* 420 (October 17, 2014): 52–57.
2. For clarity, in reference to Shondaland show *Grey's Anatomy*, the hospital is at times referred to as Seattle Grace (its original name on the show) and at other times Grey Sloan Memorial Hospital after being renamed for the second time during season 9.
3. Lisa de Moraes, "NBC Wins 2016–17 Season in Ratings Demo; CBS Takes Total Viewers," *Deadline Hollywood*, May 23, 2017, http://deadline.com/2017/05/tv-season-network-rankings -2016-2017-nbc-cbs-winners-1202100904/.
4. Rose, "Hollywood's," 54.
5. Megan Casserly, "How 'Scandal's' Shonda Rhimes Became Disney's Primetime Savior," *Forbes*, May 8, 2013, https://www.forbes.com/sites/meghancasserly/2013/05/08/how-scandals -shonda-rhimes-became-disneys-primetime-savior/#47fe97297d5a; Jason Lynch, "Thank God It's Shonda," *Adweek* 56 (2015): 9–10.
6. Lynch, 9–10.
7. John Koblin, "Netflix Signs Shonda Rhimes in Counterpunch to ABC and Disney," *New York Times*, August 14, 2017, https://www.nytimes.com/2017/08/14/business/media/shonda -rhimes-netflix-deal.html.
8. Daniel Holloway, "New 2017–18 TV Shows are Mostly White and Male" *Variety*, May 19, 2017, http://variety.com/2017/tv/news/new-2017-18-tv-shows-no-diversity-120243 6493/.
9. Shonda Rhimes, *Year of Yes: How to Dance It Out, Stand in the Sun, and Be Your Own Person* (New York: Simon & Schuster, 2015), 138–139.
10. Intersectional media critique has become more common; however, particular intersecting identities (e.g., race and gender) are far more commonly theorized than others (e.g., sexual orientation, class, nationality, ability, and religion). For example, see Rachel Alicia Griffin, "Black Feminist Thought and Disney's Paradoxical Representation of Black Girlhood in *Doc McStuffins*," in *Disney, Culture, and Curriculum*, ed. Jennifer A. Sandlin and Julie C. Garlen (New York: Routledge, 2016), 161–175; Rachel Alicia Griffin, "Olivia Pope as Problematic and Paradoxical: A Black Feminist Critique of *Scandal's* 'Mammification,'" in *Feminist Theory and Popular Culture*, ed. Adrienne Trier-Bieniek (Rotterdam, The Netherlands: Sense Publishers, 2015), 35–48; Michaela D. E. Meyer, "*The Good Wife's* Fatalistic Feminism: Televised Feminist Failures in Work/Life Balance, Romance and Feminist Alliances," in *Women, Feminism, and Pop Politics: From "Bitch" to "Badass" and Beyond*, ed. Karrin Vasby Anderson (New York: Peter Lang, 2018), 205–222; Michaela D. E. Meyer, "The 'Other' Woman in Contemporary Television Drama: Analyzing Intersectional Representation on *Bones*," *Sexuality & Culture* 19 (2015): 900–915; Michaela D. E. Meyer, "'I'm Just Trying to Find My Way like Most Kids': Bisexuality, Adolescence and the Drama of *One Tree Hill*," *Sexuality & Culture* 13 (2009): 237–251; Marian Meyers, "African American Women and Violence: Gender, Race and Class in the News," *Critical Studies in Media Communication* 21 (2004): 95–118; Danielle Stern, "It Takes a Classless, Heteronormative Utopian Village: *Gilmore Girls* and the Problem of Postfeminism," *Communication Review* 15 (2012): 167–186.
11. For a summary of these debates, see Michaela D. E. Meyer, "New Directions in Critical Television Studies: Exploring Text, Audience and Production in Communication Scholarship," *Communication Studies* 63 (2012): 263–268.
12. Katherine Sender, "No Hard Feelings: Reflexivity and Queer Affect in the New Media Landscape," in *The Handbook of Gender, Sex and Media*, ed. Karen Ross (Hoboken, N.J.: Wiley-Blackwell, 2011), 207–225.

13. For a well-constructed outline of this problem in contemporary cultural studies, see Stuart Cunningham, "Cultural Studies from the Viewpoint of Cultural Policy," in *Critical Cultural Policy Studies: A Reader*, ed. Justin Lewis and Toby Miller (Hoboken, N.J.: Wiley-Blackwell Publishers, 2002), 13–22.

14. Stuart Hall, "Encoding/Decoding," in *Media and Cultural Studies: KeyWorks*, ed. Meenakshi Gigi Durham and Douglas M. Kellner (Malden, Mass.: Blackwell, 2001), 166–176.

15. This is a common argument among television critics. See David Bianculli, *The Platinum Age of Television: From* I Love Lucy *to* The Walking Dead, *How TV Became Terrific* (New York: Random House, 2016); John Ellis, *Seeing Things: Television in the Age of Uncertainty* (New York: I. B. Taurus, 2000); or David Thomson, *Television: A Biography* (London: Thames & Hudson, 2016).

16. Alexander Dohest, "It's Not HBO: It's TV: The Views of Critics and Producers of Flemish 'Quality TV,'" *Critical Studies in Television* 9 (2014): 1–22. See also Jonathan Bignell, Stephen Lacy, and Madeline Macmurraugh-Kavanagh, *British Television Drama: Past, Present and Future* (New York: Palgrave Macmillan, 2000); Michael Newman and Elana Levine, *Legitimating Television: Media Convergence and Cultural Studies* (New York: Routledge, 2012).

17. See Janet McCabe and Kim Akass, "Introduction: Debating Quality," in *Quality Television: Contemporary American Television and Beyond*, ed. Janet McCabe and Kim Akass (London: I. B. Taurus, 2007), 1–12.

18. Jason Mittell, *Genre and Television: From Cop Show to Cartoons in American Culture* (New York: Routledge, 2004).

19. Elisabeth Leamy, "Finally Cut the Cable TV Cord in Eight Easy Steps," *Washington Post*, April 19, 2017, https://www.washingtonpost.com/lifestyle/home/finally-cut-the-cable-tv-cord -in-eight-easy-steps/2017/04/18/6cae6086–1ed8–11e7-be2a-3a1fb24d4671_story.html; Diane Bruce Anstine, "The Impact of the Regulation of the Cable Television Industry: The Effect on Quality-Adjusted Cable Television Prices," *Applied Economics* 36 (2004): 793–802.

20. Lesley Goldberg, Michael O'Connell, Bryn Elise Sandber, and Kate Stanhope, "Peak TV's Peak Players," *Hollywood Reporter* 422 (2016): 64–71.

21. Andrew Sarris, "Notes on the 'Auteur' Theory in 1962," *Kwartalnik Filmowy* 59 (2007): 6–17.

22. Goldberg et al., "Peak TV's Peak Players," 64–71.

23. Lynch, "Thank God It's Shonda," 9–10.

24. Notable examples of this important work include: Eduardo Bonilla-Silva and Austin Ashe, "The End of Racism? Colorblind Racism and Popular Media," in *The Colorblind Screen: Television in Post-Racial America*, ed. Sarah Nilsen and Sarah E. Turner (New York: New York University Press, 2014), 57–79; Amy Long, "Diagnosing Drama: *Grey's Anatomy*, Blind Casting, and the Politics of Representation," *Journal of Popular Culture* 44 (2011): 1067–1084; Kristin J. Warner, "The Racial Logic of *Grey's Anatomy*: Shonda Rhimes and Her 'Post-Civil Rights, Post-Feminist' Series," *Television & New Media* 16 (2015): 631–647.

25. Rhimes, *Year of Yes*, 234; Rose, "Hollywood's."

26. Darnell Hunt, Ana-Chirstina Ramon, and Zachary Price, *2014 Hollywood Diversity Report: Making Sense of the Disconnect* (Los Angeles: Ralph J. Bunche Center for African American Studies at UCLA, 2014).

27. Sam Lansky, Francesca Trianni, and Eliza Berman, "Shonda Rhimes on Raising the Next Generation of TV Producers," *Time Magazine*, December 1, 2017, http://time.com/collection -post/4081997/shonda-rhimes-viola-davis-scandal-kerry-washington/?iid=sr-link4.

28. Rhimes, *Year of Yes*, 235.

29. Tara-Lynne Pixley, "Olivia Pope's Scandalous Blackness," *Black Scholar* 45 (2015): 28–33.

30. Kimberly Moffitt, Simone Puff, and Ronald L. Jackson II, eds. *Gladiators in Suits: Race, Gender, and the Politics of Representation in Scandal* (New York: Syracuse University Press, forthcoming).

31. Kevin Powell, "Woman on Top," *Ebony*, March (2013), 112–117.

32. Kathryn Shattuck, "'Quantico': Should You Watch It?," *New York Times*, September 27, 2015, https://www.nytimes.com/2015/09/27/arts/television/quantico-should-i-watch.html?_r=0.

33. Greg Braxton, "Six New CBS Series, Six White Male Leads. With Prime-time Diversity Growing, How Did the Network Fall Behind?," *Los Angeles Times*, August 8, 2016, http://www.latimes.com/entertainment/tv/la-et-st-cbs-so-white-fall-20160801-snap-story.html.

34. Maryann Erigha, "Shonda Rhimes, *Scandal*, and the Politics of Crossing Over," *Black Scholar* 45 (2015): 10–15.

35. Long, "Diagnosing Drama," 1068.

36. Warner, "The Racial Logic of *Grey's Anatomy*," 645.

37. Ralina L. Joseph, "Strategically Ambiguous Shonda Rhimes: Respectability Politics of a Black Woman Showrunner," *Souls* 18 (2016): 302–320.

38. Joseph, 302–320.

39. bell hooks, *Teaching Community: A Pedagogy of Hope* (New York: Harper Collins, 2001), 83; Joseph, "Strategically Ambiguous Shonda Rhimes," 305.

40. Joseph, 305.

41. Rhimes, *Year of Yes*, 247.

42. John Fiske, "The Cultural Economy of Fandom," in *The Adoring Audience: Fan Culture and Popular Media*, ed. Lisa A. Lewis (New York: Routledge, 1992), 30.

43. See Henry Jenkins, *Textual Poachers: Television Fans and Participatory Culture* (New York: Routledge, 1992) and Henry Jenkins, *Convergence Culture: Where Old and New Media Collide* (New York: New York University Press, 2006).

44. Jonathan Gray, Cornel Sandvoss, and C. Lee Harrington, "Introduction: Why Study Fans?," in *Fandom: Identities and Communities in a Mediated World*, ed. Jonathan Gray, Cornel Sandvoss and C. Lee Harrington (New York: New York University Press, 2007), 1–16.

45. For example, see Chad Dell, *The Revenge of Hatpin Mary: Women, Professional Wrestling and Fan Culture in the 1950s* (New York: Peter Lang, 2006); Cheryl Harris and Allison Alexander, *Theorizing Fandom: Fans, Subculture and Identity* (New York: Hampton Press, 1998); Mark Jancovich, "Cult Fictions: Cult Movies, Subcultural Capital, and the Production of Cultural Distinction," *Cultural Studies* 16 (2002): 306–322; Michaela D. E. Meyer, "Something Wicca This Way Comes: Audience Interpretation of a Marginalized Religious Philosophy on *Charmed*," in *Investigating Charmed: The Magic Power of TV*, ed. Stan Beeler and Karin Beeler (London: I. B. Taurus, 2008), 3–17; and Megan Marie Wood and Linda Baughman, "*Glee* Fandom and Twitter: Something New, or More of the Same Old Thing?," *Communication Studies* 63 (2012): 328–344.

46. Karen Orr Vered and Sal Humphreys, "Postfeminist Infections in Television Studies," *Continuum: Journal of Media & Cultural Studies* 28 (2014): 155–163.

47. Cunningham, "Cultural Studies from the Viewpoint of Cultural Policy," 17.

48. Keith R. Negus, "The Work of Cultural Intermediaries and the Enduring Distance between Production and Consumption," *Cultural Studies* 16 (2002): 501–515.

49. Jon Lafayette, "They Still Love to Chase Girls," *Broadcasting & Cable*, February 6, 2012, 18. For a concise history of this trend spanning the 1990s, see Rob Becker, *Gay TV and Straight America* (Piscataway, N.J.: Rutgers University Press, 2006).

50. Brian Steinberg, "TV Ad Prices: Football Hikes, 'This Is Us' Soars, 'Walking Dead' Stumbles, 'Empire' Falls," *Variety*, November 2, 2017, http://variety.com/2017/tv/news/tv-ad-prices-football-walking-dead-empire-1202602792/.

51. Aniko Imre, "Gender and Quality Television," *Feminist Media Studies* 9 (2009): 391–407.

52. Jim McGuigan, "Cultural Policy Studies," in *Critical Cultural Policy Studies: A Reader*, ed. Justin Lewis and Toby Miller (Hoboken, N.J.: Wiley-Blackwell Publishers, 2002), 23–42.

53. Apryl Williams and Vanessa Gonlin, "I Got All My Sisters with Me (on Black Twitter): Second Screening of *How to Get Away with Murder* as a Discourse on Black Womanhood," *Information, Communication and Society* 20 (2017): 984–1004.

54. Saba Hamedy, "Twitter at the Heart of ABC's Marketing Campaign for Thursday Lineup," *Los Angeles Times*, November 25, 2014, http://www.latimes.com/entertainment/envelope/cotown/la-et-ct-tgit-abc-20141126-story.html.

55. Achille Mbembe, "Necropolitics," *Public Culture* 15, no. 1 (2003): 11–40, https://doi.org/10.1215/08992363-15-1-11.

56. Mbembe, 12.

57. Rhimes, *Year of Yes*, 89.

58. Nielsen, "TV Is Still Top Brass, but Viewing Differences Vary with Age," July 18, 2016, http://www.nielsen.com/us/en/insights/news/2016/television-is-still-top-brass-but-viewing-differences-vary-with-age.html.

59. Mahita Gajanan, "Shonda Rhimes Urges the Importance of Diversity on TV under Donald Trump," *Time Magazine*, November 22, 2017, http://time.com/4580000/shonda-rhimes-tv-diversity-trump/.

PART 1 QUALITY TELEVISION'S CULTURAL DOMINANCE

The Auteur Comes to Television Studies

1 · TRAUMA, SPIN, AND MURDER

The Carnival Spectacle in Shondaland

RICHARD G. JONES JR. AND EMILY VAJJALA

Murder, cover-ups, torture, election rigging, a penis on a dead girl's cell phone, a U.S. president killing a Supreme Court justice with his bare hands, and bodies exploding into pink mist; all of this and more is simply a day's work in Shondaland for creators, producers, actors, and crew members. Excess is a signature of Shonda Rhimes in medicine (*Grey's Anatomy*; also referred to as *Grey's*), politics (*Scandal*), and law (*How to Get Away with Murder*; also referred to as *HTGAWM*), and ABC's "Thank God It's Thursday" lineup features three Shondaland shows in a row. Rhimes's success as a showrunner has catapulted her into the spotlight as a sought-after industry powerhouse with a formidable social media presence and loyal fans. Viewers' weekly trips to Shondaland begin with *Grey's Anatomy* (2005–present), a medical melodrama in its fourteenth season. The main protagonists begin at Seattle Grace Hospital as surgical interns who eventually become attending physicians as the series progresses, with new cohorts of interns cycling through.[1] Next was *Scandal* (2012–2018), a political melodrama that ran seven seasons led by Olivia Pope as a Washington, D.C., "fixer" involved in a scandalous affair with the U.S. president. Third is *How to Get Away with Murder* (2014–present), a legal melodrama in its fourth season showcasing brilliant defense attorney and law professor Annalise Keating. Keating employs law student interns to help win unwinnable cases—which they do when they are not having sex with suspects or covering up crimes. As a signature style, the excess in *Grey's*, *Scandal*, and *HTGAWM* is as nuanced and deliberate as it is entertaining and shocking. To theorize excess in Shondaland, we analyze these shows through a Bakhtinian lens, arguing that they constitute the "Shondafication" of prime-time television.

BAKHTINIAN EXCESS IN SHONDALAND

Bakhtin's conceptualization of carnival explores literary modes that subvert or overturn dominant styles of writing.[2] He chose the metaphor of the carnival to encapsulate the various ways that literary norms can be challenged. Just as the carnival challenged the social order of Renaissance society, carnival tropes within a text can challenge readers (or viewers) to reimagine their own social worlds. Informing our work, previous scholars have employed a Bakhtinian lens to analyze media texts including *The Big Lebowski, America's Next Top Model, South Park,* and *Gimme a Break.*[3] We extend this research by focusing on multiple shows within one production company, Shondaland, and the showrunner Shonda Rhimes.

Excess is an overarching theme within the carnival. During a Renaissance carnival, revelers literally ate and drank to excess during celebratory feasts, dressed up in exaggerated costumes, and engaged with amusements ranging from freak shows to exotic musical performances.[4] Since the carnival is itself an event marked by excess, the tropes that appear within the carnival are also marked by excess. Carnival tropes that inform our analysis of Shondaland include the upheaval of social position, ritual spectacle, and grotesque realism. Inherent in each of these tropes is also the carnival cycle of degeneration and regeneration.

During the carnival celebrations the norms of polite behavior are suspended and societal roles are reversed, resulting in an upheaval of social positions and hierarchies. Those typically on the margins of society, for example, the fool, madman, rogue, or clown, may don a mask and costume and take on elite roles.[5] Conversely, the systemically privileged "people with power, history, and laws," are stripped of power as they are mocked and degraded by caricature performances of crownings and uncrownings.[6] In the carnival, those at the bottom of a social hierarchy may find themselves crowned with power, while those typically privileged with power may be uncrowned. The carnival brings forth, "in a concretely and sensuous, half-real and half-play-acted form, a new mode of interrelating between individuals, counter-posed to the all-powerful socio-hierarchical relationships of non-carnival life."[7] The world-upside-down nature of carnival is a temporary sanctioned moment during which the marginalized are regenerated and elevated as they degrade those in power. Once the carnival ends, the marginalized return to their inferior positions and the powerful rule once again, which reflects the cycle of carnival. This cycle of degeneration and regeneration is key to both the carnival and our analysis.

Ritual spectacles attract viewers by disturbing and intriguing them.[8] The carnival itself is a ritual in that it occurs annually around the same time. It is also a spectacle given the excess present in costumes, behaviors, and performances. "Exaggeration and overemphasis are indices of *value*; the greater the scale of the body's ingestion and copulation, the greater its value."[9] The cycle of degeneration and regeneration is inherent in this carnival trope. Generally, every carnival degenerates to an end point only to be ritually regenerated the following year. Additionally, ritual spectacles such as feasts and performances come to an end and are regenerated throughout one carnival. The body also becomes a site of ritual spectacle, a spectacle that is made more enthralling for the revelers through grotesque realism as bodies degenerate due to their overindulgence in food, drink, and festivities and are left to regenerate in the interval before the next carnival.

Grotesque realism is another trope of carnival, and it is the primary manifestation of carnival spirit.[10] The body and its functions are the foci of grotesque realism; eating, bleeding, dispensing waste, and having sex characterize humanness. Correspondingly, grotesque imagery includes "copulation, pregnancy, birth, growth, old age, disintegration, [and] dismemberment."[11] In addition to base corporeality that marks carnival bodies, Bakhtin specifically notes that laughter "is an explicitly expressive bodily function" tied to the carnival's rejection of ideological rules and authority. Whether it is through the size of the body or the focus on bodily functions ranging from digestion to laughter, in carnival, the more excessive these manifestations of humanness are, the more they are valued.[12] The human body and its functions are further dramatized when juxtaposed against the privileged rationality of modernity. The upper body, which holds the brain (i.e., the source of reason privileged in modernity), is highlighted through the comparison to the lower body, which houses our digestive, reproductive, and sexual parts. Bakhtin identifies degradation as essential to grotesque realism. Although we typically think of degradation, or degeneration, as negative, Bakhtin stresses that since embodied degeneration reminds us of our humanity, it is also affirmative and linked to regeneration and renewal.[13] In short, as carnival revelers behave contrary to the established social order, they achieve "renewal and revival."[14] Key to revitalization is understanding the carnival body as unfinished, as always becoming.[15] Bakhtin notes, "Degeneration digs a bodily grave for a new birth; it has not only a destructive, negative aspect, but also a regenerating one." The cycle of degeneration and regeneration is the cornerstone of our analysis of Shondaland's excess, but first we discuss how Rhimes, as a television auteur, has created the carnivalesque signature we term Shondafication.

THE SHONDAFICATION OF PRIME-TIME NETWORK TELEVISION

When ABC picked up *Grey's* in 2005, Rhimes coined "Shondaland" as an homage to Disneyland. As Everett states, "That audacious early branding move speaks volumes about Rhimes's self-confidence and business acumen."[16] Since then, especially after *Grey's* premiered to an audience of sixteen million viewers, Rhimes has emerged as a renowned showrunner who enjoys creative and executive freedom.[17] While it may seem "audacious," in Everett's words, for a relatively unknown producer and writer to name her company Shondaland, Rhimes's success validates her bold vision. Drawing on Giroux and Pollock's concept of Disneyfication, which highlights how Disney influences society, we use Shondafication to highlight Rhimes's influence on the landscape of prime-time television and the larger industry.[18] Shondaland shows' fast-paced dramatic verve, Rhimes's auteur status, the foregrounding of identity politics and diverse casting, the relatable characters in the form of broken fixers, and the integration of social media are all signatures of Shondafication.

The first element of Shondafication is the fast-paced dramatic verve of Shondaland. Even Rhimes's logo and company name elicit carnivalesque connotations, and these early choices foretold Shondafication. If Shondaland is the carnival, then Shonda Rhimes is the carnival master, a fitting metaphor given her production company's roller coaster logo, which originally appeared in bright purples, pinks, and reds but is now even more dramatic in flaming reds, oranges, and golds. The logo is appropriately symbolic of the whips and turns, highs and lows, steep climbs, and heart-racing plunges viewers experience as they ride through episodes, storylines, and seasons. One critic even suggested that the Thursday night lineup should come with warnings like those one might see on a carnival ride: "May cause narrative whiplash. Beware of injury from jaw hitting the floor. Management not responsible if you wear out the O, M, and G keys on your mobile device."[19] As cultural critics and fans of Rhimes's shows, we have personally enjoyed reveling in awe and disbelief at the tragedies that strike the characters, ranging from the devastating plane crash in *Grey's* season 8, to the attempted assassination of the president in *Scandal's* season 2, to the intense, time-bending "whodunits" in *HTGAWM's* first season. Narratively akin to riding Six Flags' Kingda Ka—the world's tallest roller coaster that transports riders from zero to 128 miles per hour in three seconds—Rhimes's shows contain "ultrafast-paced, frenetic, and head-spinning storylines, as well as mind-blowing and off-the-chain plot points that mesmerize audiences every week."[20] This fast-paced style, as evidenced by the amount and speed of dialogue, the quick-cut editing and flashbacks, and the continuing introduction and deletion of characters, is a key component of Shondafication.

The next element of Shondafication is Rhimes's influence and visibility as an auteur. Auteur theory was developed as a component of film studies and focuses primarily on film directors.[21] In television, auteur theory has been applied to producers and showrunners including Norman Lear (*Maude, The Jeffersons,* and *Mary Hartman, Mary Hartman*), Stephen Bochco (*Hill Street Blues, L.A. Law, Murder One* and *NYPD Blue*), and David E. Kelley (*Picket Fences, Ally McBeal, Chicago Hope, The Practice, Boston Public,* and *Boston Legal*).[22] Like Bochco and Kelley, Rhimes works within her own production company and often signs multishow, multiyear contracts. However, Rhimes's positionality as a black woman is unique because television auteurs are mostly white men—even more so in 2005 when Rhimes created Shondaland.[23] Shondafication brings identity politics to the forefront of television via Rhimes's presence and by turning "America's miscegenation taboo on its head," centering women of color in powerful roles, and featuring queer gender and sexuality.[24] Rhimes eschews questions about intentionally building diversity into her shows, instead discussing her practice of (color)blind casting and her focus on "writing the very types of stories that she has long waited to see on television."[25]

Rhimes and her teams' creation of compelling, diverse characters is the most important plot-oriented element of Shondafication. Protagonists are relatable broken fixers who fuel cycles of crises that keep viewers hooked. The characters in Shondaland face familiar situations; they fall in and out of love, navigate interpersonal conflict, encounter career challenges, and experience tragedy. Rhimes's longtime producing partner Betsy Beers says, "At the core [of Rhimes's shows] are these incredibly emotional, relatable, damaged characters who are vulnerable and have flaws but are really, really human."[26] Beers notes that viewers root for characters like Olivia and Huck in *Scandal* despite their horrible behaviors because we can identify with them. Their shocking acts "are acceptable within the parameters of fantasy . . . [which] is the space where the excessive and the socially problematic can be played out . . . without fear of consequences."[27] In short, the carnivalesque atmosphere of Shondaland allows for excess in fantastical storytelling which hooks audiences.

Aside from being relatable, broken fixers are another signature of Shondafication. The fixers in each show represent "high" culture as doctors, lawyers, and politicians. As fixers, the surgical interns on *Grey's* fix patients' bodies, the gladiators in suits (i.e., Olivia's employees) on *Scandal* fix clients' problems, and the lawyers and law students on *HTGAWM* fix cases to keep clients out of jail. In carnivalesque style, the interns, gladiators, and students often destabilize and dethrone the normative social order. On *Grey's*, the interns botch surgeries; on *Scandal*, the gladiators that Olivia rescued and rehabilitated literally torture each other; on *HTGAWM*, the students kill their professor's husband; and on all three shows, those with less status destabilize their professions through sexual relationships that are often asymmetrical in terms of power. These "low" culture acts create drama and overthrow, at least temporarily, the expected social order. Although doctors, politicians, and lawyers have esteem and social status, Rhimes shows us the personal, dark, and lustful underbelly of those ranks. She also invites the audience behind the curtain to witness the scandalous ascension toward the top of each esteemed profession.

Although Shondaland shows spotlight successful "fixers," the characters are tangibly imperfect. This paradoxical scripting is a key feature of plot and character development. The characters' "fatal flaws" inhibit perfection, mirroring Bakhtin's point that figures in the carnival are always becoming—never "finalized."[28] Meredith on *Grey's*, Olivia on *Scandal*, and Annalise on *HTGAWM*, for example, can be viewed as flawed "sheroes" that reflect the "demanding lives of professional . . . women" who make "cringe-worthy bad choices."[29] Rhimes's characters are "aspirational in their social status yet wildly inferior in the management of their personal lives . . . [and] practically beg audiences to tune in and offer emotional support."[30] To tune in, Rhimes's audiences often use social media to create impassioned, arguably obsessive, fan communities around the shows.

Social media buzz leading up to, during, and after Shondaland shows is the final Shondafication element we discuss. During new episodes, "Twitter feeds light up with OMGs and WTFs. The shows manipulate viewers like puppet master Olivia Pope yanking the D.C. media's strings and make old TV formats new again."[31] "Rhimes's fans relish the hypersuspended disbelief that motivates their real-time tweets of delighted shock and awe."[32] In a "post-network era," Shondaland breathed life into ABC. In 2017, *Grey's* season finale brought in 7.7 million viewers and *Scandal's* brought in 5.5 million viewers, which made ABC the most watched broadcast network by far that night.[33] The synergy created via social television, watching a television show while simultaneously on social media, plays an important role in Shondaland's success.[34] "With these kinds of numbers and ratings dominance, clearly Rhimes' auteurist vision aligns with television's millennial zeitgeist."[35]

Rhimes has been called an "auteur extraordinaire," which captures her talent for creating successful shows with relatable characters and storylines imbued with melodrama, spectacle, and excess.[36] Having established the carnivalesque lens as fitting for theorizing Shondafication, we turn to a close analysis of how the carnival functions in *Grey's, Scandal*, and *HTGAWM*. In doing so, we pay particular attention to the carnival cycle of degeneration and regeneration as well as the excess, spectacle, and grotesque realism that fuel the cycle.

THE CARNIVAL CYCLE IN SHONDALAND: DEGENERATION AND REGENERATION

The characters in *Grey's, Scandal*, and *HTGAWM* embody degeneration and regeneration within each series, each season, and sometimes within a single episode. The cycle of degeneration and regeneration is dependent on and fueled by the carnival tropes. The very process is itself a spectacle; bodies degenerate as they engage in and perform excess, which is visually identifiable through grotesque realism. For example, *Grey's* features degenerating and regenerating relationships among doctors as they are faced with grotesquely injured (degenerated) patients they must try to heal (regenerate). Relationships also degenerate and regenerate in *Scandal*. Rather than dealing with patients, Olivia and her fixers face the grotesque realism of assassination attempts and torture. In *HTGAWM*, Annalise and her students also cycle in and out of relationships but are more likely to commit murder or dispose of a body than to try to save a life as in *Grey's*. Just as each horse on a spinning carousel is vibrantly painted and dramatically posed, each show in Shondaland features a variation on carnivalesque storytelling. In the carnival, each unique horse on a carousel blends together to create a unified amusement ride. Similarly, although viewers ride through varying contexts (operating rooms, the halls of political power, and courtrooms) in each show, Shondafication is threaded through them all, creating a cohesive experience for Shondaland visitors.

Grey's Carnival

Interpersonal relationships, especially romances and hookups, are part of Grey's carnivalesque degeneration and regeneration. Within the first few minutes of the pilot, "A Hard Day's Night," Meredith's sexuality conflicts with her surgical internship.[37] Running late for work, Meredith kicks a one-night stand out of her house after he introduces himself as "Derek." It turns out that "Derek" is Dr. Derek Shepherd, a neurosurgeon at Grey Sloan Memorial Hospital (Grey Sloan) who outranks Dr. Grey. As Rhimes's first Shondaland protagonist, Grey is brilliant and often saves the day with skill and foresight, despite being only an intern. As Rhimes's first broken fixer, Grey also falls prey to teenage-like drama; she refers to Shepherd as "McDreamy" and gossips about him with her fellow interns.

Many characters on Grey's engage in conflicting sexual relationships that endanger the work environment. Their behaviors reflect the carnivalesque character of the "rogue" which is frequently the catalyst that spurs cycles of crises in Shondaland. Dr. Izzie Stevens's relationship with a patient, Denny Duquette, results in her cutting his LVAD (left ventricular assist device) wire to worsen his condition and deceitfully move him to the top of the heart transplant list.[38] Ultimately, Izzie is traumatized by Denny's death and the loss of her internship.[39] Dr. Preston Burke, an attending cardiac surgeon, is romantically involved with intern Dr. Cristina Yang, resulting in their decision to hide his hand tremor to protect his surgical reputation.[40] Their teamwork, an ethical catastrophe for surgeons and the hospital, impedes his appointment to chief of surgery and strains other relationships. When Cristina performs advanced surgical procedures under the guise of Burke's mentorship to hide his tremor, the other interns jealously credit their sexual relationship. When the tremor is exposed, hurt and anger abound, reflecting the disastrous impact sexual relationships have on the hospital. Yet in Shondaland, these omnipresent tensions fuel the carnivalesque cycle by creating degenerative strains and offering the relational support that regenerates the characters despite their degeneracy.

Meredith and Derek's romantic involvement and eventual marriage unfolds as a degeneration/regeneration cycle spanning eleven seasons. Following the drama of their initial hookup, their newly stabilized relationship degenerates when Derek's estranged wife, Dr. Addison Montgomery, shows up at Grey Sloan.[41] Meredith is shocked to learn Derek is married, and Derek's shocking secret is fully divulged when a flashback reveals Addison's long-term affair with his best friend, Dr. Mark Sloan.[42] Derek and Meredith's relationship regenerates when Addison accepts that her marriage is over and leaves Seattle to join the Ocean-side Wellness Group in Los Angeles, California, functioning as a crossover character for the second Shondaland show *Private Practice* (ABC 2007–2013).[43] This cycle transpires as Derek and Meredith's relationship goes through highs (e.g., they adopt a child, get married, have two more children), and lows (e.g., they break up and date other people, Meredith experiences problems with fertility, their career ambitions conflict). When Derek dies in a car accident, Meredith regenerates without him when she learns she is pregnant with their third child, signaling rebirth in the wake of tragic death—a dialectical extreme of the degeneration/regeneration cycle.[44] Furthering regeneration, Meredith sells their home and moves back into her mother's home where she lived at the series' outset, dates other people, and forgives the intern largely responsible for Derek's death.

The degeneration and regeneration cycle of relationships in *Grey's* is pushed along vis-à-vis grotesque realism as bodily functions are exaggerated, highlighted, and celebrated. The fact that much of the grotesque realism in *Grey's* happens within the ritual spectacle of emergency medicine heightens the carnivalesque elements. For example, season 1's "The First Cut Is the Deepest" includes a severed penis.[45] The grotesque realism begins when a beaten, bloody woman is brought into the ER followed by Dr. Burke removing something from the patients' stomach. Dr. Grey identifies the fleshy mass saying, "Oh my God! . . . She bit it off. . . . That's his penis."[46] Soon after, a man stumbles into the ER with blood soaked pants. It turns out that he sexually assaulted the woman, she fought back, and he almost bled to death. As the doctors save him, Dr. Bailey notes his penis cannot be reattached. In agreement, Dr. Grey notes that the victim's digestive stomach acids left very little to work with and the man will have to urinate out of a bag. From the image of the blurry fleshy mass to the references to gastric juices and urination, the lines and visuals in this episode exemplify the base corporeality that reflects Bakhtin's grotesque realism. Additionally, this plotline exemplifies the excessive uncrowning (severed penis) of a man who brutally raped a woman, signifying that those with power can certainly be degenerated.

Since many *Grey's* episodes literally deal with death and birth, the cycle of degeneration and regeneration is taken to its extreme. Season 2's "It's the End of the World," exemplifies the excess of the carnival as several stories are told at once, converging in a grotesque disaster involving multiple operating rooms, an evacuation, a bazooka, a car crash, and the birth of a baby. While the surgical interns are waiting on an incoming trauma, a very pregnant Dr. Bailey instructs the interns on how to handle the trauma and tells Dr. George O'Malley to page OB-GYN because "my contractions are ten minutes apart, and my water just broke all over your shoes."[47] When the ambulance arrives, we hear a screaming woman and see a paramedic's hand inside a man's chest. We soon learn the man has a live bazooka round in his chest, so the hospital is immediately evacuated. Meanwhile, Dr. Bailey's husband is in a car accident on his way to the hospital for the birth of their child and requires brain surgery. We then cut back to the paramedic, the bomb-stuffed patient, and an anesthesiologist who says, "Pink mist—that's what the bomb squad calls you when you blow up. You're liquid. You explode into a million pieces. There's nothing left. Sometimes they don't even find a finger. One minute you're a person and the next you're bloody rain."[48] Despite the omnipresence of danger and death, in the end, Dr. Bailey's baby is born, her husband survives, and Dr. Grey survives her decision to replace the paramedic who arrived with the bomb-stuffed patient. Dylan Young, the bomb squad leader who saves Grey, Burke, Yang, and the patient, walks away with the bazooka round and explodes into "pink mist" when it detonates just outside the operating room. This episode features several carnivalesque tropes including the base corporeality exhibited by amniotic fluid, the grotesque realism of reducing a human to pink mist, and the birth, death, and near-death experiences of the degeneration/regeneration cycle.

While death signifies ultimate degeneration, birth commonly represents regeneration on Shondaland's carousel. It is not unusual for a subplot involving pregnancy to be introduced when characters face trauma or near-death experiences. A major plotline spans from season 2, when Ellis Grey, Meredith's mother, first tells Meredith "the carousal never stops turning" to season 11, when Meredith realizes the parallels between her life and her mother's.[49] Both women are successful surgeons at Grey Sloan, and struggle with trust, intimacy, emotionality, marriage, and motherhood (albeit in different ways). These parallels become steadily clearer to Meredith and the audience, culminating with storylines linked to childbirth, death, and motherhood. In season 11, Meredith learns that her mother secretly had a child from an affair with Dr. Richard Webber that ended in heartbreak and the baby being put up for adoption.[50] Then, after Derek's death, Meredith leaves, has a baby, names her Ellis after her mother, but doesn't tell anyone she is pregnant or where she and her children are.[51] Both pregnancies represent rebirth in the wake of a degraded relationship and personal tragedy, while the mother/daughter parallelism signifies that the "carousel never stops turning." On *Grey's*, the carousel represents Meredith's childhood memory of her mother's and Richard's break up while she was riding a carousel and watching them fight. Another one of Meredith's childhood memories involves her calling 911 when her mother attempts suicide, which parallels Meredith's daughter Zola calling 911 when she is bleeding at the end of her pregnancy. Through a Bakhtinian lens, the carousel represents the carnival and its seemingly endless circular movement reflects the cyclical pattern of degeneration and regeneration that viewers encounter. Moreover, Ellis's suicide attempt paired with Meredith's bleeding (as well Meredith's several near-death experiences throughout the series) harken the grotesque realism of death as constantly near, a nearness also present in the next Shondaland attraction, *Scandal*.

Scandal's Carnival

In *Scandal*, the relationship between Olivia Pope, political operative and professional fixer, and Fitzgerald Grant, the president of the United States, is the central romantic plotline threaded through all seven seasons. Much like the relationship between Meredith and Derek on *Grey's*, the relationship between Olivia and Fitz cyclically degrades, only to be repetitively regenerated. Olivia's interpersonal web is taut as she pushes and pulls against past and present romantic entanglements with Fitz; with Navy captain, friend of Fitz, Pentagon official, and spy Jake Ballard; and, more sparingly, with Senator Edison Davis. Each time Olivia achieves stability in one of these relationships, it degrades due to some internal or external crisis. An interpersonal arc of degeneration/regeneration happens throughout season 2 when Fitz and Olivia are no longer speaking and Olivia is no longer working at the White House.[52] Olivia is dating Senator Davis and when Fitz learns of their relationship by unethically using his resources to spy on her, it seems their romantic involvement is over for good—until Fitz nearly dies after an assassination attempt. In addition to the grotesque realism of blood spatter when Fitz is shot in the head, the assassination attempt marks a major climax that stunned viewers in the final seconds of the episode.[53] This climax serves as the catalyst that regenerates "Olitz's" relationship; in the next episode, Olivia is standing in Fitz's White House walk-in closet, crying into his Navy sweatshirt.[54]

The constant battle to stabilize Fitz's stolen presidency from his first term to his second plays out alongside the overarching narrative of Olivia's tempestuous relationships. Over season 2, we learn that, unbeknownst to Fitz, members of his campaign—including Olivia—rigged the election results in Defiance County, Ohio. Verna Thornton, an advisor to Fitz later appointed to the Supreme Court, was involved in Defiance and was behind the attempted assassination. This storyline's cycle of death and rebirth comes full circle in a flashback when Fitz, still recovering from the shooting, visits Verna in the hospital where she is dying of cancer.[55] As Fitz delivers Verna's eulogy with her casketed corpse below his pulpit, the audience assumes she succumbed to cancer. However, the flashbacks interspersed with Fitz's eulogy show pale and bald Verna struggling to speak and relying on oxygen to breathe. When Verna tells Fitz that she plans to confess to Defiance before she dies, Fitz briefly contemplates his options and then grimly explains that he will honor her in his eulogy. Apologizing, he restrains both of her arms and removes her oxygen. Verna then struggles and gasps as Fitz holds her down and watches as her writhing weakens and she dies. Through the grotesque realism of this scene, Fitz murders an enemy who threatens uncrowning and is regenerated by a renewed drive to prove himself worthy of office and rightfully win a second presidential term.

Another degeneration/regeneration narrative in *Scandal* begins in the season 3 finale and continues through season 4's "State of the Union." The Grants' oldest son, Jerry, dies suddenly after being poisoned by Tom Larsen, a Secret Service agent who is actually working for the covert spy organization B613 headed by Olivia's father Rowan.[56] First Lady Mellie Grant, grieving the son she thinks died of meningitis, unravels amid her grief. Grotesque realism manifests as a gluttonous Mellie—far departed from the normative role of first lady—who eats chips on her son's grave, eats fried chicken on the White House balcony, and drinks moonshine out of a jar.[57] Pictures of Mellie eating on her son's grave are published with the headlines "Mental Mellie" and "Madam First Crazy" rendering her grotesque realism a public spectacle. This excessive eating and drinking is a carnivalesque trope that highlights the body's base functions as does Mellie's degenerating appearance and hygiene. Previous to Jerry's death, her appearance was impeccable; in the midst of her grief, she wears pajamas to the Oval Office and eats cereal out of the box.[58] Narrating her grotesque grief, Fitz says, "I have dealt with Drunk Mellie and Smelly Mellie and Screw-Everything-to-Hell Mellie and Crybaby Mellie and Eat-Everything-That-Is-Not-Nailed-Down Mellie and I have not complained."[59] Soon after, Fitz shows Mellie the abovementioned headlines and encourages her to attend the State of the Union as a public retort. Mellie, fried chicken in hand, erupts into cackling laughter and says, "Oh! Honey baby! Do you actually think I give a damn about what anyone thinks of me anymore?"[60] Her laughter signifies degeneration and an embodied "rejection of authority."[61] Bakhtin asserts that laughter during the carnival also represents "a capacity for survival and regeneration," exhibited when Mellie pulls herself together with a bright red dress and pearls to appear at the State of the Union.[62] After keeping up the façade of first lady for the event, Mellie shakily returns to the residence, kicks off her shoes, and desperately claws at her chest until her string of pearls breaks and she falls to her knees. Through her grief, Mellie is in a constant state of degeneration and regeneration.

While Olivia's interpersonal relationships and Mellie's well-being cyclically degenerate and regenerate, other characters endure grotesque embodied degeneration that exemplifies new heights of the carnivalesque in Shondaland. The medical trauma featured on *Grey's*, although often shocking, occurs in a context in which the audience expects bodily trauma and the base corporeality of blood, urine, and vomit. On *Scandal*, Rhimes elevates the shock factor even further, as if building a new Shondaland rollercoaster with higher hills and startling spirals. Indicative of Rhimes's pushing the limits of grotesque realism is a scene in season 3's "Yolo" in which Huck tortures his friend and fellow gladiator Quinn. Standing over a duct-taped and naked Quinn, Huck calmly tells her, "Normally, I'd start with the drill or a scalpel—peeling off the skin can be beautiful—or removing fingers, toes. I like the feeling of a toe being separated from a foot. But with you, because we're friends, because we're family, I won't do any of that."[63] Leading up to this scene we learn about Huck's past through flashbacks that explain his grotesquely degenerative history of torture and murder as a B613 agent recruited from the military. While other *Scandal* characters contribute to the carnival, Huck is consistently a curiosity as someone degenerated to the point that cyclically regenerating is questionable. We learn that he abandoned his family to keep them safe from B613 and met Oliva after defecting from B613. A destitute panhandler in the train station, after he saves Olivia from a purse snatcher, she recruits him to work for her. Olivia, often the ringleader of Huck's hellish circus, rebirths him as he regenerates into a gladiator, yet she also influences his degeneration when she calls on his torturous skills.[64] Thus, Olivia exploits the monster in Huck made by her father and B613—creating a sideshow spectacle just as the handlers of gladiators did in ancient Rome.

Huck degenerates into his sideshow so easily that he is prepared to kill his close friend and apprentice, Quinn. Returning to the abovementioned torture scene, we watch Huck manically lick Quinn's face before removing the duct-tape from her mouth and forcing it open. Amid Quinn's screaming and pleading, Huck inserts the dental pliers before being interrupted by a call from Olivia. After the fleeting distraction of Olivia's call, he rips out Quinn's molar and then suspends the torture to respond to Olivia's crisis. Thus, Olivia is perhaps the best model of the broken fixer—she repeatedly fixes Huck only to break him again and again in an ongoing degeneration/regeneration cycle replete with grotesque realism.

Scandal features grotesque torture, degenerating/regenerating love affairs, and excessively violent drama ranging from the president killing to preserve his legacy to the vice president killing her husband to Huck's slaughter of sixteen grand jury members.[65] Olivia Pope and her gladiators attempt to fix problems for clients, yet their own scandals profoundly function in service to the carnival. On the next Shondaland ride, *How to Get Away with Murder*, viewers are introduced to Annalise Keating and her team of student interns, more broken fixers who save their clients and sometimes themselves.

How to Get Away with Murder's Carnival

The degeneration/regeneration cycle appears early on *HTGAWM*. Annalise's confrontation with her husband in season 1's "Let's Get to Scooping" has become an iconic scene in which Annalise sits in front of her vanity's mirror, face neutral. Her jewelry clanks as she removes it and drops it onto the vanity. Then, she removes her wig, reaches up, and strokes her natural hair while staring at herself in the mirror. Looking down, she removes her false eyelashes and wipes the makeup from her face. Slow music plays, heightening the somber mood conveyed by her facial expression and demeanor. When her husband, Sam Keating, enters the scene, Annalise turns to him and asks, "Why is your penis on a dead girl's phone?"[66] This scene harkens the first season's central storyline, the murder of Lila Stangard, a former student of Sam Keating's at Middleton University. Annalise embodies degeneration as she breaks down the mask she wears throughout the day; her raw honesty combined with her vulnerability makes this scene emblematic of Shondaland's high-achieving yet broken fixers.[67] The empowerment that emanates from stripping herself of her wig and makeup shortly before confronting her adulterous husband, evidence literally in hand, exemplifies the liberation of carnival. The ritual unmasking of Annalise indicates the spectacle is over and the carnival has ended, leaving only real life and real consequences for her and Sam to reckon with. Yet, of course, the degeneration/regeneration cycle begins again in the next episode.

Embodied degeneration accelerates as the suspense around Lila's murder increases and as the revelation of the murderer nears. Sam is also murdered, and the audience is left pondering the role, if any, that Annalise and her interns played in his death and the subsequent cover up. Grotesque realism is foregrounded when the interns dispose of Sam's body by dismembering his corpse. Scenes of body disposal intersperse with a raucous beach party taking place within earshot of the interns. The contrast creates a carnival atmosphere as images of party goers, cheerleaders being tossed into the air, and a raging bonfire overlap with Annalise's students arguing about whether or not to set the corpse afire.[68] Connor, the suave and confident gay intern, unravels into hysterics, and flashbacks juxtapose the cool Connor with the nervous and fraught Connor. Then, the audience watches as Connor swings an axe over his head and down onto Sam's body. He delivers five blows before asking, "Hey guys I think I just detached the tibia. Or is that a fibula?"[69] Punctuating his grotesque question with unstable laughter, Connor degenerates to the point of madness, similar to Mellie's hysterical laughter on Scandal after Jerry's death. Like Mellie, Connor's laughter rejects authority as he attempts to cover up the murder of his professor and employer's husband. For Bakhtin, laughter is key to the carnival because it reminds us of our humanity. He says, "Laughter, as an embodied physiological act, facilitates a signification in and of the body."[70] Connor's speech itself (i.e., asking about human anatomy), may seem reasonable but his laughter signals the carnival's excess and degeneration.

In contrast to excessive laughter, sex and death reflect grotesque realism and the carnival's drama. Another scene in this episode shows Connor skillfully manipulating a man to get evidence to prove Annalise's client was framed. Connor walks in on a man, Paxton, alone in a copy room. Paxton takes off his belt with a flourish and drops his pants. Connor looks surprised and pleased, presumably with Paxton's endowment. The two have sex, which is shown in a series of rapid-fire jump cuts of lips, hands, and torsos. After Connor leaves, Paxton takes a call and says, "And he did this thing to my ass that made my eyes water."[71] This explicit focus on the lower stratum—the parts of the body responsible for copulation and defecation—is carnivalesque in that it references sex and excrement, vis-à-vis Paxton's penis, anus, and sexual pleasure. This is also emblematic of Shondafication as a transgression of what is typically deemed acceptable on prime time, both in the visuals of gay sex and the references to Paxton's penis and "ass." Later, consistent with the degeneration/regeneration cycle, Paxton commits suicide after

Connor and Annalise reveal that he betrayed his boss and mentor. Much like Ellis's suicide attempt in *Grey's*, Paxton's suicide, juxtaposed with the murder mysteries of Lila and Sam, reminds viewers of the constant nearness of death, which, in Paxton's case, is as near as stepping out of the window of his boss's upper floor office. Paxton's grotesque death contributes to Connor's degeneration when he frantically knocks on his boyfriend Oliver's door. As Connor shakes and hyperventilates, we are reminded of human fragility through a body/ character that is typically shown as supremely confident and sexy. Connor's breakdown also exposes his vulnerability to Oliver, and although their relationship is damaged by Connor's infidelity with Paxton, it is regenerated as Oliver comforts him.

The embodiment of sexuality on *HTGAWM* is more pervasive and explicit when compared to Shondaland's other series. The legal interns sleep with clients, witnesses, and each other—sometimes to get ahead, other times just for fun. Sex invokes grotesque realism, and the excess of sex in *HTGAWM* is part of the carnival. When the FBI shows one of Annalise's clients accused of insider trading, Marren Trudeau, a surveillance video of her having sex with someone they believe gave her insider information, she says, "Take notes. This is what Pilates can do for you."[72] Later, when Marren sees a picture of Annalise and Sam, she says, "If this were my husband, I'd never be able to walk straight again." Marren spectacles her enjoyment of sex through defiantly casual speech. Through the representation of her sexuality as excess on a normative scale, Marren becomes a clownish figure who entices the audience to laugh and cheer her on. According to Bakhtin, in the carnival, the clown can be a powerful leader, which Marren certainly is as CEO and founder of a brokerage firm who subverts social expectations about how a woman in her position should speak and act.[73] As founder of her firm, Marren started from nothing to crown herself CEO, thus upsetting the social order by being a powerful, blatantly sexual woman.

Amid *Grey's* and *Scandal's* notoriety, Shondaland audiences likely expect the excessive sexuality of *HTGAWM's* young and hot interns. Less expected is how Viola Davis as Annalise is sexualized in ways not often seen on prime-time television. The significance of how Annalise is scripted is compounded by the rarity of encountering dark-skinned black women as sexually desirable characters in complex romantic entanglements. Annalise is unapologetically sensual, witnessed via her hot affairs with Nate, a muscular black male detective, and Eve, a long-legged white female prosecutor.[74] In season 1's "Kill Me, Kill Me, Kill Me," Annalise hangs up on her husband's voicemail, gazes for a moment at a photo of Nate and his wife on their wedding day and asks Nate, "Are we terrible people?" Nate responds, "Depends on who you ask," before taking her hand, pulling her body to his, passionately kissing her as they strip, and then picking Annalise up and pressing her against a wall.[75] Commenting on how her role challenges representations of sex on television, Davis says, "Oh, I love it! . . . I wanted to be that sexy woman who took her mask off at night, the sexy woman who was not a size two, the sexy woman who looked like me and walked like me and had my skin tone."[76] As noted previously, the upheaval of social norms and expectations is key to the carnival.

In the carnival Bakhtin describes, what is usually against the rules of society is made desirable. In *HTGAWM*, Annalise is enviable, evidenced by her student Michaela yearningly stating, "I want to be her."[77] In our real-world, youth-centric society, where female sexuality is considered passive, light skin is considered desirable, and men overwhelmingly depict power, rarely would a middle-aged, dark-skinned, sexually liberated, curvy black woman be the character others idolize, yet in Shondaland's carnival, the normative social mores are off. However, like other broken fixers, the audience sees Annalise privately degenerate through grotesque realism. While school is out and Sam is "missing" (Annalise knows he is dead), Annalise retreats to a hotel where she lies on the bed in the dark, drinks from the minibar, eats room service, and rings in the new year with tears.[78] Signaling the degeneration/regeneration cycle, school returns to session, the interns return to work, Annalise has a new client to work on behalf of, and—akin to theatrics—the show must go on.

SHONDA RHIMES AS A CARNIVAL MASTER

In this chapter, we analyzed *Grey's Anatomy*, *Scandal*, and *How to Get Away with Murder* through Bakhtin's concept of the carnival. Since the carnival is literally and figuratively characterized by excess, we explored how the carnival tropes—ritual spectacle, upheaval, and grotesque realism—fuel the carnival cycle of degeneration/regeneration. While Shondaland shows are not the only televisual texts in which carnival elements manifest, we argue that these tropes are brought to new heights of excess (and popularity) through the Shondafication of prime-time television. As a carnival master, Rhimes's talent soars to new heights when she pushes the boundaries enough to shock viewers while maintaining her status. We agree with Everett that Rhimes has noticeably impacted television for the better: "Indeed, not only does Rhimes' Shondaland make possible Nowalk's new discursive success [with *How to Get Away with Murder*], but—given the copycat practices of network television—arguably, the recent increase in TV dramas featuring black women leads and co-stars in prime time can also be attributed to Rhimes' author function and televisual transdiscursivity."[79] We also believe that Shondafication has challenged the industry's status quo. Bakhtin reminds us that during the carnival, "commoners" unburden themselves—albeit momentarily—from the fear imposed by those in power who make and enforce the rule of law to their benefit. Similarly, Rhimes uses the power she has within Shondaland to unburden herself and her audience from the repressive rules of the real world. Rhimes challenges dominant logics that systematically marginalize women, especially women of color, by casting diverse female actors as powerful and complex characters in the form of Meredith Grey, Miranda Bailey, and Cristina Yang on *Grey's*; Olivia Pope, Mellie Grant, and Quinn Perkins on *Scandal*; and Annalise Keating, Michaela Pratt, and Laurel Castillo on *HTGAWM*.

As we ride Shondaland's rollercoaster through the twists and turns of high-stakes medicine, politics, and law, viewers are amazed by the main characters' savvy, while puzzled by their lack of common sense. Bakhtin's theorization of the carnival exposes how power dynamics can change, but even those crowned with power are imbued with weakness, foolishness, and depravity. Providing respite in exchange for high ratings, Rhimes and her team mirror the degeneration/regeneration cycle by introducing new twists that heal—albeit temporarily—our favorite characters, which keeps the carousel turning, the Shondaland rides operating, and amusement seekers and fans coming back for more.

NOTES

1. For clarity, Seattle Grace Hospital and Grey Sloan Memorial Hospital refer to the same hospital; Seattle Grace was renamed in Season 9 of *Grey's Anatomy*.
2. Mikhail Bakhtin, *Rabelais and His World*, trans. H. Iswolsky (Cambridge, Mass.: MIT Press, 1984).
3. Paul "Pablo" Martin and Valerie Renegar, "'The Man for His Time' *The Big Lebowski* as Carnivalesque Social Critique," *Communication Studies* 53, no. 3 (2007): 303; Tracey Owens Patton and Julie Snyder-Yuly, "Roles, Rules, and Rebellions: Creating the Carnivalesque through the Judges' Behaviors on *America's Next Top Model*," *Communication Studies* 63, no. 3 (2012): 367; Gulnara Karimova, "Interpretive Methodology from Literary Criticism: Carnivalesque Analysis of Popular Culture: *Jackass*, *South Park*, and 'Everyday' Culture," *Studies in Popular Culture* 33, no. 1 (2010): 43; Jennifer Fuller, "The 'Black Sex Goddess' in the Living Room: Making Interracial Sex 'Laughable' on *Gimme a Break*," *Feminist Media Studies* 11, no. 3 (2011): 265.
4. Linda L. Carroll, "Carnival Rites as Vehicles of Protest in Renaissance Venice," *Sixteenth Century Journal* 16, no. 4 (1985): 487–502.
5. David K. Danow, *The Spirit of Carnival: Magical Realism and the Grotesque* (Lexington: University of Kentucky Press, 1995), 4.
6. Patton and Snyder-Yuly, "Roles, Rules, and Rebellions," 367.
7. Bakhtin, *Rabelais*, 123.
8. Patton and Snyder-Yuly, "Roles, Rules, and Rebellions," 370.
9. Alastair Renfrew, *Mikhail Bakhtin* (London: Routledge, 2014), 141.
10. Renfrew, 137.
11. Bakhtin, *Rabelais*, 19–20.
12. Renfrew, *Bakhtin*, 143; Simon Dentith, *Bakhtinian Thought: An Introductory Reader* (London: Routledge, 1995), 67.
13. Dentith, *Bakhtinian Thought*, 67.
14. Bakhtin, *Rabelais*, 7–8.
15. Dentith, *Bakhtinian Thought*, 67.
16. Anna Everett, "Scandalicious: *Scandal*, Social Media, and Shonda Rhimes' Auteurist Juggernaut," *Black Scholar* 45 (2015): 36.

17. Matt Zoller Seitz, "The Year in Shonda Rhimes; What Can't She Do?," *Vulture*, December 14, 2014, http://www.vulture.com/2014/12/year-in-shonda-rhimes.html.

18. Henry A. Giroux and Grace Pollock, *The Mouse That Roared: Disney and the End of Innocence* (Lanham, Md.: Rowman & Littlefield, 2010), 164.

19. James Poniewozik, "Shonda Night in America. For Three Hours on Thursday, It's OMG TV," *Time*, September 18, 2014, http://time.com/3397088/shonda-rhimes-night-in-america/.

20. "Kingda Ka," *Six Flags*, accessed July 25, 2017, https://www.sixflags.com/greatadventure/attractions/kingda-ka; Everett, "Scandalicious," 35.

21. Patrick Colm Hogan, "Auteurs and Their Brains: Cognition and Creativity in the Cinema," in *Visual Authorship: Creativity and Intentionality in Media*, ed. Torben Grodal, Bente Larsen, and Iben Thorving Laursen (Copenhagen: Museum Tusculanums Press, 2004), 67.

22. Roberta Pearson, "The Writer/Producer in American Television," in *The Contemporary Television Series*, ed. Michael Hammond and Lucy Mazdon (Edinburgh: Edinburgh University Press, 2005), 16–25.

23. Debra Kaufman, "Inclusive Entertainment Industry Remains a Challenge," *Hollywood Reporter*, March 2, 2017, http://www.hollywoodreporter.com/news/inclusive-entertainment-industry-remains-a-131227.

24. Everett, "Scandalicious," 34–36.

25. Everett, 36.

26. Catronia Wightman, "*Scandal* Exec Betsy Beers Q&A Part 1: Fitz & Olivia, Torture, & Mellie," *Digital Spy*, June 29, 2013, http://www.digitalspy.com/tv/ustv/interviews/a493857/scandal-exec-betsy-beers-qa-part-1-fitz-olivia-torture-mellie/.

27. Kristin J. Warner, "If Loving Olitz Is Wrong, I Don't Wanna Be Right," *Black Scholar* 45, no. 1 (2015): 17.

28. Bakhtin, *Rabelais*, 19.

29. Everett, "Scandalicious," 38.

30. Eisa Nefertari Ulen, "Sisters Are Doing It for Themselves," *Crisis Magazine*, Winter 2014, 18.

31. Seitz, "The Year in Shonda Rhimes."

32. Everett, "Scandalicious," 36–37.

33. Joe Otterson, "TV Ratings: 'Grey's Anatomy,' 'Scandal' Finales Drive ABC to Easy Win," *Variety*, May 19, 2017, http://variety.com/2017/tv/news/greys-anatomy-scandal-season-finale-ratings-abc-1202436870/.

34. Ruth Deller, "Twittering On: Audience Research and Participation Using Twitter," *Participations* 8 (2011): 216–245.

35. Everett, "Scandalicious," 40.

36. Everett, 34.

37. *Grey's Anatomy*, "A Hard Day's Night," season 1, episode 1, directed by Peter Horton, written by Shonda Rhimes, aired on March 27, 2005, on ABC.

38. *Grey's Anatomy*, "17 Seconds," season 2, episode 25, directed by Daniel Minahan, written by Mark Wilding, aired on May 14, 2006, on ABC.

39. *Grey's Anatomy*, "Losing My Religion," season 2, episode 27, directed by Mark Tinker, written by Shonda Rhimes, aired on May 15, 2006, on ABC.

40. *Grey's Anatomy*, "What I Am," season 3, episode 4, directed by Dan Lerner, written by Allan Heinberg, aired on October 12, 2006, on ABC.

41. *Grey's Anatomy*, "Who's Zoomin' Who?," season 1, episode 9, directed by Wendey Stanzler, written by Harry Werksman and Gabrielle Stanton, aired on May 22, 2005, on ABC.

42. *Grey's Anatomy*, "Oh, the Guilt," season 3, episode 5, directed by Jeff Melman, written by Zoanne Clack, Tony Phelan, and Joan Rater, aired on October 19, 2006, on ABC.

43. Shonda Rhimes, *Private Practice* [television series], ABC, 2007.

44. *Grey's Anatomy*, "She's Leaving Home," season 11, episodes 22 and 23, directed by Chris Hayden, written by Stacy McKee, aired on April 30, 2015, on ABC.

45. *Grey's Anatomy*, "The First Cut Is the Deepest," season 1, episode 2, directed by Peter Horton, written by Shonda Rhimes, aired on April 3, 2005, on ABC.

46. *Grey's Anatomy*, "The First Cut Is the Deepest."

47. *Grey's Anatomy*, "It's the End of the World," season 2, episode 16, directed by Peter Horton, written by Shonda Rhimes, aired on February 5, 2006, on ABC.

48. *Grey's Anatomy*, "It's the End of the World."

49. *Grey's Anatomy*, "Bring the Pain," season 2, episode 5, directed by Mark Tinker, written by Shonda Rhimes, aired on October 23, 2005, on ABC.

50. *Grey's Anatomy*, "Puzzle with a Piece Missing," season 11, episode 2, directed by Rob Corn, written by William Harper, aired on October 2, 2014, on ABC.

51. *Grey's Anatomy*, "She's Leaving Home."

52. *Scandal*, "Defiance," season 2, episode 7, directed by Tom Verica, written by Peter Noah, aired on November 29, 2012, on ABC.

53. Lesley Goldberg, "*Scandal* Case Study: EP Betsy Beers on Who Shot Fitz and the Roller Coaster Ahead," *Hollywood Reporter*, December 6, 2012, http://www.hollywoodreporter.com /live-feed/scandal-spoilers-who-shot-fitz-398586.

54. *Scandal*, "Happy Birthday, Mr. President," season 2, episode 8, directed by Oliver Bokelberg, written by Shonda Rhimes, aired on December 6, 2012, on ABC.

55. *Scandal*, "Nobody Likes Babies," season 2, episode 13, directed by Tom Verica, written by Mark Wilding, aired on February 7, 2013, on ABC.

56. *Scandal*, "The Price of Free and Fair Elections," season 3, episode 18, directed by Tom Verica, written by Shonda Rhimes and Mark Wilding, aired on April 17, 2014, on ABC.

57. *Scandal*, "The State of the Union," season 4, episode 2, directed by Allison Liddi-Brown, written by Heather Mitchell, aired on October 2, 2014, on ABC.

58. *Scandal*, "Randy, Red, Superfreak and Julia," season 4, episode 1, directed by Tom Verica, written by Shonda Rhimes, aired on September 25, 2014, on ABC.

59. *Scandal*, "Inside the Bubble," season 4, episode 3, directed by Randy Zisk, written by Matt Byrne, aired on October 9, 2014, on ABC.

60. *Scandal*, "Inside the Bubble."

61. Renfrew, *Bakhtin*, 143.

62. Renfrew, 143.

63. Jethro Nededog, "'Scandal' Stars Weigh In on Quinn's Torture, Fallout from Olivia's Mom-Shaped Blind Spot," *Wrap*, December 12, 2013, http://www.thewrap.com/scandal-stars-weigh -quinns-torture-fallout-olivias-mom-shaped-blind-spot/.

64. *Scandal*, "Crash and Burn," season 1, episode 5, directed by Steve Robin, written by Mark Wilding, aired on May 3, 2012, on ABC.

65. *Scandal*, "A Door Marked Exit," season 3, episode 10, directed by Tom Verica, written by Zahir McGhee, aired on December 12, 2013, on ABC; *Scandal*, "You Can't Take Command," directed by Tom Verica, written by Shonda Rhimes and Mark Wilding, aired on May 14, 2015, on ABC.

66. *How to Get Away with Murder*, "Let's Get to Scooping," season 1, episode 4, directed by Laura Innes, written by Erika Green Swafford, aired on October 16, 2014, on ABC.

67. Lynette Rice and Natalie Abrams, "The Power and Glory of Viola Davis," *Entertainment Weekly*, no. 1352 (February 2015): 26–31.

68. *How to Get Away with Murder*, "Pilot," season 1, episode 1, directed by Michael Offer, written by Pete Nowalk, aired on September 25, 2014, on ABC.

69. *How to Get Away with Murder*, "Let's Get to Scooping."

70. Renfrew, *Bakhtin*, 142.

71. *How to Get Away with Murder*, "Let's Get to Scooping."

72. *How to Get Away with Murder*, "Let's Get to Scooping."

73. Danow, *Spirit of Carnival*, 3–4.

74. *How to Get Away with Murder*, "Pilot"; *How to Get Away with Murder*, "It's Time to Move On," season 2, episode 1, directed by Bill D'Elia, written by Pete Nowalk, aired on September 24, 2015, on ABC.

75. *How to Get Away with Murder*, "Kill Me, Kill Me, Kill Me," season 1, episode 9, directed by Stephen Williams, written by Michael Foley and Erika Green Swafford, aired on November 20, 2014, on ABC.

76. Nolan Feeney, "Viola Davis Says Filming *How to Get Away with Murder* Sex Scenes Should Be Uncomfortable," *Time.com*, January 29, 2015, http://time.com/3687766/how-to-get-away-with-murder-viola-davis-sex-scenes/.

77. *How to Get Away with Murder*, "Pilot."

78. *How to Get Away with Murder*, "Best Christmas Ever," season 1, episode 11, directed by Michael Katleman, written by Tracy A. Bellomo and Warren Hsu Leonard, aired on February 5, 2015, on ABC.

79. Everett, "Scandalicious," 36.

2 · WOUNDED DETACHMENTS, DIFFERENTIAL ALLIANCES

Beyond Identity and Telos in Shondaland's Heterotopia

JOAN FABER McALISTER

In my mind, I see a line. And over that line, I see green fields and lovely flowers and beautiful white women with their arms stretched out to me, over that line, but I can't seem to get there no-how. I can't seem to get over that line.' That was Harriet Tubman in the 1800s. And let me tell you something: The only thing that separates women of color from anyone else is opportunity. —Viola Davis, "Emmy Speech"[1]

On September 20, 2015, the *New York Times* reported that Viola Davis had become "the first African-American to earn an Emmy for best actress in a drama" for her starring role on ABC's *How to Get Away with Murder* (also referred to as *HTGAWM*).[2] In a speech opening with Tubman's stark portrait of the line separating her from an idealized world of white women, Davis commends Shonda Rhimes for helping to change "what it means to be beautiful, to be sexy, to be a leading woman, to be black."[3] Through this tribute, Davis underscores that prime-time television seldom features complex roles for black actresses in a medium that has stigmatized dark-skinned black women in particular, making her award-winning role as lawyer Annalise Keating even more significant.[4]

The Tubman quote Davis recites resembles the Shondaland show in which she stars, as both employ creative imagery to reveal material conditions, inciting a radically reflexive perspective on a world that is at once unreal and too real. Like Tubman's vision, *HTGAWM* places viewers in intimate proximity to the painful distance between cultural ideals and social realities. As we watch Professor Keating and her diverse group of students, staff, and clients fight to get ahead, we are shown hallowed bureaucracies designed to benefit the privileged and a criminal justice system incapable of establishing innocence. By challenging common tele-visual fantasies with real struggles endured by those at the margins of society, this legal melodrama creates revelatory reflections of U.S. culture. As its mirror image of our own society reverses conventional morality, *HTGAWM* challenges cate-gories of victim and villain and aligns audiences with widely vilified figures who are perennial targets of misogyny and bigotry. Although we witness their deprav-ity and misdeeds, audiences are nonetheless compelled to forgive them as we learn to see our legal system as a corrupt social order that requires skill without scruple.

The trajectory of the reflexive route *HTGAWM* travels is paved by shared dreams and private anguishes. It enables us to enter the looking glass of ideals while calling our attention to the exclusions making them so inaccessible for so many. As a disorienting space of otherness that forces critical reflection, *HTGAWM* recalls Michel Foucault's description of spaces termed *heterotopias*, the "counter-sites" wherein "all the other real sites that can be found within the culture" may be "simultaneously represented, contested, and inverted."[5] Heterotopias play a vital role by reflecting the real world in unreal ways that spark reflection and change. Television is heterotopic when the fictional representations it creates have the potential to mirror familiar social scenes made strange through reversals that connect sacred ideals to social critiques. Critical media scholars find Foucault's heterotopia "a useful concept to approach television as a site of contradiction" in numerous studies exploring how the medium opens "spaces of resistance."[6]

Set in recognizable places like the classroom, courthouse, and home and as a melodrama featuring narratives that contest social norms and challenge moral log-ics, *HTGAWM* utilizes heterotopia's radical openings for critical reinvention. In moments of raw intimacy, this televisual heterotopia "acts as a mirror to an increas-ingly morally complacent public who choose not to know" the pains of life at the neglected margins of society.[7] Since mediated heterotopias "reflect and refract" real settings, viewers experience the emotional journeys of characters caught in situations we cannot dismiss as entirely fictional.[8] In this way, *HTGAWM*'s het-erotopic perspective perverts familiar settings long depicted as cornerstones of U.S. society into dangerous places where exception becomes rule, deviance becomes norm, and hero becomes villain. Through such reversals, the gains of social movements recede and personal trauma governs the logic of characters con-tinually operating in survival mode as they form provisional alliances across multifarious differences.

To explore this program's heterotopic, "simultaneously mythic and real con-testation of the space[s] in which we live," I focus on how the first two seasons of *HTGAWM* invite viewers into a fictional context that exposes real ordering mech-anisms of educational, legal, and familial institutions.[9] As the strange scenes become recognizable, our own social reality and redefinitions of marginalized, counterhegemonic, or even abject existences emerge through shocking storylines. These scenarios create intimate experiences with subjects so wounded that they are incapable of the idealistic forms of trust, love, and hope central to dramatic narratives. Too damaged by daily violence, disappointment, and injustice to form stable and shared identities that might generate a common cause, *HTGAWM*'s characters have moved beyond "wounded attachments" to historical grievances that Wendy Brown locates as the foundation of identity politics.[10] But if this legal drama takes us beyond identity, it does not do so through a postracial or postfeminist fantasy of inclusion and equality. Instead, by eroding faith in conventional social movements and existing social conditions, *HTGAWM* moves us into new territory. It is a place resembling neither an inspirational utopia nor a cautionary dystopia, but a heterotopia of radically irreducible experiences that have separated subjects from shared visions of a better world, a society where shifting intimacies and forming differential alliances are the only ways to survive brutal hierarchies.

Parting company with "the genre's long-established strategies for the understanding and dramatization of deviance and criminality" by "mobilizing tropes of otherness," *HTGAWM* displaces privileged viewpoints to allow audiences to witness the traumas, humiliations, and triumphs of survivors of the oppressions that the program's heterotopia depicts as commonplace.[11] Eschewing identification with the white and male iconic figures most common in U.S. crime shows, this prime-time hit gets away with murder, exposing the audience to unapologetic queer sex, excusable adultery, and sympathetic homicide.[12] Furthermore, as viewers become attached to a legal team that blackmails witnesses, falsifies evidence, and exonerates clients guilty of violent crimes, they follow the intimate emotional journeys of women, racial minorities, working-class, and queer characters who lie, cheat, and brutalize their way up the social ladder, leaving a trail of white wealthy bodies in their wake. Creating opportunities for radical reflexivity, *HTGAWM*'s heterotopia reveals unfamiliar perspectives on the Ivy League college campus, the neoclassical county courthouse, and the Victorian family home— familiar places made strange through reversals of conventions such as rule and exception, normality and deviance, center and margin, good and evil. Flat clichés of assertive black womanhood, hypersexual gay life, and working-class masculinity are reinvented so gifted actors can embody complex characters. Responding to critics of Annalise Keating's antiheroic qualities, Viola Davis captured the force of the show's heterotopic vision when she accepted her 2016 Screen Actors Guild Award, saying "I am not who you think I am; you are who you think I am."[13]

HETEROTOPOLOGIES OF TELEVISUAL SPACE

Productive links between heterotopia and media are not new and started with Foucault's own explication of the concept. Citing the heterotopic potential of theatrical productions on stage and screen, Foucault noted how both assemble different "sites that are in themselves incompatible," creating "a whole series of places that are foreign to one another" and projecting "three-dimensional space" even through a flat medium.[14] Foucault's description suggests heterotopias serve two roles of interest to critical television scholars: "to create a space of illusion that exposes every real space, all the sites inside of which human life is partitioned, as still more illusory" or "to create a space that is other, another real space, as perfect, as meticulous, as well arranged as ours is messy, ill constructed, and jumbled."[15] The former, deemed "heterotopias of illusion," speak to the critical capacity of media to divulge counterhegemonic perspectives, while the latter, "heterotopias . . . of compensation," serve as a palliative for those most harmed by or excluded from cultural norms and social hierarchies.[16]

Communication scholars have noted heterotopic functions of television and film, with all media deemed "important agents for the production of (heterotopian) space."[17] Some have argued that heterotopic reversals are inherently "conservative" and "affirm the status quo," creating space that "offers a social safety valve from public life."[18] However, others argue that cinematic heterotopias provoke audiences to reconsider the ubiquity of racism when exposed to the experiences of those terrorized by it and can be "profoundly self-reflexive" in ways that challenge existing categories, hierarchies, and relations.[19] Studies have also explored the capacity of heterotopic film to operate "as a space that imagines and enacts heterogeneous material realities," since "heterotopias self-reflexively reinforce their otherness and expose all other real spaces as illusory, or inversely, reveal that all spaces are based on complex material conditions of lived experience."[20]

Media research has also examined political critiques offered by televisual heterotopias, exploring how fictional space "mirrors contemporary debates about domestic roles and the space of the home; multiculturalism and diversity; and the viability of democracy as a whole."[21] Nathan Stormer links the biopolitical functions of heterotopias to their temporal as well as spatial properties claiming, "The ongoing interaction of different spaces and their temporal rhythms creates the possibility of re-arranging not only the relations between those spaces but relations within them as well."[22] Foucault identifies a temporal component along with the spatial dimensions of heterotopically generated places, as they form within "slices in time" (called *heterochronies*) that interrupt existing timelines by extending or quickening flows and logics of temporality.[23] Building on this thread, John Pugliese describes media "at once grounded in reality yet invisible to some, at once marked by lived experience yet unreal," concluding "heterotopias configure complex and contradictory dimensions of space-time."[24]

The radical promise of spatial and temporal dimensions of heterotopias are crucial in examining the politics of *HTGAWM* as its places are made strange partly through concurrent yet converging timelines that unfold and rewind to reveal key details of dramatic events. Its unconventional narratives move forward from the earliest events while simultaneously moving backward from the eventual death of key characters: Lila Stangard and Sam Keating in the first season, Emily Sinclair and Annalise (who eventually survives a wound we fear is fatal) in the second season. This temporal reordering generates urgency as the distance from present time decreases and a collision between timelines becomes imminent. Crucial too is the way *HTGAWM* employs dramatic revelations, repeating but extending earlier scenes to include previously obscured information about characters and their actions. For instance, the show's pilot features Wesley Gibbins solving an urgent dispute by flipping a coin, initially evidence of his transparency and diplomacy—but we are later given a camera angle showing us Wes lied about the outcome of the toss to cover up his role in the death of Annalise's husband.

Revelatory time spaces in *HTGAWM* operate to overturn generic narrative expectations, as the audience is pulled into settings where hate crimes are commonplace, injustice is pervasive, and immorality is expected. The social reality that emerges through these heterotopic zones mirrors our own but sheds an unflattering light on the ubiquity of social privilege, inequality, and abuse. Cliché characters (ambitious black women, dangerous young thugs, promiscuous gay men) usually serving as episodic foils take center stage. Conventional authority figures (the academic elite, wealthy executives, hard-nosed police detectives) are dethroned in storylines championing deceit over veracity, rewarding those who break the rules of sacred institutions. People naïve enough to believe in the rewards of diligence, the sanctity of marriage, or the parity of law are punished with unhappy outcomes. *HTGAWM*'s portraits and plots prompt reflection on the skills and sympathies requisite in such a social order, undermining longstanding patterns of the genre.

Moreover, places associated with iconic institutions central to core cultural values are reimagined to upend traditional conventions and cherished norms. Viewers repeatedly travel to three iconic places: the classroom, the courtroom, and the home. In episode after episode, we see these benevolent sites darkly reflected as havens for humiliation, injustice, and abuse inflicted with disproportionate frequency on those who lack social privilege, those whose subsequent unethical and immoral actions then seem justified as acts of self-defense.

ANALYZING *HTGAWM*'S HETEROTOPIA

Familiar Places as Strange Spaces

From the first frames of the pilot episode, we are invited into a world that seems an unfamiliar yet feasible reflection of our own. The first shot—a dark sky streaked by toilet paper streamers and backed by aggressive music—is followed by drunken screams and the football coach's violent rallying cries to destroy a rival team burning in effigy next to a pulsing horde of half-clothed college students. Signs of danger (e.g., darkness, a mob, ritual, alcohol, fire) undermine the elevated status of campus life before we seek refuge in the woods, where we become intimate conspirators with the characters we will identify and empathize with throughout the series. While a Philadelphia university collectively erupts in drunken debauchery, members of the Keating 5 forming Annalise's legal team debate how to best hide evidence of a murder. As we repeatedly return to this place and time in scenes that show these characters dismembering and burning the body of their professor's husband, we will nonetheless feel closer to them than we do to the riotous swarm in the streets.

When we visit Middleton's campus, the hedonistic bacchanalia of the crowd on bonfire night contrasts with mundane daytime encounters in Professor Keating's introductory criminal law lecture. In scenes drawn from an anxious student's worst nightmare, Keating's lecture hall is a place of terror, humiliation, and verbal abuse. Replacing the educational ideal with its painful but plausible opposite, the college classroom becomes a place of posturing rather than learning. Intellectual exploration, skill acquisition, curiosity, and questions have no place in Keating's lecture, where students engage in a brutal competition to curry favor by demonstrating discipline, cunning, and knowledge. As they are badgered, insulted, ignored, and cross-examined by their teacher, we witness their fear and degradation.

Our attention is drawn to several students in this classroom whose struggles seem atypical of Hollywood depictions of Ivy League law schools. We see Professor Keating silence a smart and shy bilingual Latina, Laurel Castillo, whose idealism inspired her to flee her sinister father and seek the moral high ground to defend the less fortunate. We watch as an ambitious young black woman, Michaela Pratt, tirelessly and fruitlessly seeks praise from a role model who responds with personal insults and by raising the bar. We observe as a white gay man, Connor Walsh, employs a polished professionalism to hide a fear of failure that borders on hysteria in some scenes. Their struggles strike a contrast with the white son of a federal judge, Asher Millstone, whose sophomoric machismo provides comic relief in most of his scenes. But no character is more relatable than the show's Haitian American underdog, Wesley Gibbins. Viewers remain closest to Wes throughout *HTGAWM*'s first two seasons, spending time with him in his seedy apartment as he contemplates his troubled past and present quandaries. Our televisual intimacy with Wes is intensified by rarely being alone with any other character, save Annalise Keating. Fostering identification and empathy with this tall young black immigrant man—even after we have seen him holding at least three murder weapons and frequently breaking into his professor's bedroom (in a hoodie, no less)—is remarkably risky, but not unreasonable in *HTGAWM*'s topsy-turvy upheaval of the dominant social order.

We watch as Professor Keating rewards these students for illegally obtaining evidence, lying to police and members of the court, blackmailing witnesses, and using any and all means to exonerate defendants guilty of heinous crimes. We hear her profess that all clients lie and that all people, including law students and attorneys, are capable of committing terrible deeds. Since the pilot reveals that the trophy awarded to Keating's top student will become a murder weapon—and the eager and naïve Keating 5 will conspire to conceal the crime—we have no reason to dismiss her pronouncements as jaded pessimism or dramatic posturing.

The brutal environment in which *HTGAWM*'s law students compete dampens dreams of education as an equalizing means of social mobility. Furthermore, none of the lofty ideals associated with criminal law are embraced in Keating's classroom. She never asserts that all clients have a right to a fair trial, she makes no mention of the presumption of innocence, and she says little about guiding values of the justice system. In this legal world, privileges trump rights, clients are presumed guilty, and bias is the norm. Finding ways to get around the law to win cases and free clients is the explicit objective; it is a bloody arena and Keating is usually the last combatant standing as her cunning strategies and commanding courtroom performance are unbeatable.

The legal defendants introduced in Keating's classroom sketch an inverted portrait of a justice system in which the exception becomes the rule and injustice prevails. Case after case demonstrates that the police routinely falsify evidence, witnesses perjure themselves, and the state is mired in procedural inertia. District attorneys do not bother to opine about morality and the rule of law, as these iconic heroes of the courtroom drama are unapologetically motivated by personal and political gain. Similarly, television's perennial favorite, the police detective, is only interested in scoring a conviction and persistently fails to uncover the truth (or even produce a plausible version of events).

As we share secrets with Keating's firm, we keep our distance from a parade of interchangeable white, wealthy, and privileged figures on the other side of the courtroom. We root for the defense team as they exploit loopholes and shadows of doubt to keep guilty clients from paying for their crimes. The plaintiffs seem to have it coming, so we shed no tears for the philandering CEO, the pedophilic priest, or the abusive husband who have been maimed or murdered by the defendants Annalise represents. Although her victories in the courtroom free a gleeful widow, a domestic terrorist, an unrepentant stalker, and a lethal dominatrix, we know them through private conversations and intimate camera angles, and their victims seem distant and deserving.

Midway through season 1, Annalise tells her students that a death row conviction she is about to appeal destroyed her own youthful faith in the justice system. David Allen, an aging and angelic black man, shows no signs of resentment after serving twenty-one years for a crime he did not commit: the murder of his white girlfriend, a housing activist targeted for assassination by a villainous developer. Convicted by a corrupt federal judge (Asher's father), Allen's case inspires Annalise's impassioned speech as she frees an innocent man and exposes government corruption, redeeming our amoral main character while tarnishing the legal institution she serves.

In a similar season 2 case, Annalise faces the grieving mother of a boy her client killed, a black woman whose faith in restorative justice contrasts with Keating's own cynicism. Yet the trial that follows solicits Annalise's stark appraisal of a justice system that imprisons young men of color, destroys families, and erodes communities—and her speech sounds too sincere to dismiss as a courtroom ploy. Her resounding denunciation here is supported by a growing stack of case files evidencing a clear pattern of institutionalized bias, which rationalizes the dirty tricks used to outwit the transphobic cops, tainted witnesses, opportunistic attorneys, and unfeeling judges. We see Annalise encounter racism and sexism on a daily basis as she is persecuted, disrespected, and disparaged as a token by those with more power. After overhearing white women describe Annalise as an inhuman animal, the deceptions she employs to humiliate her (nearly always white and usually male) opponents seem justified.

The Keating client list shares certain characteristics that soften an otherwise shocking departure from an expectation for dramatic narrative to reward heroes and punish villains. The team nearly always represents underdogs who are up against powerful figures and oppressive forces, making them sympathetic (although usually guilty). Radical reversals position us as viewers on the side of unscrupulous survivors and against a system that would never exonerate or protect them, even if they had been innocent. The typically privileged figures victimized at the hands of Keating's defendants are often dehumanized or demonized: a maimed CEO turns out to be a habitual philanderer, a dead cop is exposed as a violent wife beater, and a defamed judge is tainted by corruption. In each case, a potential path to identification with a white male heterosexual figure of rank is closed as the character is deemed deserving of punishment or even death. Although the show's dramatic courtroom scenes reflect a moral reordering of the system most U.S. Americans have been taught to revere, we also recognize its flaws from nonfiction news accounts and real social movements. When we see police officers lie to protect their own, we are reminded of the police brutality inspiring Black Lives Matter activism, and when we learn a transgender woman staged a crime scene to deflect legal bigotry, we recall recent bathroom bills maligning transgender individuals as inherently dangerous. Annalise's world mirrors back an inequitable and discriminatory society that we know we live in.

If courthouse settings in *HTGAWM* overturn core values relating to justice, then depictions of domestic space trouble both popular feminisms and hegemonic family life—inviting strange bedfellows and bizarre public/private incursions. Annalise's legal practice operates out of a Victorian house on Middleton's campus serving as her office and residence, a situation that reverses the attainment of work/life balance. Despite familiar calls for working women to make room for family life, Keating has literally carved out a professional career in familial space. The fragile and permeable boundaries between the public and private zones in her house make for strange intimacies and open secrets in nearly every episode. Her two staff members and student employees are privy to her marital woes, intimately entangled in her mental and physical health issues, and coconspirators in her (il)legal maneuvers. Her clients' cases literally and metaphorically dominate her domestic space, as files and documents spill across every surface and skeletons and schemes leak out of every room. From damning evidence in the bedroom and litigation drafts in the library to angry confrontations in the kitchen and whispered conspiracies on the porch, the house where Annalise lives with her husband in an interracial, childless marriage is anything but an ordinary family abode. Her student Wes stumbles into her office tryst with her (also married) lover and repeatedly barges into her bedroom at night. Her home office is bugged, robbed, and broken into regularly. Rather than stealing her away from home too frequently, her professional life literally invades every corner of her personal space. There is no sanctuary for Annalise—she is physically and emotionally exposed and vulnerable in scene after scene staging devastating collisions between private and public.

The family home, long imagined as a refuge from immorality and danger, becomes a site for adultery, confrontation, and violence in *HTGAWM*'s heterotopia. We observe Annalise having sex with her current lover Nate Lahey, a police detective she blackmails into false testimony and then frames for murder, as well as her ex-lover Eve Rothlow, the attorney Annalise left to marry her therapist but later ropes into shady courtroom dealings. We watch as Annalise screams and smashes household items amid fights with her husband, her lover, and her mother. We witness her client suffocated in the basement, her husband killed in the foyer, and Annalise herself nearly strangled in the hall. We stand by as a strong black woman who rules over classrooms and courtrooms devolves into a deep, alcohol-drenched depression behind the curtains of her bedroom. As our main character totters drunkenly up the stairs, frantically searches her husband's phone for evidence of misdeeds, and hallucinates about her lost babies, we are acutely aware that her home has never been a haven from trauma. Although *HTGAWM*'s heterotopic house is the inverse of all we have long been told to associate with familial spaces (i.e., comfort, privacy, safety, intimacy, recreation, rest, morality, normalcy), we recognize that the real family homes it reflects back to us have always harbored dirty secrets. Annalise's home life may be extremely atypical, but the sorrows it houses connect viscerally with viewers' secrets and scars. None of us live in a picturesque cleaning product commercial, whatever the neighbors think.

The family Annalise forms in her house, a place where private becomes public as work becomes home, is certainly not normative. The team member who emerges as a moral compass is Connor Walsh, a hypersexual gay man who used the fictional hookup app HUMPR to have public anonymous sex and "introduced the network television masses to rimming, whether they were ready for it or not."[25] Although his morality seems unlikely, he exhibits the most conventional responses of all the students to ethical quandaries and seems most vulnerable to guilt and shame. Conner is also the only student who attempts to transfer schools to escape the immorality that surrounds him. Annalise repeatedly casts herself as abusive mother to Connor (e.g., berating him, yelling at him, threatening him with prison, telling him he is nothing and nowhere without her) as well as her other students and staff, while announcing that she never wanted children and is grateful for her miscarriages. Exposing the vulnerability of kinship structures and identity politics, intimacies are formed not through family ties or cultural legacies but through shared interests and temporary alliances. Traditional households, blood relations, and communal bonds are problematic pasts to escape, as we learn about families and communities fractured by addiction, adoption, adultery, incest, migration, sexual abuse, suicide, and violence. When relationships are formed, they emerge from exchanges we are positioned to distrust: tearful confessions are almost always lies, sexual encounters provide convenient alibis, and kindnesses turn out to be self-serving. In this heterotopic home, family is fashioned provisionally and strategically, and metaphoric blood ties spring from actual spilled blood as each character clings to coconspirators or any port in the storm.

The most genuine intimate connection we see Annalise make is with her ex-lover Eve—the one character we do not see her lie to and verbally abuse regularly. Although Annalise seems to protect and perhaps even care for her students, staff, and husband, most of her closest companions are separated from her by mutual deceptions and betrayals. She craves and enjoys the company of her lover Nate, whose muscular form and striking features exude sex appeal as his silky black vernacular conveys an effortless cool enhanced by his cocky saunter, frequent sex scenes, and shirtless appearances. But Nate seethes and barely suppresses rage in most episodes, appearing drunk and dangerous at times. Moreover, he distrusts Annalise, and we are encouraged to share his suspicions when he thinks she is lying. By contrast, Eve and Annalise share honesty and tenderness, both challenging and supporting one another. Eve's view of Annalise also provides a queer perspective on her life: when Eve sees her ex-girlfriend's belly distended with pregnancy, she reacts with disgusted disbelief. Given Annalise's own misgivings and our familiarity with the style of surrogate parenting she deploys on her students and staff, we are tempted to take Eve's position that motherhood is anything but natural for Annalise—and as the protagonist that overturns so many conventions, Professor Keating denaturalizes motherhood for viewers too.

Annalise's relationship with Eve resembles several other connections between characters in its antagonistic stance vis-à-vis dreams of shared community and collective action. Despite ever-present acts motivated by racism, sexism, classism, and other forms of discrimination (and despite the frequency with which plotlines feature rape, domestic violence, and racial profiling), common experiences with abuse and bigotry never result in intimate bonds between characters. While we see evidence of tenderness and trust in Annalise's interactions with

Eve, we also see Annalise refusing to embrace a nonheterosexual label for her own sexuality and characterizing Eve (in ugly, stereotypic terms) as a bitter, middle-aged, lonely lesbian. Other LGBTQ (lesbian, gay, bisexual, transgender, queer) characters abuse and use one another for sex, as true intimacy seems produced by happenstance rather than secured by political and cultural affinities.

Likewise, sisterhood is nowhere evident, as women battle over men and money. Black women do not support each other; Annalise has no special affection for Michaela, she refused to help her lover's terminally ill wife, and black female judges are unmoved by appeals to solidarity or evidence of racial bias. We never get a sense of black community either; class differences exacerbate the tensions between Annalise and Nate and between other black characters. Most HTGAWM families are blended and multiracial, the only black couples we meet are divided by adultery or deceit, and the friendships we see forming are usually interracial—a significant break from the pattern of segregating black female characters on television.[26] We have entered into Shondaland's heterotopia, a place profoundly altering perspectives on identity, community, and morality, radically reinventing the possibility of politics on such a terrain.

Murder through the Looking Glass

Beyond settings linked to places with near-mythic status in U.S. culture, heterotopic spaces are opened through encounters unfolding in the frequent mirror scenes featured in this legal melodrama. The reflective function of HTGAWM's heterotopia often materializes in and through literal mirror scenes that establish intimacy and empathy with deeply flawed characters that are rarely represented on prime-time television. Through this Shondaland show, we become residents of a looking glass version of our society that illuminates how we might appear to others.

The mirror serves as metaphor and exemplar in Foucault's writing, where he finds it heterotopic in that it "does exist in reality, where it exerts a sort of counteraction on the position that I occupy."[27] Elaborating on the mirror's heterotopic operations, he adds, "From the standpoint of the mirror I discover my absence from the place where I am since I see myself over there . . . the mirror functions as a heterotopia in this respect: it makes this place that I occupy at the moment when I look at myself in the glass at once absolutely real, connected with all the space that surrounds it, and absolutely unreal, since in order to be perceived it has to pass through this virtual point which is over there."[28] The critical perspective of a reflection that is real yet refracted through a virtual medium has long interested media scholars. As Paolo Magagnoli notes in an extended examination of the political potential of film to represent an altered version of reality, "as 'distorting mirrors,' heterotopias can offer a space for critical thinking from which to reflect on and contest dominant power structures."[29] Linking this function to television, Angie Knaggs argues that television can create radical heterotopic perspectives that "both reflect and contest" the real situations they represent through dramatized scenes.[30]

Always a potent trope in visual media, the use of mirrors in a program that functions heterotopically itself is particularly interesting. Fittingly, *HTGAWM* features several crucial mirror scenes central to characters that the show converts from strange to familiar. To illustrate how its reflections offer radical perspectives on educational, familial, and legal spaces, I explore three key mirror scenes in season 1. Each mirror stages critical commentary on the forces distorting the public personas and self-perceptions of characters as diverse as the images they reflect.

The pilot that launched the show contains two revealing mirror scenes that establish the legal world in which the drama takes place while exploring the social and self-images of central characters. The first features Laurel Castillo, who follows the firm's client into the courthouse restroom, eager to uncover clues that will prove her worth to the team. An extreme closeup shows us Laurel's eye peering through the crack of the bathroom stall, and then we share her perspective during a mirrored encounter between a mistress accused of attempted murder and the wife of the injured plaintiff. Instead of venomous glances or hasty departures, we witness a tender exchange as the wife gently squeezes the shoulder of the defendant and the two lock eyes in a knowing look. Shocked to find proof that Annalise is representing a guilty client, Laurel is then disillusioned to find her revelation anything but a surprise to coworkers scheming to bury evidence and misplace blame. We later learn that Laurel's father is a stern Latino patriarch, whose dirty dealings prepare her for the underbelly of a corrupt hierarchy that feels disturbingly familiar—a place she suspects she has always belonged.

The second notable mirror encounter from the pilot features Annalise and provides crucial insights into her character. When Wes meets his professor's white spouse at a cocktail party hosted by the dean, he realizes that the nude black man he glimpsed kneeling before Annalise's lifted skirt in her home office was not her husband. Coolly observing his shock, Annalise then follows Wes into the restroom. Because earlier scenes portrayed her commanding attention in the lecture hall and barking at her staff in her living room, viewers expect an unpleasant confrontation and Wes's babbled assurances that he will never expose her secret suggest he fears the same. We share his surprise when Annalise, an intimidating authority figure, neither reprimands nor threatens but dissolves into a tearful explanation of how failed pregnancies have led to marital stress. When this powerful professor then begins to reproach herself for her own unprofessionalism, it is a pitiful sight indeed. We see Wes uncomfortably backed against a large mirror that reflects Annalise's face and the disturbingly erotic motion of her hands as she caresses his shoulders, back, and chest, murmuring her gratitude for his discretion. After Wes agrees and abruptly escapes her grasp, the camera lingers over Annalise's face as she meets her own gaze in the mirror.

The crucial shot that follows is our first long and lonely moment with the protagonist, as she considers her own visage in a mirror that fills the frame. She wipes away tears and blots a running nose while we search her face for evidence of hidden motives and private thoughts, proof of sincerity, or subterfuge. As we linger on her expressions, we see pain, self-loathing, and then shame, followed by a practiced resolve as she composes herself, squaring her shoulders to confront public scrutiny once more. The mirror entices us into the interior world of this powerful black woman, a place fraught with moral ambiguities, pitiable vulnerabilities, and undeniable strengths. She is resigned to her private flaws and prepared to face public pressures we can only imagine.

Notably, this relatively long shot departs from the pilot's script in important ways. Although producer Peter Nowalk authored the first screenplay, he gives his mentor, Shonda Rhimes, and his star, Viola Davis, a great deal of public credit in developing the main character's personality, motivations, and backstory.[31] Whether it was the work of Nowalk, Rhimes, Davis, the director, or the outcome of a series of innumerable and untraceable changes, the Annalise who emerges in the first episode's cocktail party mirror scene is dramatically different from the one scripted. The written version has Annalise dispassionately removing the traces of crocodile tears as soon as Wes leaves.[32] The televised version, however, forces viewers to confront the fragility of *HTGAWM*'s most formidable figure through a mirror scene that collapses the distance otherwise enabling audiences to demonize her—a significant feat in a media culture pervaded by "controlling images" depicting black women as objects of suspicion and scorn.[33] Viewers learn eventually that the fragile subject we have just glimpsed is what remains of the child born Anna Mae Harkness, a fatherless and impoverished girl who was sexually abused by her uncle and is emotionally alienated from the mother who failed to protect her. We will see Anna Mae's posttraumatic self-loathing directed at her own reflection once again in the most celebrated segment from the first two seasons—a revelatory reflection scene that attracted widespread acclaim in the press.

These devastating mirrored moments create a dramatic ending for season 1's fourth episode that places Annalise at a dimly lit vanity (and showcases Davis's peerless talent for conveying complexities). The melodic thump of a sorrowful dance track swells while she resolutely removes her jewelry; an emphatic drop of the wedding ring creates a rewarding thud. Then, the camera offers a close up at the nape of her neck as her fingers peel off a wig to reveal close-cropped natural/ untreated hair—a part of Annalise we have never seen. Smoothing her head and mournfully lowering her gaze, she removes her false eyelashes and scrubs away a heavy layer of makeup as her face contorts (with pain or effort?) under a white tissue that might also catch unseen tears. Her eyes avoid her own reflection yet steal disparaging glances at a face moving between grief and resolution, unnervingly inscrutable. She removes the vestiges of the powerful public figure we have come to know until her familiar face is stripped bare and is barely recognizable. Exposed and raw, she then turns to confront her husband (whose entry into this private space, punctuated with a kiss on her neck, evidences rare intimacy) with an image of his own naked body on a phone recovered from a sorority house crime scene, revealing that he had an affair with his student, Lila Stangard, and may have murdered her as well. Annalise's final expression as the scene closes is perhaps the most painful: the haunted eyes of a woman accustomed to betrayal above the scornful smile of a verbal warrior who has just delivered a fatal blow.

Media coverage of this vanity scene credits Davis with the choice to remove her wig and vigorously wipe (rather than gently cleanse) the cosmetics from her face. Black women writers link the star's performance to her brave decision at the 2012 Oscars to "do what we rarely see black women in Hollywood attempt: go sans wig and let the word see her natural, chemical-free" hair.[34] Additionally, viewers read the "revelation of [her] unadorned, honest face" as a rebuke of the unkind remarks this dark-skinned, fifty-year-old actress's appearance has garnered in mainstream media and applaud her willingness to expose the main character by "removing her façade, layer by layer."[35]

Over the course of *HTGAWM*'s first two seasons, we are given ample evidence that this successful black woman hides a deep well of shame and guilt. She has not survived her unlikely climb up from the very bottom rung of the social ladder unscathed. When we join Annalise in discovering another deep family secret—the fire that killed Anna Mae's abusive Uncle Clyde was set by her mother to save her—we are offered a compelling personal and political reason for some subjects to get away with murder. Indeed, for those subjected to the triple indignities of being poor, black, and female, murder might be the only way to protect the ones you love. When Anna Mae's mother reveals that rape—by an uncle, a schoolteacher, and a priest—is a legacy shared by all of the women in their family, we are shown why one cannot rely on the rule of law or the bonds of community to prevent, police, or punish such crimes. The wounded girl we see in Annalise's reflection needed saving when a racist justice system and a sexist civil rights movement were oblivious to her pain.

Robert Reid-Pharr links the concept of heterotopia to the potential for the self-appraising gaze to symbolize the appeals and traps of identity politics. As a critic who is both gay and black, Reid-Pharr reads vanity encounters as experiences that stage a confrontation between deviance and normativity, leaving behind a wound that aches for the salve of unity or collective action. However, Reid-Pharr draws painful attention to the complexities of such calls to community: "I am aware that the label Black, Gay Man can be read as an erasure of difference. Each of our identities is crisscrossed by a multiplicity of variables. Our individual selves lie at the nexus of these."[36] For these reasons, he calls for forms of connection that will resist the unifying pull of a community that essentializes shared subjectivities at the expense of distinct differences that also matter. Such connections must acknowledge a long list of grievances without becoming dependent on preserving their own marginalized status, a posture Wendy Brown identifies as the cornerstone of identity politics. As Brown observes, such a politics relies on a "recrimination that seeks to avenge the hurt even while it reaffirms it," a position that "becomes attached to its own exclusion" and "installs its pain . . . in the very foundation of its political claim." When collective identity is grounded in such shared trauma, it falls prey to "entrenching, dramatizing, and inscribing its pain in politics."[37]

Charting a path that avoids the twin dangers observed by Reid-Pharr and Brown—disavowing complex differences and uniting as perpetually wronged—is difficult in an era that has chosen to ignore ongoing injuries of bigotry by wishing them into a past overcome. But unlike so many other programs embracing a postfeminist, postracial celebration of the end of the era of identity and identity politics, *HTGAWM* shows us a place where the wounds of the past are ever present, and we must find alternatives to idealistic hopes that a single social movement will bring about a better future for all.

BETWEEN PAST AND FUTURE, SELF AND OTHER IN SHONDALAND

In addition to drawing viewers into a heterotopic reflection highlighting the flaws of our own educational, legal, and familial realities, *HTGAWM* connects us to characters who struggle in an ongoing compromise between ethical ideals, individual desires, and protective instincts. The program's plotlines create imperfect outcomes for flawed subjects who are nonetheless worthy of empathy and whose extraordinary experiences are imaginary but feel real.

Moreover, the show reveals the degree to which domestic interiors serve as sites of violence and civic spaces are dangerous for subjects lacking the protection that privilege affords. With betrayal, brutality, and shame permeating private zones traditionally touted as sanctuaries of security and stability (e.g., the home, family, and educational and justice systems), this program indicts social hierarchies and their anointed elites for countless acts of unpunished deviance and criminality. When we see, feel, and experience the classroom with an eye toward those long excluded, the courtroom from the view of those who must get away with violence to survive, and home from the perspective of survivors of brutality and betrayal, we can sense that there is a little Annalise Keating in many of us. Commenting on the complexities of identities and diversities represented in *HTGAWM*, Viola Davis proclaims, "There is nothing about Annalise that you can define as just black." For Davis, it is this capacity to exhibit "the full spectrum of humanity" that makes Shondaland such an important place, a place where viewers encounter "characters in a narrative that reflects life, but doesn't reflect television."[38]

Indeed, through the heterotopic vision of her cultural and political context, we learn along with Annalise that we are never reducible yet always reduced to labels that cannot capture the complexities of our experiences and perspectives. We have moved beyond the possibility of identity politics, but we have lost hope that we will ever arrive at a telos of equality and justice. The best we can do with neither moral compass nor definitive destination is to fight to represent our own irreducible differences in the face of the virulent bigotries plaguing society. We are neither innocent victims nor victorious resisters but survivors who live to fight another day. Such a retreat from identity politics may represent a problematic elision of differences that risks false equivalencies—especially since privileged viewers are invited into intimacy and empathy with characters whose burdens we could not possibly share—but the show also unsettles idealistic dreams and dislodges self-congratulatory postures shielded from the material conditions that still stalk marginalized members of society.

Heterotopias are neither dystopic nor utopic in Foucault's description, but reflect places that paradoxically mirror those in our own everyday lives. As much as we might long for a narrative that offers hope of a justice system that is just, or yearn for characters to speak truth to power, the instability of the moral universe in *HTGAWM* resolutely kills off our fantasies of equality and progress. Even intersectional approaches that nuance identity politics seem simplistic in the face of the radically complex and contingent subjectivities we encounter in *HTGAWM*'s heterotopia, a place where alliances are always provisional. This Shondaland looking glass is a place of survivalist politics in crisis mode, and it leaves us with residual fears and hopes long after the credits roll.

If we look into the moral heterotopia where Annalise, Wes, and the rest of the team are surviving and see them as immoral others, we risk aligning ourselves with that idyllic and unreal white world that divides us from the humiliations, traumas, and triumphs we have come to know intimately. As the music accompanying the dramatic finale of another episode fades away and the Shondaland logo appears again, this fiery roller coaster encircling a glowing heart seems an apt metaphor for our emotional journeys into colorful lives at once far removed from and intimately connected to our own. We have taken a strange ride that shows us another prospect on our own world, and we cannot look away.

NOTES

1. Quoted in Spencer Kornhaber, "The Emmys Speech of the Night," *Atlantic*, September 20, 2015, https://www.theatlantic.com/notes/2015/09/harriet-tubman-at-the-emmys-viola-davis-first-black-woman/406360/.

2. Michael Gold, "Viola Davis's Emmy Speech," *New York Times*, September 20, 2015, http://www.nytimes.com/live/emmys-2015/viola-daviss-emotional-emmys-acceptance-speech/.

3. Gold.

4. Thomas A. Mascaro, "Shades of Black on 'Homicide: Life on the Street': Advances and Retreats in Portrayals of African American Women," *Journal of Popular Film & Television* 33, no. 2 (2013): 58–59; Beretta E. Smith-Shomade, *Shaded Lives: African-American Women and Television* (Piscataway, N.J.: Rutgers University Press, 2002), 60; Joshua K. Wright, "Scandalous: Olivia Pope and Primetime History," in *Black Women and Popular Culture: The Conversation Continues*, ed. Adria Y. Goldman, VaNatta S. Ford, Alexa A. Harris, and Natasha R. Howard (Lanham, Md.: Lexington Books, 2015), 15–32.

5. Michel Foucault, "Of Other Spaces," trans. Jay Miskowiec, *Diacritics* 16, no. 1 (1986): 24.

6. Angie Knaggs, "(Em)placing Prison Break: Heterotopic Televisual Space and Place," *Refractory Ejournal* 18 (2011), http://refractory.unimelb.edu.au/2011/05/06/emplacing-prison-break-heterotopic-televisual-space-and-place-%E2%80%93-angie-knaggs/.

7. Knaggs.

8. Paula J. Massood, "Which Way to the Promised Land? Spike Lee's *Clockers* and the Legacy of the African American City," *African American Review* 35, no. 2 (2001): 268.

9. Foucault, "Of Other Spaces," 24.

10. Wendy Brown, *States of Injury* (Princeton, N.J.: Princeton University Press, 1995), 73.

11. Yvonne Tasker, "Television Crime Drama and Homeland Security: From 'Law & Order' to 'Terror TV,'" *Cinema Journal* 51, no. 4 (2012): 44.

12. Bradley S. Greenberg and Larry Collette, "The Changing Faces on TV: A Demographic Analysis of Network Television's New Seasons, 1966–1992," *Journal of Broadcasting & Electronic Media* 41, no. 1 (1997): 7.

13. Amanda Michelle Steiner, "SAG Awards 2016: Viola Davis Isn't Worried about Being the Hero after Win," *Entertainment Weekly*, January 30, 2016, http://ew.com/article/2016/01/30/sag-awards-2016-viola-davis/.

14. Foucault, "Of Other Spaces," 24.

15. Foucault, 27.

16. Foucault, 27; 24–5.

17. André Jansson, "Beyond 'Other Spaces': Media Studies and the Cosmopolitan Vision," *Communication Review* 12 (2009): 307.

18. Andrew Wood and Anne Marie Todd, "'Are We There Yet?': Searching for Springfield and the Simpsons' Rhetoric of Omnitopia," *Critical Studies in Media Communication* 22, no. 3 (2005): 209; Andrew Wood, "'What Happens [in Vegas]': Performing the Post-Tourist Flâneur in 'New York' and 'Paris,'" *Text and Performance Quarterly* 25, no. 4 (2005): 318.

19. Nilgün Bayraktar, "Heterotopic Intersections of Tourism and Undocumented Migration in Southern Europe: The Video Essay Sudeuropa (2005–2007)," *New Cinemas: Journal of Contemporary Film* 10 (2012): 18; Robert F. Reid-Pharr, "Disseminating Heterotopia," *African American Review* 28 (1994): 347–357.

20. Hye Jean Chung, "Media Heterotopia and Transnational Filmmaking: Mapping Real and Virtual Worlds," *Cinema Journal* 51, no. 4 (2012): 89–90.

21. Aviva Dove-Viebahn, "Embodying Hybridity, (En)Gendering Community: Captain Janeway and the Enactment of a Feminist Heterotopia on *Star Trek: Voyager*," *Women's Studies* 36 (2007): 600.

22. Nathan Stormer, "Mediating Biopower and the Case of Prenatal Space," *Critical Studies in Media Communication* 27, no. 1 (2010): 15.

23. Foucault, "Of Other Spaces," 26.

24. Joseph Pugliese, "Crisis Heterotopias and Border Zones of the Dead," *Continuum: Journal of Media & Cultural Studies* 23, no. 5 (2009): 672.

25. Dennis Hinzmann, "*How to Get Away with Murder* Creator Peter Nowalk Talks Sex on the Show . . . ," *OUT Magazine*, August 19, 2015, http://www.out.com/television/2015/8/19/how -get-away-murder-creator-peter-nowalk-talks-sex-and-pressure-make-season-2.

26. Nancy Signorielli, "Minorities Representation in Prime Time: 2000 to 2008," *Communication Research Reports* 26, no. 4 (2009): 323–336.

27. Foucault, "Of Other Spaces," 24.

28. Foucault, 24.

29. Paolo Magagnoli, *Documents of Utopia: The Politics of Experimental Documentary* (New York: Columbia University Press, 2015), 29.

30. Knaggs, "(Em)placing Prison Break."

31. Laura Prudom, "'How to Get Away with Murder' Creator Peter Nowalk on Working with Shonda Rhimes, Diversity on TV," *Variety*, September 24, 2014, http://variety.com/2014/tv /news/how-to-get-away-with-murder-creator-peter-nowalk-shonda-rhimes-viola-davis -diversity-1201313779/.

32. The original script of the pilot is available at http://www.zen134237.zen.co.uk/How_To _Get_Away_With_Murder_1x01_-_Pilot.pdf.

33. Patricia Hill Collins, *Black Feminist Thought: Knowledge, Consciousness, and the Politics of Empowerment* (New York: Routledge, 2000), 7.

34. Kelly L. Carter, "Nothing Else Mattered after That Wig Came Off on 'How to Get Away with Murder,'" *Buzzfeed*, October 17, 2014, http://www.buzzfeed.com/kelleylcarter/the-wig -came-off-on-how-to-get-away-with-murder#.xmb8LE4yw.

35. Robin Givhan, "'How to Get Away with Murder': A Bare Face. Bare Emotions. No Words Required," *Washington Post*, October 17, 2014, https://www.washingtonpost.com/news/arts -and-entertainment/wp/2014/10/17/bare-face-bare-emotions-no-words-required/; Clover Hope, "*How to Get Away with Murder*'s Last Scene Was All It Was Promised to Be," *Jezebel*, October 17, 2014, http://jezebel.com/how-to-get-away-with-murders-last-scene-was-all-it-was -1647584035.

36. Robert F. Reid-Pharr, "Disseminating Heterotopia," 347–357.

37. Brown, *States of Injury*, 74.

38. Quoted in Antonia Blyth, "Viola Davis: 'How to Get Away with Murder' Season 2 'Starts with a Bang'—Emmys," *Deadline Hollywood*, August 24, 2015, http://deadline.com/2015/08 /viola-davis-how-to-get-away-with-murder-season-2-1201504592/.

3 · ABORTION IN SHONDALAND

Daring Departures from Oppressive Industry Conventions

JESSICA L. FURGERSON

Two months before the 1973 U.S. Supreme Court *Roe v. Wade* ruling to legalize abortion, groundbreaking television producer Norman Lear tackled the issue directly in *Maude* (CBS 1972–1978). In the two-part episode "Maude's Dilemma," the show's title character grapples with an unplanned pregnancy that at forty-seven years old feels impossible to continue. Despite costly backlash from television affiliates and sponsors, over sixty-five million viewers watched Maude and her husband Walter terminate her pregnancy.[1] Controversially, Maude was the first to procure an abortion on prime-time television but not the last. In their survey of film and television representations of abortion from 1916–2013, Sisson and Kimport identified 385 plotlines of which 97 appeared on television and 84 during prime time.[2] Yet, few have received as much attention as those portrayed by Shonda Rhimes in her prime-time Shondaland shows. When Rhimes caught flack for a 2015 *Scandal* (ABC 2012–2018) season 5 storyline where protagonist Olivia Pope had an abortion without discussing her choice to do so, Lear defended the bold depiction proclaiming, "I love the way it was handled . . . it was so matter of fact."[3] Recognizing the situation as serendipitous, Lear lamented the lack of societal progress since *Maude* suggesting, "The reason we're having this conversation is because it was so unusual to see such an event on television. It doesn't seem to me that much has changed."[4] Considering Sisson and Kimport identified only forty television plotlines between 2005 and 2014 featuring a character who obtained an abortion, Lear's conclusion is disappointingly accurate.[5]

Just as Maude's abortion debuted when women's reproductive rights were legally unsteady, Rhimes's daring depictions of abortion occur in an increasingly

hostile political climate characterized by legislative restrictions and vitriolic rhetoric. The 2014 progress report on the status of women's reproductive freedom in
the United States produced by the National Abortion and Reproductive Rights
Action League is grim. The federal government earned a D, twenty-five states
earned failing grades, and the report warns that abortion access is being disman-
tled by "anti-choice lawmakers [who have taken] every opportunity to restrict further the right to choose."[6] Facing the most vocal opposition to abortion since
Roe v. Wade, advocates attempt to persuade citizens and lawmakers that access to
safe and healthy abortion services is a paramount concern for humanity.[7] Four
decades after the legalization of the right to abort, the pervasiveness of anti-choice
provisions that effectively undermine the Supreme Court ruling is disturbing.
Such provisions include mandatory counseling (thirty-five states) and waiting periods (twenty-seven states), the prohibition of abortion after a set point in
pregnancy (forty-three states), and legal protections for doctors (forty-five
states) and institutions (forty-two states) refusing to provide abortions.[8] Fueling
these efforts is an unusually vocal White House with Vice President Mike Pence
becoming, in January 2017, the highest-ranking government official to speak at
an anti-abortion event.

Rhimes is a Planned Parenthood board member; therefore, that she and her
writers regularly address abortion in Shondaland is unsurprising. On *Grey's
Anatomy* (ABC 2005–present; also referred to as *Grey's*), abortion is featured
prominently in Dr. Cristina Yang's storyline in seasons 1 and 8. *Grey's* spinoff
show *Private Practice* (ABC 2007–2013) portrayed the provider's perspective in
seasons 2 and 4 with doctors Meg Porter and Addison Montgomery. *Scandal*
also includes two abortion storylines; the first involving a nonrecurring character in season 4 and the second mentioned above involving Olivia in season 5.
From 2005 to 2015, Rhimes included six different depictions of abortion, suggesting that abortion in Shondaland is not merely a plot device—it is a stylistic
choice related to her vision as a television auteur. Rhimes explains that each storyline represents an opportunity to "be serious about what's really going on" when
women grapple with unplanned pregnancy.[9] Due to their consistency and complexity, Rhimes's depictions of abortion daringly depart from previous portrayals in terms of style and substance. Utilizing Condit's analysis of televised abortion on 1980s shows such as *Cagney & Lacey* (1981–1988) and *Spenser for Hire* (ABC
1985–1988) as a framework, this chapter highlights how Shondaland challenges
television industry norms rooted in patriarchy and sexism. Thirty years ago, "Even
in the strongest cases . . . the mass cultural medium of television admitted abortion
only as an ambiguous and constrained practice."[10] Today, I argue that Shondaland
narratives succinctly and directly question the normative conventions that constrain abortion—on-screen and in real life.

REPRESENTING ABORTION ON THE SMALL SCREEN

As a conduit to unknown perspectives and narratives, television programming can alter how audiences perceive televised events that manifest themselves in real life. Because television "creates shared beliefs and perceptions as viewers adopt the messages and images presented in the symbolic world of television as accurate depictions of social reality," the critical media studies imperative to deconstruct and challenge representations of controversial issues is key.[11] Scholars critically examine small screen portrayals of abortion to document dominant tropes and interrogate the ideological functions of these portrayals. As a persuasive medium, television programs are uniquely influential because of the relationship audiences form with characters over time. This relationship "allows for a strong presentation of particular ideological sides, given that these programs engage the audience on an emotional level, base truth claims on experiential knowledge, and treat the audience as being physically present."[12] The infusion of ideology performs both rhetorical and political functions as mediated messages reify existing beliefs and political agendas in ways that indirectly advance political policies.[13] Analyzing female viewer responses to an abortion plotline in *Cagney & Lacey*, Press reveals, "when the moral language adopted by television differs from that of viewers, television viewing influences viewers to adopt its terms."[14] Television's potential to ideologically influence viewers justifies Condit's conclusion that studying television illuminates "the ways in which public, explicitly political, discourse made the crucial transition into the cultural vocabularies of everyday life."[15] By the late 1980s, it was evident that "television would not back off from televising abortion but rather would portray the motives for it in more careful and complicated fashion."[16] Almost forty years later, television programing continues to expand cultural vocabularies surrounding abortion through a diversification of complex storylines.

In her preeminent survey of televised abortion, Condit analyzes thirteen episodes from 1980s serial prime-time television programs to discern the arguments advanced through their portrayals. Heuristically, this work "provide[s] us with a framework for positing a specific set of relationships . . . between entertainment television content and socio-political opinions."[17] Condit sorts each portrayal into one of three categories based on how abortion is discussed and presented within the episode: (1) professional programs focused on the relationship between legal and medical professionals to abortion; (2) false choice/false pregnancy programs with characters who miscarry or discover they were never actually pregnant; and (3) pro-abortion programs featuring characters who implicitly or explicitly have an abortion. Despite nuanced differences, Condit argues that the categories ultimately coalesce to advance traditional ideologies concerning abortion and its acceptability or lack thereof in U.S. American culture.

Specifically, Condit's analysis reveals three narrative consistencies found within each of the abovementioned three categories of prime-time abortion depictions.

First, the choice to abort was constructed as a regrettable rejection of motherhood. During the decision-making process, characters grapple with their identity as women and potential mothers and engage in "discourse reaffirm[ing] the value of motherhood and family."[18] This discourse often resulted in the character keeping the child or being relieved of the decision via a miscarriage; for those characters who eventually abort, the portrayal entailed immense "moral guilt and personal regret."[19] Second, these portrayals narrowly defined the circumstances in which abortion is acceptable. Condit explains, abortion "was sanctioned only when it did not conflict with the values of family and motherhood—for the unmarried or those in otherwise seriously problematic situations."[20] For women with the financial and familial means to support a child, abortion was constructed as a last resort, which is why not a single show featured a married woman aborting a viable fetus. Finally, some narratives were occasionally pro-choice but were rarely, if ever, pro-abortion. She explains, these programs "support[ed] legal choice as a pragmatic necessity but defin[ed] abortion as a morally undesirable act."[21] In these circumstances, characters defended a woman's right to choose but disavowed abortion by treating it as a necessary evil rather than an acceptable option. Even those programs falling under the pro-abortion category "depicted moral disapproval of abortion, support for the concept of women's choice, and endorsement of family," which suggests that the industry standard governing representations of abortion is to endorse the right to choose while paradoxically reinforcing the moral superiority of carrying the pregnancy to term.[22] These patterns provide viewers with an unrealistic depiction of abortion as a morally permissible measure of reproductive control solely for unmarried and/or impoverished women. Utilizing Condit's categories as a framework to deconstruct representations of abortion in Shondaland, this chapter argues that *Grey's Anatomy*, *Private Practice*, and *Scandal* deviate from these normative patterns and challenge television industry norms. Specifically, I argue that the production decisions made in Shondaland challenge existing industry norms that construct abortion as a regrettable rejection of motherhood, counter established standards of acceptability, and advance pro-choice and pro-abortion discourses in opposition to messaging that covertly shames women who choose to abort.

SHONDALAND'S DARING DEPICTIONS OF ABORTION

Challenging the Regrettable Rejection of Motherhood

Abortions are inherently a rejection of motherhood. Previous televised depictions of abortion consistently reframed this rejection as temporary by reaffirming the character's desire for children under different circumstances. Depictions of abortion in Shondaland, however, are commonly accompanied by brazen rejections of motherhood signaling a significant departure from 1980s industry norms. In a 1984 episode of *St. Elsewhere* (ABC, 1982–1988), Clancy has an abortion after an unexpected pregnancy. Pleading with her unsupportive boyfriend Jack afterward, she proclaims, "I love you and someday I would like to have your baby. It's just that now wasn't the right time."[23] Clancy defends her right to make reproductive decisions that are best for her and simultaneously reassures Jack of her inevitable childbearing—reaffirming to him and the audience that she is committed to motherhood when the time is right. Such conversations were typical of pro-abortion programs with most "explicitly highlight[ing] the values of childbearing, family, and mothering in the face of the potential threat to these values abortion represents."[24] Characters on *Grey's Anatomy, Private Practice,* and *Scandal* often openly reject these values and reposition abortion as an option to prevent rather than delay motherhood. In many cases, the only mention of traditional family values in Shondaland comes from secondary characters who often do not share their concerns with the woman contemplating abortion.

On *Private Practice,* Dr. Naomi Bennett, a founder of Oceanside Wellness and an infertility specialist, openly voices her objection to abortion, yet still supports the procedure being performed at Oceanside. Ultimately, such portrayals diversify the discourse surrounding abortion by foregrounding women's agency rather than their regret or the moral authority of doctors. The most conservative portrayal of a character foregoing motherhood and choosing to abort occurs in *Private Practice*'s season 4 "God Bless the Child." Dr. Addison Montgomery's new patient Patty learns that despite having an abortion several weeks ago she is still pregnant and needs an invasive surgical procedure to fully terminate the pregnancy. Panicked, Patty declares to Dr. Montgomery, "I want kids. I do. Just not now. I mean, babies are expensive. Kids need time and attention. It seemed wrong to bring one into the world I couldn't do right by."[25] Just as Clancy assured Jack that timing opposed to a lack of maternal desire is the primary motivation for seeking an abortion, Patty narrates her commitment to family values to Dr. Montgomery. The very label, *unplanned pregnancy,* suggests a societal preference toward the willful and planned conception of children. Rhetorical appeals to timing thus have the effect of stigmatizing sexually active women who at the time of conception are unable to support a child while simultaneously implying the inevitability of childbearing and motherhood once the woman is able to plan her pregnancy. The key distinction between this *Private Practice* portrayal and those analyzed by Condit is how other characters respond to Patty's choice. Unlike Jack, who dismisses Clancy's explanation, Dr. Montgomery tells Patty that she "do[esn't] have to justify her decision" and "if you want an abortion, I'll do it. I am not here to judge you."[26] Amid a consistent plea from supporting characters that women justify their abortions, Dr. Montgomery's unwavering acceptance of Patty's choice and lack of negative judgment affirms the acceptability of abortions for women regardless of their attitude toward childbearing and motherhood.

While Patty's storyline closely mirrors traditional portrayals, the two abortion storylines from *Grey's Anatomy* involving Dr. Cristina Yang bear no resemblance to those common in the 1980s. Far from expressing regret, Cristina brazenly rejects motherhood in both instances of unplanned pregnancy. After learning that she is pregnant with Dr. Preston Burke's child in season 1, Cristina consults no one, including Preston, and immediately schedules an abortion. Learning about the pregnancy during a late night of drinking, Cristina's best friend Dr. Meredith Grey asks her what she plans to do and is bluntly told, "Look, you know what happens to pregnant interns. I'm not switching to the vagina squad or spending my life popping zits. I'm too talented, surgery is my life."[27] When Meredith later suggests that Cristina tell Preston about the pregnancy, Cristina scoffs and refers to the situation as just "a blip on [her] radar."[28] Consistent with shows encompassed by the false choice/false pregnancy category, Cristina miscarries prior to the abortion; yet, unlike normative storylines, she never shows remorse for her choice. Fellow intern Dr. Izzie Stevens is the only character to directly acknowledge the miscarriage; questioning Cristina's cold demeanor she exclaims, "She lost a baby. She lost a fallopian tube and she's acting like she doesn't even care!"[29] Izzie's concern is juxtaposed with a powerful scene of Yang tearfully proclaiming, "I was right. I was right. I'm right" in reference to her decision to abort had she not miscarried.[30] Cristina's proclamation functions as reassurance for both her and the audience that although the miscarriage was unexpected the outcome was exactly what she wanted.

Given the ease with which Cristina opted for an abortion in season 1, it is not surprising that she reached an identical conclusion in season 8 after learning she and her husband, Dr. Owen Hunt, are expecting a child. Owen, who has long wanted children, grows increasingly frustrated with Cristina's unshakable resolve to abort, pleading with her to reconsider and reassuring her that she would be a great mother. Cristina reiterates, "I don't want one. I don't hate children. I respect children. I think they should have parents who want them."[31] Owen clearly represents the traditional family values common in televised depictions of abortion. Yet, his approach differs greatly because he specifically acknowledges her career ambitions and respects her unwillingness to engage in traditional mothering. Initially he pleads, "There is a way to make this work without it ruining your life or derailing your career."[32] When Cristina reiterates her reluctance, Owen offers to assume the role of primary caretaker, suggesting that the baby will be his "problem" not hers.[33] Owen's overtures advance a popular counterargument to heterosexual married women who reject motherhood—that men can shoulder the burden of parenthood, allowing women to focus on their careers.

Despite his persistence, Owen is unable to change Cristina's mind. Acknowledging that she stands in defiance of not only her husband but societal expectations of womanhood and motherhood writ large, Cristina emotionally proclaims to Meredith, "I wish I wanted a kid. I wish I wanted one so bad, because then this would be easy. . . . But I don't. I don't want a kid. I mean, I don't want to make jam, I don't want to carpool. I really, really, really don't want to be a mother."[34]

The consistency of Cristina's rejection of motherhood culminating with this impassioned plea represents a seismic shift in how leading women on prime-time television narrate decisions to abort. No caveat is made about poor timing or a desire for future children; instead, Cristina acknowledges what motherhood entails, recognizes the demands of parenthood, and declines. Her candid decision is underscored by Meredith, drawing from her own experiences with her mother, Dr. Ellis Grey, to inform Owen how devastating it is to be the unwanted child of a surgical prodigy. Pleading with Owen, Meredith says, "Trying to pretend that she loves a kid as much as she loves surgery will almost kill her, and it'll almost kill your kid. . . . My mother was a Yang. And as the child she didn't want, I am telling you, don't do this to her. . . . The guilt of resenting her own kid will eat her alive."[35] Meredith's perspective uniquely expands the discourse surrounding abortion to include testimonial insight from the perspective of the unwanted child. Her lived experiences framed as a plea to Owen distance Cristina's decision from being convenient and selfish by signaling instead that Cristina's decision reflects self-awareness and respect for a child's quality of life. When the audience encounters Cristina and Owen in the hospital room moments before the abortion begins, viewers are asked to make the same decision Owen does by choosing to support Cristina as she terminates her pregnancy.

The tensions that animate Cristina and Owen's disagreement over children represent a common trope in contemporary conversations of childbearing—that women can have it all. Interestingly, confirmation for Cristina's rejection of this trope comes through her friendship with Meredith, who, two seasons later, finds herself struggling to balance her children and career. After performing a surgery originally assigned to Meredith, Cristina bluntly tells her that she is no longer the surgeon she once was because of her children; she remarks, "You made your choices, and they are valid choices, but don't pretend they don't affect your skills."[36] Meredith, who missed the surgery because her husband and fellow surgeon Dr. Derek Shepherd was unavailable to care for their daughter Zola, echoes the impossibility of having it all. She tells her husband, "I shouldn't have to choose between being a good mother and being a good surgeon."[37] In many ways Meredith and Derek serve as the perfect analogue to Cristina and Owen by showing viewers that Owen's promise to bear the burden of childrearing was unrealistic and validating Cristina's conclusion that she could not be a mother and a prodigious surgeon.

The choice to abort in Shondaland is markedly different from its prime-time predecessors. Women reject motherhood without persistent questioning about their motivations for doing so. Their decisions are also affirmed by doctors and husbands who, despite their reservations, are present when the procedure takes place. As with 1980s shows, contemporary portrayals of abortion remain "hemmed in by other values and principles" such as heteronormative reproduction and traditional motherhood.[38] However, the ideological values reflected in Shondaland underscore women's autonomy and agency opposed to maternal regret.

Broadening "Acceptable" Abortion

Having an abortion is one of the most personal decisions a woman can make. However, previous televised depictions of abortion frequently presented the issue as a matter of public discussion that scrutinized the woman's rationale for aborting. Confronted with a woman who needs their assistance to safely procure an abortion in a 1985 episode of *Cagney & Lacey*, the show's star characters quickly devolve into an impassioned debate over abortion's moral permissibility. Lacey prods Cagney to mock the flaws in her pro-life argument: "Well, please, let's just forget about rape victims and teenage girls and women carrying around severely damaged children."[39] Cagney retreats and admits, "I'm just trying to tell you my feelings. I don't know when it's murder."[40] Their conversation reflects how many feel toward abortion—conflicted about when, or even if, the procedure is justifiable. This interaction illuminates the real-life tensions felt by those who see abortion as murder, but also recognize that forcing women to carry to term in all instances is equally harmful. Given this conflicted societal context, it is unsurprising that abortion storylines often probe into the circumstances and motivations of the woman seeking to abort. Condit's findings suggest that an "acceptable" abortion is one necessitated by extreme situations (e.g., rape, abuse, and medically unviable fetuses) or intense economic hardships. One "acceptable" abortion occurs in Shondaland, while the other five occur without mention of mitigating factors that ideologically justify abortion in alignment with traditional values. Condit terms representations of abortion without mitigating factors to be those of convenience and explains that although the characters enact "the pro-choice position" they are shamed despite willingly pursuing a safe and legal procedure.[41] Abortions in Shondaland shatter these conventions of acceptability by supplying a wide range of motivations for abortion, and in some instances providing no explanation at all. By challenging and broadening conceptions of acceptability, audiences are forced to view the abortions enacted televisually as a legal and valid medical option—the rationale for which is irrelevant.

Signaling progress since the 1980s, *Scandal*'s season 4 "A Few Good Women" features the only abortion in Shondaland that adheres to the established template for acceptability wherein mitigating factors necessitate the procedure and thus assuage the character of the guilt she is supposed to feel. Pope is called on by Vice President Susan Ross to assist naval officer Ensign Amy Martin, a pregnant rape victim who desperately wants an abortion. Olivia does not question the ensign's choice and their dialogue focuses solely on how quickly she can get off the ship and away from her rapist. She is seen next in a hospital room with Olivia by her side—the two sit silently as the doctor performs a vacuum aspiration. The absence of dialogue debating abortion throughout the episode is a powerful production decision; it suggests that the only voice that matters is the ensign's because she gets to choose and have her choice respected.

In the absence of mitigating factors, character dialogue dispels dominant narratives of acceptability. On *Private Practice*, at Oceanside Wellness, Dr. Meg Porter boldly defends her patient's decision to abort when her pro-life coworker Dell Parker argues that rape is the only acceptable justification for an abortion. Dr. Porter lambasts Dell after his attempt to dissuade her patient not to abort by calling it murderous; she proclaims, "We don't get to know why . . . that woman agonized over a difficult choice, made it and came in here. I guarantee you she was already worried about people out there judging her only to have you make her feel ashamed."[42]

Audiences are typically provided with a backstory to contextualize a woman's choice to abort, but in this scene, we know nothing about the patient or why she wants an abortion. The absence of justification, beyond Dr. Porter's bold defense, makes it impossible to know if the patient's backstory aligns with traditional parameters of acceptability. In this moment, viewers aligned with Dell's pro-life opinion become the target of Dr. Porter's criticism. When Renee, the patient, later reveals that she only returned at Dell's insistence, the audience is forced to reconcile the possibility of being pro-life while also respecting a woman's right to choose regardless of her reasons for doing so.

Additionally, Dr. Porter's completion of the procedure (the first to be performed at Oceanside), despite Dr. Bennett's insistence that abortions "have never been done here and [should] never be done here," facilitates an important dialogue amongst other female Oceanside doctors.[43] In defense of Dr. Porter's defiance, Drs. Montgomery and Turner share their own abortion narratives which were previously unknown to the audience and to each other. Montgomery admits, "I had one, and I was embarrassed and scared. I was everything a woman shouldn't be." Then Turner confesses, "I wish that I had known a doctor like Meg or a place like our practice when I needed an abortion. I had two."[44] Amid Dr. Porter's earlier chastisement of Dell, this conversation does important rhetorical work to further expose the shame felt by many women after their abortions. That these women have known each other for years as colleagues and friends yet never shared their experiences speaks to a larger culture of silence surrounding abortion. This episode sends a strong message that all abortions are acceptable regardless of the presence of mitigating factors. Culturally, a powerful lesson about reproductive rights is conveyed to teach viewers that women seek abortions for myriad reasons that should not be subjected to external metrics of validity. Considering that an overwhelming majority of women say they don't regret having an abortion, these conversations show viewers, especially female viewers, that they should not feel ashamed either.[45] This episode is also a watershed moment for the doctors who in later storylines, including Patty's, tackle abortion with increasing nuance.

In Shondaland, abortions are not reserved solely for women whose circumstances justify them; rather, abortion is legitimated as a choice all women can make in any circumstances. These depictions challenge industry norms by framing abortion as a rightful option instead of as an option that should be avoided whenever possible.[46] Rather than constructing abortion as a last resort for desperate women, Shondaland broadens the range of acceptability to include all abortions by challenging pro-life advocates to confront the hypocrisy of circumstantially permitting abortion and shaming women for exercising their legal rights.

Safeguarding Pro-Abortion and Pro-Choice

On 1980s television, abortions were mentioned but rarely seen as characters extensively discussed them without the actual procedure being shown. Such depictions can be considered pro-choice but are hardly pro-abortion. Just one week after Cagney and Lacey debated the acceptability of abortion, the title character in *Spenser for Hire* (ABC 1985–1988) learned that his girlfriend Susan was pregnant and considering abortion. When Spenser adamantly narrates the baby's right to live, Susan rebukes, "What if I don't think it's a baby yet? What if I think there is still a choice?"[47] The two briefly continue their spat without a clear resolution of these perplexing moral questions; they reunite at the conclusion of the episode when Spenser brings Susan flowers at the hospital. These questions are not answered nor is the audience privy to the particularities of Susan's decision-making, which leaves viewers to reconcile Susan's questions and actions with their own ideology. Like *Spenser for Hire*, previous prime-time portrayals vaguely advocated for a woman's right to choose and failed to position the enactment of rights as "matter[s] of principle."[48] These portrayals also avoided "philosophical or scientific arguments about the status of the fetus," as was the case with Spenser and Susan who invoke questions of when life begins.[49] Conversely, in Shondaland viewers encounter multilayered ideological discussions and witness the mechanics of the procedure. By framing abortion in this way, Rhimes defends a woman's right to choose, plunges viewers into complex conversations concerning when and how to perform abortions, and invites audiences into the surgical room to experience the procedure.

The most ardent pro-choice defense in Shondaland emerges from medical professionals. Unlike Condit's professional programs category set primarily in a law enforcement context, *Private Practice* is a medical melodrama that lends itself to philosophical discussions of abortion that were notably absent on 1980s television. In the breakroom at Oceanside, the doctors become embroiled in a tense discussion about the practice and politics of abortion when Dr. Montgomery tells them about her patient Patty. Patty is nineteen weeks pregnant after an unsuccessful attempt to abort several weeks prior. Patty's abortion, considered late term, sparks a heated debate that escalates when Dr. Bennett refers to the procedure as "a partial birth abortion" and insists that Dr. Montgomery cannot perform it.

Mentioning that Patty used condoms to reassure Dr. Bennett that she is not using abortion as a contraceptive, Dr. Montgomery proclaims, "There is no judgment from us. We are doctors, and we all know birth control sometimes fails, and . . . the doctor she went to the first time was a quack. . . . And now she's come to me, and my job is to help her."[50] As with Dr. Porter's resistance toward Dell, Dr. Montgomery reiterates that abortion should not be a shameful experience and that nobody, especially not a medical professional, has the right to judge women for choosing to abort.

Mirroring 1980s television, Rhimes incorporates ideological claims from varying sides of the abortion debate, yet this production choice does not adhere to industry norms. Rather, as she explains, "You have to portray all different sides of who people can be" to create a realistic take on divisive issues.[51] Unlike past portrayals relying primarily on vague value-laden claims to prioritize choice or childbearing, the *Private Practice* conversation among female doctors focuses viewers on the pragmatics rather than the politics of the situation. Dr. Montgomery directly chastises Dr. Bennett for her use of political and not medical terminology, and Dr. Turner reminds everyone that, regardless of personal feelings, the procedure is legal. When Dr. Bennett, clearly the show's pro-life advocate, expresses her frustrations to Dr. Gabriel Fife, she is again prompted to think about abortion pragmatically when he reminds her that "a fetus may be a life, but it's not a biologically independent life, so in my mind and in the mind of the Supreme Court, the right of termination belongs to the mother."[52] When Dr. Bennett voices pro-life claims that appeal to conservativism, she is rebuked at every turn by reminders that abortion is legal and must be made available to all women regardless of her personal beliefs. Just as Dell succumbs to Dr. Porter's persuasive insight and calls Renee to apologize and reschedule her abortion, this episode ends with Dr. Bennett holding Patty's hand as the abortion is performed. This scene powerfully symbolizes the acquiescence of pro-life perspectives to the legality and legitimacy of abortion.

Shondaland's largest, and arguably most important, deviation from 1980s abortion portrayals is the literal depiction of medical procedures rather than simply inferring that an abortion took place. Breaking with industry norms wherein abortion is discussed but rarely seen, Shondaland viewers are privy to the private decision-making process *and* the actual procedure. Media critics quickly noted this deviation. Dusenbery praises the realness of Cristina's season 8 abortion on *Grey's* explaining, "She didn't just consider it. . . . She didn't even do it off screen. They showed her in the stirrups and the doctor even talked about numbing her cervix."[53] Four years later, after *Scandal's* Ensign Martin underwent the procedure, Dyson notes, "It's rare to see a character on the table with the machines whirring and a trusted friend at her side as the procedure takes place."[54] Depicting the actual medical procedure is rhetorically important because it pictorially reaffirms "abortion as an actual practice in real lives."[55] If abortion is never seen, akin to 1980s television, it is difficult for viewers to develop shared beliefs about the procedure itself. Thus, prior portrayals fail to accurately depict social reality by neglecting to literalize abortion beyond dialogue. Although previous portrayals adequately depict the difficult decision to abort; Shondaland storylines are some of the first on television to literally portray a woman's right to choose.

When Dr. Porter's patient Renee returns to Oceanside for her abortion, this is the only Shondaland storyline that does not show the procedure. In all other instances, viewers are taken into the surgical room for an intimate view. Aside from Cristina's prior decision to abort and Patty's abortion, the remaining abortion scenes in Shondaland look remarkably similar. For example, Cristina, accompanied by Owen, and the ensign, accompanied by Olivia, are shown in a surgical room with a doctor who remains obscured throughout the procedure. Although the full procedure is not shown, the instruments present in Cristina's room and the machine shown in the ensign's convey that both are undergoing a surgical abortion. These scenes punctuate abortion as a routine medical procedure that women choose to have in a safely sterile environment. Olivia's abortion is notable in this context because the audience first learns about her pregnancy and choice to abort in the procedure room. Prior to the procedure, we see her sitting in a beautiful space indistinguishable from a hotel lobby. The first hint of a medical appointment appears when the nurse accompanies Olivia to the exam room. This scene differs only slightly from Rhimes's previous portrayals because the audience observes a more detailed procedural view when the doctor turns the suction machine on as the camera pans out to show the initial phase of the abortion being performed. Unlike Cristina and the ensign, who viewers last see in the procedure room, Olivia is shown leaving the clinic. She is neither sullen nor ashamed; instead, she carries herself with the ease and confidence viewers have come to expect of her.

Overall, none of the women are anesthetized and very little, if any, physical pain registers on their faces. Noting the "straightforward fashion" of Olivia's scene, Skoski remarks, "The doctor works methodically, like a dentist filling a cavity. And when we pan up to Olivia, her face is not tearstained. . . . In fact, she is smiling."[56] Viewed outside this episode's context, these depictions bear a striking resemblance to a routine gynecological exam and portray abortion in a way that reiterates the procedure's simplicity. Even when the procedure is more complicated, as was the case with Patty, every abortion in Shondaland is safely executed without medical complications. Collectively, these portrayals counteract the high prevalence of television storylines that "narratively lin[k] the consideration of pregnancy termination with violence and death."[57] In the United States' current political context, countering this narrative is increasingly important as politicians regulate abortion access under the guise of protecting women's health via false narrations of abortion as dangerous.

The choice to depict abortions with such minimalism also exemplifies a powerful counterargument against pro-life imagery portraying abortion as inhumane, immoral, and unsafe. Condit argues that pro-choice images have not historically harnessed the same persuasive power as pro-life images because they "merely summarized arguments, rather than grounding them" in visually commanding imagery.[58] Though rarely shown on television, pro-life imagery commonly includes bloody fetal remains and hyperrealistic embryos emblazoned on protest signs. Rhimes's depictions avoid this pitfall by portraying abortion as a nonviolent, low risk, and relatively noninvasive medical procedure. That viewers see the abortion for themselves concretizes the legitimacy and safety of the procedure to those who have never personally experienced it. In doing so, these scenes challenge the condemnation conveyed by pro-life images of aborted fetuses and botched abortions. These scenes also solidify abortion as a prudent, viable alternative to unwanted pregnancy.

Unencumbered by dialogue or voiceover, the Shondaland scenes depicting the medical procedures are straightforward. When conversation does take place, its purpose is either confirmatory or explanatory. Prior to beginning the procedure on *Private Practice*, Montgomery gently asks Patty, "We're ready. Are you sure about this?"[59] Although Patty admits to being scared and feeling alone, she confidently reiterates her decision. On *Grey's* Cristina's procedure follows a similar script when the doctor instructs her that he will numb the cervix before saying, "I want to ask you one more time, are you absolutely sure you want to do this?"[60] Nodding yes, Cristina sets her gaze on Owen who stands by the bed holding her hand. Since both women contemplated alternative options, albeit briefly, the confirmatory dialogue in these scenes reaffirms their agency and functions as a respected enactment of their right to choose. However, not all Shondaland abortions are accompanied by confirmatory or explanatory dialogue. Not a single word is spoken on *Scandal* during Olivia's or Ensign Martin's abortions. Instead, both women are shown in a procedure room, and sound emerges only from the machine. Confirmation is not sought in these scenes because no additional confirmation is needed. Ensign Martin explicitly rejected all other options and viewers learn of Olivia's choice to abort once she is already on the table. The silence is undoubtedly intentional. *Scandal's* executive producer Betsy Beers explains, "It just happens, there's no lead-up. That's what I thought was so brilliant about it."[61] The fact that Olivia's abortion consumes less than one minute of air time whereas similar storylines in Shondaland are the focus of entire episodes elevates the significance of Olivia's portrayal by telling audiences they are not entitled to an explanation when a woman chooses abortion.

Additional episodic elements situate Olivia's decision as an empowered choice that should be respected. For instance, Senator Mellie Grant's impassioned filibuster to prevent the defunding of Planned Parenthood is a running thread that ideologically endorses a woman's right to choose—a right Olivia later exercises. The supportive dynamic between Olivia and Mellie as women advocating for other women is also telling. Olivia negotiates a bathroom break for Mellie that leaves her filibuster intact, and Mellie surreptitiously insists that the government, and the audience, protect and respect Olivia's choice. The absence of confirmatory dialogue is the ultimate expression of each character's agency (Olivia, the ensign, and Cristina)—their silent resolve assures viewers that dialogue is unnecessary because their decisions are right and legal. The removal of dialogue also counters industry norms that grant other characters permission to judge and comment on women's reproductive choices. Also noteworthy is the overt sexuality of Olivia on *Scandal* and Cristina on *Grey's* before and after their abortions. Although abortion is certainly an unintended consequence of sex, both women unabashedly continue to routinely engage in steamy sex scenes. In Shondaland, female sexuality is celebrated, unintended consequences are directly addressed, and abortions occur without consultation—solidifying for viewers that a woman's sexual agency is not tied to her reproductive capacity.

Featuring the medical procedure is a marked departure from industry norms; nonetheless, for viewers who have had abortions, these scenes are unrealistic at best. The average U.S. American woman seeking an abortion does not have the same unfettered access to private abortion providers that Shondaland characters enjoy. Cristina makes the short walk up a flight of stairs to her appointment; in comparison, one-third of women in the United States travel outside their county to find an abortion provider.[62] Patty can access care at Oceanside Wellness's private practice while Olivia sits in a swanky waiting room and departs from the doctor's office devoid of protestors. After *Roe v. Wade* (1973), the number of women receiving abortions at hospitals fell dramatically from two-thirds in the 1970s to just 7 percent by 1995.[63] This decline is attributed to wary hospital administrators who outsource the procedure to clinics to eliminate political backlash and patient backlog.[64] Factor in the rapidly growing Targeted Restrictions on Abortion Providers (TRAP) laws implemented since the early 2000s, and abortion access for the average U.S. American woman looks bleak at best. Therefore, while Cristina effortlessly schedules her abortion in season 1 without leaving the hospital and Olivia awaits her procedure in a luxurious setting that looks nothing like a Planned Parenthood clinic, millions of real world women are forced to navigate massive legal, medical, and financial hurdles to access these services. These hurdles include: fees ranging from $600, if performed in the first trimester, and up to $6000 for late term abortions; traveling, possibly across state lines if you live in North Dakota, South Dakota, Missouri, or Wyoming, which each have only one abortion provider; and enduring required ultrasound viewings and mandatory waiting periods.[65] In Shondaland, characters who have the means to access private physicians easily surpass these obstacles. The ease with which they navigate securing an abortion is unrealistic, but also provides a chilling reality check concerning the class divides that permeate reproductive health care in the United States.

One exception to this idyllic portrayal is Patty's storyline on *Private Practice*. She ends up at Oceanside after beginning her abortion experience like most women—at a clinic surrounded by protestors. Patty confides in Dr. Montgomery, "The things they were yelling—calling me a murderer, a baby killer. I couldn't go in. I tried to find a private doctor, but most of them won't do abortions."[66] Patty's narrative addresses two harrowing aspects common to U.S. American abortion experiences—the fear felt by many seeking the procedure and the back alley abortions that have killed thousands of women since the early 1900s. Forced to see a disreputable doctor recommended by a friend, Patty's struggle provides a small glimpse into the difficulty many women face in finding a physically and emotionally safe provider. Dr. Montgomery also acknowledges these difficulties when she pleads with Dr. Bennett prior to performing Patty's procedure: "It is not enough to just have an opinion, because in a nation of over 300 million people, there are only 1,700 abortion providers and I'm one of 'em."[67] Here, viewers are cued in to the harsh reality that 38 percent of reproductive-aged women are without an abortion provider in their county.[68] In the corpus of Shondaland's abortion storylines, Patty's experience resonates most with the typical abortion experience. She does not have unprecedented access to private physicians; she is scared and desperate to avoid childbearing and lucky to have found a doctor and medical facility willing to perform an abortion.

Shondaland abortion depictions shatter industry norms, especially considering Condit's observation that none of the programs in her study even showed the medical procedure. Rather than only capturing characters' feelings before and after abortion, these shows expose viewers to abortion experiences in their entirety. This production choice makes it difficult for audiences to separate a woman's right to choose from her enactment of that choice, and both are major focal points of current political debates. Shondaland demonstrates that it is not enough to just talk about abortion, it also needs to be seen. This stance reflects the difference between pro-choice and pro-abortion television programming.

PRO-CHOICE AND PRO-ABORTION IN SHONDALAND

Television audiences of the 1980s were shown a myopic view of abortion that struck a delicate balance between emerging discourses of choice and existing pro-life sentiments. Although Rhimes provides an obligatory nod toward pro-life discourses, Shondaland brazenly adopts rhetorics of choice and, more importantly, visually portrays that choice. The range of experiences depicted in Shondaland is also noteworthy—Patty needs a second abortion after the first doctor failed, Cristina chooses to terminate two pregnancies, and Oliva aborts the child of a sitting U.S. president. Though dramatized for entertainment, the scope of these depictions reiterates the diversity among unplanned pregnancies in the United States wherein one in three women will have an abortion in their lifetime.[69] The fact that abortion is an option for any woman in Shondaland reflects a desperate need for real world change amid how inaccessible abortions have steadily become since *Roe v. Wade*. As the landscape of women's reproductive rights becomes increasingly hostile, progressive depictions are now more important than ever. Seeing beloved characters have abortions and unapologetically move on with their lives reaffirms women's legal rights at a time when lawmakers are quickly eroding them.

The very nature of this chapter illuminates Shondaland's intensive labor to challenge industry practices governing abortion portrayals on prime-time television. Condit's analysis relied on thirteen distinct television shows airing on different channels and rarely in the same season. To find six storylines dedicated to abortion involving episodic characters and permanent cast members all airing on the same network within a few years of each other is (sadly) remarkable. Their presence signifies an important stylistic choice from the perspective of a television auteur. The diversification and more common appearance of abortion on television expands our cultural understanding of the practice in ways that meaningfully dispel myths of maternal regret, challenge normative boundaries of acceptability, and insist that abortion is a safe medical solution to unwanted pregnancy. Additionally, Cristina's two divergent abortion storylines exemplify progress within Shondaland. Akin to many 1980s storylines, Cristina's first unplanned pregnancy was resolved via a medical emergency that eliminated the need for an abortion. This outcome, however, was not originally scripted. Rhimes explains that she wanted Cristina to have an abortion but opted for the ectopic pregnancy after "some very strong conversations with Broadcast Standards and Practices."[70] Six years later, after tackling abortion on *Private Practice*, Rhimes scripted Cristina's second unwanted pregnancy on her own terms; she remarks, "it made sense for the character of Cristina Yang and the network [stands] behind my choice to do that."[71] Capitalizing on her earned credibility, rapport with ABC, and Shondaland's success, Rhimes consistently pushes the envelope—even joking that "I don't necessarily have to ask anybody anymore."[72] This is not to say that Shondaland's controversial storylines are crafted solely for shock value, but rather that Rhimes has cashed in her political capital to portray the complexity of abortion candidly and challenge industry norms. Abortion is not merely a plot device in Shondaland, it is a common occurrence epitomizing real world women's lives. Other shows are taking note and following suit. "*Scandal* set a new standard" on television for the "drama-free abortion."[73] Programs such as *BoJack Horseman* (Netflix 2014–present), *Jane the Virgin* (CW 2014–present), *You're the Worst* (FXX 2014–present), and *Crazy Ex-Girlfriend* (CW 2015–present), include storylines wherein abortion is framed as hopeful as opposed to tragic, making 2016 "the year abortion was destigmatized on TV."[74]

NOTES

1. Sarah Erdreich, "More Than 40 Years after Maude, Abortion Remains Taboo on TV," *Talking Points Memo*, May 19, 2014, https://talkingpointsmemo.com/cafe/cristina-yang-s-anatomy-abortion.

2. Gretchen Sisson and Katrina Kimport, "Telling Stories about Abortion: Abortion-Related Plots in American Film and Television, 1916–2013," *Contraception* 89, no. 5 (2014): 415.

3. Charlotte Alter, "Norman Lear: Why Oliva Pope's Abortion on *Scandal* Was 'Frank and Bold,'" *Time Magazine*, November 24, 2015, http://time.com/4125345/norman-lear-why-olivia-popes-abortion-on-scandal-was-frank-and-bold/.

4. Alter.

5. Gretchen Sisson and Katrina Kimport, "Facts and Fictions: Characters Seeking Abortion on American Television, 2005–2014," *Contraception* 93, no. 5 (2016): 447.

6. NARAL Pro-Choice America, *Who Decides? The Status of Women's Reproductive Rights in the United States* (Washington, D.C.: NARAL Pro-Choice America Foundation, 2014), 4.

7. Heather D. Boonstra and Elizabeth Nash, "A Surge of State Abortion Restrictions Puts Providers—and the Women They Serve—in the Crosshairs," *Guttmacher Policy Review* 17, no. 1 (Winter 2014): 9–15.

8. Guttmacher Institute, *An Overview of Abortion Laws* (Washington, D.C.: Guttmacher Center for Population Research Innovation and Dissemination, 2017).

9. Laura Stampler, "Why 2014 Should Be the Year We Talk about Abortion on TV," *Time Magazine*, January 23, 2014, http://entertainment.time.com/2014/01/23/why-2014-should-be-the-year-we-talk-about-abortion-on-tv/.

10. Celeste Michelle Condit, *Decoding Abortion Rhetoric* (Champaign: University of Illinois Press, 1994), 131.

11. Deborah A. Fisher, Douglas L. Hill, Joel W. Grube, and Enid L. Gruber, "Sex on American Television: An Analysis across Program Genres and Network Types," *Journal of Broadcasting & Electronic Media* 48, no. 4 (December 2004): 530.

12. Lance R. Holbert, Dhavan V. Shah, and Nojin Kwak, "Political Implications of Prime-Time Drama and Sitcom Use: Genres of Representation and Opinions Concerning Women's Rights," *Journal of Communication* 53, no. 1 (March 2003): 47.

13. Beth K. Jaworski, "Reproductive Justice and Media Framing: A Case Study Analysis of Problematic Frames in the Popular Media," *Sex Education* 9, no. 1 (February 2009): 109.

14. Andrea L. Press, "Working-Class Women in a Middle-Class World: The Impact of Television on Modes of Reasoning About Abortion," *Critical Studies in Mass Communication* 8 (1991): 438.

15. Condit, *Decoding Abortion Rhetoric*, 123.

16. Condit, 124.

17. Holbert, Shah, and Kwak, "Political Implications of Prime-Time Drama and Sitcom Use," 58.

18. Condit, *Decoding Abortion Rhetoric*, 135.

19. Condit, 138.

20. Condit, 138–139.

21. Condit, 133.

22. Condit, 136.

23. *St. Elsewhere*, "Playing God: Part 2," season 3, episode 2, directed by Bruce Paltrow, written by John Masius and Tom Fontana, aired on September 26, 1984, on CBS.

24. Condit, *Decoding Abortion Rhetoric*, 139.

25. *Private Practice*, "God Bless the Child," season 4, episode 21, directed by Jeannot Szwarc, written by Jennifer Cecil and Barbie Kligman, aired on May 12, 2011, on ABC.

26. *Private Practice*, "God Bless the Child."

27. *Grey's Anatomy*, "Raindrops Keep Fallin' On My Head," season 2, episode 1, directed by Peter Horton, written by Stacy McKee, aired on September 25, 2005, on ABC.

28. *Grey's Anatomy*, "Make Me Lose Control," season 2, episode 3, directed by Adam Davidson, written by Krista Vernoff, aired on October 9, 2005, on ABC.

29. *Grey's Anatomy*, "Deny, Deny, Deny," season 2, episode 4, directed by Wendey Stanzler, written by Zoanne Clack, aired on October 16, 2005, on ABC.

30. *Grey's Anatomy*, "Deny, Deny, Deny."

31. *Grey's Anatomy*, "Unaccompanied Minor," season 7, episode 22, directed by Rob Corn, written by Debora Cahn, aired on May 19, 2011, on ABC.

32. *Grey's Anatomy*, "Unaccompanied Minor."

33. *Grey's Anatomy*, "Unaccompanied Minor."

34. *Grey's Anatomy*, "Free Falling," season 8, episode 1, directed by Rob Corn, written by Tony Phelan and Joan Rater, aired on September 22, 2011, on ABC.

35. *Grey's Anatomy*, "Free Falling."

36. *Greys Anatomy*, "I Bet it Stung," season 10, episode 5, directed by Mark Jackson, written by Jeannine Renshaw, aired on October 17, 2013, on ABC.

37. *Grey's Anatomy*, "I Bet it Stung."

38. Condit, *Decoding Abortion Rhetoric*, 140.

39. *Cagney & Lacey*, "The Clinic," season 5, episode 6, directed by Alexander Singer, written by Judy Merl and Paul Eric Myers, aired on November 11, 1985, on CBS.

40. *Cagney & Lacey*, "The Clinic."

41. Condit, *Decoding Abortion Rhetoric*, 138.

42. *Private Practice*, "Crime and Punishment," season 2, episode 8, directed by Mark Tinker, written by Shonda Rhimes, aired on December 3, 2008, on ABC.

43. *Private Practice*, "Crime and Punishment."

44. *Private Practice*, "Crime and Punishment."

45. According to a 2015 study conducted by the University of California–San Francisco School of Medicine, of the six hundred women surveyed, 95 percent of women felt the decision was right for them. Maria Caspani, "Overwhelming Majority of U.S. Women Don't Regret Abortion: Study," *Reuters*, July 17, 2015, https://www.reuters.com/article/us-usa-women-abortion/overwhelming-majority-of-u-s-women-dont-regret-abortion-study-idUSKCN0PR1KP20150717.

46. Condit, *Decoding Abortion Rhetoric*, 139.

47. *Spenser for Hire*, "The Killer Within," season 1, episode 7, directed by Don Chaffey, written by Robert B. Parker, John Wilder and Robert M. Young, aired on November 12, 1985, on ABC.

48. *Spenser for Hire*, "The Killer Within."

49. Condit, *Decoding Abortion Rhetoric*, 129.

50. *Private Practice*, "God Bless the Child."

51. Willa Paskin, "Shonda Rhimes on *Grey's Anatomy*'s Recent Abortion Story Line," *Vulture*, September 27, 2011, http://www.vulture.com/2011/09/shonda_rhimes_talks_about_grey.html.

52. *Private Practice*, "God Bless the Child."

53. Maya Dusenbery, "A Character on *Grey's Anatomy* Had an Abortion," *Feministing*, September 27, 2011, http://feministing.com/2011/09/26/a-character-on-greys-anatomy-had-an-abortion/.

54. Cicely K. Dyson, "'Scandal' Recap: Season 5, Episode 21, 'A Few Good Women,'" *Wall Street Journal*, May 8, 2015, https://blogs.wsj.com/speakeasy/2015/05/08/scandal-recap-season-4-episode-21-a-few-good-women/.

55. Condit, *Decoding Abortion Rhetoric*, 123.

56. Elizabeth Skoski, "Oliva Pope's Abortion on 'Scandal' is Progress—But We Need to Talk about That Warning," *Bustle*, November 20, 2015, https://www.bustle.com/articles/125307-oliva-popes-abortion-on-scandal-is-progress-but-we-need-to-talk-about-that-warning.

57. Sisson and Kimport, "Telling Stories," 417.

58. Condit, *Decoding Abortion Rhetoric*, 92.

59. *Private Practice*, "God Bless the Child."

60. *Grey's Anatomy*, "Free Falling."

61. Emily Yahr, "'Scandal' Stuns Viewers with Abortion Scene in the Season's Winter Finale," *Washington Post*, November 20, 2015, https://www.washingtonpost.com/news/arts-and-entertainment/wp/2015/11/20/scandal-stuns-viewers-with-abortion-scene-in-the-seasons-winter-finale/?noredirect=on&utm_term=.9d959fa4391b.

62. Boonstra and Nash, "A Surge of State Abortion Restrictions," 9–15.

63. Eyal Press, *Absolute Convictions: My Father, A City, and the Conflict That Divided America* (New York: Picador, 2007), 62.

64. Press, 64.

65. Erica Hellerstein, "Pricing American Women Out of an Abortion, One Restriction at a Time," *Think Progress*, February 25, 2015, https://thinkprogress.org/pricing-american-women-out-of-abortion-one-restriction-at-a-time-c545c54f641f/.

66. *Private Practice*, "God Bless the Child."

67. *Private Practice*, "God Bless the Child."

68. Boonstra and Nash, "A Surge of State Abortion Restrictions," 9–15.

69. Boonstra and Nash, "A Surge of State Abortion Restrictions," 9–15.

70. Paskin, "Shonda Rhimes."

71. Paskin.

72. Paskin.

73. Ariane Lange, "The Year Abortion Was Destigmatized on TV," *Buzzfeed*, December 19, 2016, https://www.buzzfeed.com/arianelange/abortions-on-tv-2016?utm_term=.tsGeoQDvOd#.sfBR1aBw6n.

74. Lange.

4 · SOUNDTRACKING SHONDALAND

Televisual Identity Mapped through Music

JENNIFER BILLINSON AND
MICHAELA D. E. MEYER

Longtime fans of Shonda Rhimes know the premium she places on music in Shondaland; when a scene or episode hits an emotional crescendo, viewers can count on a poignant musical surge. *Grey's Anatomy* (ABC 2005–present; also referred to as *Grey's*) viewers experienced this in season 11 as Dr. Meredith Grey watches a nurse switch off Dr. Derek Shepherd's life support. He was her husband and longtime scene partner, a character that many fans never envisioned leaving the show, let alone dying. What made the soundtracked storyline especially noteworthy was not a new, devastatingly sad ballad accompanying a shocking on-screen death. Rather, Rhimes recalled a familiar tune—a gentle, minimalist cover of "Chasing Cars" by Snow Patrol.[1] First heard in the season 2 finale and again in *Grey's* season 7 musical episode, the song serves as a gateway to previous episodes and plotlines. This time, it journeys through the evolution of Meredith and Derek's romantic relationship with flashbacks to them flirting in a bar, stealing glances over microscopes, and adopting and birthing their children. We also revisit their "post-it" wedding vows, impassioned elevator rides, and Derek professing his love for Meredith in a monologue. This remembrance functions as a highlight reel of one of television's most iconic romantic duos, accompanied by what has become one of television's most iconic soundtracks. We then see their first scene together before transitioning back to the hospital room where Derek lies dying. Thus, "Chasing Cars" on *Grey's* highlights Rhimes's signature rule for the marriage between popular music and prime-time melodrama practiced in Shondaland.

This chapter examines how Rhimes's rise to fame is informed by her innovative approach to using popular music for bolstering her show's identities, framing television narrative, and developing storylines by strategically using background music alongside character, plot, and genre devices. Throughout Shondaland, musical soundtracks are tantamount to narrative development and audience engagement. More broadly, they establish a key facet of Rhimes's signature as a showrunner and Shondaland's style as a production company. To examine the important relationship music plays in constructing the stylistic vision of Rhimes's work, we examine the soundtracking of three Shondaland shows to reveal the distinct ways music is employed for affect and style. Collectively, *Grey's Anatomy*, *Scandal* (ABC 2012–2018), and *How to Get Away with Murder* (ABC 2014–present, also referred to as *HTGAWM*) span Rhimes's prime-time career, demonstrate her evolution as an auteur, and signal the increasing influence of digital media on television. The rise and crest of digital media as a means of distributing popular culture is a defining feature of the technological revolution defined, in part, by widespread internet accessibility and mobile media devices (e.g., smart phones).[2] Linking new media developments to Rhimes's industry ascendance, this chapter unravels how Shondaland deploys music to uniquely brand each show, evoke emotion, and critique contemporary identity politics.

THE MARRIAGE OF POPULAR MUSIC AND TELEVISION NARRATIVE

Characterizing the relationship between music and television as "uneasy," Simon Frith asserts that television, as a rule, is not sound centered.[3] He offers several reasons for why the relationship between music and television is fraught, including technical quality, portability, and the foregrounding of visual experience.[4] Despite these tensions, music has become significant to television, albeit usually in the background unless linked directly to narrative elements (e.g., characters in the show seeing a particular band, a musician guest starring as themselves). Three aesthetic conventions of music use on television are predominant in Shondaland: (1) to ground what we see, (2) to tie a moment to a familiar song, and (3) to provide ironic commentary on what is seen.[5] More often than not, these conventions consumptively sell music that accompanies the televisual format. Even in the melodramatic formats that Shondaland is known for, music is rarely the main focus of narrative television programming.[6] In the fifteen years since Frith's essay, television has become portable and music has become more accessible, legally or otherwise. These industry changes have influenced television production by altering the dynamic between television and music.[7] Shondaland's catalogue of popular prime-time shows feature a wide variety of musical ensembles and thus serve as important terrain for exploring how television auteurs utilize music.

Although Shondaland features incredibly gifted melodic storytellers, by no means did they pioneer the melding of popular music and scripted television.[8]

The rise of corporate media mergers following the Telecommunications Act of 1996 led to higher network involvement in cross marketing, substantially elevating the music-on-TV game throughout the 1990s and early 2000s.[9] Adding music to television creates a symbiotic relationship—when television features music, the series develops a musical signature that contributes to a series' identity while simultaneously increasing popular exposure for music artists and their labels. Television narratives like *Buffy the Vampire Slayer* (WB/UPN 1997–2003), *Charmed* (WB 1998–2006), *One Tree Hill* (WB/CW 2003–2012), and *Ally McBeal* (Fox 1997–2002) heavily featured popular music, but typically did so by featuring musical performances that added to the "realism" of the on-screen experience. For example, on *One Tree Hill*, the main characters hosted a benefit for breast cancer at a night club called Tric featuring performances by Jack's Mannequin and Fall Out Boy.[10] Instead of a faceless soundtrack, the artists performed and sometimes interacted with the fictional characters, providing audiences with the illusion of attending a live concert. This practice, common in the late 1990s, departs from earlier music-on-television conventions that assumed that seeing an actual musician on screen would ruin both the music and televisual experience.[11] This practice also intensified market synergy when the same parent companies contracted the series and the artist.[12] This model of promoting musicians on screen continued throughout the 2000s yet has dwindled as alternate technological means for artists to gain exposure have emerged.

Alongside including music in scripted television, the reality television genre provided a "real world" format whereby artists could appear more fluidly as themselves rather than as part of a scripted narrative. *Big Brother* (CBS 2000–present) often has musicians playing backyard concerts for houseguests, and the series has a long tradition of featuring upcoming films, shows, and new products (often produced or owned by the series' parent company CBS) during the reality competition.[13] This cross marketing is a blatant form of advertising that works well on reality television; however, if cross marketing is not scripted with finesse on melodramas, it often disrupts viewers' immersive viewing experience.[14] This is the foremost challenge that scripted television producers face when trying to use music as a signature feature of the televisual experience.

Despite criticism for its inherently commercialized nature, popular music is a facet of mass media with tangibly nuanced influence on emotions, identity, and cultural rituals. Using media to transmit culture and ritual is one of the oldest uses of communication and one of the primary roles that music plays in modern society, both religiously (using, for example, prayers and hymns) and secularly (as, for example, when a romantic couple picks "their song" or when "Auld Lang Syne" is the first song played after the ball drops on New Year's Eve in the United States).[15] The emotional connections that humans have with music are well documented.[16] Biologically, the mechanisms that make music essential to the human condition are driving questions for neuro-musicologists and psychologists. Neurologist

Oliver Sacks uses case studies of traumatic brain injuries to explore how music and the brain are linked in *Musicophilia*, asserting that humans are intrinsically musical beings.[17] This research is supported throughout the field of neuromusicology, with studies finding that even nonmusicians are able to understand the emotionality of music after trauma or injury.[18] This neurological connection provides an important motivation for television producers to employ music. Television shows like *Cold Case* (CBS 2003–2010) and *Mad Men* (AMC 2007–2015) explicitly use music to evoke nostalgia, and these music/television pairings heighten the emotionality of the scripted televisual moment. Emotions such as nostalgia are nebulous concepts, and the experiences that individual viewers have with popular culture are not necessarily shared ones.[19] Thus, television industry norms for using music emotionality are often laden with normative assumptions of a default privileged audience (e.g., white, middle-to-upper class, heterosexual), ignoring identity differences that diversify audience experiences.[20]

Beyond television's use of music to establish emotional tone, setting, and time period, music can also function as an explicit marker of a character's or a group's identity. Too often, audiences see this devolving into stereotypical melodies of Mariachi music for Latinx characters, unidentifiable rap beats for young men of color, or mystical chimes for a character of Asian descent. These stereotypical practices are common in reality television; for example, *Survivor* divided up contestants based on race and used stereotypical musical distinctions to differentiate between tribes.[21] Parallel to musical expressions of character identity, music also expresses producers' desire for lyrics and melodies to easily identify the characters appearing on screen. To theorize Rhimes's musical signature, it is important to note that Shondaland intentionally attempts to challenge these stereotypical industry norms.

MUSIC IN AN AGE OF DIGITIZATION AND NEW MEDIA

Early academic debates about the role and value of popular music centered largely on mapping emotional authenticity and distinguishing between listening to recordings versus live performances.[22] Corresponding with Theodor Adorno's work in the 1940s, many contemporary critiques of popular music distinguish between listening to recordings and experiencing live performances.[23] However, the late-twentieth-century rise of digital music opened a Pandora's Box that some analysts think has yet to be closed; thus, once people experience "free" music, it is very difficult to get them to pay for recordings or live concerts.[24] Moreover, radio—offering the original "free" form of recorded popular music—has trouble competing with consumers' desires to hear music on demand. The epic boon of digital piracy, led by Napster, helped incite digital music production and significantly altered the industry's ability to control access to musical recordings and artists. Economically, this yielded a decrease in sales and a dramatic cultural shift in how consumers experience and share music.[25]

This globalized shift in consumption plummeted the popular music industry into an identity crisis from which it is still attempting to emerge and recover. If artists can distribute music directly to listeners and digital users can trade music among themselves, what use is the music industry and how profitable can it be?[26] Furthermore, how are physical musical spaces impacted by listeners' easy access to music online? Brick-and-mortar record stores such as Tower Records and Sam Goody were traumatically impacted by the loss of their customer base; many rebranded or closed for good.[27] Apple's creation of iTunes and the iTunes store is credited with saving the industry as much as it could be salvaged.[28] Apple resolved the overpriced CD issue, a criticism often used to justify piracy, by selling songs individually to allow consumers to pick and choose à la carte instead of buying entire albums. iTunes also eased the purchasing process by storing credit card information and offering iTunes gift cards in service to highly accessible digital music. iTunes's early 2000s model has since morphed into subscription streaming services. Spotify, Tidal, and Apple Music offer unlimited access for a monthly fee, with artists like Jay-Z, Beyoncé, Kanye West, and Taylor Swift offering exclusive music to specific platforms.

Ultimately, these dynamic shifts in consumption, distribution, and sales dramatically altered the status quo for featuring music in televisual contexts. Historically, the typical scripted format would feature an artist on a series to increase their popularity and skyrocket sales of their new artistic work. However, a rise in broadcast regulation and legal entanglements spearheaded by the ever-changing music industry created barriers for artists seeking to appear on or have their music used on television.[29] While the mix of music and television should theoretically be expected to continue given longstanding practice, industry crises have led to licensing conflicts which, in turn, have substantially complicated the union. *The Wonder Years* (ABC 1988–1993) has long been a cautionary tale in soundtracking television. Because the series existed prior to the age of music digitization, the forethought to secure music copyrights and clearances was simply unnecessary. Many tracks, including the beloved theme song "With a Little Help from My Friends" (a Beatles song covered by Joe Crocker), were not legally cleared for streaming rights until 2014.[30] In 2011, this forced Netflix to stream the series with several altered songs until the series with its original music tracks became available in 2014.

Shondaland's *Grey's Anatomy* emerged in 2005 just as the cultural conflux of television, popular music production, and licensing was fundamentally shifting. A leader among broadcast networks, ABC has placed a premium on maintaining and increasing the connection between television and music. The ABC Music Lounge website is "the place for all music-related content from your favorite ABC shows, including songs featured on TV, video clips, cast playlists, music supervisor blogs, and more."[31] The rise of *Grey's* came just after legal online music downloading sites (along with illegal sites still utilized post-Napster) conditioned consumers to browse for singles online in lieu of buying entire CDs at brick-and-mortar stores. Replacing the traditional shopping experience, the ABC Music Lounge directs viewers to purchase singles heard in conjunction with episodes. Even more pointedly, viewers are given purchasing instructions during live airings of shows. With industry and analytical focus increasingly on digital streaming rights, app wars between Apple and Tidal, and artists like Beyoncé blazing new distribution and publicity pathways, Rhimes and her team carved out creative space for popular music to flourish on "old-fashioned" network television.

SOUNDTRACKING SHONDALAND'S MUSICAL SIGNATURE

Shondaland's rise, with its focus on music as well as providing new artists with airtime in concert with digital music's increasing popularity, stands as a contemporary exemplar of successfully blending art and business. On *Grey's Anatomy*, *Scandal*, and *How to Get Away with Murder*, music is commercially featured and sold via ABC's promotional efforts; however, it is also deliberately used for different narrative purposes on each show. As Rhimes built her empire, melding popular music and television emerged as a key element of her signature style which consistently led to emotional musical moments that Frith feared would be lost amid the colossal increase of media and media consumption.[32] Rhimes has been vocal about fighting to secure the music to soundtrack her shows; she set a precedent for doing so early on in her career when *Grey's* premiered in 2005:

> For *Grey's*, I remember having the battle in the editing room . . . when I was just the little girl who had a show. I put all of that music that you heard in the pilot. The guys came in and said, "You can't have this music in the show," and they scored the show with this very testosterone-y music that made it sound like an action movie and the show looked ridiculous. I [thought], "They're the executive producers and I'm screwed," and having [television executive] Betsy [Beers] come in and go "This is ridiculous. Put that music back," and getting my voice heard. But [I was] also watching how a show can become a completely different animal with different kinds of music.[33]

Early on, Shondaland's use of music was intentional, determined, and groundbreaking in a flustered entertainment industry trying to figure out how to preserve the longstanding relationship between music and television and how to survive the technological revolution. The era and context in which Shondaland became a powerhouse production company under Rhimes's leadership establishes Shondaland's creative products as rich sites to analyze the synergistic storytelling that emerges when popular music and scripted television are combined. Moreover, Rhimes's direct involvement in the creative process establishes her as an auteur whose signature style is partly defined by her use of music—albeit rarely mentioned in debates about how she has impacted the television industry. Commonly lauded for colorblind casting and expanding the ongoing conversation about diversity and representation on television, Rhimes has also repeatedly promoted artists on the fringes of popularity, particularly queer female artists such as Teagan and Sara, Brandi Carlisle, and the Ditty Bops.[34] Suturing additional links between music and identity politics, Shondaland often employs familiar songs in new and sometimes tongue-in-cheek or ironic ways that offer cultural commentary. Consequently, Rhimes leverages Shondaland as a pedagogical opportunity to advocate for increased diversity in listening as well as viewing while exposing prime-time network television as a cultural space that has historically excluded marginalized artists.[35]

Traditionally, television scholars focus on the tensions between narrative and visual on-screen elements, as both are significant and arguably necessary for a (traditionally) successful episode of television.[36] By comparison, Shondaland's soundtracks warrant analysis for what they do narratively *and* how they heighten musical presence and emotionality to push the boundaries of what constitutes successful television. In Shondaland, soundtracking is sometimes allowed to compete with traditional elements such as visual staging and verbal dialogue and, at times, steals the show. This is not only allowable but often preferable to more holistically tell a story. *Grey's* musical episode "Song beneath the Song" from season 7 provides the most transparent example of this interplay between music and traditional television scripting.[37] The result is inherently melodramatic, lifting viewers out of the day-to-day action in the series and directing them toward the background music blasted in the forefront. To illustrate how Rhimes provokes synergy between popular music and television narrative, in the analysis that follows, we offer a close reading of Shondaland's signature style by soundtracking key music and narrative moments in three series—*Grey's Anatomy*, *Scandal*, and *How to Get Away with Murder*.

"How to Save a Life:" Soundtracking *Grey's Anatomy*

The importance of music to Rhimes is immediately evident in *Grey's* because every episode is named after a song. While not a novel move (e.g., shows like *Degrassi: The Next Generation* [CTV/MuchMusic 2001–2015] did this prior to *Grey's*), this practice makes music a foregrounded focal point. From *Grey's* pilot onward, the series' musical point of view is also repetitively emphasized by having each episode pivot around key melodic scenes. As viewers watch and listen from the very beginning, light electronic dance pop juxtaposed with indie ballads mirrors the frenetic lives of Seattle Grace interns who go from dancing in bars to the operating room, literally moving between life and death while learning how to save a life. In episode 1, "A Hard Day's Night," Rilo Kiley's "Portions for Foxes" is the audience's introduction to the tone of the show—the young indie-pop vibe, concurrent with the times, offers immediate insight into lead character Meredith Grey's "dark" personality; the song discloses that she is (or she believes herself to be) "bad news."[38] It also starkly contrasts the professional and private worlds of Meredith and her fellow interns while signaling that both worlds are messy, complicated, and frequently blurred. For example, the pilot's first scene is Meredith waking up on the floor next to a nude man she brought home from the bar the night before who, unbeknownst to her, also works at Seattle Grace. The song begins as Meredith ushers the stranger out and transitions into our first shot of a dark operating room. We listen and watch as the light is flicked on and interns trickle in, jaws slightly agape at their new surroundings. It plays in the background as chief of surgery Dr. Richard Webber explains that most of them will fail, with the camera panning the faces of Grey's main characters. The song's narration of what life is like "for a walking corpse like me" parallels the line the characters will walk between life and death and incites the audience to contemplate which of the interns will survive the program.

This explicit focus on music from the get-go led both Grey's and its featured musical artists to economic and commercial success. When The Fray's single "How to Save a Life" was first featured in season 2's "Superstition," it skyrocketed to the number three position on the Billboard charts.[39] In the episode, the song fades in and becomes audible as Dr. Derek Shepherd says his trademark phrase "It's a beautiful day to save lives" just before he makes the first cut of a neurosurgery. The song, mirroring a typical Grey's storyline, references an intervention on behalf of someone in trouble. In the context of the show, its meaning vacillates between literally saving lives and surviving the complex social relationships of the hospital's staff. As a musical anchor throughout the series, the song is returned to as a signifier of Derek and Meredith's relationship. "How to Save a Life" is also the title of the season 11 episode in which Derek dies. Grey's early success and emotive music/television pairings led to more overnight musical sensations akin to the overnight popularity of The Fray. In 2006, being featured on Grey's launched indie-rocker Ingrid Michaelson from relative obscurity to hypervisibility, despite not having a major record label behind her.[40] Her song "Keep Breathing" was used at a dramatic climax of season 3's "Didn't We Almost Have It All" as Meredith helps a sobbing Dr. Cristina Yang break free from her constrictive wedding dress and choker after she is left at the altar by Dr. Preston Burke.[41]

Now Grey's is recognized as a prime avenue for artists to gain exposure and debut new music to large audiences. Similar to Michaelson, although already a well-known artist, John Legend's now ubiquitous "All of Me" debuted in the season 9 finale, soundtracking a montage of several of Grey's couples reconciling and embracing, most notably Jackson and April after he was injured in a bus explosion.[42] Musical artists such as Legend, Snow Patrol, and The Fray have not only debuted music in Shondaland, some have also recorded songs specifically for the show (including the covers of iconic *Grey's* songs like "How to Save a Life" and "Chasing Cars"). On *Grey's*, the relationship between an artist's music and the television narrative as a showpiece poised to engage in melodic storytelling frequently launches both the artist and song into stardom.

In addition to featuring relatively unknown artists and new music, the series also employs cover songs, or alternate versions of familiar scores, in a manner that reinspires popularity for classic popular songs. In a departure from *Grey's* common use of new singer-songwriters and electronic pop, the soundtrack of *Grey's* season 10 was populated by covers of 1980s songs. Some were wildly reimagined, reinterpreted, and rendered barely recognizable, while others were modernized only slightly; the cover of "Just like Heaven" by Joy Zipper sounds like an update of the original, while the Bootstraps's rendition of "I Wanna Dance with Somebody" is sung as a slow, melancholic ballad.[43] By creating musical moments built on collective cultural memory on *Grey's*, and to a less successful degree on *Private Practice* (ABC 2007–2013), Rhimes and her team are heavy-handedly guiding the emotionality of scenes and storylines. This use of cover material fosters a complex reference to the past, while showcasing a contemporary musical style performed by relatively unknown fringe artists. This is particularly meaningful for season 10 when original cast member Sandra Oh, playing Dr. Cristina Yang, left the series. The use of cover songs as a nostalgic reference throughout the season built the emotional crescendo for viewers as they witnessed her final goodbyes and were invited to contemplate what her departure means on screen for her and Meredith and off screen for the series. Another more recent example occurs in the season 14 episode "Who Lives, Who Dies, Who Tells Your Story," the three-hundredth episode of the series.[44] Described as a "love letter" to the original cast, the episode features a number of musical references to prior episodes, including "Cosy in the Rocket" by Psapp, which served as the original opening credit theme music for the series.[45]

These careful, emotionally saturated production practices fashion music as part and parcel of Rhimes's showrunning signature, the identity of the show and its characters. Specific songs that have become canonical in the *Grey's* universe aid in the creation of a series identity particular to Shondaland and cue up memories of past content for viewers. Songs like "How to Save a Life" and "Chasing Cars" are utilized in this way. Another strong example of this is Teagan and Sara's "Where Does the Good Go."[46] Debuting in season 1's "No Man's Land," it plays in the background as Cristina utters the first time-of-death call of her medical career.[47] The tone of the song—slow at first with minimalistic acoustic guitar, accompanied with pop vocals ultimately escalating into a full upbeat crescendo—does not match the dire circumstances playing out on screen, although, contradicting the melody, the lyrics are a bit morose and deal with heartbreak. Fast-forward to season 10's "Fear (of the Unknown)," Cristina prepares to say her goodbyes to coworkers and friends before she moves to Switzerland for her dream position as the director of cardiothoracic surgery at the Klausman Center for Medical Research.[48] The emotional buildup occurs as she prepares her goodbyes for those who have been her family for over a decade. At the episode's emotional climax, Cristina and her best friend Meredith finally face off to say goodbye and end up doing what they always do when things get too emotionally heavy—they dance it out. Slow-motion shots of them dancing with abandon in an on-call room to "Where Does the Good Go" heightens the dramatic effect of the scene while harkening back to that first significant time-of-death goodbye for Cristina.

Dancing to blow off emotional steam is a recurrent theme for Meredith, Cristina, and other characters at key episodic moments and exemplifies how Shondaland's musical choices breathe additional life into the narrative structure of the series. In a show that is narratively populated by romantic entanglements, Meredith and Cristina are framed as each other's "person." Their deep friendship is repeatedly positioned as the most significant relationship on the show—despite romantic relationships, marriages, and other friendships for both women, and Meredith's having children. This is an important statement by Rhimes that she punctuates with music to convey that friendships between women, which are all too often frivolously portrayed as secondary to a heterosexual romantic pairing or motherhood, are essential and irreplaceable. We witness Cristina and Meredith navigate and nurture their friendship through conversation (or a lack thereof) about love, fear, and pain. We watch as they grow into a friendship that is marked by unconditional love and respect when Cristina leaves for Switzerland. When the audience encounters their dancing to music as their goodbye, it is a ritualized dance of empowerment—absent the male gaze and imposition of frivolity—for women who struggle with intimacy in varying degrees. In this context, "Where Does the Good Go" functions as a Shondaland anthem for the profound friendship between these two central Grey's characters.

"Don't You Worry 'bout a Thing:" Soundtracking Scandal

Unlike its predecessor Grey's Anatomy, Scandal's soundtracking is largely populated by well-known artists of slick 1970s funk and soulful rhythm and blues such as Booker T & the M.G.s, Marvin Gaye, Sly & the Family Stone, Otis Redding, and Stevie Wonder. Scandal is the first television series to feature a black woman in the leading role since Get Christie Love in 1974, thus, that the series relies heavily on 1970s music performed by artists of color demonstrates a clear musical and narrative arc connecting historical resistance to the present.[49] Throughout the series, music by black artists is specifically connected to Olivia Pope's character and storylines. In season 3's "YOLO," Olivia says goodbye to her mother Maya Pope—previously assumed dead and suspected of terrorism—at an airfield while Michael Jackson's "Ben" plays in the background.[50] As the scene unfolds with the music, the audience experiences Olivia's flashbacks documenting her growing realization that perhaps her father's advice not to trust her mother was right. If so, by securing a plane for Maya's escape, she is helping a terrorist escape as opposed to saving her mother from her oppressive father. The use of "Ben" is notable here because the song details an eerie relationship between a young boy and a rat. Michael Jackson originally recorded the song for the film *Ben* (1972), a sequel to the film *Willard* (1971).[51] In *Willard*, Ben is a pet rat who is trained by a human named Willard to kill for him, but at the end Ben and the rats turn against him. In *Ben*, a young boy befriends the rat, but the rat turns evil and recruits other rats to attack humans. For this *Scandal* scene, the historical reference underscores the tenuous relationship between "humans" and "rats" and punctuates *Scandal*'s series theme of who can trust whom? From one episode to the next, Olivia strategically decides who to trust and who to betray even when (especially when) it comes to her parents. On the tarmac, the song parallels Olivia's emerging suspicions about her mother; both she and the audience watch as the plane takes off and she cognitively grasps that her mother has been a "rat" all along. It is also historically significant that "Ben" was Michael Jackson's first U.S. number one solo hit on the *Billboard* charts. From a critical vantage point, nothing in Shondaland is accidental. Therefore, we interpret the song's use as a televisual opportunity to honor the late artist's long-ago emergence as an icon.

Pairings between *Scandal* narratives and popular black music artists consistently highlight the classic melodramatic blurring of binary distinctions between right and wrong and good and evil. Christine Geldhill notes that in order for melodrama to exist in conjunction with modernity, there is a narrative need to complicate the moral compass between traditional Victorian sensibilities and the rise of progressive modernism.[52] Addressing this tension, Shondaland's emphasis on underscoring the moral compass of the series through music creates poignant statements about contemporary ethics in Washington, D.C., politics. Holding up a mirror to the modern U.S. political landscape, high-ranking *Scandal* characters have adulterous affairs, dabble in substance abuse, and engage in questionable and outright illegal and amoral behavior. Thus, *Scandal*'s soundtracking is far more mature in its articulation of professionalism than *Grey's*. Whereas *Grey's* follows interns, students learning where they fit into the professional system of medicine, *Scandal*'s narrative landscape necessitates far more savvy, wisdom, and violence to ensure success and survival. *Scandal*'s characters, who are similar in age to *Grey's* interns, have already established themselves as central to the political system and are consumed with leveraging their respective power toward their end goals, often at the behest of others. Logistically then, it makes sense that *Grey's* musical score focuses primarily on emerging or unknown young artists, while *Scandal* pulls from established artists of color known for their groundbreaking, gritty forays into the music industry—battles that were often politically charged in a racist and classist music industry.[53]

From an industry perspective, Rhimes's early commercial success with *Grey's* likely made it possible for her to successfully negotiate rights and licenses for the use of songs from well-known artists with established reputations on Shondaland's later shows. *Billboard Magazine* even ponders, "You'd think that with such sinister plots that legacy artists like Marvin Gaye would be hesitant to have their music used"; Rhimes responds with the following explanation: "Some artists really care. Stevie Wonder is an artist who really, really cares. It's kind of delightful. I will submit the scene and he comes back and says, 'Absolutely you can use this song,' or 'Absolutely you can't use this song.' And his reasons are always very smart, very clear, and he has parameters. And I respect that. It's been so helpful to us for this genre of music."[54] Shondaland's production team notes that "the clearance process has certainly been more complicated" with popular, established artists featured in *Scandal's* soundtrack, but that they have "had great luck in clearing all of her [Rhimes's] first choices."[55]

Additionally, Rhimes often uses music on *Scandal* as a means to disseminate sophisticated cultural criticism frequently in conversation with contemporary cultural politics. One particularly salient example occurs in the much-discussed abortion scene in "Baby, It's Cold Outside."[56] Rhimes employs an Aretha Franklin cover of the Christmas classic "Silent Night" as the soundtrack playing while Olivia takes her place on a medical table for her abortion procedure.[57] Though the word *abortion* is never uttered and viewers were unaware that Olivia was pregnant until she arrived at the doctor's office, the entire abortion "scene" lasts for less than a minute and is not treated as the episode's focal point. This representation is a stark departure from how abortion has traditionally been depicted on television—as a huge decision that women agonize over in a continuous narrative arc. Instead, Olivia's pregnancy is introduced and terminated within the span of a minute, and a speech by Olivia's father, Rowan Pope, conveys some of the cultural complexities surrounding abortion that rarely see television airtime. As a result, the episode has a strong, clear message about women's reproductive health in a political era when women's reproductive choices are under fire.

The use of "Silent Night" in the abovementioned scene is rife with meaning. The traditional Christmas hymn celebrates the birth of Jesus—a baby his mother Mary was unprepared for yet accepted into her arms with joy and reverence. The lyrical content of the piece worships the sacred bond between mother and child. Using this song in conjunction with an abortion offers a very pointed critique of contemporary cultural stances on abortion, especially those imbued with religious ideology. Rhimes explicitly draws attention to our privileged ideological preference for valorizing unplanned pregnancy as something women should and must go through with. Through Olivia's demeanor juxtaposed against the song, the audience is invited to question this hegemonic preference as Olivia willingly and resolutely, without emotionality, terminates her unplanned pregnancy. Moreover,

"Silent Night" is also about silence. In the political sphere, debates about abortion are not often explicitly about abortion. Rather, advocates and politicians typically employ silence about abortion to direct the political conversation to sexual health issues that have more common ground. For example, on *Scandal*, Republican senator Mellie Grant skirts around abortion as a women's health issue and focuses instead on sexually transmitted infections when she filibusters for women's health care.[58] In the real world, Planned Parenthood also often employs this tactic to direct public attention to other aspects of their services including routine gynecological care. That Olivia's abortion occurs in relative silence illustrates the stigmatized nature of conversations about abortion in the United States. Therein, Shondaland clearly offers an alternative use of silence via Olivia's experience to challenge a real-world political climate that strongly opposes a woman's right to choose.

"No One's Here to Sleep": Soundtracking *How to Get Away with Murder*

How to Get Away with Murder differs in its soundtracking from both *Grey's* and *Scandal*, but some key stylistic features are shared in this 2014 addition to Shondaland. *HTGAWM*'s soundtrack is comprised almost exclusively of electronic music with heavy bass, largely featuring DJs rather than bands or individual artists. The soundtracking is similar to *Grey's* in that both shows emphasize what was popular music at the time of the premiere. Singer-songwriters and indie ballads were at the height of popularity in 2004, while the most popular music in 2014 was dominated by a DJ culture much less focused on the celebrity, personality, or branding of musical artists. While music sets the dark tone of the series, as of its fourth season, its commercial connection to music is tenuous at best. The series has yet to "launch" and popularize artists in the same way that *Grey's* has for years. This distinction could be a direct result of creative difference (Peter Nowalk is the lead creator, not Rhimes), or it could signal a shift away from the commercialization of music as a primary goal in Shondaland.

An illustration of this tension occurs with OneRepublic's single "Love Runs Out," which was used for *HTGAWM* previews and promotions but does not appear in the series' soundtrack.[59] Slightly similar to some of the other Shondaland shows' soundtrack choices, it differs significantly from other *HTGAWM* musical selections because OneRepublic is a relatively well-known pop-punk group and the song sounds more mainstream than you would expect from the show's genre of musical ensembles. With a catchy hook and beat, the song provided ABC with a commercial, marketable soundbite for the series. It is possible the song was selected due to the lessened commercial appeal of the soundtrack overall. It is also possible that traditional commercialized goals for soundtracking have become less important or restrictive in the wake of Shondaland's continued popularity. In other words, the success of Shondaland from an auteur perspective may afford the creators more leeway to utilize music solely as a storytelling device without the traditional cross-promotional marketing that generally accompanies the marriage of music and television.

Creatively, Rhimes utilizes lyrical meaning in music for *Grey's* and *Scandal* where she serves as the primary showrunner; however, *HTGAWM* is guided by the creative direction of Peter Nowalk. Intentionally or not, the soundtrack conveys more masculine characteristics, foregrounding a dark mood for the series, inspiring fear and rage, and providing little connection to lyrical content. In season 1's "He Deserved to Die," the electronic "Vagaries of Fashion" by Fujiya & Miyagi plays as we cut between two scenes; in one, Rebecca and Wes are having sex for the first time. The other, in stark juxtaposition, is of Lila's exhumed body being reautopsied.[60] The white sheets on the bed beneath Rebecca become the sheet pulled down in the morgue, revealing Lila's decomposing face. A closeup of Lila's bitten neck being photographed by a mortician flips to Rebecca's neck and collarbone as Wes kisses her and slides the strap of her shirt down. Rapid shots switch between Rebecca's alive frame being touched by Wes, and Lila's dead body being handled by morticians, complete with bloody surgical instruments and biohazard bags presumably housing organs. The frames quickly switch as the sex scene progresses to a climax, with Rebecca's and Lila's faces almost melding together. The result is the visual conflation between violence and sex, linked by aggressive sonic elements that also highlight a connection between the two (mirroring the connection between sex and violence in season 1's plotline). The implicit focus of the scene draws attention to the consumption of women's bodies—in life and in death—through the male gaze; the song choice stylistically creates a dark, electronic vibe where lyrical content and dialogue are not the focus.[61]

In fact, because lyrical content in the electronic genre is often difficult to process audibly, it would be tempting to assert that song lyrics have little to do with *HTGAWM*'s narrative framing beyond general tone. However, upon closer examination, some overlap between lyrical content and television representation does occur. In the previous example, a line about "unraveling the seams" of a garment plays as morticians cut open crude stitches on Lila's corpse and Wes unzips Rebecca's pants. Similarly, upon our introduction to protagonist Annalise Keating in the pilot, music establishes her character's defining features. Annalise, a law professor whose ruthless persona is seen in the classroom and courtroom, is involved with plots to murder, attempts to frame individuals for crimes they did not commit, and routinely involves her students in criminal cover-ups. She is introduced in the pilot to the song "Dark and Stormy" by Hot Chip, but the song that best encompasses her sharp-witted character is what plays as the episode ends in a closeup of her face as she stares at her husband, who viewers now know she suspects of murder.[62] "I Come with Knives" by IAMX gradually gets louder in the background, the lyrics switching from German to English just in time to hear a snippet of the chorus: "I come with knives and agony."[63] Audibly splashed across her face, the melody and lyrics convey that while her husband may have murdered his young girlfriend, it is Annalise who is to be feared. Annalise is equipped with all kinds of weapons, and, as she proves in the pilot, she is skilled at manipulation. Not only does she get the police detective she is sleeping with to commit perjury in open court, she also convinces Wes to keep her affair a secret. She depicts no shame in using these weapons as the lyrics "I never promised you an open heart or charity" accompany the credit roll. The soundtracking of *HTGAWM* shares some common elements with the shows Rhimes actually showruns, but the musical signature of Nowalk's series differs in its significantly lessened commercial appeal.

SHONDALAND'S MUSICAL SIGNATURE: SOUNDTRACKING FOR SUCCESS

Through an analysis of three shows in Shondaland (two written and showrun by Rhimes and one supported by her production company but run by Nowalk), key aspects of soundtracking in contemporary television come to light. One of cultural studies' classic criticisms of popular music comes from Adorno: "The whole structure of popular music is standardized, even where the attempt is made to circumvent standardization. Standardization extends from the most general features to the most specific ones. Best known is the rule that the chorus consists of thirty two bars and that the range is limited to one octave and one note."[64] In other words, the strict structural formality and limitation of the genre of popular music was seen as an important consideration in early cultural studies work on music. More "serious" constructions of music—such as classical composing—were lauded as more creative, "high" cultural forms, while the popular, formulaic constructions were relegated to "low" class status.[65] However, as this analysis shows, the standardized form and structure of popular music, particularly in stylistic choices of genre and lyrics, is particularly useful for underscoring and elevating key narrative moments on television. Ultimately, these choices can signal a signature style developed by a television auteur as they do for Rhimes's Shondaland. Highlighting the pairing between popular music and television, a repetitive musical signature literally builds the public identity of a show as concretely as traditional elements like character and plot devices.

One key facet of Rhimes's showrunner strategy has been to use popular music purposefully in her television work. Shondaland's rise during the digital music crisis offered a smooth transition for contemporary industry coexistence between television and music. Rhimes's style as an auteur utilized an old model (new songs premiering on must-see-television) in a new way (incorporating digital media and online purchasing options), establishing a groundbreaking new formula for television showrunners. One can easily track music trends from 2004 to the present through Shondaland's television shows. For instance, in the early 2000s (i.e., *Grey's* debut), singer-songwriters soared in popularity, giving way to a boom of nostalgic classic music in the late 2000s (i.e., *Scandal's* debut) (now all easily accessible through Apple Music, Pandora, or Spotify), ultimately leading to digitized techno with thumping bass lines in the 2010s (i.e., *HTGAWM's* debut). Thus, her creative works, and those produced through her company, follow a particular formula: capitalize on popular music trends, connect these trends to characters and storylines within a series, and tie in commercial purchasing options. Though the process is not a stark deviation from pre-digitization models, it seamlessly integrates existing business models (that music executives struggle to hold on to) with new technological progress in a way that is commercially profitable for all stakeholders involved. This purposeful blend of television narrative and music commercialization is a signature that Rhimes and her production team have employed successfully enough that other production companies, networks, and auteurs are copying its format.

While the construct of popular music and its commodification can and should be criticized, televisual identities are built and strengthened in and through popular music. If, indeed, the role of music in television is to "aestheticize the reality we see . . . to ground what we see, to tie a moment to a familiar song . . . [and to provide] ironic commentary on what is seen," it is evident that Shondaland meets these conditions through its productive use of popular music.[66] Music is used for irony, for familiarity, and to offer on-screen and offscreen sociohistorical context and commentary. At the same time, burgeoning artists in an industry radically transformed by advances in technology needed new economic models for popular music. ABC's embrace of the Music Lounge as a digital place where television and music synergistically benefit each other offers musical content readily available at the click of a button. These kinds of corporate tie-ins should be an anticipated feature in the future of the television industry, particularly as the number of media monopolies continues to dwindle.

NOTES

1. Sleeping at Last, "Chasing Cars," *Covers* vol. 2, released November 4, 2016, https://www.youtube.com/watch?v=Yun3N6pI128.

2. Mark Cooper, "From Wifi to Wikis and Open Source: The Political Economy of Collaborative Production in the Digital Information Age," *Journal on Telecommunications & High Technology Law* 5 (2006): 125–157.

3. Simon Frith, "Look! Hear! The Uneasy Relationship of Music and Television," *Popular Music* 21 (2002): 277–290.

4. Frith.

5. Frith.

6. Keith Negus, "Musicians on Television: Visible, Audible and Ignored," *Journal of the Royal Musical Association* 131 (2006): 310–330.

7. Patrick Burkart and Tom McCourt, *Digital Music Wars: Ownership and Control of the Celestial Jukebox* (Lanham, Md.: Rowman & Littlefield, 2006).

8. Anna Everett, "Scandalicious: Scandal, Social Media, and Shonda Rhimes' Auteurist Juggernaut," *Black Scholar* 45, no. 1 (2015): 34–43.

9. Patricia Aufderheide, *Communications Policy and the Public Interest: The Telecommunication Act of 1996* (New York: Guilford Press, 1999).

10. *One Tree Hill*, "Just Watch the Fireworks," season 3, episode 15, directed by Billy Dickson, written by James Patrick Stoteraux and Chad Fiveash, aired February 15, 2006, on The CW.

11. Negus, "Musicians on Television."

12. See Will Brooker, "Living on *Dawson's Creek*: Teen Viewers, Cultural Convergence, and Television Overflow," *International Journal of Cultural Studies* 4, no. 4 (2001): 456–472; Glyn Davies and Kay Dickinson, eds., *Teen TV: Genre, Consumption & Identity* (London: British Film Institute, 2000); Michaela D. E. Meyer and Megan M. Wood, "Sexuality and Teen Television: Emerging Adults Respond to Representations of Queer Identity on *Glee*," *Sexuality & Culture* 17, no. 3 (2013): 434–448.

13. *Big Brother*, series directed by Mark W. Roden, aired 2000–2019, on CBS

14. Randall L. Rose and Stacy L. Wood, "Paradox and the Consumption of Authenticity through Reality Television," *Journal of Consumer Research* 32 (2005): 284–296. For a wider variety of scholarly perspectives on the interplay between narrative television and music, see Ronald Wayne Rodman, *Tuning In: American Narrative Television Music* (New York: Oxford University Press, 2010).

15. James W. Carey, *Communication as Culture, Revised Edition: Essays on Media and Society* (Abingdon, U.K.: Routledge, 2008).

16. Daniel J. Levitin, *This Is Your Brain on Music: The Science of a Human Obsession* (New York: Penguin, 2006).

17. Oliver Sacks, *Musicophilia: Tales of Music and the Brain* (Toronto: Vintage Canada, 2010).

18. Isabelle Peretz, Lise Gagnon, and Bernard Bouchard, "Music and Emotion: Perceptual Determinants, Immediacy, and Isolation after Brain Damage," *Cognition* 68 (1998): 111–141.

19. Clare Birchall, "'Feels like Home': *Dawson's Creek*, Nostalgia, and the Young Adult Viewer," in *Teen TV: Genre, Consumption and Identity*, ed. Glyn Davies and Kay Dickinson (London: British Film Institute, 2004), 176–189.

20. For a concise history of this trend spanning the 1990s, see Rob Becker, *Gay TV and Straight America* (Piscataway, N.J.: Rutgers University Press, 2006).

21. Richard E. Crew, "Viewer Interpretations of Reality Television: How Real Is *Survivor* for Its Viewers?," in *How Real Is Reality TV? Essays on Representation and Truth*, ed. David S. Escoffery (Jefferson, N.C.: McFarland, 2006), 61–77.

22. Theodor W. Adorno, "How to Look at Television," *Quarterly of Film Radio and Television* 8 (1954): 213–235.

23. Theodor W. Adorno, "On Popular Music," in *Essays on Music*, ed. Richard Leppert (Los Angeles: University of California Press, 2002), 437–469; Christopher Small, *Musicking: The Meanings of Performing and Listening* (Middletown, Conn.: Wesleyan University Press, 2011).

24. Rajiv K. Sinha and Naomi Mandel, "Preventing Digital Music Piracy: The Carrot or the Stick?," *Journal of Marketing* 72 (2008): 1–15.

25. Jerald Hughes and Karl Reiner Lang, "If I Had a Song: The Culture of Digital Community Networks and Its Impact on the Music Industry," *International Journal on Media Management* 5, no. 3 (2003): 180–189.

26. Marcus Breen, "The Music Industry, Technology and Utopia—An Exchange Between Marcus Breen and Eamonn Forde," *Popular Music* 23 (2004): 79–89.

27. Neda Ulaby, "2006 and the Death of Tower Records," *NPR*, December 29, 2009, https://www.npr.org/2009/12/29/121975854/2006-and-the-death-of-tower-records.

28. Valerie L. Vaccaro and Deborah Y. Cohn, "The Evolution of Business Models and Marketing Strategies in the Music Industry," *International Journal on Media Management* 6 (2004): 46–58.

29. Bethany Klein, *As Heard on TV: Popular Music in Advertising*. (Burlington, Vt: Ashgate, 2010).

30. John Jurgenson, "A Second Life for *The Wonder Years*," *Wall Street Journal*, October 2, 2014, https://www.wsj.com/articles/a-second-life-for-the-wonder-years-1412287481.

31. The ABC Music Lounge, http://abc.go.com/shows/music-lounge.

32. Frith, "Look! Hear!"

33. Melinda Newman, "Shonda Rhimes on Her Early Battles over Music for Her Shows and the Artist She's Obsessed With," *Billboard*, September 17, 2015, http://www.billboard.com/articles/news/magazine-feature/6700362/shonda-rhimes-music-greys-anatomy-scandal-how-to-get-away-with-murder-shondaland.

34. Bambi Haggins, "The Cultural Politics of Colorblind TV Casting, by Kristen Warner," *Transformative Works and Cultures* 22 (2016), July 30, 2017, http://journal.transformativeworks.org/index.php/twc/article/view/962/627.

35. For an historical overview of cultural forces shaping television soundtracking, see Kevin Donnelly, *The Spectre of Sound: Music in Film and Television* (London: British Film Institute, 2005) or Ron Rodman, *Tuning In: American Narrative Television Music* (New York: Oxford University Press, 2010).

36. Andrew Darley, *Visual Digital Culture: Surface Play and Spectacle in New Media Genres* (New York: Routledge, 2002).

37. The Marque Blog, "*Grey's Anatomy* Gets All *Glee* on Us: What's the Verdict?," *CNN Entertainment*, April 1, 2011, http://marquee.blogs.cnn.com/2011/04/01/greys-anatomy-gets-all-glee-on-us-whats-the-verdict/.

38. *Grey's Anatomy*, "A Hard Day's Night," season 1, episode 1, directed by Peter Horton, written by Shonda Rhimes, aired on March 27, 2005, on ABC; Rilo Kiley, "Portions for Foxes," Warner Brothers Records, 2005, https://www.youtube.com/watch?v=qtNV3pOqcjI.

39. *Grey's Anatomy*, "Superstition," season 2, episode 21, directed by Tricia Brock, written by Shonda Rhimes and James Parriott, aired on March 19, 2006, on ABC; Corey Moss, "The Fray Hit It Big, with Some Help from Dr. McDreamy," *MTV News*, December 4, 2006, http://www.mtv.com/news/1547078/the-fray-hit-it-big-with-some-help-from-dr-mcdreamy/.

40. "Ingrid Michaelson Flips the Script: She's Climbing Our Charts, Scored a Hit TV Series and a Blockbuster Commercial, and She Still Has No Label," *Billboard*, January 12, 2008, 24–27.

41. *Grey's Anatomy*, "Didn't We Almost Have It All?," season 3, episode 25, directed by Rob Corn, written by Tony Phellan and Joan Rater, aired on May 17, 2007, on ABC.

42. *Grey's Anatomy*, "Perfect Storm," season 9, episode 24, directed by Rob Corn, written by Stacy McKee, aired on May 16, 2013, on ABC.

43. Joy Zipper, "Just like Heaven," American Laundromat Records, 2008, https://www.youtube.com/watch?v=xSGlcsZJU6s; Bootstraps, "I Wanna Dance with Somebody," Atelier Recordings, 2016, https://www.youtube.com/watch?v=L4Ed2_bfnFo.

44. *Grey's Anatomy*, "Who Lives, Who Dies, Who Tells Your Story," season 14, episode 7, directed by Debbie Allen, written by Shonda Rhimes and Krista Vernoff, aired on November 9, 2017, on ABC.

45. Jayme Deerwester, "*Grey's Anatomy* 300th Episode Is a 'Love Letter' to the Original Cast," *USA Today*, November 8, 2017, https://www.usatoday.com/story/life/tv/2017/11

/08/greys-anatomy-300th-episode-ellen-pompeo-shonda-rhimes/840545001/; Psapp, "Cosy in the Rocket," Hollywood Records, 2005, https://www.youtube.com/watch?v=VwjZGyc 6VNE

46. Tegan and Sara, "Where Does the Good Go?," Sanctuary Records, 2004, https://www.youtube.com/watch?v=8RDdmfWsrsw.

47. *Grey's Anatomy*, "No Man's Land," season 1, episode 4, directed by Adam Davidson, written by Shonda Rhimes and James Parriott, aired on April 17, 2005, on ABC.

48. *Grey's Anatomy*, "Fear (of the Unknown)," season 10, episode 24, directed by Bill D'Elia, written by Shonda Rhimes and Austin Guzman, aired on May 15, 2014, on ABC.

49. Tanzina Vega, "A Show Makes Friends and History; *Scandal* on ABC Is Breaking Barriers," *New York Times*, January 16, 2013, http://www.nytimes.com/2013/01/17/arts/television/scandal -on-abc-is-breaking-barriers.html.

50. *Scandal*, "YOLO," season 3, episode 9, directed by Oliver Bokelberg, written by Shonda Rhimes and Chris Van Dusen, aired on December 5, 2013, on ABC; Michael Jackson, "Ben," Motown Records, 1972, https://www.youtube.com/watch?v=A0LiYT1tXhA.

51. *Ben*, directed by Phil Karlson (1972; Los Angeles, Calif.: Shout! Factory, 2017), DVD; *Willard*, directed by Daniel Mann (1971; Los Angeles, Calif.: Shout! Factory, 2017), DVD.

52. Christine Gledhill, *Home Is Where the Heart Is: Studies in Melodrama and the Woman's Film* (London: British Film Institute, 1987).

53. Mark Anthony Neal, "Sold Out on Soul: The Corporate Annexation of Black Popular Music," *Popular Music & Society* 21, no. 3 (1997): 117–135.

54. Mike Ayers, "The Soul of *Scandal*: How Shonda Rhimes Soundtracks TV's Most Dramatic Show," *Billboard*, April 17, 2014, http://www.billboard.com/articles/columns/pop-shop /6062363/the-soul-of-scandal-how-shonda-rhimes-soundtracks-tvs-most.

55. Ayers.

56. *Scandal*, "Baby, It's Cold Outside," season 5, episode 9, directed by Tom Verica, written by Shonda Rhimes and Mark Wilding, aired on November 19, 2015, on ABC.

57. Aretha Franklin, "Silent Night," DMI, 2008, https://www.youtube.com/watch?v=y _hUsoUZNLk.

58. *Scandal*, "Baby, It's Cold Outside."

59. OneRepublic, "Love Runs Out," Interscope Records, 2013, https://www.youtube.com /watch?v=oOWjoCiM8WU.

60. *How to Get Away with Murder*, "He Deserved to Die," directed by Eric Stoltz, written by Warren Hsu Leonard, aired November 6, 2014, on ABC; Fujiya & Miyagi, "Vagaries of Fashion," Yep Roc, 2014, https://www.youtube.com/watch?v=lN6hRYLQS70.

61. Laura Mulvey, "Visual Pleasure and Narrative Cinema," in *Media and Cultural Studies: Keyworks*, ed. Meenakshi Gigi Durham and Douglas M. Kellner (Malden, Mass.: Blackwell, 2001), 393–404.

62. *How to Get Away with Murder*, "Pilot," season 1, episode 1, directed by Michael Offer, written by Peter Nowalk, aired September 25, 2014, on ABC; Hot Chip, "Dark and Stormy," Domino, 2013, https://www.youtube.com/watch?v=J4f2el1M-Pw.

63. IAMX, "I Come with Knives," 61 Seconds, 2012, https://www.youtube.com/watch?v =WjQM-AkCA08.

64. Adorno, "On Popular Music," 438.

65. This is well documented among many cultural theorists. A strong overview and discussion can be found in Angela McRobbie, *In the Culture Society: Art, Fashion and Popular Music* (New York: Routledge, 1999).

66. Frith, "Look! Hear!" 277–290.

PART 2 SHONDALAND'S PARADOXICAL IDENTITY POLITICS AND THE FANTASTICAL "POST"

5 · RACE (LOST AND FOUND) IN SHONDALAND

The Rise of Multiculturalism in Prime-Time Network Television

JADE PETERMON

In the summer of 1999, the president of the National Association for the Advancement of Colored People (NAACP), Kweisi Mfume, threatened action against ABC, CBS, NBC, and Fox—the Big Four television networks. Mfume noted that, "not a single prime-time show among 26 to be introduced on the major broadcast networks this fall has an ethnic minority character in a leading role."[1] The previous season (1998–1999) featured eleven black prime-time network shows including *Sister, Sister* (WB 1994–1999), *Moesha* (UPN 1996–2001), *The Jamie Foxx Show* (WB 1996–2001), *The Steve Harvey Show* (WB 1996–2002), and *The Hughleys* (ABC/UPN 1998–2002). Most of these shows aired on the WB [Warner Brothers] and UPN [United Paramount Network], two fledgling networks known for catering to "urban markets," which is the problematic term that media conglomerates typically use in reference to black markets. Although Mfume's advocacy against the media's systematic exclusion of people of color is well founded, it is intriguing that this issue reached a boiling point at a time when the televisual landscape was rich with images created by and for black people.

Network experimentation with niche programing in the late 1980s and early 1990s led to an increase in shows that addressed racialized identities. This time period saw success of numerous black-produced shows as well as shows like Margaret Cho's *All American Girl* (ABC 1994) and George's López's *George López* (ABC 2002–2007). However, beginning with the 2005 WB/UPN merger that created the CW (parent companies CBS and Warner Brothers), this type of niche programming has since sharply declined; consequently, prime-time network television shows featuring, written, and produced by people of color in general and African Americans specifically have also declined. The popular and lucrative black sitcoms on Fox and the CW in the 1990s through the early 2000s have largely been replaced by reality television. Additionally, after the merger, black shows were largely shifted to cable and the network space reserved for scripted shows reflected a strengthened commitment to multiculturalism. For example, Mara Brock Akil's *The Game* (The CW/BET 2006–2015), a *Girlfriends* (UPN/CW, 2000–2008) spin-off, moved to cable in 2009 and *Girlfriends* was canceled the same season that Shonda Rhimes's *Private Practice* (ABC 2007–2013) premiered.

Krystal Brent Zook's analysis of early 1990s black shows on Fox is particularly useful in trying to understand the difference between the niche shows of the 1990s and the multicultural shows that replaced them after the 2005 WB/UPN merger. Zook distinguishes between black-produced shows (i.e., shows created and/ or produced by black showrunners) and those that feature a black cast. She identifies four aspects of black-produced television: autobiography, improvisation, aesthetics, and emotionally challenging subject matter; also noted is the importance of black-produced shows featuring black issues and themes alongside black casts.[2] The shows Zook describes are different from multicultural shows in their willingness to embrace cultural specificity rather than using cultural ambiguity to appeal to the widest audience.

On television, multiculturalism often masquerades as diversity, presenting different creeds of people while obscuring, erasing, or objectifying their differences. While on-camera racial diversity is indeed progressive, the entertainment industry often capitalizes on the visibility of people of color without regard for cultural specificity. Therefore, multiculturalism leads to a multicultural colorblindness characterized by featuring people of various identities and hues minus any social, historical, or political background to construe their racial or ethnic identities. Today, many of the scripted shows on broadcast television look more like *Private Practice* than *Girlfriends*. Enter Shonda Rhimes and Shondaland's mass popularity.

Rhimes's first television show, *Grey's Anatomy* (ABC 2005–present; also referred to as *Grey's*), debuted during the niche model decline and dovetailed with the merger that ended nearly a decade of black-produced shows matching Zook's description. Early on, Rhimes vocally supported colorblind casting and, more broadly, postracial ideology via comments such as: "On *Grey's* we don't have the black character who is 'the black character.' He has issues way beyond being, 'the black character.'"[3] Mirroring postracialism, Rhimes's characters, for whom racism is not a barrier to success, are progressive. In Zook's analysis, in contrast to Rhimes's approach, racially marginalized actors are cast and their visibility is meaningful; however, their storylines rarely explore racialized struggles or politicize characters' intersectional identities. Therefore, according to Zook, the mere inclusion of people of color is not progressive. Postracial ideology served Rhimes well early on because she gained exposure as a showrunner without rocking the boat. From a critical television studies perspective, her projects were nonthreatening and starkly nonpolitical, in turn, bolstering their appeal to mainstream (i.e., predominantly white) audiences.

In the early days of her television career, Rhimes's high ratings positioned her within a neoliberal moment of tokenism. Hall reminds us that "neoliberalism is grounded in the 'free, possessive individual,' with the state cast as tyrannical and oppressive."[4] The United States' eminence as the Promised Land rests on the idea that anyone—regardless of identity/identities—through hard work can become successful. While this is true for some, Rhimes included, meritocratic success is not feasible for most.[5] The bootstraps narrative, on which neoliberalism's cult of individual responsibility hinges, requires that tokens exist as examples of what is possible if only an individual works hard enough.[6] Linking neoliberalism to media, Hasinoff says, "The increased visibility of racial identities is deployed to commodify race and maintain its political invisibility."[7] In this way, driven by neoliberal tokenism, Rhimes's palatability to white audiences was an attractive commercial choice for ABC. The network could forefront a talented black showrunner producing multicultural shows and simultaneously abandon black-produced shows while pointedly escaping accusations of racism by tokenizing Rhimes's identities.

Over a decade into *Grey's* popularity, coupled with the unprecedented success of *Scandal* (ABC 2012–2018) and *How to Get Away with Murder* (also referred to as *HTGAWM*) (ABC 2014–present), Rhimes has more outwardly engaged "black" and "woman" as politicized identities for herself, which aligns with her shows becoming more political as well. In 2012, she called out Amy Sherman-Palladino on Twitter for *Bunheads's* (ABC Family, 2012–2013) lack of diversity: "Hey @abcbunheads: Really? You couldn't cast even ONE young dancer of color so I could feel good about my kid watching this show? NOT ONE?"[8] Shondaland's storylines echo this shift from silence to outspokenness; *Scandal*'s season 4 episode "The Lawn Chair" addresses police violence against unarmed black men, and *HTGAWM*'s season 1 episode "Let's Get Scooping" addresses racialized beauty standards.[9] These storylines, among others, demonstrate Rhimes's growing willingness to actively contribute to public discourses on diversity and the lack thereof on television. This approach, albeit imperfect, marks a sincere departure from her earlier style, which I argue was purposefully apolitical and did not seriously engage race or racism.

Rhimes's takeover of ABC's prime-time slots is more clearly understood when situated within the context of broader industry shifts over the past twenty years. In this chapter, I examine the content of shows like *Grey's* and *Scandal* against the historical backdrop of patterned industry changes to demonstrate how Rhimes's increasingly political engagement is key to exploding the postracial myth that gained momentum in the 2000s. I highlight the distinct relationship between Rhimes's early success, her avid defense of colorblind casting, and postracialism in stark contrast to her current showrunning practices. Additionally, turning toward the larger television industry, I link Rhimes's feats to the success of shows like *Black-ish* (ABC 2014–present), *Fresh off the Boat* (ABC 2014–present), and *Empire* (Fox 2014–present). Overall, my analysis of Rhimes and Shondaland exposes how neoliberalism manipulates the ability to see, comprehend, and deconstruct the power dynamics that deeply inform the television industry. Intersectional identity politics and race, particular to this essay, are omnipresent; yet, neoliberalism appropriates the look and language of progress to renew oppressive mechanisms and stifle bona fide societal transformation.

To deconstruct patterned industry shifts disguised as progressive multicultural inclusivity, I deploy hyper(in)visibility as a concept that underscores how black bodies in the neoliberal era are paraded across the visual field, signifying progress and promise, while the humanity of black people is obscured. The recent works of scholars including Safiya Noble, Rachel Alicia Griffin, Amber Johnson, and Robin Boylorn provide foundational insight into the paradox of black visibility characterized by total objectification. Noble recognizes the hypervisibility of black women's and girls' oversexed bodies through Google searches as intimately linked to commercial processes that prioritize paid advertising within search results. This hypervisibility of black girls' sexuality ultimately renders them invisible via objectification. Noble also links the hyper(in)visibility of black girls to postracial and colorblind ideologies via Google's corporate outlook, which "places the onus of discrimination or racism on the individual or on the algorithm."[10] Similarly, Griffin argues that the film *Precious* (2009) features a black female protagonist only to commodify her suffering and reaffirm white superiority, rendering "Precious hypervisible and yet largely unseen."[11] Johnson and Boylorn use "hyper/in/visibility" to analyze the complicated uses and values of visibility for oppressed groups; specifically, LGBTQ (lesbian, gay, bisexual, transgender, queer) individuals. They call attention to how queer hypervisibility can often be just as harmful as invisibility depending on the context. Furthermore, it is not enough to simply create a space where bodies are visible, but "how, when, where, and to whom we share those bodies are just as important as the sharing itself."[12] Closely informed by these works in the realms of digital media and film, I use hyper(in)visibility to illuminate how neoliberalism produces a racialized paradox on television, namely, a cultural moment in which black people are more visible than ever before yet stripped of corresponding black experiences, which often leaves black audiences craving effective representation.[13] The industry embrace of generic multiculturalism and the decline in shows about black culture suggest a strong connection between neoliberal ideology and the television industry. Deconstructing this connection reveals an added layer of complexity that necessitates examining the influential linkages between the social institutions of media and government.

Conceptually anchored by hyper(in)visibility, I also utilize Havens, Lotz, and Tinic's critical media industry studies approach.[14] This approach considers mid-level operations and culture as departure points for analysis to highlight how power-laden media practices produce ways of seeing. This framework, through theoretically informed ethnography as well as textual and discursive analysis, values the analytical space of contradiction because "contradictions account for instances of creativity, resistance, and change."[15] Characterized by conducting "empirical (not empiricist) research into the media industries with an eye toward the *struggle* over ideological hegemony in the production of popular culture," this approach is critical to my reading of Rhimes's shows and Shondaland's success.[16] Thus, the contradictions that emerge when Rhimes's early public discourse and showrunning decisions are compared with her overall career trajectory proffer an opportunity to examine power in television. Next, to provide context for my close analysis, I explain how black-produced shows on prime-time network television were replaced by exposing neoliberalism's role in creating a space for multiculturally colorblind shows to take over.

THE RISE OF MULTICULTURALISM ON PRIME TIME

Several scholars have troubled black representation and participation in network television and voiced black audiences' dissatisfaction with television.[17] Gray delineates three categories of black shows: assimilationist, pluralist, and multicultural.[18] Assimilationist shows eliminate the social issues and cultural differences of blackness altogether while pluralist, or separate but equal, shows present black people in a world of their own or as peripheral to the central white world. Multicultural shows present black experiences parallel to white experiences and champion integration over the separatism espoused on pluralist shows. At the time of Gray's 1995 study, there were several assimilationist and pluralist shows. Comparatively, in the past decade, pluralist shows such as *Everybody Hates Chris* (UPN/CW 2005–2009), have been in constant decline while multicultural shows such as *Modern Family* (ABC 2009–present) have dominated prime time. For Gray, multicultural shows may or may not include those with a predominately black cast and his category differs from my literal use of the term. A multicultural show, according to Gray's classification, "invites viewers, regardless of race, class or gender locations, to participate in black experience from multiple subject positions."[19]

Late 1980s/1990s multicultural shows like *A Different World* (NBC 1987–1993) and *Roc* (Fox 1991–1997) "explicitly examined issues of racism, apartheid, discrimination, nationalism, masculinity, color coding, desegregation, and poverty from multiple and complex perspectives within blackness."[20] However, a key difference between then and now is that contemporary multicultural shows are not regularly concerned with examining racial issues as outlined by Gray. Rather, multicultural ideology, rhetoric, and representation has increasingly become synonymous with colorblindness. Prashad argues, "The shallow divide between multi-culturalism as a liberal doctrine and colorblindness as a conservative one masks the dialectical interrelationship between the two: both doctrines in tandem, occlude any discussion of the means of subordination of certain people along class, gender, and racial lines."[21] For Prashad, although multiculturalism and colorblindness appear oppositional, both prize progress toward a postracial society, thereby undermining centuries of activism against systemic inequality. The urgency to declare society postracial is closely linked to the hegemonic structures of neoliberalism and postracial rhetoric functions in service to neoliberal regimes. The merge between multiculturalism and colorblindness has impacted how race is understood in society at large and, more specifically, representations of black people on television.

According to Prashad, "Conceiving of television as a dense site or place of struggle over the symbolic meanings (and uses) of blackness in the production of the nation admittedly gives television a central role in cultural politics."[22] Equally insightful, Gray's analysis critically intervenes in neoliberalism by highlighting the meaning of blackness and how it is constantly in flux on television. In this context, the decline of black-produced shows is particularly revealing. Trends toward multicultural, colorblind representations are reflective of a national desire to erase race and embrace postracial nationalism, which is more consequential than a mere change in what is on television. Next, I examine a series of political moments that illustrate the progression of postracial desire.

NEOLIBERAL HYPER(IN)VISIBILITY: SETTING THE POLITICAL SCENE

According to Harvey, "Neoliberalism is a theory of political economic practices proposing that human well-being can best be advanced by the maximization of entrepreneurial freedoms within an institutional framework characterized by private property rights, individual liberty, unencumbered markets and free trade."[23] The implementation of these practices has shifted global finance, commerce, and, more broadly, culture. Hall reminds us that "questions of culture are not superstructural to the problems of economic and political change; they are constitutive of them."[24] This means significant political and economic changes consequentially necessitate changes in culture. Foucault further explains how this process occurs by theorizing neoliberalism as a shift *of* ideology rather than a simple shift *in* ideology.[25] This distinction is meaningful because it is not solely limited to the workings of the state but extends to "the entirety of human existence."[26] Foucault claims that subjects under neoliberalism become entrepreneurs of one.[27] We are each our own business in the marketplace seeking ways to increase our bottom line. Read asserts, "As a form of governmentality, neoliberalism would seem paradoxically to govern without governing; that is to function, its subjects must have a great deal of freedom to act."[28] In other words, neoliberalism presumes to create freedom by limiting freedoms. As a result, it is imperative to examine how neoliberalism creates subjects.

Neoliberalism creates varying subjects complicated by identities such as race and gender because such identities can foster marginalization thereby limiting one's ability to monetize their personhood. Noble states, "Formulations of postracialism presume that racial disparities no longer exist, within which color-blind ideology finds momentum."[29] Therefore, postracialism inhibits the ability of racially marginalized individuals to function (let alone succeed) in a neoliberal state because it obscures the mechanisms (e.g., racism, xenophobia, ethnocentrism, white privilege) by which they are oppressed. To further elucidate the relationship between neoliberalism and postracialism before detailing how these constructs manifest in Shondaland, I examine key political moments that demonstrate how this multicultural/colorblind pairing contributed to a shift in the national rhetoric toward postracialism in service of a neoliberal regime which, in turn, seriously impacted television industry production.

This contemporary history begins with the racially motivated codification of blackness by the Reagan administration in the 1980s. Using racialized codes, Republican president Reagan reignited a long-standing us/them dichotomy that united conservatives across the country. Allegiant to the black/white binary, Reagan used television to position blacks (i.e., "them") as moral deviants in the cultural imaginary, while whites (i.e., "us") were positioned as "the workers, the tax payers, the persons playing by the rules and struggling to make ends meet while brazen minorities partied with their hard-earned tax dollars."[30] Reagan criminalized "them" with inflammatory antiblack rhetoric, including his oft noted welfare queen from Chicago with "eighty names, thirty addresses, [and] twelve Social Security cards who is collecting veteran's benefits on four non-existing deceased husbands. She's got Medicaid, getting food stamps and is collecting welfare under each of her names. Her tax-free income is over $150,000."[31] Offering a "solution" to the "problem," Reagan promised, if elected president, to attack racially conscious policies and implement colorblindness as a corrective enactment of fairness.[32]

Colorblindness and multiculturalism, as conservative and liberal yearnings for the state of race relations, exist in the societal imagination as opposing ideals; however, they concurrently mirror each other perfectly. According to Brown et al.:

When segregation was legal and racial classification determined whether one sat or drank or lived or went to school, color-blindness meant abolishing the color-coded laws of southern apartheid. . . . [However] with the clarity of hindsight, we can now see that it was naïve to believe America could wipe out three hundred years of physical, legal, cultural, spiritual and political oppression based on race in a mere thirty years.[33]

Brown et al.'s insight on the incongruity of historical and contemporary uses of colorblindness is compelling. Thus, although colorblindness may have been a lofty, even respectable, goal long ago, it is no longer a productive path to racial equality. Unfortunately, colorblindness has shapeshifted over the past sixty years to the benefit of neoliberalism; it ideologically prevails in political debates on social issues (e.g., affirmative action, education, poverty) while conveniently ignoring institutional racism. Brown et al. explain how several scholars and politicians have used colorblind ideology to discount racism as a present-day problem in U.S. American society.[34] Similarly, Bonilla-Silva argues that white people subscribe to colorblind ideology to mask racist opinions about blacks and other people of color. He asserts, "Whites have developed powerful explanations—which have ultimately become justifications—for contemporary racial inequality that exculpate them from any responsibility for the status of people of color. These explanations emanate from a new racial ideology I label *color-blind racism*."[35] The seeds for colorblind racism, planted on the heels of civil rights and feminist movements, were nurtured during Reagan's era and bloomed during the Bush Sr. and Clinton eras.

Republican president George H. W. Bush's racialization of politics closely mirrored Reagan's. His campaign rhetoric capitalized on the Willie Horton narrative to make his Democratic rival, Michael Dukakis, appear soft on crime. Horton was a black man who committed violent crimes against whites while on a prison furlough program comparable to those Dukakis supported. Bush's use of racialized dog whistle politics saved his campaign.[36]Once elected, Bush worked to end affirmative action and refused to sign the Civil Rights Act of 1990, which offset the effects of several Supreme Court decisions that weakened Title VII of the Equal Employment Opportunity Law.[37] These policy decisions align with Reagan's and further established the foundation for colorblind politics that, in effect, reproduced racism.

Although William J. Clinton's rhetoric sounded considerably different than Reagan and Bush, his presidency demonstrates how commitments to "diversity" foster neoliberal hyper(in)visibility and affirm postracialism. Interestingly, Reagan and Bush were widely perceived as "old boys club" conservatives, whereas Clinton was widely perceived to be an ally to people of color, so much so that Toni Morrison referred to him as the United States' first black president, citing the ways his biography contained many tropes of the black experience in the United States including: being born into poverty, raised by his single mother in the working class, and even playing the saxophone.[38] Notably, one of his first acts as president was to purposefully diversify his cabinet. When asked about why he included so many people of color he said, "to prove we could build a 21st century community that was truly diverse and committed to excellence, to me that was a very important job of being president."[39] Clinton's visible increase of diversity aligns with the logic of neoliberal hyper(in)visibility, that is, when people of color are highly visible, there is no need to address institutional racism. Cloaked by the premise of progress, hyper(in)visibility allowed many of Clinton's domestic policies to covertly increase racialized inequity and sustain white supremacy. Most famously, his federal "three strikes" law dramatically increased the prison population, continued the disproportionate imprisonment of racial minorities, and advanced the prison industrial complex.[40] Clinton also cut welfare rolls in half, disproportionately affecting women of color.[41] Clinton's presidency marks a turning point from the 1980s colorblindness to contemporary postracial neoliberalism. His rhetoric and policies demonstrate the agility of colorblind ideology. More specifically, his use of hyper(in)visibility and appropriation of blackness facilitated the expansion of neoliberal policies and racial disparity.

Following Clinton, George W. Bush avoided blatantly coding blackness in the ways that Reagan and his father did, but racial markers worked rather differently during his presidency than they did in the 1980s because both our lexicon of racialized terms and our racial rhetoric shifted. Gray writes, "The politically conservative administration of George W. Bush has . . . systematically weakened the role of the state in civil rights protections . . . [concurrently] it is easy for conservatives to conclude from the presence of blacks in music videos, in sports, on television, and on the big screen that we have arrived at that idealized American landscape of racial equality and color-blindness."[42] By pointing out normative assumptions about black visibility, Gray outlines how essential black hyper(in)visibility is to neoliberalism. The hypervisibility of black people in the cultural sphere functions as a prop. Hyper(in)visible black people such as Oprah are cited as evidence of racial equality and the eradication of racism. Additionally, hypervisibility is strategically utilized to make social inequity seemingly disappear. This dynamic reflects the kinship between hyper(in)visibility and neoliberalism in accordance with dominant ideologies of whiteness that employ multicultural colorblind rhetoric to mask the omnipresence of racism and white privilege. Bush's use of colorblind rhetoric during Hurricane Katrina renders these entanglements clear.

After Katrina, Bush said, "The storm didn't discriminate, and neither will the recovery effort. When those Coast Guard choppers . . . were pulling people off roofs, they didn't check the color of a person's skin."[43] Hiding behind his presidential assertion that race was irrelevant, Bush avoids the fact that people were concerned about the racialized distribution of aid before and after the storm. By evoking colorblind rhetoric, Bush unmasks the impulse of neoliberalism and reveals his, and more broadly white America's, anxiety about perceived and real racialized inequalities. Once the government's neglect to swiftly respond to storm survivors' needs was publicly exposed, Bush went to New Orleans, Louisiana, and spoke in a decidedly different tone. "As all of us saw on television, there's also some deep, persistent poverty in this region . . . that poverty has roots in a history of racial discrimination, which cut off generations from the opportunities in America"[44] The blatant contradiction between the former statement and the latter, which acknowledges class disparity at the expense of race, highlights how racism informs colorblindness. Bush's initial affirmation of colorblindness failed to recognize the tangible racial disparities on display for the world to see. This political moment provides insight into how blackness was circulated under Bush's leadership, which helped to propel us toward postracial ideology.

President Barack Obama's landmark election succeeded Bush's tenure. Nationally and internationally, the United States' election of a black president signified a departure from our nation's brutally racist history. For instance, global headlines announced, "Obama Elected President as Racial Barriers Fall" and "Change Has Come to America."[45] These headlines demonstrate the prevalence of neoliberal hyper(in)visibility regardless of how a president racially identifies or how a presidency unfolds. Merely *seeing* a black man in the White House signified progress in U.S. race relations despite the reality that visibility alone has never been indicative of actualized change for those targeted by systemic racism. Cobb highlights the complexity of postracialism and its attempt to erase the concept of blackness:

> Blackness is rendered hypervisible as a symbol in a post-race United States; yet, it is also made invisible in terms of its own social and cultural relevance. Media narratives mobilize Obama "to 'celebrate' blackness conceived in terms of sameness," while circumscribing "blackness as *otherness*" (Watts & Orbe, 2002, p. 3). Circulating as willful delusion, postraciality asks us to treat the U.S.'s legacy of slavery, Reconstruction, civil rights, and overall discrimination like one long, bad dream. Despite our nightmarish past and present of prejudice, the possibility (and later inauguration) of President Obama on January 20, 2009 represented a national wake-up to a new day.[46]

Here Cobb connects neoliberal hyper(in)visibility to the election of Obama, and the resulting assumption of progress presents contradictory logics. Electing a black president is perceived as an essentially American act precisely because of the history of racial oppression juxtaposed against transcendent narratives. Moreover, no matter how much Obama is framed as the *same*, he will always be the *first*, a racialized *other*. This postracial articulation of Obama's symbolism excuses white U.S. Americans from racial guilt without addressing racism as an everlasting societal force. Despite the overwhelming cultural desire to celebrate Obama's presidency—especially amid Donald Trump's current presidency—a critical lens exposes how Obama fertilizes and subsequently sustains the neoliberal growth that occurred during the Reagan, Bush Sr., Clinton, and Bush Jr. eras.

This political review functions as a bedrock to expose the relationship between racialized political rhetoric and media industry practices. Pointedly, in 2008, President Obama was elected, and the last black-produced television show, *Everybody Hates Chris*, was canceled on prime-time network television. Obama's rise to power not only coincides with the end of black-produced television but also with the surges in multicultural programming and postracial rhetoric. The logic around the cancellation of black shows, alongside the much cheaper production of reality television, is that since U.S. American society is postracial and race no longer matters, segregated audience consideration is also an antiquated practice. However, segregated audience considerations remain an industry practice because white mainstream audiences set the norm for who the industry actively caters to; this outcome is amplified by examining the replacements for black shows on prime-time network television.

INDUSTRY LOGICS AND BLACK EXPENDABILITY

The Cosby Show (NBC 1984–1992) was particularly useful to quietly promote colorblind ideology.[47] While the racist rhetoric of the Reagan administration played out on the nightly news, once a week, a "perfect" black family entertained black and white America in very different ways. Black families took pride in seeing a fun, loving, well-to-do black family who looked like them, while white families viewed a welcoming world of palatable black citizens who worked hard, raised their children well, and never encountered the perils of race.[48] "The representations and expressions of African American life on *The Cosby Show* seemed little more than soothing symbolic props required to affirm America's latest illusion of feel-good multiculturalism and racial cooperation."[49] Symbolically, the show was a multicultural inaugurating moment in the landscape of television. For the Reagan administration and for conservatives, neoconservatives, and liberals alike, it functioned as a space where whites could embrace racial tolerance through their acceptance of the Huxtables. Jhally and Lewis make a compelling point when they argue,

> Most white people—certainly those who watch *The Cosby Show*—no longer see skin color as a barrier to liking someone or treating them as an equal. Unimpeded by such all-encompassing prejudice, they are able to discriminate between black people some of whom have succeeded, and some of whom have not. However, they quietly (and perhaps unconsciously) retain the association of blackness as an indicator of cultural inferiority, albeit one from which African Americans, if they are talented enough or hard working enough, can escape.[50]

In effect, *The Cosby Show* facilitated neoliberal absolution for white audiences.

The Cosby Show aired on NBC, overlapping with *The Fresh Prince of Bel-Air* (NBC 1990–1996) and *Family Matters* (ABC/CBS 1989–1998); however, the influx of black-produced shows accompanied two new networks in the mid-1990s: UPN and the WB. According to Carter, to compete for audiences with the Big Four, "UPN and the WB were relying heavily on comedies with black casts."[51] This is unsurprising because WB's founding president was Jamie Kellner, a former executive at Fox when it was well known for cornering "urban markets" in the early 1990s.[52] This strategy was purely financial; UPN and the WB sought to gain a foothold in the industry, and they looked to black audiences as the most lucrative underserved market to help them do so because industry executives knew that "black households naturally tend to favor programs with black casts."[53] This untapped market was especially important for UPN, which was completely dependent on advertising dollars for revenue.[54]

Black-produced shows are significant for black audiences in having their interests meaningfully considered, but the value was eventually lost on studio executives and advertisers who were merely invested in profit, not diversity. After the disappearance of black shows in the mid-2000s, concurrent with the proliferation of multicultural and colorblind rhetorics in political spheres, "diverse" casts appeared more frequently in sitcoms and dramas. Shows like *30 Rock* (NBC 2006–2013), *The Office* (NBC 2005–2013) and *Modern Family* (ABC 2009–present) broke barriers of racial segregation, absurdly, by distancing themselves from racial specificity. These shows do not engage identities as political categories outside of cheap punch lines based on stale stereotypes. Ironically, the neoliberal disappearance of race on prime-time network television as a political identity marker happened just when a black woman showrunner began to flourish.

RACE (LOST AND FOUND) IN SHONDALAND

Today, most television shows try to achieve multicultural casting. Although focused overwhelmingly on white characters, token characters of color are present to signify racial inclusion, because all-white casts are generally socially unacceptable. Multicultural shows are not at all concerned with the cultural specificity of racial others; thus, although black characters (as well as other people of color) are present and are, perhaps, major characters, issues concerning blackness or race relations are rarely, if ever, progressively broached. *Grey's Anatomy*, in its insistence on multicultural colorblindness, especially in the early seasons, supports this premise. *Grey's* debuted as a show about five surgical interns who begin their residency at Seattle Grace Hospital as a multiracial cohort. The white protagonist is Meredith Grey; however, her fellow intern and best friend Cristina Yang is Korean, and they are surrounded by black characters in meaningful roles including: Richard Webber, chief of surgery; Preston Burke, head of cardiothoracic surgery; and Miranda Bailey, chief resident.

According to Fogel, "Shonda Rhimes has conceived Seattle Grace as a frenetic, multicultural hub where racial issues take a back seat."[55] Mirroring this interpretation, Rhimes—aligning with neoliberalism—uses a system of multicultural colorblind casting. Originally, Miranda's role was meant for a blond white woman and Isaiah Washington was going to be cast as Meredith's love interest Derek Shepherd.[56] Rhimes's early outlook on race relations and colorblind casting are made clear by her quote: "My friends and I don't sit around and discuss race. . . . We're post-civil rights, post-feminist babies, and we take it for granted we live in a diverse world."[57] This comment is provocative because of the possible, yet unlikely, nature of the fictional world that Rhimes and her team of writers have created. In real life, there are black people who occupy chief of surgery positions in hospitals, but surgical staffs are not nearly as diverse as *Grey's*.[58] Additionally, it is quite remarkable that all of the black characters are in positions of power. This fictive authority structure of color creates a dynamic in which the visual presence of racial diversity on the show allows writers to conveniently avoid real-world issues of racism in the workplace that can manifest as segregation of tasks by race, denial of promotions based on race, and microaggressions such as offensive language, humiliation, and gossip. Shondaland's *Grey's* depicts a multicultural world in which race is not and does not need to be a factor. The result is an idealistic, multicultural, yet colorblind world that has yet to be achieved offscreen and therefore disregards the reality of racism.

A key feature of multicultural programming, in addition to actors being easily swapped between roles (e.g., without rewriting the characters, Miranda could have been a white woman and Derek could have been a black man), is underdeveloping characters of color to ensure they can be easily stereotyped. On *Grey's*, particularly in the early seasons, black characters' storylines are thin and mostly exist to provide substance for other characters. Miranda is known throughout the hospital as "the Nazi" for her strict treatment of her interns; when the interns catch first sight of the short black woman, Cristina exclaims, "*That's* the Nazi?" and Meredith replies, "Well, I thought she would be more like . . . a Nazi."[59] Their comments function as code for whiteness and masculinity and imply that a black woman who looks like Miranda is not expected to be in a position of power or to have high professional standards. The implicit surprise is that this woman would make more stereotypical sense as a workplace mammy rather than a disciplinarian. Initially, as promised by her stern racist moniker, Miranda is very hard on the residents. Conversely, by season 3, she has shifted from a stern boss to a stern motherly figure whose primary concern is her interns. Despite Miranda's alignment with "mammification" throughout the first few seasons of *Grey's*, Rhimes claims that this character is only accidentally black.[60]

Other black characters receive similar underdeveloped treatment. Most notably, we learn very little about characters of color beyond Seattle Grace, whereas we learn much more about their white counterparts' lives outside of the hospital. The audience does not learn about Richard's wife until season 2, and by then, their marriage is in trouble. Additionally, Preston is more developed than Richard, but his romantic involvement with Cristina places his character development—and Cristina's—in service to Meredith. While Miranda, Richard, and Preston were not initially written as black characters, once they were cast, their scenes were written with these actors in mind and thereby reflect racialized stereotypes. Miranda is mammified as a black woman; in accordance with stereotypes about black men, Richard is a philandering husband; and Preston is morally bankrupt when he puts many patients at risk by performing surgeries with a hand tremor. While the show improves in its representations of marginalized characters over time, it unequivocally reproduces historically situated racial tropes. This is particularly problematic amid multicultural colorblind programming replacing shows created by and for black audiences. It is important for disenfranchised groups not only to see themselves represented, but also to see their distinct cultures, practices, and struggles represented holistically, which is not the same as positively. Multicultural colorblind shows are desperately lacking these attributes.

Exemplary of Shondaland, Grey's major problem is the showrunner's and writers' failure to address racism even when storylines beg the question or can bear the weight. Exposing the ideological alignment between the U.S. social institutions of media and government, this is problematic precisely because the show mirrors constant denials of the significance of race and racism in real life. Rhimes is quick to congratulate herself on the diversity of her shows, and this celebration is mirrored by an industry committed to neoliberalism and in need of ammunition against accusations of racism.[61] Mindful of neoliberalism, multicultural colorblind casting is an easy escape from racial specificity and the realness of racism.

Shondaland's Scandal is different from Grey's insofar as the protagonist, Olivia Pope, is a black woman. However, the show still reflects multicultural colorblind logics. Partly based on the real-life career of Judy Smith, who was a press aide for George W. Bush's administration, Pope is a Washington, D.C., fixer who leads a team of gladiators that resolve intense political crises. The central narrative conflict is her affair with President Fitzgerald Grant, a white, married Republican. The president's chief of staff, Cyrus Beene, is openly gay, married, and has an adopted black daughter. Although Pope drives Scandal's storylines and the show is populated with characters of color and interracial relationships, as with Grey's, race and racism are rarely addressed as societal issues. Calling out this paradox and its detrimental impact on race consciousness in the real world, McKenzie says, "You cannot have a black woman in an affair with a white Republican president and pretend that race does not exist. . . . Americans don't need another excuse to ignore race, especially when such a good opportunity exists to pay attention to it."[62]

Although distinctly multicultural in its casting, Scandal demonstrates a tacit desire to affirm itself as a black-produced show. This occurs largely in two ways. The first is in Scandal's soundtracks, which are prominently featured in each episode; the second is Rhimes's eventual willingness to address race directly in season 3—albeit fleeting attention as the series unfolds. The music featured is almost exclusively soul music performed by black artists from the sixties and seventies. Over the first two seasons, artists such as Stevie Wonder, Sly and the Family Stone, and Nina Simone are featured in minor and pivotal scenes. These choices are rather stark, especially in comparison to *Grey's* soundtracks which are consistently racially indistinct. Likewise, considering how seldom the show outwardly addresses race, the music's close association with the civil rights movement stands out. As a key element of television production, Shondaland's habitual inclusion of soul and civil rights music on *Scandal* reflects a choice to align Rhimes's work with black artistry that is more explicitly political. By choosing music from this era, the songs also evoke cultural memories that signal racialized resistance and political progress.

At the end of season 2, viewers are introduced to Olivia's father, Rowan Pope. In the first episode of season 3, he delivers a monologue in which he rebukes Olivia with "You have to be TWICE as good as them to get HALF of what they have."[63] This is an ideological expression common among black people reminding one another of racism's systemic disadvantages for black people versus the systemic privileges afforded to white people. Scripting black characters with black cultural sayings marks a tremendous change in Shondaland, especially amid Rhimes's hesitance, and at times outright refusal, to explicitly address race. I find it significant that she is attempting to broach racism at all given the history of Shondaland. By doing so, Rhimes departs from industry norms and her steadfast multicultural colorblind strategies.

Well beyond her prime-time network debut and well into the mass popularity of *Grey's*, *Scandal*, and *HTGAWM*, Rhimes now regularly addresses race as a public figure. She is also publicly supporting the work of other black women including actor Viola Davis and internet sensation Issa Rae.[64] In her autobiography, *Year of Yes: How to Dance It Out, Stand in the Sun and Be Your Own Person*, race comes up several times. She extensively describes what she calls being an "F.O.D.—a First. Only. Different." and addresses her earlier ambivalence about race as a racial category.[65] She says, "As the shows got more popular, I was acutely, painfully aware of what was at stake. I smiled, refused to answer the question, pretended I didn't know what reporters were asking me about when they asked about race. But you can't be raised black in America and *not* know. This wasn't just my shot. It was *ours*."[66] This public acknowledgement of blackness as a source of profound difference is new for Rhimes. Clearly a different stance than ardently aligning with "post" logics; she continues:

> When I made my first television show, I did something I felt was perfectly normal: in the twenty-first century, I made the world of the show look the way the world looks. I filled it with people of all hues, genders, backgrounds and sexual orientations. And then I did the most obvious thing possible: *I wrote all of them as if they were . . . people*. People of color live three-dimensional lives, have love stories and are not funny sidekicks, clichés or criminals. Women are the heroes, the villains, the badasses, the big dogs. This, I was told over and over, was trailblazing and brave.[67]

Here Rhimes not only acknowledges the history of racial stereotyping and its nor-malization in the industry, she also narrates the hefty responsibility she felt to challenge these stereotypes.

Rhimes's early success is clearly tied to her embrace of multicultural colorblind programming that reinforced neoliberalism as the prevailing political ideology and whiteness as normative. However, as she has gained more industry power, she has more openly engaged intersectional identity politics both personally and pro-fessionally. Her third and fourth ABC shows, *Scandal* and *HTGAWM*, more readily embrace racial themes. Additionally, as *Grey's* progressed, Miranda's and Richard's storylines took on more sophisticated and less stereotypical arcs. After Miranda has a baby and gets divorced, she nervously learns how to date again, earns accolades and promotions at work, and remarries. Her representation as a complex plus-sized middle-aged black professional woman negotiating sex, rela-tionships, motherhood, and health and well-being is a significant departure from Miranda's earlier portrayal. Contextualizing these changes, Warner observes, "The more money showrunners make for the network, the less the network interferes" in the narrative construction of a series.[68]

The problem with multicultural colorblind television is that it reinforces the idea that race is no longer an important societal issue, further instantiates post-racialism, and floods the visual field with hyper(in)visible characters of color to the benefit of white society and the detriment of people of color. Just like neoliberalism in the political realm, neoliberal media deepens the problem of unexamined structural racism. Nevertheless, blackness remains a powerful cul-tural signifier and whether or not television addresses race explicitly, institutional racism persists. Equally important is acknowledging how hyper(in)visibility is perpetuated by the television industry, which is largely owned and controlled by white people who benefit from neoliberalism. Admittedly, there has been a recent shift with culturally specific network shows like *Black-ish*, *Fresh off the Boat*, *Cristela* (ABC 2014–2015), *Jane the Virgin* (CW 2014–present), and *Empire* reclaiming the market space left void when the NAACP intervened in 1999. Although this shift is surely related to Shondaland's success—especially since three of the five abovementioned shows debuted on ABC—it is also important to note that each of these shows feature characters whose racial identity is central to their motivations, narrative arcs, and commercial success. Despite this shift, the intricate linkages between political rhetoric and media representation coupled with the networks' cyclical interest in profitable niche markets cause me to question the longevity of these changes. Sadly, I imagine that neoliberalism will eventually tire of even Shondaland's mitigated, albeit steadily and progressively upgraded, approach to underscoring race and racism on television.

NOTES

1. Lawrie Mifflin, "N.A.A.C.P. Plans to Press for More Diverse TV Shows," *New York Times*, July 13, 1999, https://www.nytimes.com/1999/07/13/us/naacp-plans-to-press-for-more-diverse-tv-shows.html.

2. Kristal Brent Zook, *Color by Fox: The Fox Network and the Revolution in Black Television* (Oxford: Oxford University Press, 1999), 5.

3. Producers Guild of America, "Case Study: Shonda Rhimes," produced by magazine of the Producers Guild of America (Beverly Hills, Calif.: Producers Guild of America, Spring 2006), 18.

4. Stuart Hall, "The March of the Neoliberals," *Guardian*, September 12, 2011, https://www.theguardian.com/politics/2011/sep/12/march-of-the-neoliberals.

5. Vijay Prashad, "Second-Hand Dreams," *Social Analysis: The International Journal of Social and Cultural Practice* 49, no. 2 (2005): 191–198.

6. Prashad.

7. Amy Hasinoff, "Fashioning Race for the Free Market on America's Next Top Model," *Critical Studies in Media Communication* 25 (2008): 327.

8. Philiana Ng, "'Bunheads' Creator Amy Sherman-Palladino Sounds Off on Shonda Rhimes Comments," June 18, 2012, http://www.hollywoodreporter.com/live-feed/amy-sherman-palladino-shonda-rhimes-bunheads-338681.

9. *Scandal*, "The Lawn Chair," season 4, episode 14, directed by Tom Verica, written by Zahir McGhee, aired on March 5, 2015, on ABC; *How To Get Away With Murder*, "Let's Get to Scooping," season 1, episode 4, directed by Laura Innes, written by Erika Green Swafford, aired on October 16, 2014, on ABC.

10. Safiya Umoja Noble, "Google Search: Hyper-Visibility as a Means of Rendering Black Women and Girls Invisible," *InVisible Culture* 19 (2013), http://hdl.handle.net/1802/28018.

11. Rachel Alicia Griffin, "Pushing into *Precious*: Black Women, Media Representation, and the Glare of the White Supremacist Capitalist Patriarchal Gaze," *Critical Studies in Media Communication* 31, no. 3 (2014): 182–197.

12. Amber Johnson and Robin M. Boylorn, "Digital Media and the Politics of Intersectional Queer Hyper/In/Visibility in *Between Women*," *Liminalities: A Journal of Performance Studies* 11, no. 1 (2015): 7–8.

13. Nicole Fleetwood, *Troubling Vision: Performance, Visuality, and Blackness* (Chicago: University of Chicago Press, 2011).

14. Timothy Havens, Amanda Lotz, and Serra Tinic, "Critical Media Studies: A Research Approach," *Communication, Culture and Critique*, no. 2 (2009): 234–253.

15. Havens, Lotz, and Tinic, 238.

16. Havens, Lotz, and Tinic, 249.

17. See Zook, *Color by Fox*; Beretta A. Smith-Shomade, *Shaded Lives: African American Women and Television* (New Brunswick, N.J.: Rutgers University Press, 2002); and Catherine Squires, *African-Americans and the Media* (Cambridge, U.K.: Polity Press, 2009).

18. Herman Gray, *Watching Race: Television and the Struggle for Blackness* (Minneapolis: University of Minnesota Press, 1995).

19. Gray, *Watching Race*, 90.

20. Gray, 91.

21. Prashad, "Second-Hand Dreams," 196.

22. Prashad, xiv.

23. David Harvey, "Neoliberalism as Creative Destruction," *Annals of the American Academy of Political and Social Science* 610 (March 2007): 22–44.

24. Stuart Hall, "Subjects in History: Making Diasporic Identities," in *The House That Race Built* (New York: Vintage Books, 1998), 289.

25. Jason Read, "A Genealogy of Homo-Economincus: Neoliberalism and the Production of Subjectivity," *Foucault Studies*, no. 6 (2009): 28.

26. Read, 26.

27. Read, 26.

28. Read, 29.

29. Noble, "Google Search," http://hdl.handle.net/1802/28018.

30. Ian Haney López, *Dog Whistle Politics: How Coded Racial Appeals Have Reinvented Racism and Wrecked the Middle Class* (London: Oxford University Press, 2014), 59.

31. López, 58.

32. Sarah Nielsen and Sarah Turner, "Introduction," in *The Colorblind Screen: Television in Post-Racial America* (New York: New York University Press, 2014), 3.

33. Michael K. Brown, Martin Carnoy, Elliott Currie, Troy Duster, David B. Oppenheimer, Marjorie M. Shultz, and David Wellman, *Whitewashing Race: The Myth of a Colorblind Society* (Berkeley: University of California Press, 2003), 3–4.

34. Brown et. al, 3–4.

35. Eduardo Bonilla-Silva, *Racism without Racists: Color Blind Racism and the Persistence of Racial Inequality in the United States* (Oxford: Rowman & Littlefield, 2001), 2.

36. López, *Dog Whistle Politics*, 106.

37. H. Prentice Baptiste, Heidi Orvosh-Kamenski, and Christopher J. Kamenski, "American Presidents and Their Attitudes, Beliefs and Actions Surrounding Education and Multiculturalism," *Multicultural Education* 12, no. 2 (2004): 33.

38. López, *Dog Whistle Politics*, 12.

39. Baptiste, Orvosh-Kamenski, and Kamenski, "American Presidents," 36.

40. Michelle Alexander, *The New Jim Crow: Mass Incarceration in the Age of Colorblindness* (New York: New Press, 2013), 56–57.

41. Alexander, 35–36.

42. Gray, *Watching Race*, xviii.

43. Robert C. Lieberman, "The Storm Didn't Discriminate: Katrina and the Politics of Color Blindness," *Dubois Review* 3, no. 1 (2006): 9.

44. Lieberman, 10.

45. Adam Nagourney, "Obama Elected President as Racial Barriers Fall," *New York Times*, November 5, 2008, https://www.nytimes.com/2008/11/05/us/politics/05elect.html; Dan Rather, "Change Has Come to America," *Seattle Post-Intelligencer*, November 5, 2008.

46. Jasmine Cobb, "No We Can't! Postracialism and the Popular Appearance of a Rhetorical Fiction," *Communication Studies* 62, no. 4 (2011): 407.

47. Mike Budd and Clay Steinman, "White Racism and the Cosby Show," *Jump Cut* 37 (1992): 5–12.

48. Sut Jhally and Justin Lewis, "White Responses: The Emergence of 'Enlightened' Racism," in *Channeling Blackness: Studies on Television and Race in America*, ed. Darnell M. Hunt (New York: Oxford University Press, 2005), 74–88.

49. Gray, *Watching Race*, 82.

50. Jhally and Lewis, "White Responses," 77–78.

51. Bill Carter, "Two Upstart Networks Courting Black Viewers," *New York Times*, October 7, 1996, https://www.nytimes.com/1996/10/07/arts/two-upstart-networks-courting-black-viewers.html.

52. Michele Hilmes, *Only Connect: A Cultural History of Broadcasting in the United States* (Boston: Wadsworth, 2010), 349.

53. Carter, "Two Upstart Networks Courting Black Viewers."

54. Carter.

55. Fogel, "*Grey's Anatomy* Goes Colorblind," 16.

56. Kristen Warner, "The Racial Logic of *Grey's Anatomy*: Shonda Rhimes and Her 'Post-Civil Rights, Post-Feminist' Series," *Television & New Media* 16, no. 7 (2015): 631–647.

57. Warner, 636.

58. Dorothy A. Andriole, Donna B. Jeffe, and Kenneth B. Schechtman, "Is Surgical Workforce Diversity Increasing?," *Journal of the American College of Surgeons* 204, no. 3 (2007): 469–477.

59. *Grey's Anatomy*, "A Hard Day's Night," season 1, episode 1, directed by Peter Horton, written by Shonda Rhimes, aired on March 27, 2005, on ABC.

60. Fogel, "*Grey's Anatomy* Goes Colorblind"; see also Barbara Omolade, *The Rising Song of African American Women* (New York: Routledge, 1994).

61. See Paige Albiniak, "Why 'Grey' Seems So Bright," *Broadcasting & Cable* 135, no. 22 (2005): 18–24; and Jeanne McDowell, "A Woman and Her Anatomy," *Time* 167, no. 21 (2006): 70–71.

62. Mia McKenzie, "*Scandal*: Why I Kinda Love It, Why I Kinda Hate It," *Black Girl Dangerous*, January 30, 2013, http://www.blackgirldangerous.org/2013/01/2013128scandal-why-i-hate-it-why-i-kinda-love-it/.

63. *Scandal*, "It's Handled," season 3, episode 1, directed by Tom Verica, written by Shonda Rhimes, aired on October 3, 2013, on ABC.

64. Jenna Wortham, "The Misadventures of Issa Rae," *New York Times*, August 4, 2015, https://www.nytimes.com/2015/08/09/magazine/the-misadventures-of-issa-rae.html.

65. Shonda Rhimes, *Year of Yes: How to Dance It Out, Stand in the Sun and Be Your Own Person* (New York: Simon and Schuster, 2015), 138.

66. Rhimes, 138.

67. Rhimes, 139.

68. Kristen Warner, *The Cultural Politics of Colorblind TV Casting* (New York: Routledge, 2015), 24.

6 · EMB(RACE)ING VISIBILITY

Callie Torres's (Im)Perfect Operation of Bisexuality on *Grey's Anatomy*

SHADEE ABDI AND BERNADETTE
MARIE CALAFELL

Now in its fourteenth season, *Grey's Anatomy* (also referred to as *Grey's*) debuted on ABC in March 2005. Created and produced by Shonda Rhimes and her production company, Shondaland, the show is centered around the lives of surgical interns, residents, and attendings at the fictional Grey Sloan Memorial Hospital in Seattle, Washington. Focused on the medical pursuits, friendships, and romantic relationships of the main characters, the show is largely narrated by Dr. Meredith Grey, who is the daughter of famed surgeon Dr. Ellis Grey. *Grey's* has been recognized with multiple Emmy, Screen Actors Guild, Golden Globe, American Latino Media Arts (ALMA), National Association for the Advancement of Colored People (NAACP), and Gay and Lesbian Alliance Against Defamation (GLAAD) awards.[1] One of *Grey's* most well liked and developed characters is Dr. Calliope "Callie" Iphegenia Torres, portrayed by openly bisexual, Tony Award winning, Mexican American actress Sara Ramirez.[2] Since joining the cast in season 2, Ramirez's character emerged as one of the most multidimensional bisexual characters on network television, and her performance was recognized by the National Council for La Raza (NCLR) and the NAACP through multiple nominations for ALMA and Image Awards.[3] Ramirez describes Callie as a "kickass orthopedic surgeon, who happens to be smart, driven, strong, vulnerable, funny, female, Latina, and bisexual."[4]

While Callie's race is not often depicted as the central aspect of her character, she is coded as Latina via specific clues, including her upbringing in Miami, Florida, which marks her as Cuban American. She is also marked as a Catholic, wealthy, well-educated woman who pairs with only white romantic partners. We argue that Callie's proximity to whiteness constructs her bisexuality to satisfy white heteronormative

U.S. audiences. These audiences, traditionally targeted by television networks, often disregard overtly diverse identities, resulting in poor ratings. ABC intermittently addresses some of these challenges; for example, *Black-ish* (ABC 2014–present) and *Cristela* (ABC 2014–2015) premiered in 2014 as two diverse new series although the latter was canceled after the first season.[5]

To cater to normative audiences and thwart accusations of homophobia, networks typically create palatable queer characters that are cisgender, homonormative, and not necessarily transgressive. As such, we argue that Callie's bisexuality is cushioned by her romantic relationships with white partners. Whether intentional or not, keeping Callie's bisexuality in close proximity to whiteness gives Rhimes leeway to pursue storylines through Callie that attempt to complicate representational queer politics in the media. Thus, we specifically theorize how Callie complicates discourses surrounding sexuality by examining how her bisexuality achieves palatability through a careful negotiation of her intersectional identities as an upper-class, Catholic Latina. Interestingly, these identities work to both privilege and disenfranchise Callie by situating her sexuality in relation to the possible loss of money, family, and religiosity. Moreover, because of her likability as a holistically developed character, the showcasing of her other identities mark her as a positive depiction of a Latina character. The implications of these perceptions have been measured in a study by Tukachinsky, Mastro, and Yarchi that theorized how blacks and Latinxs[6] are perceived by white audiences.[7] The study revealed that "the number of highly professional and social Latinos characters had a significant positive effect on Whites' attitudes toward Latinos."[8] Therefore, theorizing the implications of how Callie's identities are presented is imperative to underscoring how she is perceived by wider audiences. We present our argument through queer of color and feminist theories that guide our analysis by situating Callie within the historical landscape of mediated representations of Latinas. Doing so allows us to examine how the character of Callie—always in close proximity to whiteness—represents a pedagogy of bisexuality.

QUEER OF COLOR THEORIES, CHICANA FEMINISMS, AND BISEXUALITY

Queer scholars of color challenge the progress narrative that governs coming out of the closet by pointing out how whiteness and Eurocentrism uphold this narrative.[9] Ross argues, "(White) queer theory and history are beset by what I call 'claustrophilia,' a fixation on the closet function as the grounding principle for sexual experience, knowledge, and politics, and that this claustophilic fixation effectively diminishes and disables the full engagement with potential insights from race theory and class analysis."[10] Opposed to whitewashing queerness, it is important to consider how coming out for queer people of color may lead to the potential loss of not only familial relationships, but also racial and ethnic identity connections and support.[11] Furthermore, Cohen adds that scholars must challenge the dominant heterosexual/homosexual binary that governs most queer scholarship by addressing intersectionality and the matrix of domination—concepts that emerge from black feminist and critical race inquiry.[12] Nero echoes this call by advocating for scholars to be attentive to the racial privilege and potential class privilege afforded to white queers.[13] Additionally, Muñoz asserts that queers of color are subject to what he terms "the burden of liveness," meaning that our everyday lived experiences are constantly being surveilled.[14] Therefore, queer people of color are always performing under the surveillance of whiteness in everyday life. Perhaps no one's bodies are more surveilled than those of women of color.[15] Cultural surveillance is particularly omnipresent in the media, where the visibility of women of color caters to palatability for wider (read: whiter) audiences.

Though often overlooked within the queer canon, Chicana feminist scholars Gloria Anzaldúa and Cherríe Moraga are foundational to queer theorizations of identity, embodiment, performance, and representation. These scholars richly contribute to understandings of how *mestizaje*, family, and religion inform Chicana (queer) identities, which in turn expands queer scholarship by challenging privileged homogeneity within the canon.[16] Anzaldúa argues for understanding Chicanx identities through the lens of *mestizaje*, which embraces mixed-race or hybrid identities created via colonialism and the slave trade.[17] *Mestizaje* can be likened to intersectionality as Anzaldúa calls for us to understand how class, gender, sexuality, and ability inform Chicanx mixed-race identities. Queerness is at the heart of Anzaldúa's understanding of *mestizaje*; this is important because it places at the center that which has been historically maligned in Chicana/o movement rhetorics. Deepening theorizations of race and sexuality, Calafell highlights the ways that *mestizaje* marks Chicanxs and Latinxs as queer within the exclusionary black/white racial binary; for those who are lesbian or bisexual, this queerness is magnified.[18]

Like Anzaldúa, Moraga argues for an unapologetically queer Chicana feminism that attests to the queer complexities of Chicanas.[19] Additionally, both she and Anzaldúa understand the importance of religion in the lives of Chicanas. Moraga argues that the virgin/whore dichotomy governs and disciplines Chicana sexuality. This dichotomy operates in relationship to the Virgin of Guadalupe, the patron saint of Mexico, and Malintzin Tenepal (La Malinche), the symbolic Eve figure who aided Spaniard Hernán Cortés in the Spanish colonization of what is now Mexico. Through the story of Malintzin and Hernán Cortés, heterosexual and interracial violence is at the core of the "origin" narrative of Chicanas and Mexicanas. While the Virgin of Guadalupe is upheld as an impossible standard for Mexicanas and Chicanas, Malintzin is seen as the whore/traitor who could not control her sexuality. Though these cultural and religious figures are connected specifically to Mexicana and Chicana histories, it is important to note that the virgin/whore dichotomy governs a great deal of Latina experience, regardless of country of origin. For example, one of the central ways Spanish colonialism was enacted was through meshing Indigenous mother goddess figures with the Virgin Mary, which shifted some of the religious beliefs of Indigenous peoples while still allowing them to hold onto Indigenous practices.[20] While Mexicans and Chicanxs worship the Virgin of Guadalupe, many Cubans and Cuban Americans worship Our Lady of Charity.[21]

Religion plays a prominent role in the lives of Chicanas and Latinas and often holds them to an unattainable and often undesirable patriarchal standard. Supported by a family structure that can be very patriarchal, religion also informs how Latinas are socialized to think about their sexuality.[22] While Latinxs may have some shared histories, they lead to different lived experiences because of factors such as colonialism, religion, gender role expectations, and language.[23] *Latinidad* is what allows us to think about possibilities for connection across differences among various Latinx groups.[24] For example, the virgin/whore dichotomy often governs media representations of Latinas and typically results in stereotypical and one-dimensional characterizations.[25] Thus, *Grey's* portrayal of Callie's religion as elemental to her desire to perform the good, heterosexual, obedient daughter (i.e., virgin-like coding) as part of her core identity is imperative to understanding how Latinas exist within these complicated intersections.

Moraga further articulates the multiple challenges faced by many Chicana lesbians who are often constructed symbolically as Malinches: betrayers of their culture, patriarchy, and religion.[26] Additionally, Moraga argues that Chicana lesbians must negotiate shame both as colonized people and because of their queerness. Rodriguez elaborates that the "connection of shame and the inhibition of pleasure has particular resonance for racialized women for whom victimization functions as an ontological condition."[27] Anzaldúa challenges the shame associated with *mestizaje* or colonial mixed-race identities as well as queerness, instead seeing these liminal or borderland places as spaces of radical possibility through *mestiza* consciousness.

Similar to the ways queer theories often recenter white gay male experiences at the cost of white queer women and queer women of color, much of the work in gay, lesbian, bisexual, transgender, and queer (LGBTQ) studies ignores the experiences of bisexuals. Michaela D. E. Meyer argues that, in many cases, bisexuality is seen as a stop on the road to one's "true" identity as either gay or straight.[28] She contends that "those who profess bisexuality past this intermediate stage are seen as promiscuous swingers or sexual predators. Often, bisexuality is defined *in relation to* gay/lesbian identities rather than being defined as a unique sexual identity."[29] Meyer further argues that bisexuality is often challenged by the LGBTQ community.[30]

Bisexual characters in dramatic television narratives are typically depicted as "female[s], portrayed by non-white actors, thus signifying a cultural struggle over the matrix of oppression through gender, race, and sexuality."[31] Meyer argues that these characters are "intersectional hybrids" who "serve hegemonic and counter-hegemonic functions simultaneously."[32] Meyer further contends that when a television character is already marginalized, the acceptance of bisexuality by other characters showcases the readiness of others to be accepting or tolerant.[33] Among the characters Meyer discusses is *Grey's* Dr. Callie Torres, whose "instability" makes the behaviors of the bed-hopping heterosexual characters seem more stable.[34] She calls for scholars to critically unpack how these types of characters both challenge and uphold hegemony.[35] We take up Meyer's call by critically reading Callie through queer of color and Chicana/Latina feminist theories. We examined all of the episodes of *Grey's* available at the time of this writing, seasons 1 to 11, focusing primarily on Callie's familial storylines and relational partners. We critique *Grey's* episodes as the primary text as well as their extra-textual elements to critically examine the impact of Callie's representation of bisexuality. We begin with Callie's coming out narrative as it relates to her family, proximity to whiteness, and her relational partners.

DECONSTRUCTING DR. CALLIE TORRES'S WHITENED VISI(BI)LITY

Callie's "Coming Out" as Bi

Meyer notes that in many cases, bisexual characters "do not 'come out' as bisexual, rather their sexuality is introduced casually, usually as a secondary plot device."[36] This was certainly the case with Callie, as she was first introduced as heterosexual. Following a failed marriage to Dr. George O'Malley, Callie developed romantic feelings for another surgeon, Dr. Erica Hahn. While sorting out her feelings, Callie slept with Erica and Dr. Mark Sloan—from whom she solicited tips on how to sexually please Erica. Ultimately, with Mark's guidance as her best friend and sexual partner, Callie accepts that she enjoys sex with both of them, marking herself as bisexual without labeling herself as such. This is best exemplified when Erica realizes she is, in fact, a lesbian, comparing the revelation to putting on eyeglasses and finally being able to clearly see leaves on trees. Erica's coming out is framed through Callie's reaction, which indicates, by comparison, that while Callie enjoys sex with Erica, she did not have the same epiphany. Biphobia is articulated here through the metaphor of eyeglasses, wherein Erica inevitably "chose" one preferred gender and could see clearly while Callie could not. Because heteronormative scripts necessitate the heterosexual/homosexual binary, bisexuality is often seen as a temporary pit stop toward one or the other. Erica's rejection of Callie's bisexuality underscores how biphobia exists within the lesbian-gay (LG) community, highlighting the disbelief or questioning of unclear sexual identities. In their final scene, Erica and Callie argue over the actions of a surgical intern, which leads to Erica steadfastly dismissing the notion of 'grey' areas. In the end, Erica responds resentfully, "You can't *kind of* be a lesbian," before walking to her car, never to be seen again.[37] Here, Erica's discomfort with Callie's bisexuality acts as a catalyst for the character's departure.

Following fan outrage about Erica's sudden departure as a series regular and its implications for LGBTQ visibility on television, Rhimes determinedly set out to continue telling Callie's story.[38] Rhimes cast Jessica Capshaw as Arizona Robbins, an openly lesbian pediatric surgeon who became Callie's new love interest.[39] Callie and Arizona begin dating in season 5 and quickly became a fan-favorite couple.[40] Thereafter, many fans and media commentary reactions marked Callie as a lesbian and not bisexual, since she had gone from one relationship with a woman to another.[41] Rhimes vehemently disagreed with this assertion and turned to Twitter to clarify, "Callie's not a lesbian. Arizona is a lesbian. Jessica, Sara and I really wanted to tell both experiences."[42] Rhimes further elaborates, "I love that she's determinedly bisexual. She's not somebody who is straight who discovers she's a lesbian; she's bisexual and feels very strongly about that."[43] Presenting an authentic account of Callie's sexuality has been one of Rhimes's major objectives, in hopes of deviating from the typical trope of bisexuals on a path to choosing one side of the binary. In fact, Rhimes has been so committed to telling Callie's bisexual story that she and her team of writers have scripted Callie to explicitly name her sexual identity on a number of occasions. During a pivotal scene when Meredith and Callie are intoxicated at Joe's Bar, the popular postshift hangout across from the hospital, Callie drunkenly turns to Meredith and exclaims, "So I'm bisexual! So what! It's a thing, and it's real. I mean, it's called LGBTQ for a reason. There's a B in there, and it doesn't mean badass. OK, it kinda does, but it also means bi."[44] Callie's statement, while seemingly inconsequential, is poignant as one of the only times a prominent prime-time television character has confidently self-identified as bisexual.

Once Callie's bisexuality has been firmly established, her story unfolds as she: gets pregnant and has a baby named Sofia Robbin Sloan Torres with her best friend Mark, marries Arizona, raises Sofia with Mark and Arizona, hooks up with Dr. Alex Karev (in a flashback), divorces Arizona, dates women both on and off screen, and—at the writing of this chapter—begins a new relationship with Dr. Penelope Blake.[45] Interestingly, as Callie and Arizona's relationship progresses, Callie's bisexuality is a constant point of contention within their relationship. Callie's sexuality is understood as an area of mistrust and is regularly brought up during arguments. Early in their relationship, after their first breakup, Callie confronts Arizona's insecurity during a hospital lockdown, asking her, "When are you going to forgive me for not being a good enough lesbian for you?"[46] In this context, Arizona reifies negative stereotyping of bisexuals within the LGBTQ community by imploring Callie to prove that she and their relationship are different than Callie's previous loves. Arizona's discomfort with bisexuality is best exemplified by her reactions to Callie's relationship with Mark. Arizona is scripted as extremely jealous, fearing Callie will eventually leave her for him. In season 6 she says, "Oh my God, you're breaking up with me. Mark? Is it Mark? Are you sleeping with Mark again? Are you one of those fake lesbians having a va-va-vacation in lesbian land?"[47]

During season 7, Arizona earns a grant to offer pediatric care in Malawi, Africa, which ultimately leads to their second breakup. Realizing she cannot live without Callie, Arizona returns to Seattle to mend their relationship. When she arrives, Arizona discovers that Callie is pregnant with Mark's baby. Obviously upset, Arizona cries, "I'm mad that you slept with someone else, and I know we were broken up, but you slept with someone else. And I'm even madder that that person has a penis," suggesting that her worst nightmare had come true.[48] Not only had Callie embodied her bisexuality and slept with a man while they were broken up, but that man was Mark. Arizona's jealousy, conceptually examined through biphobia, is common in the gay and lesbian community. According to Weiss, internalized homophobia causes many gays and lesbians to exclude bisexuals from the community, feeling instead that "bisexuality and transgenderism are detrimental to the social and political acceptance of gays and lesbians."[49] Several factors ranging from internalized homophobia to ignorance inform biphobia, yet the most common struggle often has to do with a fear that bisexual women will eventually choose a heterosexual relationship. In other words, they are not quite gay enough.[50] Symbolically, this can be read as a subtle articulation of heteronormative patriarchy winning out, displacing lesbianism to center the phallus. It offers a pedagogy of bisexuality that conveys bisexuals cannot be trusted, will never truly be able to commit to one partner, and therefore, are a threat to heteronormativity and homonormativity.

After eventually reconciling and committing to tri-parent the baby, Arizona's insecurities heighten and her critique of Mark's role in their lives becomes even more explicitly linked to Callie's sexuality. When discussing Mark's role as a father, Arizona exhaustedly exclaims that Callie is living "some kind of 'bi' dream come true" because she gets to be with the woman she loves and "the guy best friend who's also a great lay."[51] She continues, "Then you get a baby. I mean you get it all. And me? This is not my dream. My dream does not look like this."[52] Soon after, Mark gets brought up again during another fight, leading to Callie suggesting that Arizona is jealous of Mark. Arizona asks, "Do you blame me? I mean he gets most of you. The straight you, the Catholic you, the girl who loves baby showers. I just get, you know, the gay you, which is really only about twenty minutes a night."[53] This theme of mistrust, steeped in biphobia, is bookended during a scene in which Callie and Arizona attend couples therapy. When Arizona explains to their therapist that their issues began when she returned from Africa to find Callie pregnant, Callie interrupts and clarifies, "I'm bisexual. I'm attracted to both men and women and that freaks her out."[54] Once again, Callie's bisexuality is marked as the cause of their relational troubles, glossing over all other potential sources of tension and conflict. The repetitious implication here points to how biphobia catalyzes most of Callie's relational troubles. Despite the fact that Arizona agreed to raise Sofia as her child, married Callie, and ultimately was the one who cheated, Arizona repeatedly blames their relational turbulence on not trusting Callie because she is bisexual. This works to construct bisexuality as "abnormal," positioning heterosexuality and queerness on opposite static poles in accordance with dominant logics.

Familial Reactions

While *Grey's* clearly defines Callie's sexual identity and racialized partner preference, there has been less clarity in naming Callie's ethnicity other than as Latina. Moreman and Calafell mark a similar strategy in *Chasing Papi*, which, after the media constructed the "Latino explosion" in the late 1990s and early 2000s, relied on generically Latinx characters devoid of specific ethnic origin.[55] The characters in the film, though generically identified as Latina, did have some regional coding that could be identifiably interpreted as Mexican American, Puerto Rican, and Cuban American to Latinx viewers.[56] Creating characters and casting actors that can still be ethnically read through markers of whiteness (e.g., light skin), but are marked with palatable undifferentiated differences (e.g., accented speech without regional distinction or slang, stereotypical behaviors) is marketable to white audiences and their desire for otherness. However, these images flatten and homogenize a very heterogeneous Latinx community.[57] Similarly, Callie's racial and ethnic coding are particularly important to theorizing her sexuality in relation to her religious Latinx family. In this context, the generic coding of Latinx characters is important to challenge in order to comprehend how various ethnic communities underneath the umbrella of Latinx may understand and perform queerness differently due to factors including, but not limited to, citizenship, immigration history, and class.

Callie's family joins *Grey's* storyline when her father Carlos visits shortly after she and George are married during season 5, only to discover they had already divorced.[58] When Carlos sees George, he grabs him by the shirt and manhandles him for committing adultery. Callie distracts her father by screaming that she too committed adultery with Mark, who then receives Carlos's angry attention. Callie stops the attack by sharing that she is happily in a new relationship, to which her father responds, "I'd like to meet this new gentleman suitor."[59] A nervous Callie glances over at a nearby Arizona as she begins her pronoun-void elucidation, "They're pretty busy because they're a doctor here. But you will love them. You will love them. Because they're smart and funny and handsome and beautiful. And very supportive. Daddy, please be okay with this."[60] A second later she brings Arizona over and shares, "Dad, this is Arizona Robbins. This is who I'm dating now."[61] A short time later we see Arizona watching from a distance as Callie and her dad argue in Spanish. We learn that her father has given her an ultimatum. He threatens to cut her off financially unless she "comes home," and much to Arizona's surprise, Callie tells her that she "cut him off."[62] This leads to financial woes, causing Callie to contemplate Dr. Cristina Yang's suggestion to lie to her family by telling them that she and Arizona have broken up. Thus, we see another woman of color (Cristina) advocating for familial nondisclosure marking the reification of homophobia that can exist within nonwhite families and cultures. Callie briefly entertains this option but ultimately decides against it, telling Mark, "I can't lie. Even if they think I'm wrong. Even if they don't understand. Even if they think I'm crazy. I'm me. They're supposed to accept me. They're supposed to support me. They're supposed to love me. You know? I can't lie."[63] The tension Callie experiences, and that Cristina understands, is the stress that queer of color scholars such as Ross and Moraga allude to—the need to at times be closeted because of fear of losing not only family and cultural ties but also in this case financial support. Callie understands that if she plays the good dutiful daughter, symbolically located at the virgin end of the virgin/whore dichotomy, she can maintain her connection to her family versus being ousted if she is the symbolic "traitor" or whore figure, Malinche, who is often connected to discussions of Chicana lesbianism.

In season 6, Carlos returns to the hospital with a priest, Father Kevin.[64] Imploring Callie to talk with him, Carlos says, "We'd always work it out *mija*."[65] Seeing her father with the priest, Callie asks outright, "You think you can pray away the gay?" followed by, "You can't pray away the gay!"[66] Her father yells after her as she walks away, clearly enunciating the Spanish pronunciation. She yells back, "You can't pray away the gay!"[67] Her clear, unaccented English response stands in contrast to his accented English, marking her family as Latinx and her queerness as white. In this way, we see Callie's anger toward her father's reaction to her queerness as a rejection of his intolerance. Presumably, much of the conversation about LGBTQ identity that surrounds Callie is consistent with the white homonormative understanding of queerness (i.e., visibility equals power or "it gets better"). The divisionary juxtaposition between Callie's race and sexuality continues throughout the show and is hypervisibly noticeable because all of Callie's relational partners are white.

After her argument with her father, Callie vents to Arizona. To Callie's surprise, Arizona merely encourages her to have a conversation with her father, suggesting that she shocked him by coming out after thirty years of what he experienced as his daughter's heterosexuality. Callie, presuming that Arizona had a similar coming out experience, believes she should be more understanding of the situation. However, Arizona shares that her being a lesbian was not a surprise to her family because she never dated men. Drawing a comparison between her and Callie, Arizona explains that she feels that Callie's father has a right to be shocked. Here, Arizona, the white woman who has always been queer, counsels Callie to ease up on her Latinx father. While Arizona's race is not the only factor determining how she and her family understood her sexuality, it does underscore how LGBTQ identity is communicated differently within families of color. Furthermore, Arizona gets to appear caring, benevolent, and rational while Callie is marked as overly emotional, a coding that is commonly associated with Latinas. Arizona's statements about always knowing she was a lesbian also assume a fixed identity narrative steeped in white privilege—a trope we see more often with gay men. This is interesting given that gay white male narratives are the most common in representations of queerness in the popular imagination, rhetorically silencing the experiences of queer white women and queer people of color.

Later in the episode, Callie is seated at a table with the white priest and her father. Symbolically, the priest sits between Callie and Carlos, mediating Callie's symbolic move toward white queerness and her intersectional Latina Catholic identity. Callie challenges her father to see that queerness has been present in their family for some time whether he has chosen to acknowledge it or not. She mentions her Uncle Berto who has not been single for six years "for no reason."[68] This is both a familiar queer code of the lifelong bachelor and a common way that Latinxs frame family members who are not out of the closet officially, though their queerness is a well-known secret. Callie tells her father, "You should have adjusted by now."[69] Carlos responds, "I love you with all my heart. . . . I'm scared for you. It's an abomination. It's an eternity in hell."[70] Father Kevin, a literal and symbolic source of righteousness, interjects in his role as mediator and the white voice of patriarchal reason, "Let's not start with words like hell."[71] After Carlos refuses to apologize and pleads against Callie's queerness, she and her father passionately exchange Bible verses. At the end, Callie retorts, "Jesus is my savior daddy, not you. And he would be ashamed of you for judging me. And he would be ashamed of you for turning your back on me."[72] Her response is important because she refuses to let go of her Catholicism or her queerness, both of which are fundamental to her intersectional Latina identity.

After comforting a devastated Callie, Arizona decides to speak to Carlos herself. Arizona explains that she was named after the USS Arizona, the ship her grandfather died on during the bombing of Pearl Harbor after saving nineteen men from drowning. His heroism and love of country was a cornerstone of Arizona's upbringing. When she came out to her father, a colonel in the Marine Corps, she was prepared for him to kick her out of the house, but instead he asked, "Are you still who I raised you to be?"[73] She tells Carlos, "My father believed in country the way that you believe in God. And my father is not a man who bends, but he bent for me because I'm his daughter. I'm a good man in a storm. I love your daughter. And I protect the things that I love."[74] By relating strict military life to religiosity, Arizona appeases some of Carlos's fears. After their exchange, Carlos waits for his daughter outside of the hospital and Callie scoffs and walks past him. Carlos asks her if there is hope for a wedding between her and Arizona and eventually grandchildren. Pacified by Callie's affirmation of marriage and children, Carlos hugs his daughter. Again, we see how Arizona's military upbringing and masculine narrative style provides the white voice of "reason," which ultimately prompts Carlos to forgive Callie, underlining the resolution of the conflict via Callie's Catholic Latinx family being swayed by and adhering to norms associated with white queer familial acceptance. Arizona functions as a normative buffer of sorts between Callie and Carlos. Importantly, Carlos's inquiries about a wedding and children highlight his need to negotiate his daughter's sexuality while simultaneously retaining and emphasizing his ties to culture and religion. These ties reinforce his reliance on traditional Catholic and Latinx values concerning honor and family, and they point to a desired performance of homonormativity rather than queerness.

Carlos's reaction is complicated in that while it maintains associations of Latinx families as homophobic and unsupportive, it also disrupts the hegemonic coming out narrative that is governed by white queers' access to racial privilege. Through Carlos, we witness how coming out has the potential to cut Callie off from her cultural and familial ties, which visually makes her angry and breaks her heart. In the end, Callie's coming out is a triumph mediated by whiteness, which results in associating Latinx identities with primitivism because they do not perform 'correctly' within the white queer progress narrative of coming out. This interpretation is further supported by Carlos's furious reactions to George and Mark; in defense of his daughter, he was driven by a sense of overprotective machismo. Importantly, throughout all of these relationships, Callie vehemently refuses to be cast in the trope of the bad woman/whore that must be atoned back into the virginal, dutiful daughter. She does so by standing up for herself, her sexuality, her autonomy, and her intersectional identities.

As previously mentioned, Callie and Arizona eventually marry. Callie's father and mother, Lucia, are set to attend the wedding. However, from the moment they arrive, we see Lucia's discomfort overshadow the joy of the event and all subsequent familial interactions. During the rehearsal dinner attended by both sets of parents, Carlos displays his newfound acceptance by attempting to connect with Arizona and (over)excitedly sharing, "We sat next to a charming young man on the plane today, and he said he was going with his partner to march in a parade. For pride."[75] Sensing Lucia's agitation, Callie interjects by asking if she would like to hold her grandchild, Sofia, for the first time. Lucia quickly declines by offering eating as an excuse and tensions thicken. Then Callie sits Lucia down and explains that she has tried hard to please Lucia's Catholic sensibilities throughout the wedding planning process, including wearing Lucia's veil. Lucia retorts, "Don't you dare imply that there's anything about a wedding to a woman or a baby out of wedlock that's for me."[76] Callie responds, "So what bothers you more? My bastard child or my lesbian fiancée?"[77] Lucia, mournfully homophobic, replies that she will not see Callie in heaven and that her marriage to another woman does not make her a bride.

Eventually, Lucia resolves not to attend the wedding. At Callie's insistence, Carlos reluctantly leaves with his wife. However, during the wedding reception, we see Carlos return when he realizes he cannot miss the opportunity to dance with his daughter on her wedding day. This is significant as Latinx families have traditionally been framed within the trope of machismo and marianismo, meaning that men are seen as the head of the household who may hold sexist qualities, while women are seen as virginal, religious makers of home. Carlos's attendance at the wedding serves as a sign of support from the patriline; however, to Callie, her mother's absence signifies her failure to perform proper (i.e., heterosexual) Latina identity and homemaking. This is highlighted during the conversation between Callie and Dr. Miranda Bailey after Callie's painful interaction with her mother. Callie says, "My mom's right. It's a joke. It's not a wedding. It's not happening. I can't have a priest. I no longer have a minister. I'm not being given away by my dad. The wedding isn't legal. What's the point? This isn't a wedding. It's not even in a church. It's nothing. It's a couple of girls playing dress up."[78] Following this emotional exchange, Callie tearfully calls off the wedding. Thus, although Callie has the blessing of her father; her mother, as the symbolic keeper of culture reflecting a trait often associated with women, refuses to give her blessing. This portrayal stigmatizes women of color while framing patriarchy in a positive light because it is Carlos who shows up for his daughter despite Lucia's homophobic inability to do so.

Whiteness and Romantic Relationships

Callie's relationships play an imperative role in her life and, therefore, in interpreting the pedagogy of her bisexuality. In addition to theorizing her race-culture and her family, it is important to recognize that all of Callie's relational partners have been white. Callie's steady stream of white romantic partners marks the manifestation of Callie's palatable queerness. According to Meyer, "Bisexual characters are typically non-White women whose unstable discourses serve as a 'contemporary site for the production and consumption of identity.'"[79] Meyer further argues that,

> The bisexual character serves to stabilize heterosexuality in his or her immediate relational and work environment. Bisexual female characters are not the leads and are often the foils to White, heterosexual women protagonists, whereas bisexual men exist only to complicate existing relationships between White, male protagonists. Although the presence of characters that embody intersectionality can potentially unfix dominant discourses of identity, scholars must pay close attention to the ways in which these images serve to challenge and maintain the status quo simultaneously.[80]

Meyer's insight fittingly extends to Callie because she is a bisexual Latina whose character both fits within and functions outside of the status quo.

Each of Callie's partners, including the aforementioned George O'Malley and Erica Hahn, have been white. Because Callie inhabits multiple intersectional identities simultaneously, we argue that Callie being paired with only white partners is a missed opportunity to contest normativity on television. We see Callie's proximity to whiteness as an intentional industry practice employed to connect with white heteronormative audiences and to foster normative comfort, thus taming both her sexuality and her Latina identity. As Holtzman and Sharpe contend,

> While Asian and Pacific Islander and Latina/Latino characters such as Grey's Anatomy's Cristina Yang and Callie Torres are prominent and complex characters, their onscreen life partners and best friends are white, and they rarely, if ever, have to face either individual prejudice or racial barriers to their personal and professional success. These kinds of characters and themes are choreographed to assimilate in such a way that allows the characters to be treated as white to keep audiences in a comfort zone that discourages any observation or analysis of racial tension or discrimination.[81]

Similarly, Callie's selection of white partners who identify either as solely gay or solely straight and her serial monogamy frames her bisexuality as less intimidating because she is always in close proximity to normativity.

Because promiscuity is stereotypically assigned to bisexuality, Callie's adherence to and belief in monogamy works to defy the stereotype, which we believe is done intentionally to, once again, keep her in acceptable proximity to normativity. In other words, Callie is never given the benefit of the doubt, despite her proclivity for monogamy. For example, Callie's fidelity is constantly called into question by Arizona in relation to her bisexuality; however, she is paradoxically shown to consistently want a strictly monogamous relationship. This paradox contributes to Arizona's suspicions and is made evident through an underscoring of biphobia, even within the LGBTQ community. This is of particular interest because the type of monogamy attributed to Callie's romantic relationships differs from that of the straight characters on the show, many of whom are in monogamous relationships but have cheated on their relational partners. Moreover, in season 9, Arizona cheats on Callie with Lauren Boswell, which leads to Callie and Arizona's subsequent divorce.[82] While Arizona's cheating is portrayed as a marital transgression, it is not portrayed as innate to her sexuality. Conversely, mirroring Arizona's constant fears that Callie would cheat, we believe that if Callie had cheated—especially with a man—that her doing so would have been read by audiences as an inevitable circumstance of her bisexuality. In this context, Callie's scripted monogamy should be read as a purposeful narrative move to counter longstanding tropes of bisexuality that suggest bisexual women are sexually promiscuous and, as such, incapable of monogamy. While many of the straight characters on the show such as Mark Sloan and George O'Malley were incapable of monogamy throughout the series, Callie's racialized, lived experiences seemingly make any potential indiscretions on her part appear more prominent, particularly when read against the larger context of heteronormativity.

GREY'S (IM)PERFECT PEDAGOGY OF BISEXUALITY

Callie Torres provides us with an interesting example of what Meyer terms an "intersectional hybrid"[83] character. She offers a complicated intersectional performance of bisexuality connected to her Catholic, upper-class, and Latina identities; all of which she importantly refuses to sacrifice. Overall, we interpret and experience Callie as a progressive representation of queer women of color. However, as noted earlier, some of her transgressive potential is tempered by the ease with which her storylines reify progress narratives that associate being "out" with liberation and being closeted as primitive, while ignoring the complex presence of race, ethnicity, and religion alongside sexuality. Progress narratives position white lesbian and gay politics in conversation with assimilationist tendencies (e.g., middle- or upper-class respectability, homonormativity) and thus are liberatory, while Latinx identities are positioned as comparatively oppressive. Therefore, Callie's stream of white relational partners and the positioning of her family in relation to this progress narrative offers important implications to consider with regard to the workings of normativity and acceptability as presented on television.

After ten years, Callie Torres left Grey Sloan Memorial Hospital to move to New York City with another white partner, intern Penny Blake, in season 12.[84] Though Ramirez requested the time off, catching Rhimes off guard, Callie's exit cements much of the critique we lay out in this chapter.[85] Leaving her friends and career behind for yet another white partner underscores how Callie subscribes to many of the normative depictions of queer characters of color we continue to see in the media. Though it is unclear if Callie will return to Seattle at some point before Grey's ends, it is clear that despite being unanticipated, Callie's departure is a telling punch line to the potential end of her storyline.

Overall, our critique of Grey's pedagogy of bisexuality through Callie complicates theorizations of queer women of color and offers a nuanced intersectional analysis of bisexuality. Latinx media figures are the most palatable when they are marked with ambiguous difference but still situated within close proximity to whiteness.[86] As we can see with Callie's character, this trend continues with queer Latinx representations in television. Certainly, Callie adds an *other* sexuality to Grey's narrative canon; however, her otherness is tempered by white gay male norms of coming out and class politics of respectability, which ultimately work to recenter white patriarchy. While we see the potential of having had such an unapologetically bisexual Latina character on screen, we also recognize the multiple ways transgressive possibilities function in service to discourses of whiteness and homonormativity. Thus, we must ask: who benefits from these representations? As Griffin demonstrates in her critical analysis of *The Help*, a film that exploits black women's experiences to bolster white femininity, perhaps Callie's narrative is less about the empowerment of bisexual women of color and more about normalizing discourses of white (patriarchal) queerness.[87] One of Rhimes's newer characters, Annalise Keating, on *How to Get Away with Murder* (ABC 2014–present), is a bisexual African American woman. Differently from Callie, she has been portrayed with at least one romantic partner of color in addition to her white husband. Shondaland's expansion offers an opportunity for Rhimes and her team of writers to develop the pedagogy of bisexuality far beyond appeals to normativity; it will be interesting to see what the future of bisexuality looks like on television, within and beyond Shondaland.

NOTES

1. "Awards," *IMDB*, accessed February 24, 2017, http://www.imdb.com/title/tt0413573/awards?ref_=tt_awd.

2. Ramirez came out after departing the show in its twelfth season. See Elizabeth Wagmeister, "Sara Ramirez Leaving 'Grey's Anatomy' after More Than 10 Years," *Variety*, May 19, 2016, http://variety.com/2016/tv/news/sara-ramirez-callie-torres-leaving-greys-anatomy-shonda-rhimes-reaction-1201779222/.

3. "Sara Ramirez Awards," *IMDB*, accessed February 19, 2017, http://www.imdb.com/name/nm0708381/awards?ref_=nm_awd.

4. Sara Ramirez, "HRC Speech," *Who Say*, 2015, http://www.whosay.com/status/sararamirez/1077633.

5. Esther Breger, "Primetime TV Is More Diverse Than It's Ever Been. Why Now?," *New Republic*, August 25, 2014, https://newrepublic.com/article/119196/black-ish-cristela-network-tvs-diversity-push-fall.

6. We use Latinx as a gender neutral term.

7. Riva Tukachinsky, Dana Mastro, and Moran Yarchi, "Documenting Portrayals of Race/Ethnicity on Primetime Television over a 20-Year Span and Their Association with National-Level Racial/Ethnic Attitudes" *Journal of Social Issues* 71, no. 1 (2015): 17–38.

8. Tukachinsky, Mastro, and Yarchi, 17–38..

9. Marlon B. Ross, "Beyond the Closet as Raceless Paradigm," in *Black Queer Studies: A Critical Anthology*, ed. E. Patrick. Johnson and Mae G. Henderson (Durham, N.C.: Duke University Press, 2005), 161–189.

10. Ross, 162.

11. Cathy Cohen, "Punks, Bulldaggers, and Welfare Queens," in *Black Queer Studies*, 21–49; E. Patrick Johnson, "Quare' Studies, or (Almost) Everything I Know about Queer Studies I Learned from My Grandmother," in *Black Queer Studies*, 124–157.

12. Cohen, "Punks, Bulldaggers, and Welfare Queens," 21–49.

13. Charles I. Nero, "Why Are Gay Ghettos White?," in *Black Queer Studies*, 228–245.

14. José Esteban Muñoz, *Disidentifications: Queers of Color and the Performance of Politics* (Minneapolis: University of Minnesota Press, 1999).

15. Bernadette Marie Calafell, *Latina/o Communication Studies: Theorizing Performance* (New York: Peter Lang, 2007); Bernadette Marie Calafell, *Monstrosity, Performance, and Race in Contemporary Culture* (New York: Peter Lang, 2015).

16. Gloria Anzaldúa, *Borderlands/La Frontera: The New Mestiza*, 4th ed. (San Francisco: Aunt Lute Books, 2012).

17. We use Chicanx as a gender neutral term.

18. Calafell, *Monstrosity*.

19. Cherrie Moraga, *Loving in the War Years: Lo Que Nunca Pasó Por Sus Labios*, 2nd ed. (Boston: South End, 2000).

20. Anzaldúa, *Borderlands/La Frontera*.

21. Mary Murray, "Cuba Celebrates Our Lady Charity, Island's Patron Saint." *NBC News*, September 8, 2014, http://www.nbcnews.com/news/latino/cuba-celebrates-our-lady-charity-islands-patron-saint-n198396.

22. Murray.

23. Calafell, *Latina/o Communication Studies*.

24. Calafell, *Latina/o Communication Studies*.

25. Charles Ramírez Berg and Charles Ram, *Latino Images in Film: Stereotypes, Subversion, and Resistance* (Austin: University of Texas Press, 2002).

26. Moraga, *Loving in the War Years*.

27. Juana Maria Rodriguez, *Sexual Futures, Queer Gestures, and Other Latina Longings* (New York: New York University Press, 2014).

28. Michaela D. E. Meyer, "'I'm Just Trying to Find My Way like Most Kids': Bisexuality, Adolescence and the Drama of *One Tree Hill*," *Sexuality & Culture* 13, no. 4 (2009): 237–251.

29. Meyer, 239–240.

30. Michaela D. E. Meyer, "Drawing the Sexuality Card: Teaching, Researching and Living Bisexuality," *Sexuality & Culture* 9, no. 1 (2005): 3–13.

31. Michaela D. E. Meyer, "Representing Bisexuality on Television: The Case for Intersectional Hybrids," *Journal of Bisexuality* 10, no. 4 (2010): 366–387.

32. Meyer, 367.

33. Meyer, 367.

34. Meyer, 375.

35. Meyer, 379.

36. Meyer, 380.

37. *Grey's Anatomy*, "Rise Up," season 5, episode 7, directed by Joanna Kerns, written by William Harper, aired on November 6, 2008, on ABC.

38. Melissa Silverstein, "Why the Firing of Brooke Smith Is Bigger Than ABC Wants Us to Think," *Huffington Post*, December 11, 2008, http://www.huffingtonpost.com/melissa-silverstein/why-the-firing-of-brooke_b_142603.html. Shortly after the character's exit, news broke that the network had terminated the actor who played Erica—Brooke Smith. Smith sat down for an exclusive interview with *Entertainment Weekly*, where she shared that it was an upset Rhimes who broke the news to her, and that she believed ABC had given Rhimes little choice in the matter. Smith conveyed her disappointment in ABC for cutting what could have been a transgressive story of two women falling love, maintaining, "They just suddenly told me they couldn't write for my character anymore." Michael Ausiello, "Exclusive: 'Grey's Anatomy' Discharges Dr. Hahn," *Entertainment Weekly*, November 3, 2008, http://www.ew.com/article/2008/11/03/brooke-smith-le.

39. Michael Ausiello, "'Grey's' Exclusive: Jessica Capshaw Inks Contract!" *Entertainment Weekly*, February 26, 2015, http://ew.com/article/2009/02/26/greys-exclusi-1-3/.

40. Maggie Furlong, "'Grey's Anatomy': Callie and Arizona's Relationship Repair Is 'Not Gonna Be Easy,' Sara Ramirez Says," *Huffington Post*, October 25, 2012, http://www.huffingtonpost .com/2012/10/25/greys-anatomy-callie-and-arizona_n_2012974.html.

41. Kristen Benson, "Kirstin Says: Callie the Lesbian Hooks Up with McSteamy & Dr. Bailey Gets Wasted on 'Grey's Anatomy'!" *Hollywood Life*, November 9, 2010, http://hollywoodlife .com/2010/11/19/kirstin-says-greys-anatomy-recap-watch-bailey-drunk-callie-lesbian-mark -mcsteamy-sex-7x09-video/.

42. Shonda Rhimes, "Callie's Not a Lesbian." *Twitter*, November 12, 2010, https://twitter.com /shondarhimes/status/3236123782418432.

43. Lesley Goldberg, "'Grey's Anatomy': Callie and Arizona Dating Others," *Hollywood Reporter*, January 21, 2015, http://www.hollywoodreporter.com/live-feed/greys-anatomy-callie -arizona-dating-765764.

44. *Grey's Anatomy*, "I Feel the Earth Move," season 11, episode 15, directed by Thomas J. Wright, written by Jen Klein, aired on March 12, 2015, on ABC.

45. *Grey's Anatomy*, "The Time Warp," season 6, episode 15, directed by Rob Corn, written by Zoanne Clack, aired on February 18, 2010, on ABC; *Grey's Anatomy*, "White Wedding," season 7, episode 20, directed by Chandra Wilson, written by Stacy McKee, aired on May 5, 2011, on ABC; *Grey's Anatomy*, "It's a Long Way Back," season 7, episode 19, directed by Steve Robin, written by William Harper, aired on April 28, 2011, on ABC; *Grey's Anatomy*, "Guess Who's Coming to Dinner," season 12, episode 5, directed by Debbie Allen, written by Mark Driscoll and Meg Marinis, aired on October 22, 2015, on ABC.

46. *Grey's Anatomy*, "Sanctuary," season 6, episode 23, directed by Stephen Cragg, written by Shonda Rhimes, aired on May 20, 2010, on ABC.

47. *Grey's Anatomy*, "Suicide Is Painless," season 6, episode 18, directed by Jeannot Szwarc, written by Tony Phelan and Joan Rater, aired on March 25, 2010, on ABC.

48. *Grey's Anatomy*, "Don't Deceive Me (Please Don't Go)," season 7, episode 13, directed by Kevin McKidd, written by Mark Wilding, aired on February 3, 2011, on ABC.

49. Jillian Todd Weiss, "GL vs. BT," *Journal of Bisexuality* 3, no. 3–4 (2003): 29.

50. Amy Andre, "Biphobia: The Attitude That Plagues the LGBTQ Community," *One Equal World*, October 7, 2013, http://www.oneequalworld.com/2013/10/07/biphobia-attitude -plagues-lgbtq-community/.

51. *Grey's Anatomy*, "Not Responsible," season 7, episode 16, directed by Debbie Allen, written by Debora Cahn, aired on February 24, 2011, on ABC.

52. *Grey's Anatomy*, "Not Responsible."

53. *Grey's Anatomy*, "This Is How We Do It," season 7, episode 17, directed by Edward Ornelas, written by Peter Nowalk, aired on March 24, 2011, on ABC.

54. *Grey's Anatomy*, "Bend & Break," season 11, episode 5, directed by Jesse Bochco, written by Meg Marinis, aired on October 23, 2014, on ABC.

55. Shane T. Moreman and Bernadette Marie Calafell, "Buscando Para Nuestra Latinidad: Utilizing La Llorona for Cultural Critique," *Journal of International and Intercultural Communication* 1, no. 4 (2008): 309–326.

56. Moreman and Calafell.

57. Moreman and Calafell.

58. *Grey's Anatomy*, "Sweet Surrender," season 5, episode 20, directed by Tony Phelan, written by Sonay Washington, aired on April 23, 2009, on ABC.

59. *Grey's Anatomy*, "Sweet Surrender."

60. *Grey's Anatomy*, "Sweet Surrender."

61. *Grey's Anatomy*, "Sweet Surrender."

62. *Grey's Anatomy*, "Sweet Surrender."

63. *Grey's Anatomy*, "No Good at Saying Sorry (One More Chance)," season 5, episode 21, directed by Tom Verica, written by Krista Vernoff, aired on April 30, 2009, on ABC.

64. *Grey's Anatomy*, "Invasion," season 6, episode 5, directed by Tony Phelan, written by Mark Wilding, aired on October 15, 2009, on ABC.

65. *Grey's Anatomy*, "Invasion."

66. *Grey's Anatomy*, "Invasion."

67. *Grey's Anatomy*, "Invasion."

68. *Grey's Anatomy*, "Invasion."

69. *Grey's Anatomy*, "Invasion."

70. *Grey's Anatomy*, "Invasion."

71. *Grey's Anatomy*, "Invasion."

72. *Grey's Anatomy*, "Invasion."

73. *Grey's Anatomy*, "Invasion."

74. *Grey's Anatomy*, "Invasion."

75. *Grey's Anatomy*, "White Wedding."

76. *Grey's Anatomy*, "White Wedding."

77. *Grey's Anatomy*, "White Wedding."

78. *Grey's Anatomy*, "White Wedding."

79. Meyer "Representing Bisexuality," 379.

80. Meyer, 379.

81. Linda Holtzman and Leon Sharpe, *Media Messages: What Film, Television, and Popular Music Teach Us about Race, Class, Gender, and Sexual Orientation* (New York: M. E. Sharpe, 2014), 356.

82. *Grey's Anatomy*, "Readiness Is All," season 9, episode 23, directed by Tony Phelan, written by William Harper, aired on May 9, 2013, on ABC.

83. Meyer, "Representing Bisexuality," 367.

84. Natalie Abrams, "Grey's Anatomy: Sara Ramirez Exits after 10 Years as Callie Torres," *EW*, May 19, 2016, http://ew.com/article/2016/05/19/greys-anatomy-callie-sara-ramirez-exit/.

85. Lauren Piester, "Shonda Rhimes 'Had a Different Plan' for Callie before Sara Ramirez' *Grey's Anatomy* Exit," *E News*, May 22, 2016, http://www.eonline.com/news/767003/shonda -rhimes-had-a-different-plan-for-callie-before-sara-ramirez-grey-s-anatomy-exit.

86. Calafell, *Latina/o Communication Studies*.

87. Rachel Griffin, "Problematic Representations of Strategic Whiteness and 'Post-Racial' Pedagogy: A Critical Intercultural Reading of *The Help*," *Journal of International and Intercultural Communication* 8, no. 2 (2015): 147–166.

7 · THE PROBLEMATICS OF POSTRACIAL COLORBLINDNESS

Exploring Cristina Yang's Asianness in *Grey's Anatomy*

STEPHANIE L. YOUNG AND VINCENT PHAM

"Oh, screw beautiful. I'm brilliant! If you want to appease me, compliment my brain!" says Dr. Cristina Yang to Dr. Owen Hunt on *Grey's Anatomy* (ABC 2005–present; also referred to as *Grey's*).[1] Played by Sandra Oh, Cristina is one of the most complex characters on television; she has been praised as "a downright revolutionary character" and described as combining "the type-A Asian, the frigid ballbuster, [and] the unlikable shrew" with "humor, swag, and a sex drive."[2] Since *Grey's* 2005 debut, Oh has been nominated for five Emmy Awards and in 2006, won a Golden Globe and Screen Actors Guild Award.[3] Spanning ten seasons and over two hundred episodes previous to her departure from *Grey's*, Cristina is one of the longest-running and most popular portrayals of an Asian American woman on network television. Her popularity and complexity can be traced throughout her portrayal as a hypercompetitive, hardworking, career-driven woman of color who is sarcastic, blunt, and deeply loyal to *Grey's* lead character, Dr. Meredith Grey. Cristina is key to major storylines and deals with a plethora of drama, including a miscarriage, being stood up at her first wedding, a mass shooting, posttraumatic stress disorder (PTSD) following a plane crash, an abortion, and numerous cutting-edge surgeries that she earns, swindles her peers out of, and prioritizes as the most important part of her life. "To her, her career always, unarguably came first—and in a world, even a TV one, where women are expected to rearrange their priorities around the age of 30, Cristina's path was incredibly brave."[4]

Grey's Anatomy exemplifies casting, scripting, and storyline choices that progressively depart from television industry norms that limit roles for women of color, particularly Asian American women. In their analysis of 414 films and television series (broadcast, cable, and digital streaming), the Institute for Diversity and Empowerment at Annenberg found "at least half or more of all cinematic, television, or streaming stories fail to portray one speaking or named Asian or Asian American on screen."[5] Additionally, although there has been an increase in depictions of Asian Americans, they continue to be represented stereotypically.[6] However, Cristina stands out as one of few intricately developed Asian American characters on network television. Rather than being reduced to a proverbial sidekick, Cristina is Meredith's equal, her "person." As showrunner Shonda Rhimes notes, their friendship, not Meredith's romantic relationship with Dr. Derek Shepherd, is "the big relationship of the show" because "Cristina is her [Meredith's] soul mate."[7] While research has focused on Cristina's character reinforcing stereotypes such as the Dragon Lady and the model minority, her "dark and twisty" platonic relationship with Meredith, her feminist sensibilities, and her interracial relationship with Dr. Preston Burke, there has been little theorization of how Cristina functions in service to postracialism as a Jewish Korean American woman.[8]

In this chapter, we engage in a close textual analysis of Cristina on *Grey's* in response to Ono's call to investigate mediated "postracial strategies" that antiquate racial inequalities and systematic racism while (ironically) commodifying race for white audiences.[9] Deconstructing Shondaland's representation of Cristina reveals the unique ways an Asian American character problematically promotes postracialism by minimizing both race and racism. We explore Cristina's portrayal by paradoxically pairing the absence of racial discourse with the presence of the visually marked Asian body.[10] We argue that she, because of and despite being Asian American, sporadically functions in service to three strategies of postracial colorblindness. First, when on-screen dialogue about race and racial identity is relevant in storylines, Cristina is selectively "race-silenced" to recirculate Asian American stereotypes and position her as an "honorary white" character.[11] Second, Cristina's honorary white status is secured through religious identification via her intersectional yet ambivalent embodiment of Asian American Jewish identity. Finally, Cristina's portrayal operates relationally to perpetuate racial hierarchies that position characters of color against a postracial backdrop.

Organized into four parts, we first contextualize the landscape of television where *Grey's* is commonly situated and celebrated as a progressive, postracial medical melodrama in its casting and storytelling. Next, we define close textual analysis as the method used to select and theorize representative examples of Cristina's embodiment of postracialism. Then, we expose two problematic patterns within Cristina's racialization that foster what we term *postracial colorblindness*. The first problematic pattern exposed is that the only prominent Asian American character on *Grey's* is imprinted by fragmented Asian tropes, specifically the model minority and the Dragon Lady. The second problematic pattern exposed is how Cristina's identities are leveraged to reinforce dominant racial hierarchies in relation to other characters. Deconstructing these two patterns allows us to highlight postracial strategies that reinforce white superiority despite representing a society devoid of race and racial inequality—which, in turn, births our conceptualization of postracial colorblindness. Despite Grey's attempts at blazing new ground for women of color, the series ultimately undermines such efforts by confining Cristina's legacy as one of the foremost Asian American characters in the history of network television to postracial colorblindness.

A NEO-PLATOON SHOW WITH COLORBLIND CASTING: THE POSTRACIAL HOSPITAL OF GREY'S ANATOMY

Much scholarship and popular press has explored racial diversity on Grey's, particularly its diverse cast.[12] In the first season, four of the nine main characters were people of color—two African American men (Dr. Preston Burke and Dr. Richard Webber), an African American woman (Dr. Miranda Bailey), and an Asian American woman (intern Cristina Yang). With a large cast of ethno-racially diverse characters partaking in melodramatic storylines, Grey's is what Brook terms a neo-platoon show that "present[s] a multicultural and transnational universe in which not only everything is interconnected but also interconnectedness provides the key to salvation."[13] As Grey's creator and executive producer, Rhimes is commonly praised for casting roles without considering race, that is, colorblind casting. This approach, common throughout Shondaland, allows ethno-racially diverse actors to erect and inhabit the neo-platoon hospital setting. "Rhimes has conceived Seattle Grace as a frenetic, multicultural hub where racial issues take a back seat to the more pressing problems of hospital life: surgery, competition, exhaustion and—no surprise—sex."[14] While representational diversity is visible on neo-platoon shows, Brook notes that "convergent ethnicity" erases identifiable difference and cultural specificity; a cast "may look different, but they tend to act the same" and "historical and cultural distinctions, not to mention persistent ethno-racial inequities, are ignored . . . if not denied altogether."[15] On Grey's this translates into the aforementioned "pressing problems" that characters face being distanced from race, as if race and racism matter far less than interpersonal hospital dynamics. In place of meaningful portrayals of ethno-racial differences, Grey's focuses on highly motivated and often egotistical surgeons and surgeons-in-training who practice medicine in a colorblind and postracial context.[16] This pattern of employing diverse casts without directly addressing their ethno-racial differences reinforces U.S. American meritocratic ideologies that appear in shows such as Lost (ABC 2004–2010) and The Walking Dead (AMC 2010–present).[17]

Rhimes is seemingly cognizant of the limitations of neo-platoon shows and mainstream television. In an interview, she explains for example how the absence of racial discourse within interracial relationships on *Grey's* reflects a conscious decision. She says, "I think that issues of race are a larger conversation that people project on a relationship, but for the two people in it, that's not the primary thing on their minds . . . part of a truly diverse world is not needing to make a statement about the fact that it's a diverse world. When we get to that point, we've gotten somewhere."[18] Rhimes's justification for casting characters of color without explicitly addressing race shifts the burden of responsibility from the industry (e.g., showrunners, production companies, and networks) to the audience. In effect, this practice aligns with obscuring racism, reproducing white privilege, and reinforcing postracialism to the benefit of whiteness despite the visibility of people of color.

By identifying a lack of discussion about diversity as a marker of progress, Rhimes also reinscribes postracial understandings of the role of race. As articulated, discussions concerning diversity and colorblind casting practices are not prioritized to challenge racism in the television industry. Instead, such discussions and practices modernize the look of shows in exchange for increased viewership and profit. While "at the heart of colorblind casting is the belief that race doesn't affect character," Rhimes's colorblindness problematically situates characters as "raceless" and situates women of color like Cristina in a postracial world that ignores whiteness and systemic racism.[19] Both colorblindness and postracialism posit that individuals should be treated equally regardless of race or ethnicity while masking normative whiteness and overlooking structures that maintain racial disenfranchisement.[20] Additionally, colorblind and postracial discourses proclaiming "racism no longer exists" deny racism's contemporary presence and impact.[21] Such proclamations assert that racial identities and racialized barriers are no longer significant in shaping relationships, educational opportunities, professional achievements, and lived experiences even though race continually impacts myriad facets of everyday life. *Grey's* is a prime example of how television constructs "a fictional colorless world in which the ideology of the American dream dictates that anyone can succeed with hard work."[22] One is "free from racial group identification" and individually responsible for "her lot in life."[23] In this context, the empty presence of racial identity exemplifies a neoliberal postracialism in which U.S. society, in service to whiteness, embraces individual racial difference but ignores systematic racial inequalities.[24]

In Shondaland, colorblindness problematically operates as a "race-neutral" strategy; one that eradicates racial conceptions but not racism, removes considerations of race as part of decision-making processes without remedying racial inequity, and situates race as irrelevant despite its continued significance.[25] Via Rhimes's showrunning logic, merely seeing racial diversity on screen is satisfactory, even though characters of color are consumed by whiteness's commitment to postracial colorblindness. Admittedly, Shondaland's prevailing use of colorblind casting has resulted in more ethno-racial actors in roles, which, in turn, undeniably fosters greater visibility of racial diversity on television. However, colorblind casting does not adapt the role to the person of color and thereby ignores racialized nuance to instead reinscribe white normativity. For example, Meredith and Cristina are oversimplified and reduced to being two seemingly raceless women who are best friends and work at the hospital. Race and its impact on their friendship is never directly discussed; however, the absence of talk upholds Meredith's whiteness by denying that Cristina's Koreanness *matters*. While the characters may not outwardly consider race, *Grey's* discursively functions within real world racial dynamics and therefore affects our material world.

Through neo-platoon trends, televisual representations have shifted from explicitly racist stereotypes to colorblindness. While there is greater visibility of racial diversity on the screen, these representations are merely superficial depictions of "symbolic inclusion" that normalize colorblindness and fuel postracialism to the detriment of holistic representations of people of color.[26] More specifically, television lacks developed storylines and characters that directly address racial differences and systematic racism as significant factors that impact individuals, relationships, and society. By superficially foregrounding race and emphasizing multiracial assimilation, television perpetuates colorblindness and avoids overtly politicized discussions about the differences between the world we watch on TV and the world we live in.

Within colorblindness, the strategic erasure of race naturalizes whiteness and invisibly fosters white superiority to the benefit of white audiences.[27] Furthermore, the presence of ethno-racially diverse characters ironically centers whiteness instead of deconstructing it and production strategies such as colorblind casting inconspicuously shape the industry to seem, rather than actually be, racially inclusive. As Bastién writes, "White actors can end up taking roles for non-white characters, as in *Aloha* and *Pan*," and "Productions can slot minority actors into secondary roles and get praised for diversity."[28] Thus, colorblind casting in *Grey's* whitewashes characters of color and the cast's composition perpetuates postracialism, making the show a multicultural vehicle for white normativity. Because television "plays an important role in maintaining a racialized social order," it is vital to explore *how* mediated texts visually and discursively enact postracial colorblindness.[29] To do so, we pay close attention to the absence or presence of racialized speech and storylines in relation to Cristina's portrayal as an Asian American Jewish woman.

CLOSE TEXTUAL ANALYSIS: A METHODOLOGICAL APPROACH

To examine constructions and contradictions, we follow McGee's approach to text as inherently fragmented.[30] As Dow argues, criticism is a process of meaning creation, and a text is "assembled" by the rhetorical critic for analysis.[31] Our approach mirrors how audiences often piece together discontinuous media across time and place—different shows, news outlets, websites, and other sources of public discourse.[32] Television series require viewers to piece together discontinuous scenes within the show to interpret characters and narrative. Particular to our focus, Cristina Yang is constructed in scenes interspersed with scenes focused on other characters. Additionally, the show's format as a medical melodrama weaves characters' stories together to deepen the plot. Audiences are subjected to fragments of the character and therefore must piece together the character from dialogue, interactions, and storylines.

Amid this fragmentation, we selected episodes where Cristina is central to the narrative. To do so, we watched 130 episodes and often fast-forwarded to scenes where Cristina visually appears. While this approach does not mimic the typical viewer experience, it allowed us to construct a holistic storyline in order to deconstruct Cristina's role and the normative tropes she is scripted to convey. In the sections that follow, we highlight two strategies of postracial colorblindness perpetuated through Cristina's character—her enactment of Asian American tropes and her reinforcement of dominant racial hierarchies.

CONNECTING FRAGMENTED ASIAN AMERICAN TROPES

Because Dr. Cristina Yang is the only Asian in the primary cast of *Grey's*, she serves as a slate for intermittently displaying a variety of stereotypical Asian American tropes.[33] These tropes construct her as both exceptional and threatening amid her fierce intellectual and sexual prowess; such prowess often hastens how she is stereotyped as an Asian American woman. The model minority and Dragon Lady tropes appear, fade away, and reappear as necessitated by storylines that function to reinforce a stratified racial order in which Asian Americans are simultaneously valorized and ostracized to mask and maintain hegemonic whiteness.[34] While sporadic references are made to Cristina's identities as a Korean Jewish woman, her racial identity is not represented as central to her character or meaningfully understood by her peers. For example, early on in season 1, Izzie Stevens misidentifies her as Chinese.[35] Cristina retorts that she "grew up in Beverly Hills. The only Chinese I know is from a Mr. Chow's menu. Besides, I'm Korean."[36] In this interaction, her racial identity is part of a snappy response to discipline Izzie rather than an articulation of Cristina's intersectional identities or the cultural differences between Asian ethnic groups. In season 3, Cristina meets the parents of her boyfriend Dr. Preston Burke.[37] When Preston's mother, an African American woman, overhears Cristina calling Dr. Bailey "the Nazi," she confronts her, stating that "the Nazis were responsible for the worst genocide in the history of man. And a racist genocide at that. I would think that as a woman of color and as a doctor, no less, that you would think twice before using that word as a punch line." Preston's mother shames Cristina as a woman of color for using such language casually.

Calling Dr. Bailey, a black woman, "the Nazi" is not only deemed disrespectful but also a racist slur that is complicated by Cristina's positionality as Jewish. For the remainder of the episode, Cristina worries that Preston's mother considers her racist. However, the episode fails to address Cristina's relationship to the Holocaust, how race and faith impact her, or the challenges of an interracial black-Asian romance.

Moreover, at no point in the series does Cristina address how racial differences impact her interracial romantic relationships—first with Dr. Burke, who is black, and second with Dr. Owen Hunt, who is white. The overarching absence of dialogue across ten seasons about the politics of interracial relationships reflects what Chidester describes as rhetorical silencing via what is not said more so than by what is said.[38] Silence about the complexity of romantic, platonic, and professional interracial relationships communicates a sense of inevitable racial progress that substantiates colorblind and postracial discourses.[39] As a Korean woman constantly engaged in interracial relationships without talking about race or how to navigate racial differences, Cristina conveys to audiences that racism no longer impacts interpersonal relationships in U.S. society.

Rhetorical silencing also functions as "equipment for living" that allows people to thrive and survive in a delusional, postracial colorblind world.[40] This is reflected in Rhimes's accounts of her own life that narrate her success and survival in the predominantly white male Hollywood industry. However, this translation into the cultural phenomenon of *Grey's* (and Shondaland writ large) also provides "equipment for living" for its viewers on how to approach race in their own lives. In Cristina's case, it is through silence—either the subject is never broached or is explicitly avoided to alleviate social embarrassment. While Cristina is chagrined at having her "Nazi" comment brand her as racist, Preston's mother is the disciplinary figure who utilizes race to shame Cristina instead of using their marginalization as women of color to foster solidarity. Thus, deflection and avoidance can be viewed as survival mechanisms for succeeding in a supposedly postracial world that deems race a dangerous and embarrassing topic of conversation.

Grey's also addresses racism comically or tangentially rather than purposefully centering it as a "real" issue. In season 4, Dr. Erica Hahn discloses to Dr. Addison Montgomery that she disapproves of Cristina's needy behavior as it reminds her of her younger self. When she refuses to let Cristina scrub in on surgeries because she interprets her as a "brownnoser," Cristina gingerly asks, "[I]s it 'cause I'm Asian? Is that your problem? You don't like Asian people?"[41] The subtext of Dr. Hahn's concerns signal that Dr. Yang is desperately leveraging an accusation of racism in an attempt to perform surgery; in turn, racism is not depicted as a serious issue in the medical profession. Beyond these rare racial quips, there is a marked absence of meaningful conversation about Cristina being Korean American. Conversely, despite the trivialization and dismissal of her racial identity, various stereotypical Asian American tropes are mapped onto her in fragmentary ways. As Shoba Sharad Rajgopal points out, Cristina does not have the feminine qualities of the show's white female characters.[42] While Meredith is intensely neurotic and Izzie is a sweet, sexy blonde, Cristina is consistently cold, enigmatic, and fiercely committed to professional perfectionism, signaling the archetypal model minority and Dragon Lady. At the intersections of race and gender, these stereotypical tropes function to reduce Asian women to manipulative workaholics.

Cristina's portrayal as a complex Asian character is unusual since media depictions of Asian Americans are often simplistic and stereotypical. Studies of Asian American representation in popular culture have revealed a long history of frequent racist tropes that broadly essentialize across several Asian ethnic groups. While Asian American women are generally represented as submissive Lotus Blossoms, sacrificial Madame Butterflies, and sexually dangerous and cunning Dragon Ladies; Asian American men have been largely relegated to smart but subservient Charlie Chan sidekicks, diabolical Fu Manchus, or emasculated and sexually undesirable.[43] Collectively, Asian Americans have been construed as a dangerous yellow peril that invades and negatively influences the U.S. body politic or, conversely, a model minority whose intelligence is deemed exceptional but threatening. As a hard-charging surgeon-in-training pursuing excellence, Cristina sporadically calls forth the Dragon Lady trope by leveraging her sexuality and the model minority trope by leveraging her intelligence and embracing robotic emotionlessness. According to Nakayama, Asian Americans are viewed as the robotic "model minority" or the "super minority" and are subsequently stereotyped as excessively hardworking, ambitious, emotionless, and economically successful "geniuses."[44] Cristina is just that—a highly educated, hypercompetitive workaholic from Beverly Hills who aspires to be the best. In several episodes, she verbalizes her educational pedigree, an MD from Stanford and a PhD from Berkeley, to command respect and convey superiority. She also uses cutthroat methods to excel by foregoing sleep, bragging, and vying for the best surgeries. When Cristina hits the eighty-hour weekly limit, for example, Dr. Bailey tells her to go home and enjoy the day. "I'll enjoy my day if I can help retrieve a heart," she replies.[45] Even on her and Preston's wedding day, she indicates that she is happier prepping a patient than preparing for her nuptials.[46] Cristina is so hypercompetitive that she is willing to exceed the workweek limit and arrive late to her own wedding in hopes of being selected as chief resident.[47]

As demonstrated thus far, Cristina privileges her career over all other aspects of her life. In season 2, when she reveals her unplanned pregnancy to Meredith, she says, "I'm not switching to the vagina squad or spending my life popping zits. I'm too talented. Surgery is my life."[48] For her, having a child would ruin her career aspirations. Cristina's decision not to have a child is not just that of a woman choosing a career over motherhood but it is inevitably demonstrative of an *Asian* woman whose ambition leads to a mechanical decision devoid of the nurturance motherhood requires. Moreover, in season 6 she pleads with Dr. Teddy Altman, a close friend of her boyfriend Dr. Owen Hunt and a cardiothoracic surgeon, to mentor her.[49] Unbeknownst to Cristina, Teddy is in love with Owen. When Cristina demands that Teddy tell her what she wants in exchange for mentorship, Teddy blurts out that she wants Owen. "Fine! Done! Take him!" Cristina gasps in response. While her response can be minimized as a moment of sheer desperation, since losing Dr. Altman will thwart her budding career, Cristina's offer reveals that she is willing to sacrifice love in exchange for becoming the best cardiothoracic surgeon. When juxtaposed against Teddy, a white woman willing to sacrifice the opposite—her career for love, Cristina emerges as an emotionless model minority whose ultimate goal is surgical excellence.

As a stereotypically career-driven and robotic Asian model minority, Cristina is repeatedly criticized for emotional ineptitude. When Dr. Bailey assigns her to talk with a patient's family, she replies, "I'm not a people person. I can't do that. I can't talk to the families of patients."[50] Additionally, Cristina's peers covet her stoic emotional control. In season 2, after Cristina's miscarriage, Dr. George O'Malley and Izzie discuss her emotional well-being.[51] Voicing the paradox, Izzie describes her as traumatized, "like she's missing a soul," while George admires her for being "hard-core. She's got ice in her veins."[52] Paradoxically, while George admires Cristina's cold precision (i.e., Asianness), he also implores her to be more emotionally responsive (i.e., feminine). In season 3, George's father is admitted to Seattle Grace with cancer and George explains to Cristina that he chose her as his dad's intern because she's "a freakin robot in a white coat who never makes a mistake"; yet, he also pleads with her to "try to be a human being."[53] Akin to Izzie's characterization (above), Cristina is both admired and admonished for being unemotional yet highly skilled. After George's dad dies, Cristina comforts him by disclosing that her father died and expressing sorrow that he has joined the "dead dad's club."[54] This scene is a startling departure from Cristina's typical portrayal. That a rare display of genuine compassion emerged in response to a white male's grief is significant because his experience—not hers—is the conduit for her "proper" emotional display and he—not her—is the benefactor of her emotional labor.

Despite the smattering of scenes where Cristina embodies relational emotions, she is repetitively confined within the stereotype of the hypersuccessful Asian medical doctor who lacks interpersonal skills. When promoted to teaching resident, which involves mentoring interns, Cristina is portrayed as lacking empathy, being condescending, and refusing to let them work on patients because her intelligence and skills are superior. After overhearing her yell at Lexie Grey, a first-year intern and Meredith's half sister, Dr. Shepherd calls her out for being a bully. By the end of the episode, Cristina has changed her approach and guides Lexie through a bleed during surgery.[55] Similar to George's critique of Cristina, Dr. Shepherd's insistence that she be more "human" and assimilate to white U.S. American norms of emotional expression functions as a disciplinary technique. Dr. Yang conforms to the norms of medical professionalism saturated in identity politics only after Dr. Shepherd, a white male attending doctor, threatens not to allow her to assist him with surgeries.

In accordance with the model minority trope, Cristina further embodies being the hypersuccessful Asian medical doctor and best cardiothoracic intern by lacking humility. In season 7, Teddy tells Owen, one attending doctor to another, that she finds Cristina's professional hubris dangerous.[56] The ideological implication is subtle because Cristina is incredibly confident and skilled, and unapologetically advocates for herself. Yet from a critical stance, mindful of how Cristina is scripted in relation to several white characters (e.g., Meredith, Izzie, George, and Derek), white dominance and postracial colorblindness are once again secured through Teddy. As a woman of color, Cristina is "dangerous" because her arrogant confidence functions as a symbolic threat to the white U.S. American majority. Dr. Altman's interpretation of Dr. Yang, despite Cristina's proven surgical acumen, echoes historical discourses of the "yellow peril."[57] These echoes are especially clear amid Teddy's status as an attending and access to Owen (as an attending and Cristina's boyfriend); both their status and their friendship allows Teddy and Owen to have a (white) conversation about Cristina. The underlying message is that a "good" doctor should not glorify these "Asian" characteristics (e.g., being unyielding, egotistical, emotionally detached, and unapologetically skilled). That "Asian" characteristics are often regularly on display via white surgeons signals that Cristina is being disciplined as a woman of color in ways that her coworkers are not.

Cristina also exhibits aspects of the Dragon Lady, the scheming seductress who uses sex to manipulate men. Although sexual promiscuity is normalized at the hospital and Cristina's sexual desires mirror those of her peers, she is scripted in alignment with this racist and sexist caricature that confines Asian women to being "witty, clever, and calculating; powerful, but lacking empathy or maternal instinct."[58] Early on in the series, Cristina departs from the Dragon Lady caricature through her reluctance to engage in romantic relationships. Once involved with Preston, she is depicted as genuinely caring for him as opposed to merely manipulating him.[59] Yet over time, Cristina's sexual desire and romantic relationships are scripted in closer proximity to the Dragon Lady. For example, her sexual urges for Preston appear uncontrollable, and Cristina's mother chastises her for privileging sexual relationships over emotional ones.[60] Moreover, in season 7, Cristina withholds sex from Owen to "assist" him with making an "objective" decision in choosing a new chief resident.[61]

While Cristina is covertly scripted as a Dragon Lady through her romantic relationships, Dr. Erica Hahn articulates her sexuality overtly in alignment with the trope. When she eagerly volunteers to scrub in on Dr. Hahn's heart transplant, Hahn calls Cristina out for having sexual relationships with previous mentors. She says, "You sleep with them, right? Preston Burke, Colin Marlowe, that's your thing?" followed by "My theory is if you had the chops in the O.R., you wouldn't need to try to impress in the bedroom."[62] By slut-shaming Dr. Yang for her sexual past with surgical superiors, Dr. Hahn belittles her intellect and skill by insinuating that she seduces powerful men to access top surgeries. Cristina later defends herself by arguing, "I did not sleep my way to the top. I'm attracted to a talent that resembles my own."[63] This exchange between the two women reflects an interesting dynamic amid the intersecting politics of sexuality and race. Cristina, a Korean heterosexual woman, is shamed for her sexual promiscuity by Erica, a white lesbian woman. Erica's queer sexuality is framed as nonthreatening, private, and professionally acceptable by comparison as it does not complicate her workplace relationships, while Cristina's Korean hyperheterosexuality is depicted as uncontrollable, manipulative, and inappropriate. Functioning as a disciplinarian, Erica perpetuates the patriarchal oppression of female sexuality in accordance with whiteness by shaming Cristina for her sexual relationships and disregarding her actualized excellence (i.e., Cristina did not sleep her way to the top).

Cristina's continual characterization as a hypersuccessful "robot" also draws on model minority logics, illustrating extraordinary technical abilities that save lives but sacrifice normative standards for social well-being. Cristina has her own standards about friendship, motherhood, marriage, and emotional expression, but these are deemed wrong. Mirroring discourses of the bamboo ceiling, she is penalized for her emotions—whether she shows them or not.[64] While her Asianness is not explicitly addressed in meaningful ways, race is omnipresent via the use of historical tropes that discipline Asian identity. The overall lack of explicit racial dialogue obscures racial difference and subsequently reinforces postracial colorblindness in service to white superiority. As a Korean Jewish woman, Cristina is permitted to transcend systematic racism intermittently through her sheer excellence and sexually manipulative ways without encountering the very real racist and sexist barriers that exist in present-day U.S. American society. What is provocatively telling is the absence of Asian female characters on *Grey's* or elsewhere comparable to Cristina's significance. While Rhimes may tout a fantastical, racially diverse postracial world, Cristina continues to be the token Asian.

NAVIGATING THE MINEFIELD OF RACIAL HIERARCHIES

While Cristina's race and ethnic background are mentioned only a few times throughout ten seasons, issues of race and racism are particularly evident in a two-episode storyline in season 4 titled "Crash into Me."[65] In these episodes, Dr. Yang's Asianness is central in relation to Dr. Bailey's blackness and their medical treatment of a white supremacist patient. Instead of viewing Cristina as an Asian American character in isolation, we approach this storyline paying particular attention to the hierarchical relationships among whiteness, blackness, and

Asianness to analyze how race is configured in the postracial setting of *Grey's*. Washington has addressed interracial relationship dynamics and how they "reproduce power relations that support the white privileged racial hegemony."[66] Extending her argument along a different trajectory, we focus on how these episodes explicitly address racism through hierarchical relationships—the doctor-patient relationship between Dr. Yang and a white supremacist patient alongside the supervisor-subordinate relationship of Drs. Bailey and Yang as those who perform his surgery.

After one ambulance crashes into another, a white male paramedic named Shane is injured but refuses to let Dr. Bailey treat him by initially asking for a male doctor. Dr. Webber, the black male chief of surgery, is then brought in to check Shane's abdomen. Shane refuses again and requests a "different doctor."[67] Dr. Webber quickly realizes that he wants a white doctor and tasks Dr. Bailey to take care of the situation. This storyline is anchored by Dr. Bailey's attempt to treat Shane and "rise above" the racist ideology that he represents. To do so, Dr. Bailey orders Dr. Yang to treat Shane since she is neither black nor white. To reveal how postracial strategies work in a storyline about two female doctors of color treating a white supremacist, we focus on the interactions between the characters as they navigate fulfilling their Hippocratic Oath amid Shane's refusal to be treated by black doctors.

First, Dr. Yang has little agency; she is trapped within the black/white binary and between black and white characters as a Korean woman. When pulled off Dr. Hahn's surgery to treat Shane, she caustically demands an explanation. Dr. Bailey responds, "You're not black, but you're not white either."[68] Knowing that undiagnosed internal injuries could kill Shane, Dr. Bailey instructs Dr. Yang to provide high quality treatment in accordance with the law. Dr. Yang lifts his shirt, exposing a large swastika tattooed on his stomach. This is disconcerting because she is Jewish, which Dr. Bailey does not yet know. Here, Dr. Yang is chosen because of her race without consideration of her religion. Equally problematic is that she was not chosen because of her medical skills; rather, Dr. Bailey tokenized her Korean identity and required that she perform the relatively menial function of examining a patient rather than gaining surgical experience. While medical care is typically understood as scientifically driven and socially neutral, these episodes reveal that sometimes it is not. While Drs. Bailey and Webber get to make choices about whether or not to confront Shane's racist tattoo, buttressed by their firm positionality in the black/white binary, Dr. Yang does not. Shane gets to choose not to have a black doctor, Drs. Bailey and Webber choose not to exercise their positional power and treat Shane regardless of his request, and Dr. Bailey chooses to "rise above" during Shane's surgery—all of these choices were made at Dr. Yang's expense since Shane's interests as the patient and Drs. Bailey and Webber's interests as her superiors were all prioritized above hers.

Nonetheless, Dr. Yang attempts to assert her agency and vocalizes that Dr. Bailey exploited her Korean identity by assigning Shane to her. Dr. Bailey's brash demeanor and her decision not to assign a white doctor reveal that she did so to challenge swastika-tattooed Shane's explicit representation of white supremacy. Dr. Yang calls Dr. Bailey out and says, "You know, what you did, pulling me off of Hahn's surgery was an abuse of power. . . . You used me because of the color of my skin. I mean, you compromised the quality of my education because of my color. I resent it."[69] In this scene, Dr. Yang regards Dr. Bailey's authorial choice to leverage her Korean identity in her fight against racism as disempowering and a reproduction of racism because Dr. Bailey's actions reduce Dr. Yang to skin color and bolster the black/white binary upon which white supremacist ideology thrives. While Dr. Bailey may view her actions as directly confronting white supremacist ideology, a way to refuse Shane what he wants (a white doctor) and an opportunity to train Dr. Yang in a multicultural work setting, Dr. Yang experiences Dr. Bailey's decision-making as misguided and professionally harmful.

Dr. Yang's racialized role in this storyline reaffirms the threat of blackness, specifically black intelligence, rather than challenging white supremacy. The swastika, as a symbol of racism and anti-Semitism, is not perceived by Dr. Yang as the primary threat. Rather, it is Dr. Bailey, who compromises Dr. Yang's excellence and education to reinscribe racial hierarchy by insisting that she treat Shane solely because she is Korean. This thread of the storyline focuses viewers' attention on the micro conflict between two women of color and away from how racism systemically manifests in medicine. Furthermore, Dr. Bailey falls prey to the "angry black woman" stereotype and becomes a threat to Asianness (e.g., Cristina's agency) and whiteness (e.g., Shane's body). When Dr. Bailey stitches up Shane's swastika unevenly near the end of his surgery, she scars his white body, damages the symbol of white supremacy, and challenges white superiority.

Captured by Dr. Bailey's transcendent emphasis on rising above, race and racism are depicted as a hindrance to medicine in these episodes. As Dr. Yang treats Shane, he states, "You gotta treat me like anyone else. That's the beauty of this country."[70] Later, when Drs. Yang and Bailey prep for a surgery, Dr. Yang indicates that her presence is unnecessary and informs Dr. Bailey that "he has a swastika on his abdomen, a giant black swastika. My stepfather's parents died in Auschwitz."[71] Dr. Bailey responds, "You and I will do this. We will do this, and we will consider ourselves having risen above. We'll rise above."[72] Here, to "rise above" can be viewed as an antiracist act; they will be better than the white supremacist patient by providing the same medical attention to him as to anyone else. Yet, Dr. Bailey upholds the postracial status quo by failing to apologize to Dr. Yang for unintentionally perpetuating racism and anti-Semitism and failing to acknowledge her intersectional hybrid identities as a racially Asian, ethnically Korean, and religiously Jewish woman.[73] Furthermore, intersectional identity differences function to discipline attempts at antiracist coalition building. When

Dr. Bailey attempts to forge a racial alliance despite the many ways she insults Dr. Yang, Dr. Yang reiterates that racism is not her primary concern as a surgeon and highlights Dr. Bailey's limited knowledge about her identities beyond tokenized Asianness. Led by Dr. Bailey's "rise above" attitude as a postracial emblem, viewers learn that race, racism, and anti-Semitism are to be transcended through individual actions and personal triumph that reaffirm postracial color-blindness in medicine. They also learn that blackness and whiteness are the natural default in racialized conflicts; consequently, Asian Americans are left somewhere in between.

CRISTINA'S TELEVISION LEGACY

Seldom in television has an Asian American character been as central to a show as Sandra Oh's Cristina Yang. Paradoxically, Cristina's significance on Grey's is typically partnered with the absence of racialized storylines that mirror the real world. While Grey's outwardly embraces postracialism as Shondaland's longest-running show, this chapter illustrates how race plays a highly functional role in constructing Cristina's character and juxtaposing Asian inferiority against white superiority. Over many seasons, interspersed throughout many episodes and specified in relation to non-Asian characters, Cristina is racialized in fragmented ways that build a pastiche of Asian American tropes that affirm the dominant racial hierarchy. With her robotic model minority presence and Dragon Lady–like manipulations to progress up the ranks, Cristina's excellence is formidable and distrusted. The omnipresence of these stereotypical tropes undermines her medical excellence and achievements as a steady reminder that she is not white. Moreover, her Asianness is seldom addressed to meaningfully highlight how race and racism impact the social institution of medicine. Rather, Grey's elides progressive racial discourse to reinforce postracial rhetorics of success and colorblindness—both are especially problematic because health disparities, access to health insurance and quality medical care, and opportunities to become medical professionals are highly racialized and influenced by institutional racism.[74] On the rare occasion that race is explicitly addressed on Grey's, it is often visually and narratively juxtaposed to triangulate whiteness and blackness, with Asianness caught in the middle. Absent the complex consideration of her intersectional identities, Cristina is portrayed in alignment with colorblindness, postracialism, whiteness, and the denial of racial justice as she attempts to become a revered cardiothoracic surgeon.

Whether race and racial dialogue are silent, absent, or present at any particular moment on Grey's Anatomy, the optics of race permeate the show. While we laud Cristina's character for her central role and complexity, the lack of racial discourse surrounding her character is a missed opportunity to re-envision and further complicate Asian American tropes. Shows like Grey's have racially diverse casts well-poised to critically address how race and racism function in the real world. Shonda Rhimes and Shondaland could script characters to openly discuss interracial differences, include more nuanced depictions of people of color, and directly interrogate whiteness and white privilege in storylines. In the absence of their willingness to do so, critical media scholars must continually question racialized power dynamics, examine limited representations of Asian Americans, and expose how television simultaneously supports and resists hegemonic discourses in a supposedly colorblind and postracial society. Simply stated, visible racial diversity and superficial representations of racial harmony should not be understood as an indication of racial equality on television or in the real world.

NOTES

1. *Grey's Anatomy*, "This Is How We Do It," season 7, episode 17, directed by Edward Ornelas, written by Shonda Rhimes and Peter Nowalk, aired on March 24, 2011, on ABC.

2. Lauren Hoffman, "Why Cristina Yang Leaving 'Grey's Anatomy' Is So Devastating," *Cosmopolitan*, May 15, 2014, http://www.cosmopolitan.com/entertainment/celebs/news/a6823/goodbye-cristina-yang/; Willa Paskin, "How Cristina Yang Changed Television," *Slate*, August 15, 2013, http://www.slate.com/blogs/browbeat/2013/08/15/sandra_oh_leaves_grey_s_anatomy_cristina_yang_her_character_changed_tv.html.

3. IMDb, "Sandra Oh Awards," February 20, 2016, http://www.imdb.com/name/nm0644897/awards.

4. Rachel Simon, "*Grey's Anatomy* Sandra Oh Deserves an Emmy Nomination & Here's Why," *Bustle*, June 5, 2014, http://www.bustle.com/articles/27044-greys-anatomys-sandra-oh-deserves-an-emmy-nomination-heres-why.

5. Stacy L. Smith, Marc Choueiti, and Katherine Pieper, "Inclusion or Invisibility? Comprehensive Annenberg Report on Diversity in Entertainment," *Media, Diversity, & Social Change Initiative* (Los Angeles: University of Southern California, Annenberg School for Communication and Journalism, 2016), 19.

6. See Amanda Hess, "Asian-American Actors Are Fighting for Visibility. They Will Not Be Ignored," *New York Times*, May 25, 2016, http://www.nytimes.com/2016/05/29/movies/asian-american-actors-are-fighting-for-visibility-they-will-not-be-ignored.html; Qin Zhang, "Asian Americans beyond the Model Minority Stereotype: The Nerdy and the Left Out," *Journal of International and Intercultural Communication* 3, no. 1 (2010): 20–37.

7. Sandra Gonzalez, "Sandra Oh, 'Grey's' Creator Shonda Rhimes Say Goodbye to Cristina," *Entertainment Weekly*, May 15, 2014, http://ew.com/article/2014/05/15/sandra-oh-greys-anatomy-cristina-farewell/.

8. See Kent A. Ono and Vincent N. Pham, *Asian Americans and the Media* (Malden, Mass.: Polity, 2009), 66, 84–86; Myra Washington, "Interracial Intimacy: Hegemonic Construction of Asian American and Black Relationships on TV Medical Dramas," *Howard Journal of Communication* 23, no. 3 (2012): 259; Kirthana Ramisetti, "What *Parks and Recreation* Could Learn from *Grey's Anatomy* about Friendship," *Atlantic*, October 31, 2013, http://www.theatlantic.com/entertainment/archive/2013/10/what-i-parks-and-recreation-i-could-learn-from-i-greys-anatomy-i-about-friendship/281036/; Mikaela Feroli, "A Deeper Cut: Enlightened Sexism and *Grey's Anatomy*," in *Smart Chicks on Screen: Representing Women's Intellect in Film and Television*, ed. Laura Mattoon D'Amore (Lanham, Md.: Rowman & Littlefield, 2014), 119–124; Erica

Chito Childs, *Fade to Black and White: Interracial Images in Popular Culture* (Lanham, Md.: Rowman & Littlefield, 2009), 40; Kristen J. Warner, "The Racial Logic of *Grey's Anatomy*: Shonda Rhimes and Her 'Post-Civil Rights, Post-Feminist' Series," *Television & New Media* 16, no. 7 (2015): 642; Washington, "Interracial Intimacy," 262.

9.   Kent A. Ono, "Postracism: A Theory of the 'Post' as Political Strategy," *Journal of Communication Inquiry* 34, no. 3 (2010): 227.

10.   Robert L. Scott, "Dialectical Tensions of Speaking and Silence." *Quarterly Journal of Speech* 79, no. 1 (1993): 16.

11.   Eduardo Bonilla-Silva, "From Bi-racial to Tri-racial: Towards a New System of Racial Stratification in the USA," *Ethnic and Racial Studies* 27, no. 6 (2004): 933.

12.   Norma Jones, "Beyond Suzie Wong? An Analysis of Sandra Oh's Portrayal in *Grey's Anatomy*" (master's thesis, University of North Texas, 2011), 1–180; Amy Long, "Diagnosing Drama: *Grey's Anatomy*, Blind Casting, and the Politics of Representation," *Journal of Popular Culture* 44, no. 5 (2011): 1067–1084; Washington, "Interracial Intimacy," 253–271.

13.   Vincent Brook, "Convergent Ethnicity and the Neo-Platoon Show: Recombining Difference in the Postnetwork Era," *Television & New Media* 10, no. 4 (2009): 331–332.

14.   Matthew Fogel, "*Grey's Anatomy* Goes Colorblind," *New York Times*, May 8, 2005, http://www.nytimes.com/2005/05/08/arts/television/greys-anatomy-goes-colorblind.html.

15.   Brook, "Convergent Ethnicity," 348.

16.   Wen Shen, "Is the Quest to Build a Kinder, Gentler Surgeon Misguided?," *Pacific Standard*, July 14, 2014, http://www.psmag.com/health-and-behavior/bloody-nice-better-cold-heartless-surgeons-84256.

17.   Michaela D. E. Meyer and Danielle M. Stern, "The Modern(?) Korean Woman in Prime Time: Analyzing the Representation of Sun on the Television Series *Lost*," *Women's Studies: An Interdisciplinary Journal* 36, no. 5 (2007): 313–331; John Greene and Michaela D. E. Meyer. "The Walking (Gendered) Dead: A Feminist Rhetorical Critique of Zombie Apocalypse Television Narrative," *Ohio Communication Journal* 52 (2014): 64–74.

18.   Colleen Oakley, "Interview with Shonda Rhimes: Five Questions for *Grey's Anatomy* Writer, Creator, and Executive Producer, Shonda Rhimes," *Marie Claire*, April 8, 2007, http://www.marieclaire.com/celebrity/a333/greys-anatomy/.

19.   Angelica Jade Bastién, "The Case against Colorblind Casting," *Atlantic*, December 26, 2015, http://www.theatlantic.com/entertainment/archive/2015/12/oscar-isaac-and-the-case-against-colorblind-casting/421668/.

20.   Monnica T. Williams, "Colorblind Ideology Is a Form of Racism," *Psychology Today*, December 27, 2011, https://www.psychologytoday.com/blog/culturally-speaking/201112/colorblind-ideology-is-form-racism; Mark Orbe, "#AllLivesMatter as Post-Racial Rhetorical Strategy," *Journal of Contemporary Rhetoric* 5, no. 3–4 (2015): 94.

21.   Ono, "Postracism," 22.

22.   Amy Adele Hasinoff, "Fashioning Race for the Free Market on *America's Next Top Model*," *Critical Studies in Media Communication* 25, no. 3 (2008): 330.

23.   Warner, "Racial Logic of *Grey's Anatomy*," 637.

24.   David C. Oh and Omotayo O. Banjo, "Outsourcing Postracialism: Voicing Neoliberal Multiculturalism in *Outsourced*," *Communication Theory* 22, no. 4 (2012): 453.

25.   David Theo Goldberg, *The Threat of Race: Reflections on Racial Neoliberalism* (Malden, Mass.: Blackwell, 2009).

26.   Eduardo Bonilla-Silva and Austin Ashe, "The End of Racism: Colorblind Racism and Popular Media," in *The Colorblind Screen*, ed. Sarah Nilsen and Sarah E. Turner (New York: New York University Press, 2014), 67.

27. Ann Louise Keating, "Interrogating 'Whiteness,' (De)Constructing 'Race,'" *College English* 57, no. 8 (1995), 905; Thomas Nakayama and Robert L. Krizek, "Whiteness: A Strategic Rhetoric," *Quarterly Journal of Speech* 81, no. 3 (1995): 293.

28. Bastién, "The Case Against Colorblind Casting."

29. Ono and Pham, *Asian Americans and the Media*, 7; Michael Omi and Howard Winant, *Racial Formation in the United States*, 3rd ed. (New York: Routledge, 2015).

30. Michael Calvin McGee, "Text, Context, and the Fragmentation of Contemporary Culture," *Western Journal of Speech* 54, no. 3 (1990): 274–289.

31. Bonnie J. Dow, "Response Criticism and Authority in the Artistic Mode," *Western Journal of Communication* 65, no. 3 (2001): 336–349.

32. Vincent N. Pham, "Our Foreign President Barack Obama: The Racial Logics of Birther Discourses," *Journal of International and Intercultural Communication* 8, no. 2 (2015): 86–107.

33. *Grey's Anatomy* has been praised for being racially diverse; however, few have critiqued the series for the lack of representation of Asian American medical professionals that would be more demographically typical of "real" U.S. hospitals. According to the Association of American Medical Colleges, in 2013, 11.7 percent of all active physicians in the United States were Asian. The other recurring Asian character in *Grey's* is Bokhee, a scrub nurse, who is present in many surgeries but speaks few lines.

34. Claire Jean Kim, "The Racial Triangulation of Asian Americans," *Politics & Society* 27, no. 1 (1999): 105.

35. *Grey's Anatomy*, "The First Cut Is the Deepest," season 1, episode 2, directed by Peter Horton, written by Shonda Rhimes, aired on April 5, 2005, on ABC.

36. *Grey's Anatomy*, "The First Cut Is the Deepest."

37. *Grey's Anatomy*, "I Am a Tree," season 3, episode 2, directed by Jeff Melman, written by Krista Vernoff, aired on September 28, 2006, on ABC.

38. Phil Chidester, "May the Circle Stay Unbroken: *Friends*, The Presence of Absence, and the Rhetorical Reinforcement of Whiteness," *Critical Studies in Media Communication* 25, no. 2 (2008): 157.

39. Washington, "Interracial Intimacy," 267.

40. Kenneth Burke, *The Philosophy of Literary Form*, 3rd ed. (Berkeley: University of California Press, 1973), 293–304.

41. *Grey's Anatomy*, "Piece of My Heart," season 4, episode 13, directed by Mark Tinker, written by Stacy McKee, aired on May 1, 2008, on ABC.

42. Shoba Sharad Rajgopal, "'The Daughter of Fu Manchu': The Pedagogy of Deconstructing the Representation of Asian Women in Film and Fiction," *Meridians: Feminism, Race, Transnationalism* 10, no. 2 (2010): 155.

43. Ono and Pham, *Asian Americans and the Media*, 83.

44. Thomas Nakayama, "Model Minority and the Media: Discourse on Asian America," *Journal of Communication Inquiry* 12, no. 1 (1988): 70.

45. *Grey's Anatomy*, "Begin the Begin," season 2, episode 13, directed by Jessica Yu, written by Kip Koenig, aired on January 15, 2006, on ABC.

46. *Grey's Anatomy*, "Didn't We Almost Have It All?," season 3, episode 25, directed by Tony Phelan and Joan Rater, written by Rob Corn, aired on May 17, 2007, on ABC.

47. *Grey's Anatomy*, "I Will Survive," season 7, episode 21, directed by Zoanne Clack, written by Tom Verica, aired on May 12, 2011, on ABC.

48. *Grey's Anatomy*, "Raindrops Keep Falling on My Head," season 2, episode 1, directed by Peter Horton, written by Stacy McKee, aired on September 25, 2005, on ABC.

49. *Grey's Anatomy*, "Blink," season 6, episode 11, directed by Randy Zisk, written by Debora Cahn, aired on January 14, 2010, on ABC.

50. *Grey's Anatomy*, "Winning a Battle, Losing the War," season 1, episode 3, directed by Tony Goldwyn, written by Shonda Rhimes, aired on April 10, 2005, on ABC.

51. *Grey's Anatomy*, "Deny, Deny, Deny," season 2, episode 4, directed by Wendy Stanzler, written by Zoane Clack, aired on October 16, 2005, on ABC.

52. *Grey's Anatomy*, "Deny, Deny, Deny."

53. *Grey's Anatomy*, "Staring at the Sun," season 3, episode 8, directed by Jeff Melman, written by Gabrielle Stanton and Harry Werksman Jr., aired on November 16, 2006, on ABC.

54. *Grey's Anatomy*, "Six Days (Part 2)," season 3, episode 12, directed by Greg Yaitanes written by Krista Vernoff, aired on January 18, 2007, on ABC.

55. *Grey's Anatomy*, "The Heart of the Matter," season 4, episode 4, directed by Randall Zisk, written by Allan Heinberg, aired on October 18, 2007, on ABC.

56. *Grey's Anatomy*, "White Wedding," season 7, episode 20, directed by Chandra Wilson, written by Stacy McKee, aired on May 5, 2011, on ABC.

57. Ono and Pham, *Asian Americans and the Media*, 38.

58. Sheridan Prasso, *Asian Mystique: Dragon Ladies, Geisha Girls, and Our Fantasies of the Exotic Orient* (New York: Public Affairs, 2006), 86; Ono and Pham, *Asian Americans and the Media*, 66.

59. *Grey's Anatomy*, "If Tomorrow Never Comes," season 1, episode 6, directed by Scott Brazil, written by Krista Vernoff, aired on May 1, 2005, on ABC.

60. Washington, "Interracial Intimacy," 259.

61. *Grey's Anatomy*, "I Will Survive."

62. *Grey's Anatomy*, "Haunt You Everyday," season 4, episode 5, directed by Bethany Rooney, written by Krista Vernoff, aired on October 25, 2007, on ABC.

63. *Grey's Anatomy*, "Haunt You Everyday."

64. Jane Hyun, *Breaking the Bamboo Ceiling: Career Strategies for Asians* (New York: Harper Business, 2006). The bamboo ceiling (like the "glass ceiling") refers to the characteristics of bad communication and leadership skills commonly ascribed to Asians.

65. *Grey's Anatomy*, "Crash into Me: Part 1," season 4, episode 9, directed by Michael Grossman, written by Shonda Rhimes and Krista Vernoff, aired on November 22, 2007, on ABC; *Grey's Anatomy*, "Crash into Me: Part 2," season 4, episode 10, directed by Jessica Yu, written by Shonda Rhimes and Krista Vernoff, aired on December 6, 2007, on ABC.

66. Washington, "Interracial Intimacy," 256.

67. *Grey's Anatomy*, "Crash into Me: Part 1."

68. *Grey's Anatomy*, "Crash into Me: Part 1."

69. *Grey's Anatomy*, "Crash into Me: Part 2."

70. *Grey's Anatomy*, "Crash into Me: Part 2."

71. *Grey's Anatomy*, "Crash into Me: Part 2."

72. *Grey's Anatomy*. "Crash into Me: Part 1."

73. Beyond superficial acknowledgment of her Jewishness (e.g., her disclosure to Burke that she does not celebrate Christmas; her explanation of shivah to Izzie after Denny's death), Yang's Jewish identity plays a relatively small role within the show.

74. See Centers for Disease Control and Prevention, "CDC Health Disparities & Inequalities Report (CHDIR)—United States, 2013" in *Morbidity and Mortality Weekly Report (MMWR)*, Supplement 62, no. 3 (November 22, 2013), 1–186, http://www.cdc.gov/minorityhealth /chdireport.html; Lesley Russell, *Fact Sheet: Health Disparities by Race and Ethnicity* (Washington, D.C.: Center for American Progress, 2010), https://www.americanprogress.org/issues /healthcare/news/2010/12/16/8762/fact-sheet-health-disparities-by-race-and-ethnicity/.

8 · INTERRACIAL INTIMACIES
From Shondaland to the Postracial Promised Land

MYRA WASHINGTON AND TINA M. HARRIS

On small and silver screens alike, interracial couplings of Black women and White men expose the layered tensions between recognizing the salience of race and the desire to transcend race as a quotidian force.[1] This tension has created critical opportunities for entertainment media to challenge hegemonic ideologies by creating truly transformative representations that allow the widest range of progressive images to flourish. Interracial pairings and the opportunities they create for change are noteworthy because White men are instrumental in highlighting the desirability of Black women, who have long been framed as undesirable partners for long-term and serious romantic relationships on television.[2] In nearly fifty years—from Captain Kirk and Lieutenant Uhura's first interracial kiss on U.S. television in 1968 on *Star Trek* (NBC 1966–1969) to Helen and Tom Willis on *The Jeffersons* (CBS 1975–1985) to current Shondaland shows—the historical rarity of Black female/White male interracial romantic relationships has shifted toward increasing prominence and familiarity.[3] Since media and cultural texts are polysemic and therefore allow myriad audience interpretations, interracial relationships can, for example, be simultaneously interpreted as barometers of racial reconciliation, corruption of Whiteness, and fetishization of Blackness.[4]

SHONDALAND'S TRANSDISCURSIVITY

Examining these divergent readings of interracial intimacies is paramount to deconstructing Shonda Rhimes's problematic reliance on colorblindness coupled with her postracial vision of society. Portraying these twisted logics on television is crucial to "articulations of post-racialism" in the real world.[5] Though the terms colorblindness and postracialism are often erroneously used interchangeably, we, like Haney-López, situate postracial narratives as "the rhetorical response to color-blindness."[6] Furthermore, postracialism "constitutes a liberal embrace of color-blindness . . . in a way likely to limit progress toward increased racial equality."[7] Support for postracialism is rooted in the belief of a race-neutral universalism because racial divisions have been transcended. To critique representations of interracial romance between Black women and White men in Shondaland's *Scandal* (ABC 2012–2018) and *How to Get Away with Murder* (also referred to as *HTGAWM*) (ABC 2014–present), this chapter is conceptually grounded in what Foucault terms a *transdiscursive authorship*.[8] Transdiscursive authorship refers to the "possibilities and the rules for the formation of other texts."[9] Amid Shonda-land's clout, transdiscursive authorship highlights how the production company cultivates industry standards for a nascent genre of television shows implementing Shondaland's discursive practices. Kincheloe and Berry remind us that "discourse cannot be removed from power relations and the struggle to create particular meanings and legitimate specific voices."[10] Therefore, critiques of Shondaland must first engage the tensions around intersectional identity politics (e.g., race and gender) that contextualize Rhimes's vision of the televisual landscape and then subsequently deconstruct the influence of her vision and success in the larger television industry.

Theorizing *Scandal* and *HTGAWM* requires situating these shows amid con-textual factors that inform and frame televisual representations of interracial relationships. Particular to our argument about race, distinguishing between colorblindness and postracialism is essential because they overlap and differ in ways that are often overlooked. Colorblindness, as Bonilla-Silva defines it, con-fines racism to individual actions and preferences, cultural practices, or instances that should be minimized or ignored rather than recognizing racism as an institutionalized system of oppression.[11] Childs notes that framing interracial relationships via colorblind discourses is "problematic because it ignores, even disguises, the power and privilege that still characterize race relations in this country."[12] While colorblindness acknowledges race but negates its significance, postracialism necessitates the contemporary erasure of race via transcendent logics—even though both continue to shape and structure life in the United States. Postracial discourses allow "whites to oppose civil-rights remedies and advocate for race-neutral policies because society has transcended the racial moment, or civil rights era. Under post-racialism, race does not matter, and should not be taken into account or even noticed."[13] Postracialism and colorblindness are racial logics that function to benefit Whiteness and manifest in myriad ways including opposition to integration efforts, mass incarceration of people of color, rejection of affirmative action policies, and continued voter disenfranchisement.

On *Scandal* and *HTGAWM*, the romantic relationships between Black women and White men are essential to each show's narrative arc and each coupling has incited audience investment in how the relationships evolve. Olivia Pope and

Fitzgerald Grant and Olivia and Jake Ballard on *Scandal* and Annalise Keating and Sam Keating on *HTGAWM* are three highly popular Black women/White men pairings on prime-time television, and the subjects of our analysis. Viewers commonly pledge their support for particular couples via social media and partake in polls online where, for example, *Scandal* viewers cast votes for Jake or Fitz.[14] Additionally, memes mock the embroiled love triangle between Olivia, Fitz, and Jake mirroring ABC's official promotional materials that visually position Olivia between the two men.[15] Similarly invested, *HTGAWM* viewers on Twitter renamed the show "How to have an interracial relationship" because nearly all of the characters are or have been part of an interracial pair.[16] Memes on the Annalise and Sam relationship focus on and mock the failures of their interracial pairing—affairs, miscarriages, death.[17] Generally, Shondaland's extremely popular interracial unions are typically praised for offering postracial dreams or criticized for representations that are racially regressive. For example, *New York Times* columnist Alessandra Stanley lauds Rhimes's lead characters because they struggle with "everything except their own identities, [they are] so unconcerned about race that it is barely ever mentioned."[18] Stanley is echoing *New Yorker* columnist Emily Nussbaum's thoughts on *Scandal's* series debut, where she predicts "that *Scandal's* post-racial fantasy will feel refreshing, for black viewers and non-black ones, in varying ways. It removes the weight of both race and racism: Pope is never referred to as the 'first black' anything."[19] In contrast, Rosenberg pointedly objects in the *Washington Post* by noting that *Scandal* exists in a "fantasy-land" that makes "racism seem like an easier foe than it actually is."[20] The dichotomy revealed in critics' interpretations can also be mapped onto similar binaries like inclusion versus exclusion, desirable versus undesirable, and good versus bad. That these dichotomies mirror the Black/White racial binary is not coincidental; rather, these dichotomies highlight how Shondaland strategically relies on and abjures race. We make this tension visible by centering our focus on specific interracial couplings and analyzing the contested, ambiguous space between binary opposites. Key to our argument is a close examination of how postracial and colorblind discourses in Shondaland minimize race and its structuring power. These reductive treatments of race transdiscursively function as a problematic guide for other showrunners, television shows, and networks to similarly and profitably navigate the current racial terrain.

CASTING DIVERSITY

Analyzing casting decisions and interracial representations in Shondaland highlights the conflicts between what viewers see on screen and Rhimes's racialized objectives, illustrating how discourses of colorblindness and postracialism work in concert to maintain normative Whiteness cloaked in the façade of racial progress. We also situate key casting decisions within extradiegetic contexts including Rhimes's interviews and speeches for insight into the workings of production. Taken altogether, these elements form a transdiscursive body of work that provides signs, tropes, character and narrative archetypes, norms, and structures for other showrunners to replicate Shondaland's highly successful signature formula. Focusing on formulaic representations of interracial relationships, we critique *Scandal* and *HTGAWM* in order to complicate reductionist readings by recognizing the tensions produced by colorblind and postracial representations. Significantly, our analysis undermines Shondaland's embrace of colorblind and postracial discourses—we do not read interracial relationships as singularly exceptional or deviant. Ultimately, we conclude that Shondaland's colorblind efforts to usher in a postracial utopia work to reinscribe the significance of race from production to audience reception.

Debates about diversity in television; more specifically, the lack of diversity *on* television have been happening since its invention.[21] When *Scandal* premiered in 2012 and *HTGAWM* in 2014, shows such as HBO's *Girls* (2011–2017) were heavily criticized for the absence of people of color, despite being set in New York City.[22] ABC Family's *Bunheads* (2012–2013) was similarly criticized by Rhimes for not casting "even one dancer of color" in the show.[23] Additionally, discussions about whether including token representation was better than having all-White casts populated the news cycle, and media commentators highlighted how few shows, particularly on network channels, featured actors of color.[24] Amid these debates and discussions, Rhimes's Shondaland programming was praised for influencing the televisual landscape by showcasing how well racially diverse shows could do in the ratings.[25] Rhimes's showrunner ethos emerged against this backdrop, and she described her approach to casting and representation as one that neutralizes the racial differences between and among characters by "crafting complex, original characters unconstrained by such singular definitions as 'Black,' 'Asian' or 'gay.'"[26] She uses colorblindness to create shows where race "no longer correlates with privilege or disadvantage, and so carries no meanings tied to established hierarchies."[27] When asked about her casting choices, in reference to diversity on TV, Rhimes replies, "I think it's sad, and weird, and strange that it's still a thing."[28]

Rhimes's explicit reliance on the combination of colorblindness and postracialism allows for the creation of her ideal multicultural televisual space where she can "ignore race and racism and celebrate the invisibility of racial identity."[29] Rhimes's, and by extension Shondaland's, disavowal of the salience of race and other identity markers is a critical component of Shondaland's transdiscursive authorship. Analyzing her shows within these twinning discourses of colorblindness and postracialism push critical scholars to read Shondaland as something other than solely progressive and woke. Thus, despite the outward appearance of racial diversity, Shondaland shows partake in a discursive assemblage that purposely reifies racial normativity.

According to Rhimes's interviews, the success of Shondaland as an industry model for other shows is rooted in casting practices. This process is referred to as open or blind-casting, meaning the characters are not written with an ethnicity in mind and are open to all auditioning actors.[30] Rhimes defends her reliance on, and the importance of, blind-casting by pointing out that "it works. Ratings-wise, it works."[31] However, blind-casting, like colorblindness, is a counterintuitive strategy that presumes to solve the issue of race by ignoring race. Still Rhimes favors this strategy while paradoxically noting that diversity is necessary. She says, "It's not necessarily intentional. We have a really diverse cast, which was important to me that we bring in actors of every color for every role. I wanted a world that looked like the world I lived in. . . . I feel like they're three-dimensional characters, which, when you only have one character of color in a show, doesn't necessarily get to happen."[32]

Blind-casting's problematic nature is revealed through Rhimes's contradictory positions on the importance of diversity for character development coupled with the insignificance of diversity for casting the characters themselves. Rhimes's utilization of these conflicting strategies transdiscursively promotes the industry's standard commitment to Whiteness by offering cover for industry professionals who similarly justify their all-White, predominately White, and stereotypical casting choices as the result of a meritocratic, colorblind audition process. After all, according to dominant racial logics, not getting a role reflects lack of talent rather than persistent systemic inequalities. The prevailing view in the industry is that "it's a perfectly efficient system and it's entirely meritocratic, so if women aren't as successful, and if people of color aren't as successful they're simply not as good at it as good white men."[33] The long history of mediated Whitewashing, or racebending, demonstrates that casting has always worked to the benefit of Whiteness.[34] White actors, including those who pass for White or appear racially ambiguous in close proximity to Whiteness, like Vin Diesel, are already over-whelmingly cast—even when the roles are meant or written for people of color.[35] When producers like Rhimes choose not to see color and their industry practices declare its irrelevance, they perpetuate the idea that race no longer matters even though institutionalized racism continues to be a significant determinant regarding who auditions and which roles they are ultimately cast in.

Critically attending colorblindness reveals the contradiction between Rhimes's discouragement of purposefully diverse casting and her encouragement of purposeful diversity for character development. This tension is not unexpected, as Doane explains how the allure of colorblind discourses lies in the ability "to hold simultaneous—and contradictory—positions—for example, that racial inequality and white privilege persist, but that racism is not widespread. This allows for such conflicting phenomena as colorblind diversity, the condemnation of racists, minority racism/white victimization, racial awareness in a 'colorblind' society, and reverse exceptionalism, all supported by an overarching belief that

American society is fundamentally meritocratic."[36] Doane's insight reveals how Rhimes ensconces herself within a discourse of colorblindness that fuels postracialism and reinforces racial hierarchies that ultimately prize Whiteness through her refusal to attend to the material effects of race and structural inequality.[37] Interestingly, this is how she can criticize *Bunheads* for not featuring "even one" dancer of color while simultaneously bristling at the request to address race more complexly in her own shows.[38]

Alongside her narrations of Shondaland's production practices, Rhimes unequivocally invokes postracialism in interviews and profiles when diversity in Hollywood is featured. In a *New York Times* interview she notes, "My friends and I don't sit around and discuss race. We're post-civil rights, post-feminist babies, and we take it for granted we live in a diverse world."[39] This sort of refrain is echoed by White showrunners like *House of Cards*'s (Netflix 2013–present) Beau Willimon who when asked about his approach to diversity replied "I think that our responsibility is to tell the truth, and if you're telling the truth about your given sliver, however narrow or wide it is, then you're contributing to the overall diversity of our collective story."[40] If telling any story—even those told time and time again as Willimon advocates—is a demonstration of diversity in action, diversity then becomes everything and is subsequently rendered inconsequential. Rhimes repeatedly activates this response when asked to explain her production decisions: "It's not shocking if the guy running the hospital is Black. It's not shocking if the surgeon is Black. If you accept it as reality instead of making it a very special episode of *Grey's Anatomy* where people discuss race which would make me crazy, it seems like the show could be about something more. And once you start seeing these people as people [as opposed to] the color of their skin, you begin to maybe see the people in your grocery store as more than the color of their skin."[41]

Coupling Rhimes's very public embrace of postracialism with her blind-casting strategy is the only way Shondaland's attempt at unspoken diversity can operate successfully. Having a Black surgeon (or Black showrunner) who never addresses or is forced to confront the materiality of race happens because postracial discourses flatten "cultural markers—such as vernacular, diction, fashion, hairstyles, extended family, or accompanying traditions associated with kinfolk," ensuring racialized struggles are never resolved.[42] For Rhimes, race becomes a nonfactor as she recognizes "race but only as a signal of its legacies having been defeated."[43] She also conflates race with skin color and the mere visibility of people of color with racial progress and inclusion. This allows her, and other showrunners who follow Shondaland's transdiscursive model, to ignore obligations to address and challenge racism. By merging the treatment of characters' racial identities with the treatment of race in her personal life, Rhimes refuses to explicitly address its influence, which functions as a detriment to progressive societal understandings of race and racism: "[When producers] have one character of color on their show, that character spends all their time talking about the world as 'I'm a black man blah, blah, blah,' . . . that's not how the world works. I'm a black woman every day, and I'm not confused about that. I'm not worried about that. I don't need to have a discussion with you about how I feel as a black woman, because I don't feel disempowered as a black woman."[44] Tellingly, Rhimes's comment frames race as an individualized experience and discounts the reality of racism as systemic. Since she does not feel disempowered as an individual Black woman, her postracial emphasis on its unimportance cuts off the possibility of recognizing that many others can be and actually are disempowered because of race.

FORMULA FOR SUCCESS

If colorblindness "aspires to retreat from race," then postracialism "authorizes the retreat from race,"[45] and Rhimes's commitment to these twin discourses ignores and erases how power, culture, and race shape U.S. society. Much of Shondaland's appeal as a transdiscursive force is that it rescues media from having to structurally change the industry. Both colorblind and postracial discourses allow for the proliferation of normative ideologies as both strategically deploy racial progress to silence critiques of persisting inequalities. Furthermore, both discourses push media to create representations and narratives in "which race is no longer a basis for differential treatment, grievance, or remedy."[46] Therefore, instead of utilizing race to connect and enlighten viewers, Shondaland's formula, and by extension, the shows that follow its transdiscursive lead, replaces racial differences with a brand that universally caters to Whiteness.

In *Scandal* and *HTGAWM*, key series plotlines revolve around the romantic relationships between Black women and White men. These relationships, rarely featured between lead characters on prime-time television, are so central to each show that the storylines would falter without them as sources of epitasis. In *Scandal*, Olivia Pope is a Washington, D.C., political fixer who alternates between romantic involvement with the married president of the United States Fitzgerald Grant and his military confidante Jake Ballard. In *HTGAWM*, Annalise Keating is a criminal attorney and law school professor married to psychologist, professor, and philanderer Sam Keating. The importance of these interracial relationships outwardly seems to counter the colorblind and postracial discourses deployed by Rhimes and Shondaland. However, we argue that these discourses actually deracialize the interracial component of the relationships, emptying them of "any particular histories, social structures, or structural inequalities."[47] In addition to serving as crucial plot devices, these interracial relationships symbolize "a transgression of symbolic racial borders and provide a space for groups to express and play out their ideas and prejudices about race and sex . . . since interracial couples exist at the color line within society, the ideas and beliefs about these unions are a lens through which we can understand contemporary race relations."[48] In the sections that follow, we offer pointed examples of how Shondaland has created a successful formula that simultaneously relies on racial stereotypes while dismissing the significance of race.

During its first season, *Scandal* took great pains not to address race. As a woman of color, Olivia enabled the elision of racial tensions through her "exceptional presence," keeping with the utopic postracial viewing experience provided by Shondaland; one that "removes the weight of both race and racism."[49] Her crisis management firm, Pope and Associates, successfully fixes problems for mainly White clients ranging from politicians to judiciaries to White House aides and interns. In a city as racially, ethnically, and culturally diverse as Washington, D.C., the lack of people of color should be distractingly obvious, yet it is barely noticeable. The lack of diegetic racial diversity aligns with Rhimes's colorblind philosophy; as such, *Scandal* is deeply "concerned with adapting to White cultural norms rather than devoting any significant attention to the real, material concerns of Black society."[50] Olivia is positioned as a desirable and attractive woman, but never specifically as a desirable and attractive Black woman. As her affair with the president unfolds throughout the first season, the extraordinariness of a Black woman having an affair with a White, Republican president is largely ignored. During an exchange with the president's chief of staff, Cyrus Beene, Olivia and Fitz's relationship is reduced to mere tabloid fodder instead of the explosive news dominating scandal it becomes by season 5. As Cyrus berates Olivia, he revealingly barks, "What happened? You danced? He said he loved you? What, are you gonna go meet him right now? You're being played by the best politician in the world. The upside? The tell-all book that you can write when you're old: *The President's Whore*."[51]

Calling Olivia a "whore" signals the interlocking discourses of race, class, gender, and sexuality, which offers a perfect opportunity for Rhimes and her team to address how the insult degrades Black women's sexuality. Instead, the show conveys the banality of the insult through literal silencing as Olivia is escorted out of the scene and unable to respond. This exchange ignores the racialized specter of Black hypersexuality that Cyrus conjures up to shame Olivia as a Black woman having an affair with a much more powerful White man. In scenes like these, when identity politics clearly surface, they are quickly shunned in favor of the postidentity politics fantasy. For instance, although mutually volatile anger in this scene is featured, the political dynamics of a Black woman being called a whore by a gay White man are obvious but unnamed. Aligning with colorblind and postracial discourses, this regrettably allows audiences to disarticulate both characters from their racial identities. In turn, their disarticulation and dismissal of race—vis-à-vis Shondaland's separation of race from any mooring in political, economic, and cultural structures—remains loyal to Whiteness and ensures viewers have an uninterrupted normative televisual experience.

Race also plays a central role in framing the relationship between Olivia and Fitz. *Scandal*'s success is predicated on the audience's ability to recognize racialized tropes, such as the hypersexual Black woman, and their attendant anxieties regarding the power of Black sexuality to corrupt Whiteness. A key scene in season 5 shows First Lady Mellie Grant informing Olivia's imprisoned father, Rowan Pope, about the unfolding scandal around the affair. Mellie tells Rowan the news coverage is framing Olivia as "a whore, a homewrecker, a slut who repeatedly spread her legs to get to the top."[52] When audiences watch Cyrus berate Olivia or Mellie take pleasure in Olivia's ruin, we are implicated in historical scripts that denigrate Black women's bodies as provocative, excessive, oversexed, and without value unless they are used for the sexual pleasure and sustainment of White others. Fitz and Olivia's inability to refrain from sex regardless of the setting and the professional jeopardy and personal risk they are courting reflects a narrative saturated with stereotypical portrayals of Blackness framed by an overreliance on the body, underreliance on intellect, and the inability to transcend baser instincts. In contrast, Cyrus and Fitz are not essentialized reflections of terrible White men everywhere. The generalizability of Blackness contrasted against the specificity of Whiteness are manifestations of the deployment of postracialism and colorblindness. This is because Whiteness is so often unremarked upon—it exists without any narrative constraints that might disrupt what Frankenberg and hooks refer to as its myth of sameness.[53] The myth of sameness is rooted in the belief that we share a universal humanness that removes the need to address "differences" such as race. So while Olivia's treatment so clearly aligns with familiar racist and sexist tropes, viewers can easily disregard how race has constituted the representations they see on screen.

HEADING TO THE PROMISED LAND

During *Scandal*'s second season, in response to the criticism regarding the portrayal of race, the show attempted to overtly acknowledge the significance of race. Using Olivia and Fitz's relationship as its continued epitasis, their interracial romance triggered all of the main characters to behave badly, which led to multiple attacks against the presidency, Olivia's firm, and their relationship. In its most obvious reference to race and interracial dynamics, the show compared Olivia and Fitz's relationship to that of Sally Hemings and the third U.S. president, Thomas Jefferson. Hemings was the Black woman enslaved by Jefferson and therefore victimized by his state-sponsored sexual coercion. Flashing back to Fitz's early days as president, Olivia attempts to end their relationship through a reference to Hemings and Jefferson. She says, "I'm feeling a little, I don't know, Sally Hemings/Thomas Jefferson about all this."[54] Later in the episode, Fitz confronts Olivia, describing her comparison as "below the belt":

FITZ: The Sally Hemings/Thomas Jefferson comment—was below the belt.
OLIVIA: Because it's so untrue?

FITZ: You're playing the race card on the fact that I'm in love with you? Come on. Don't belittle us. It's insulting and beneath you and designed to drive me away. I'm not going away . . .

OLIVIA: . . . You own me. You control me. I belong to you, I—

FITZ: . . . There's no Sally or Thomas here. You're nobody's victim, Liv. I belong to you.

Olivia's agency to choose their relationship and consent to sex, despite the very real power differential between her and Fitz, renders the Hemings/Jefferson comparison flawed and offensive. Olivia's comparison fits within the Shondaland formula as it allows the show to mention race, which acknowledges the parallel racial composition, without addressing the attendant ramifications of racism, such as a relationship between a master and slave. Fitz's accusation that Olivia's glib reference to a historically antecedent and racist relationship is insulting fits seamlessly within postracial discourse. Only within this discourse could a racist not be the person who racially subjugates and oppresses like Fitz and Jefferson before him. Rather, the racist hitting below the proverbial belt is the person who draws any attention whatsoever to race. Via postracialism, accusations of playing the race card are the ultimate way to shut down critiques of racism by attempting to shame the person who brings up race. Fitz's dismissal of Olivia's comparison also highlights how Whiteness disregards the perspectives of people of color in its quest not to see or consider race while invoking colorblindness. His insistence that Olivia not play the victim, in addition to the way he frames himself as the injured party, is an example of how colorblind discourses manipulate the language and remedies of race-based programs. His dismissal also depicts him as more knowledgeable than Olivia about both racism and Blackness.

Another penultimate scene in season 2 of *Scandal* offers a key moment when the twisted logics of colorblindness and postracialism combine to promote the show as racially progressive only to reveal it as anything but. Fitz delivers a fiery monologue to his wife, First Lady Mellie Grant, after demanding a divorce:

> My relationship with Olivia is going to spark a real dialogue about race in this country, and it is going to blow the Republican party wide open and let some light and air into places that haven't seen change in far too long. So the party will love her. And you want to be on the right side of history here. . . . If you refuse to go gently, well, it only takes a few whispers of the word "racist" for the feminist groups and the religious groups and even the Republican national committee to turn up their noses at your stink.[55]

Interracial relationships have existed for as long as there have been races, and yet these relationships have not eradicated racism because while they appear to be signs of racial progress, they are rarely leveraged to structurally dismantle White supremacy. Fitz's assertion that his interracial relationship with Olivia will substantially change the Republican Party, and his threat to brand Mellie as "racist" for decrying their extramarital-perhaps-soon-to-be-legitimate relationship converges colorblindness and postracialism into a neat package that maintains normative Whiteness. The relationship between Olivia and Fitz does not advocate for race-based action or remedies; hence, racist ideologies and policies remain unchallenged. In short, the presence of one Black woman in the White House, whether her presence is personal or professional, does nothing to abate anti-Black racism and unseat White dominance. Fitz ends his tirade with an invitation for Mellie to embrace his interracial relationship with Olivia and join him "as a living, breathing monument to redemption and second chances and the America we all hope still exists."[56] He sees racism as an entity that used to plague the United States and distances himself from the retrograde, conservative people who continue to believe in its salience. *Scandal* idealizes the United States as a country in which this interracial romance conveniently becomes a barometer of racial acceptance that progressively challenges and changes both the political landscape and ostensibly racist White U.S. Americans.

The third season of *Scandal* finds Olivia in a love triangle with Fitz and his friend Jake Ballard, the military officer charged by Fitz to surveil and protect her. In the season finale, Olivia makes the choice to leave Washington, D.C., and to leave both men behind. Jake confronts her as she sets out to leave:[57]

OLIVIA: This is not a pity party. This is me doing what I do best. I'm handling this. I'm fixing this. . . . I'm the thing that needs to be fixed, I'm the thing that needs to be handled. I'm the scandal. And the best way to deal with a scandal is to shut it down.
JAKE: Take me with you. Take me with you. Run away with me. Save me.

This exchange highlights how postracial discourse reduces the fallout from the relationship between Olivia and Fitz to her individual failings rather than an outcome conditioned by centuries of oppression. Furthermore, Jake's demand that Olivia save him by choosing their relationship doubles as mammification and a means for them to become racially transcendent.[58] As the protagonist, Olivia must choose between being a good Black woman and nurturing Whiteness at the expense of her Blackness or being the bad Black woman who rejects Whiteness. Should she choose the latter, colorblindness affirms that Olivia is the problem as a discomfiting object whose presence ensures race cannot be ignored unless she (and by extension race) is removed. Ultimately, her choice to take Jake with her gives the show a reprieve from having to reckon with Olivia's Blackness and race. The tension that arises from relying on both postracial and colorblind discourses are the same tensions that arise between fixing Olivia's disruptive raced and gendered presence and rejecting the focus on her raced and gendered body.

BROKEN (POSTRACIAL) PROMISES

As the scene between Jake and Olivia ends with a promise to "stand in the sun," the season ends by convincingly encouraging viewers to embrace *Scandal*'s color-blind and postracial discourses in the name of love and idyllic locales.[59] We interpret standing in the sun as a metaphor for Rhimes's postracial Promised Land, which is also a command (or endorsement) to ignore identity politics and inequality by "leaving everything else behind."[60] Darkness then signifies not just the systemic oppressions that shape our material conditions but the critique of those structures and the work needed to "handle" them. Though biblically, the Promised Land referred to a specific place, for Black slaves (and later Black people), the Promised Land stood for emancipation and heaven. Du Bois writes that for the enslaved, "Emancipation was the key to a promised land."[61] He goes on to explain that after emancipation, "the freedman has not yet found in freedom his promised land," determining that the Promised Land for Blacks is actually a space free from oppression.[62] The day before his assassination, Martin Luther King Jr. similarly noted that though there were still "difficult days ahead," eventually Black people would reach the Promised Land where they would no longer face racial discrimination.[63] Despite these historically situated visions of the Promised Land, Shondaland's transdiscursive formula diminishes it to a society free from *race* rather than a society free from *racial discrimination*.

Comparatively, *Scandal* works hard not to acknowledge race, while *HTGAWM*'s characters and storylines explicitly acknowledge race. This contrast is provocative because both shows reify colorblind and postracial discourses despite their different approaches. In this context, Shondaland—through a show under Peter Nowalk's leadership—is further popularizing its signature formula that production companies can emulate to produce normative television. This formula includes presenting a vision of equality focused "more on individual (or micro) experiences as opposed to institutional (or macro) analyses."[64] It also advocates "minimiz[ing] the reality of racism" mainly through dehistoricizing the impact and salience of race.[65] Ultimately, the formula transdiscursively advances the indistinctness of race and attacks identification with racial identities as being complicit in racism.[66]

In the first season of *HTGAWM*, Annalise and her law students try to solve the murder of Lila Stangard, an undergraduate student having an affair with Annalise's husband Sam. As they solve the mystery, the audience learns that Annalise is having an affair with the detective tasked with solving the murder. In addition to the murder of Sam's mistress, Annalise and the students have a different legal case to resolve in each episode. These cases range from a millionaire accused of brutally murdering his wife to a son accused of murdering his abusive police officer father to a friend accused of insider trading. Approximately halfway through the first season, *HTGAWM* addresses race openly when their case is a final effort to save a Black man on death row accused of killing his White girlfriend. The episode's secondary plot highlights Annalise's bond with her client through their shared Blackness and familiarity with interracial romance. Meanwhile, in the primary story arc, Sam is increasingly concerned that he will be arrested for Lila's murder and accuses Annalise of being more concerned about her client than him. In response, she says, "When I filed the petition I didn't know you were screwing some White whore."[67]

Racially identifying Lila seems to violate normative colorblind and postracial discourses; however, in Shondaland, this retort gives Whiteness the moral high ground. By calling out Sam's mistress racially, Annalise violates a key component of colorblindness which contends that only racists notice race. Like Olivia in *Scandal*, in this scene, Annalise is a Black woman shamed as racist for drawing attention to race. This allows Sam as a White male to distance himself from this unacceptable behavior, despite the role that his affair plays in Annalise's racialized anger. Furthermore, although Sam's extramarital activities should be the focus of audiences' scorn, it is Annalise who is positioned to receive viewers' disapprobation because it is her "prejudice" that maligns an innocent murder victim. Unlike *Scandal*, this time it is a Black woman calling a White woman a whore, which is promptly repudiated in the scene by Sam. This postraciality allows Whiteness, represented by Sam, to claim the superior position, since he (unlike Annalise) is appropriately not concerned with race and defends Lila's womanhood.

Eventually, evidence implicates Sam as Lila's killer and Annalise forcefully confronts him:

SAM: I am still the man you married.

ANNALISE: You are not that man anymore, and I don't think you ever were. Which is why you chose me isn't it? I've been window dressing for you. The Black woman on your arm so you can hide, so that people only saw the good guy . . .

SAM: You want the truth? You are nothing but a piece of ass. That's what I saw when I first talked to you in the office that day. I knew you'd put out, that's all you're really good for . . . you disgusting slut.

ANNALISE: At least you're finally able to tell the truth.[68]

Shondaland's presumed certainty that bluntly mentioning race is sufficiently redemptive is problematic. Annalise's indictment of Sam's racialized motivation for entering into their interracial marriage conveniently doubles as the most obvious indictment of Shondaland's reliance on interracial relationships as narrative devices that protect the shows from accusations of racism. Superficially acknowledging race is not the same as actively engaging in antiracist efforts. Yet audiences who are not taught otherwise likely believe the mere visibility of diversity on television is not only enough, but also reason enough to refrain from challenging the representations of that diversity. As previously mentioned, Rhimes and her production company are uninterested in using raced characters as a critique of racist (and sexist, classist, ableist, etc.) structures that constrain her life or the lives of her marginalized characters and the actors who play them. Moreover, Annalise's accusation that Sam used their relationship as a pretense for benevolence supports postracial emphasis on the symbolic redemption of Whiteness through acts of racial transcendence.

In Shondaland, interracial intimacies are a key element of its transdiscursive signature formula that threads colorblindness and postraciality throughout character and storyline development, shows, and the production company. The veneer of progress disappears completely when Sam tells Annalise what he really thinks of her; that he does so by sexually objectifying her signals the ease with which Black women are stripped of their humanity. Sam's allegiance to Whiteness and his enactment of racism undermines interracial intimacy by highlighting how these relationships are still "bound by class, gender, and racial hierarchies," as demonstrated by his disparagements of Annalise's body and sexuality.[69] While *HTGAWM* imbues Annalise with the agency to choose her husband, it is merely an illusion as she is never free from the racist and sexist ideologies that frame Black women. As Henderson points out, "Sometimes counternarratives of sexuality that attempt to occupy a revolutionary and insurrectionist space within the public body politic run the risk of perpetuating the very thing one hopes to reuse to reclaim one's agency."[70] Throughout the show, Annalise is depicted as empowered through her sexual agency, which is showcased through her marriage, affairs, and multiple lovers only to be eventually reduced to her body. Thus, Shondaland teaches us, despite aiming for the contrary, that the bodies of women and in this case, the bodies of Black women, are always exposed to scrutiny and surveillance. In his tirade against Annalise, Sam also refers to their relationship as dirty and shameful, effectively depicting Black womanhood as unacceptable and interracial relationships as scandalizing. His rant highlights the failures of both colorblind and postracial discourses, because he embodies how one can both be in an interracial relationship and continue to hold racist ideologies. This key moment also exposes how these twinned discourses are powered by the desire to return to a normative Whiteness that revels in its ability to decide when and how race should matter.

SHONDALAND'S DANGEROUS TRANSDISCURSIVITY

Whether race is explicitly addressed as in *HTGAWM* or mostly ignored as in *Scandal*, both approaches abide by and ultimately strengthen colorblind and postracial discourses. Shondaland's commitment to featuring diverse casts and interracial relationships while openly deriding the material impact of race creates an interesting paradox. The attempts to merely present race and usher in a colorblind and postracial utopia only work to reinforce the normative significance of race from production to audience reception. Importantly, our analysis reveals that the praise for these shows as racially progressive is misplaced. While we note that interracial relationships, particularly Black women/White men pairings, remain rare on television, their reliance on normative racial ideologies make the representations of these relationships familiar. The ways these relationships have been scripted reinforce Shondaland's decision to draw from "individualistic approaches and ahistorical frameworks" to convince viewers we are finally colorblind and beyond race. For Olivia and Annalise, the twinned discourses of colorblindness and postracialism ensure that audiences are unable (or unwilling) to culturally account for their Blackness since it is rendered into something they have dismissed as irrelevant.

Rhimes's considerable efforts to minimize the significance of race only foreground its importance; this is notable because Shondaland functions transdiscursively in the television industry. The formulaic success of Shondaland consistently featuring normative interracial intimacies, settings that are racially diverse in the real world but mostly White on screen, denial of racism's effects, and Whiteness as the central organizing force means that other showrunners and production companies will certainly mimic these signature elements, hence our concern with the popularity of Rhimes's shows. Though discourses of colorblindness and postraciality make audiences feel good about society, examining her shows exposes how these narratives do not address or resolve enduring institutionalized inequalities.

Our critique resists the prevailing urge to laud Rhimes and Shondaland for merely depicting diversity. To envision and enact transformative representations of romantic interracial relationships, we recommend that Shondaland actually deal with the entrenched effects of institutionalized racism. This entails having White characters reflect on their own racial identity and the privileges they are afforded by Whiteness. Additionally, this recognition of Whiteness, both behind and in front of the camera, would effectively shake the shows out of their self-satisfied superficial embrace of diversity and into an unmistakably antiracist stance. Finally, and importantly, Shondaland needs to address the material impact of race in perpetuating social inequalities. We purposefully do not offer ideal depictions or suggest how scenes and plots can be recreated to be "better" because to do so would presume a singular authentic and correct representation. Instead, we end by highlighting how adopting our suggestions would allow Shondaland to creatively engage with rather than disavow racial difference. In practice, doing so may finally get us to the Promised Land.

NOTES

1. Some of the more recent pairs: Molly and John on *Extant*, created by Mickey Fisher, aired 2014–2015 on CBS; Abbie and Ichabod on *Sleepy Hollow*, created by Phillip Iscove, Alex Kurtzman, and Roberto Orci, aired 2013–2017 on FOX; Veronica and Kevin on *Shameless*, created

by John Wells and Paul Abbott, aired 2011–present on Showtime; Jasmine and Crosby on *Parenthood*, created by Jason Katims, aired 2010–2015 on NBC; Angela and Shawn on *Boy Meets World*, created by Michael Jacobs and April Kelly, aired 1993–2000 on ABC; Nicole and Sam on *True Blood*, created by Alan Ball, aired 2008–2014 on HBO; Candace and James on *The Haves and the Have Nots*, created by Tyler Perry, aired 2013–present on OWN; Joanna and Julian on *Deception*, created by Chris Fedak, aired 2018–present on ABC; Joss and John on *Person of Interest*, created by Jonathan Nolan, aired 2011–2016 on CBS; Guinevere and King Arthur in *Merlin*, created by Johnny Capps, Julian Jones, and Jake Michie, aired 2008–2012 on BBC; April and Richard on *Mistresses*, created by K. J. Steinberg, aired 2013–2016 on ABC; Bonnie and Jeremy on *The Vampire Diaries*, created by Julie Plec and Kevin Williamson, aired 2009–2017 on The CW; Naevia and Crixus on *Spartacus*, created by Steven S. DeKnight, aired 2010–2013 on STARZ; Isabelle and Shawn on *The 4400*, created by René Echevarria and Scott Peters, aired 2004–2007 on USA; and Jack and Allison on *Eureka*, created by Andrew Cosby and Jaime Paglia, aired 2006–2012 on SYFY. Some of the more recent films include *Magic Mike XXL*, directed by Gregory Jacobs (2015; Los Angeles: Warner Brothers and Iron Horse Entertainment, 2015), DVD; *Best Man Holiday*, directed by Malcolm D. Lee (2013; Los Angeles: Universal Pictures Home Entertainment, 2014), DVD; *Shame*, directed by Steve McQueen (2011; Los Angeles: Momentum Pictures, 2011), DVD; *Belle*, directed by Amma Asante (2013; Los Angeles: FOX, 2013), DVD; *Cloud Atlas*, directed by Lana Wachowski, Andy Wachowski, and Tom Tykwer (2012; Los Angeles: Warner Brothers, 2013), DVD; *Animal*, directed by Brett Simmons (2014; Los Angeles: Shout! Factory, 2015), DVD; *Joyful Noise*, directed by Todd Graff (2012; Los Angeles: Warner Brothers, 2012), DVD; *Colombiana*, directed by Olivier Megaton (2011; Los Angeles: Sony Pictures Home Entertainment, 2011), DVD; *The Words*, directed by Brian Klugman and Lee Sternthal (2012; Los Angeles: Sony Pictures Home Entertainment, 2012), DVD; *Zookeeper*, directed by Frank Coraci (2011; Los Angeles: Sony Pictures Home Entertainment, 2011), DVD; *From the Rough*, directed by Pierre Bagley (2013; Los Angeles: Freestyle Digital Media, 2014), DVD; *The Losers*, directed by Sylvain White (2010; Los Angeles: Warner Home Video, 2010), DVD; *Retreat*, directed by Carl Tibbetts (2011; Los Angeles: Sony Pictures Home Entertainment, 2012), DVD; *Seven Psychopaths*, directed by Martin McDonagh (2012; Los Angeles: Sony Pictures Home Entertainment, 2013), DVD; *Skyfall*, directed by Sam Mendes (2012; Los Angeles: MGM Video & DVD, 2015), DVD; *Star Trek: Into the Darkness*, directed by J. J. Abrams (2013; Los Angeles: Paramount, 2013), DVD; *Think like a Man*, directed by Tim Story (2012; Los Angeles: Screen Gems, 2012), DVD; *Think like a Man Too*, directed by Tim Story (2014; Los Angeles: Sony, 2014), DVD; and *A Madea Christmas*, directed by Tyler Perry (2013; Los Angeles: Lionsgate, 2014), DVD. We capitalize "Black" and "White" in this chapter because their use refers to culture, ethnicity, or a group of people in the same way as Asian, Latinx, Arab, and so on. We do not capitalize these words in direct quotes unless those authors capitalized their usage.

2. Myra Washington, "Interracial Intimacy: Hegemonic Construction of Asian American and Black Relationships on TV Medical Dramas," *Howard Journal of Communication* 23 (2012): 253–271; Roland G. Fryer Jr., "Guess Who's Been Coming to Dinner: Trends in Interracial Marriage over the 20th Century," *Journal of Economic Perspectives* 21, no. 2 (2007): 71–90; Rachel F. Moran, *Interracial Intimacy: The Regulation of Race and Romance* (Chicago, University of Chicago Press, 2001); Maria P. P. Root, *Love's Revolution: Interracial Marriage* (Philadelphia, Pa.: Temple University Press, 2001); Cynthia Feliciano, Belinda Robnett, and Golnaz Komale, "Gendered Racial Exclusion among White Internet Daters," *Social Science Research* 38 (2009): 39–54; Patricia Hill Collins, *Black Sexual Politics: African Americans, Gender, and the New Racism* (New York: Routledge, 2005); Kyle D. Crowder and Stewart E. Tolnay, "A New Marriage Squeeze for Black Women: The Role of Racial Intermarriage by Black Men," *Journal of*

Marriage and the Family 62 (2000): 792–807; Jerry A. Jacobs and Teresa G. Lobov, "Gender Differentials in Intermarriage among Sixteen Race and Ethnic Groups," *Sociological Forum* 17 (2002): 621–646; Zhenchao C. Qian and Daniel T. Lichter, "Social Boundaries and Marital Assimilation: Interpreting Trends in Racial and Ethnic Intermarriage," *American Sociological Review* 72 (2007): 68–94.

3. Sharon Bramlett-Solomon, "Interracial Love on Television: What's Taboo Still," in *Critical Thinking about Sex, Love, and Romance in the Mass Media: Media Literacy Applications*, ed. Mary-Lou Galician and Debra L. Merskin (London: Routledge, 2006), 85–93.

4. Stuart Hall, "Encoding/Decoding," in *Media and Cultural Studies: Keywords*, ed. Meenakshi Gigi Durham and Douglas M. Kellner, (Malden, Mass.: Blackwell Publishing, 2001), 166–176; Wendy Wang, "The Rise of Intermarriage," Pew Research Center, Executive Summary, February 16, 2012, http://www.pewsocialtrends.org/2012/02/16/the-rise-of-intermarriage/?src=prc -headline; Moran, *Interracial Intimacy*.

5. Roopali Mukherjee, "Rhyme and Reason: 'Post-Race' and the Politics of Colorblind Racism," in *The Colorblind Screen: Television in Post-Racial America*, ed. Sarah Nilsen and Sarah E. Turner (New York: New York University Press, 2014), 39–56.

6. Ian F. Haney-Lopez, "Is the Post in Post-racial the Blind in Colorblind," *Cardozo Law Review* 32 (2010): 807–831.

7. Haney-López, 808.

8. Michel Foucault, "What Is an Author?," in *The Foucault Reader*, ed. Paul Rabinow, (New York: Pantheon Books, 1984), 101–120.

9. Foucault, 113–114.

10. Joe Kincheloe and Kathleen Berry, *Rigour and Complexity in Educational Research: Conceptualizing the Bricolage* (New York: Open University Press, 2004).

11. Eduardo Bonilla-Silva, "'New Racism', Color-blind Racism, and the Future of Whiteness in America," in *White Out: The Continuing Significance of Racism*, ed. Ashley W. Doane and Edward Bonilla-Silva (London: Routledge, 2003), 271–284.

12. Erica Chito Childs, "Listening to the Interracial Canary: Contemporary Views on Interracial Relationships among Blacks and Whites," *Fordham Law Review* 76 (2008): 2771–2786.

13. Sumi Cho, "Post-racialism," *Iowa Law Review* 94 (2009): 1589–1649.

14. Anna Everett, "Scandalicious: Scandal, Social Media, and Shonda Rhimes' Auteurist Juggernaut," *Black Scholar* 45 (2015): 34–43; Rachel Roberts, "The People's Poll: Would You Choose 'Scandal's' Fitz or Jake?," *Bravo*, September 24, 2015, http://www.bravotv.com/the -peoples-couch/blogs/the-peoples-poll-would-you-choose-scandals-fitz-or-jake.

15. For examples of the memes, please see the following links: "Will go down in history as a side bae to a side chick," (meme), accessed May 1 2018, https://s-media-cache-ako.pinimg.com /736x/aa/54/da/aa54da9bf4f89e6f1df7ddo3572c861b.jpg; katrinapavela.tumblr.com, "If she was your girlfriend, she wasn't last night," (meme), accessed May 1, 2018, https://s-media-cache-ako .pinimg.com/736x/cc/1b/25/cc1b25538a53913de57dbc68340dc76d.jpg; katrinapavela.tumblr .com, "I better not catch your punk ass alone in the streets son," (meme), accessed May 1, 2018, https://s-media-cache-ako.pinimg.com/736x/21/31/3b/21313ba61b6e224538d951e1dc089795 .jpg; Itah Hod, "'How to Get Away with Murder,' 'Grey's,' 'Scandal' Stars Tease ABC's Big 'TGIT' Mid-Season Return," *Wrap*, January 30, 2015, http://www.thewrap.com/how-to -get-away-with-murder-greys-scandal-stars-tease-abcs-big-tgit-mid-season-return.

16. For a summary of this discourse, use the following link: https://twitter.com/search?q =htgawm%20%2B%20interracial&src=typd.

17. Alex Kritselis, "Why Is 'How to Get Away with Murder' Character Annalise So Upset with Sam When She's a Cheater Too?," *Bustle*, November 18, 2014, https://www.bustle.com/articles /49866-why-is-how-to-get-away-with-murder-character-annalise-so-upset-with-sam-when-shes.

18. Alessandra Stanley, "Wrought in Rhimes's Image: Viola Davis Plays Shonda Rhimes's Latest Tough Heroine," *New York Times*, September 18, 2014, https://www.nytimes.com/2014/09/21/arts/television/viola-davis-plays-shonda-rhimess-latest-tough-heroine.html?_r=1.

19. Emily Nussbaum, "Primary Colors: Shonda Rhimes's 'Scandal' and the Diversity Debate," *New Yorker*, May 21, 2012, http://www.newyorker.com/magazine/2012/05/21/primary-colors.

20. Alyssa Rosenberg, "The Racial Education of Scandal's Olivia Pope," *Washington Post*, March 9, 2015, https://www.washingtonpost.com/news/act-four/wp/2015/03/09/the-racial-education-of-scandals-olivia-pope/?utm_term=.39afe1d68d2f.

21. David M. Blank, "The Quest for Quantity and Diversity in Television Programming," *American Economic Review* 56 (1966): 448–456; Mara Einstein, "Broadcast Network Television, 1955–2003: The Pursuit of Advertising and the Decline of Diversity," *Journal of Media Economics* 17 (2004): 145–155.

22. Judy Berman, "'I'm a White Girl': Why 'Girls' Won't Ever Overcome Its Racial Problem," *Atlantic*, January 22, 2013, https://www.theatlantic.com/entertainment/archive/2013/01/im-a-white-girl-why-girls-wont-ever-overcome-its-racial-problem/267345/.

23. Sandra Gonzalez, "Bunheads Amy Sherman-Palladino Responds to Shonda Rhimes' Twitter Criticism," *EW.com*, June 17, 2012, http://ew.com/article/2012/06/17/bunheads-amy-sherman-palladino-shonda-rhimes-diversity/.

24. Maureen Ryan, "HBO's Girls Isn't Racist, Television Is Racist (and Sexist)," *Huffington Post*, June 25, 2012, http://www.huffingtonpost.com/maureen-ryan/girls-hbo-racist_b_1451931.html; Dennis Romero, "How Hollywood Keeps Minorities Out," *LA Weekly*, February 25, 2015, http://www.laweekly.com/news/how-hollywood-keeps-minorities-out-5402815; Gillian B. White, "Hollywood Has No Business Case for Booking All-White Casts," *Atlantic*, May 16, 2016, https://www.theatlantic.com/business/archive/2016/05/hollywood-diversity/482700/; Melena Ryzik, "What It's Really Like to Work in Hollywood* (*If You're Not a Straight White Man)," *New York Times*, February 24, 2016, https://www.nytimes.com/interactive/2016/02/24/arts/hollywood-diversity-inclusion.html; Laura Lorenzetti, "Hollywood Still Has a Major Diversity Problem," *Fortune*, August 6, 2015, http://fortune.com/2015/08/06/hollywood-diversity-white-men/; Mark Harris, "TV's Diversity Dilemma," *Entertainment Weekly*, May 4, 2012, http://www.ew.com/article/2012/05/04/mark-harris-tvs-diversity-dilemma; Britney Cooper, "Hollywood's Post-racial Mirage: How Pop Culture Got Gentrified," *Salon*, March 24, 2014, http://www.salon.com/2014/03/25/hollywoods_post_racial_mirage_how_pop_culture_got_gentrified/.

25. Willa Paskin, "Network TV Is Broken. So How Does Shonda Rhimes Keep Making Hits?," *New York Times*, May 9, 2013, http://www.nytimes.com/2013/05/12/magazine/shonda-rhimes.html?pagewanted=all&_r=0; Lacey Rose, "Shonda Rhimes Opens Up about 'Angry Black Woman' Flap, Messy 'Grey's Anatomy' Chapter and the 'Scandal' Impact," *Hollywood Reporter*, October 8, 2014, http://www.hollywoodreporter.com/news/shonda-rhimes-opens-up-angry-738715; Neil Drumming, "ABC's Recent Ratings Success Says Diversity Is Good Business," *Salon*, May 20, 2014, http://www.salon.com/2014/05/20/abcs_recent_ratings_success_says_diversity_is_good_business/.

26. Rose, "Shonda Rhimes Opens Up."

27. Haney-López, "Is the Post in Post-racial the Blind in Colorblind," 809.

28. Paskin, "Network TV is Broken."

29. Washington, "Interracial Intimacy," 257.

30. Vorris L. Nunley, "*Crash*: Rhetorically Wrecking Discourses of Race, Tolerance, and White Privilege," *College English* 69 (2007): 335–346; Amy Long, "Diagnosing Drama: 'Grey's Anatomy', Blind Casting, and the Politics of Representation," *Journal of Popular Culture* 44 (2011): 1067–1084.

31. Paskin, "Network TV Is Broken."

32. Mark Robichaux, "Rhimes' Anatomy," *Broadcasting & Cable*, February 26, 2006, http://www.broadcastingcable.com/news/news-articles/rhimes-anatomy/78998.

33. Alyssa Rosenberg, "How Hollywood Stays White and Male," *Washington Post*, May 14, 2015, https://www.washingtonpost.com/news/act-four/wp/2015/05/14/how-hollywood-stays-white-and-male/?utm_term=.e44c6e3aa9b0.

34. Albert S. Fu, "Fear of a Black Spider-Man: Race and the Colour-line in Superhero (Re)casting," *Journal of Graphic Novels and Comics* 6 (2015): 269–283.

35. Norman K. Denzin, *Reading Race: Hollywood and the Cinema of Racial Violence* (Thousand Oaks, Calif.: Sage, 2001); Sean M. Tierney, "Themes of Whiteness in *Bulletproof Monk, Kill Bill*, and *The Last Samurai*," *Journal of Communication* 56 (2006): 607–624.

36. Ashley Doane, "Shades of Colorblindness: Rethinking Racial Ideology in the United States," in *Colorblind Screen*, 17.

37. Bonilla-Silva, "New Racism."

38. Gonzalez, "Bunheads."

39. Matthew Fogel, "Grey's Anatomy Goes Colorblind," *New York Times*, May 8, 2005, http://www.nytimes.com/2005/05/08/arts/television/greys-anatomy-goes-colorblind.html?_r=2.

40. Stacey Wilson Hunt and Lacey Rose, "Lee Daniels, Damon Lindelof, A-List Writers on Race, Ignoring Critics, an 'Empire' Axing," *Hollywood Reporter*, May 11, 2015, http://www.hollywoodreporter.com/features/lee-daniels-damon-lindelof-a-794430.

41. *Nightline*, "America in Black and White: *Grey's Anatomy*," season 25, episode 56, hosted by Vicky Mabrey, aired on March 20, 2006, on ABC.

42. Maryann Erigha, "Shonda Rhimes, Scandal, and the Politics of Crossing Over," *Black Scholar* 45 (2015): 10–15.

43. Mukherjee, "Rhyme and Reason," 51.

44. Paskin, "Network TV Is Broken."

45. Cho, "Post-racialism," 18.

46. Cho, "Post-racialism," 18.

47. Rona Tamiko Halualani, "Abstracting and De-racializing Diversity: The Articulation of Diversity in the Post-race Era," in *Critical Rhetorics of Race*, ed. Michael G. Lacy and Kent A. Ono (New York: New York University Press, 2011), 247–264.

48. Erica Chito Childs, *Fade to Black and White: Interracial Images in Popular Culture* (Lanham, Md.: Rowman & Littlefield Publishers, 2009), 1.

49. Nussbaum, "Primary Colors."

50. Erigha, "Shonda Rhimes," 12.

51. *Scandal*, "Hell Hath No Fury," season 1, episode 3, directed by Allison Liddi-Brown, written by Shonda Rhimes and Matt Byrne, aired on April 19, 2012, on ABC.

52. *Scandal*, "Baby, It's Cold Outside," season 5, episode 9, directed by Tom Verica, written by Shonda Rhimes and Mark Wilding, aired on November 19, 2015, on ABC.

53. Ruth Frankenberg, *White Women, Race Matters: The Social Construction of Whiteness* (Minneapolis: University of Minnesota Press, 1993).

54. *Scandal*, "Happy Birthday Mr. President," season 2, episode 8, directed by Oliver Bokelberg, written by Shonda Rhimes, aired on December 6, 2012, on ABC.

55. *Scandal*, "White Hat's Back On," season 2, episode 22, directed by Tom Verica, written by Shonda Rhimes, aired on May 16, 2013, on ABC.

56. *Scandal*, "White Hat's Back On."

57. *Scandal*, "The Price of Free and Fair Elections," season 3, episode 18, directed by Tom Verica, written by Shonda Rhimes and Mark Wilding, aired on April 17, 2014, on ABC.

58. Rachel A. Griffin, "Olivia Pope as Problematic and Paradoxical: A Black Feminist Critique of Scandal's 'Mammification,'" in *Feminist Theory and Popular Culture*, ed. Adrienne Trier-Bieniek (Rotterdam, Netherlands: Sense Publishers, 2015), 35–48.

59. *Scandal*, "The Price of Free and Fair Elections."

60. *Scandal*, "The Price of Free and Fair Elections."

61. W.E.B. Du Bois, "Of Our Spiritual Strivings," in *Race and Racialization: Essential Readings*, ed. Tania Das Gupta (Toronto: Canadian Scholars' Press, 2007), 144–148.

62. Du Bois, 145.

63. Martin Luther King Jr., "I've Been to the Mountaintop" (speech, Memphis, Tenn., April 3, 1968), *American Rhetoric*, http://www.americanrhetoric.com/speeches/mlkivebeentothe mountaintop.htm.

64. Ralina L. Joseph, *Transcending Blackness: From the New Millennium Mulatta to the Exceptional Multiracial* (Durham, N.C.: Duke University Press, 2013), 28.

65. Kent A. Ono, "Postracism: A Theory of the 'Post'—as Political Strategy," *Journal of Communication Inquiry* 34 (2010): 228.

66. Ralina. L. Joseph, "'Tyra Banks is Fat': Reading (Post-) Racism and (Post-) Feminism in the New Millennium," *Critical Studies in Media Communication* 26 (2009): 237–254; Jonathan P. Rossing, "Deconstructing Postracialism: Humor as a Critical, Cultural Project," *Journal of Communication Inquiry* 36 (2012): 44–61.

67. *How to Get Away with Murder*, "Freakin' Whack-a-Mole," season 1, episode 6, directed by Bill D'Elia, written by Peter Nowalk and Michael Foley, aired on October 30, 2014, on ABC.

68. *How to Get Away with Murder*, "Kill Me, Kill Me, Kill Me," season 1, epidsode 9, directed by Stephen Williams, written by Peter Nowalk and Michael Foley, aired on November 20, 2014, on ABC.

69. Washington, "Interracial Intimacies," 267.

70. Carol E. Henderson, "AKA: Sarah Baartman, the Hottentot Venus and Black Women's Identity," *Women's Studies* 43 (2014): 946–959.

PART 3

CONSUMPTION, ETHICS, AND MORALITY

Shondaland Fandom as Cultural Meaning Making

9 · #BLACKLIVESMATTER ON *SCANDAL*

Analyzing Divergent Fan Reactions to "The Lawn Chair" Episode

MARK P. ORBE

"What would Ferguson have looked like if there had been an Olivia Pope there?" This question begins an *Entertainment Weekly* review of *Scandal's* (ABC 2012–2018) season 4 episode "The Lawn Chair."[1] *Scandal* is a political melodrama set in Washington, D.C., that follows the crisis management firm Pope and Associates; this episode's plot mirrored the death of Michael Brown at the hands of a Ferguson, Missouri, police officer, Darren Wilson. It aired on March 5, 2015—the same week the U.S. Department of Justice outlined the rationale for clearing the Ferguson, Missouri, police officer of civil rights violations.[2] Gravely collapsing the distance between fiction and reality, "The Lawn Chair" features an unarmed African American male teenager, Brandon Parker, being shot and killed by a white American male police officer. The consummate political fixer, Olivia Pope, is hired by the police department to "handle" the crisis that unfolds as Brandon's father, Clarence, and the community unite in racialized protest against Brandon's death and larger issues of police brutality and racism. Throughout the episode, Olivia struggles with the tension between her professional obligations, the realities of antiblack racism and police brutality, and her identity as an African American. Pope and Associates eventually locate a video establishing that a knife was planted on Brandon's body—a discovery that prompts the police officer suspected of murder to go on an incriminating rant that ultimately results in multiple charges. The climatic ending of the episode features President Fitzgerald Grant embracing Clarence in the Oval Office of the White House. This emotional meeting, orchestrated by Olivia, shows both men commiserating the premature deaths of their sons across their racial differences.

Shonda Rhimes via Shondaland Productions has successfully created television programming that appears progressive but largely takes a colorblind approach, through which African American characters are steeped in an evasion of blackness.[3] According to Erigha, this strategy is necessary to achieve mainstream success: "Crossover brands simultaneously embrace and transcend blackness, albeit paradoxically."[4] "The Lawn Chair" is unique because it is the first episode in four seasons of *Scandal* to overtly focus on race, racial identity, and racial injustice; in fact, it breaks the colorblind televisual experience that has come to define the show.[5] Dedicating an entire episode to the core issues of #BlackLivesMatter— although this well-known hashtag is never seen or spoken explicitly on air— represents a break from Rhimes's colorblind approach to achieving mainstream success.

#BlackLivesMatter is an internationally recognized symbol for resisting the "virulent anti-Black racism that permeates our society."[6] Created by women of color, this oft-seen hashtag emerged as George Zimmerman was found innocent in the death of Trayvon Martin and gained momentum in subsequent years as more unarmed African Americans were killed by armed police officers and citizens. #BlackLivesMatter fostered a collective stream of consciousness about several deaths including Martin, Michael Brown, Eric Garner, Tamir Rice, Tony Robinson, Walter Scott, and Freddie Gray and prompted thousands of assemblies, vigils, rallies, marches, and die-ins worldwide.[7] The core objective of this formidable protest movement is to confront racial profiling, police brutality, mass incarceration, and the militarization of policing in black communities.[8] Rhimes reportedly drew from the harsh racialized realities that define the #BlackLivesMatter movement to create this episode's storyline.[9] In this chapter, I explore the paradox of "The Lawn Chair" episode—one that importantly highlights the persistence of racism and racial inequality while ironically achieving significant crossover success on television by de-emphasizing race.[10] More specifically, I analyze audience reactions via social media to explore a number of interrelated questions: What reactions did self-identified fans have to the episode? What scholarly theories exist that allow for increased insight into comparative and divergent perceptions? Finally, will the episode mark an increase in the explicit saliency of race on *Scandal*, or stand apart as an exception to the show's televisual colorblind reality?

STANDPOINT THEORIES

Standpoint theories are based on one simple idea: The world looks different depending on your social standing.[11] Traditionally, scholars used standpoint theories to understand how women and men experience the world differently; more recently, communication scholars have used them to describe and theorize how people from different racial and ethnic groups experience the world differently.[12] Standpoint theories are also useful for theorizing diverse audience reactions to mass media texts.[13] All of this scholarship begins with the same premise: individuals have similar and different vantage points from which they interpret the world. According to Collins, these vantage points, or locations, are established through one's field of experience and informed by social group membership.[14]

Social locations—including those informed by intersecting identities, such as gender, race, and class—shape people's lives, experiences, and perceptions of the world.[15] Grounded in critical analyses of the master-slave relationship, scholars theorized that each social position represented a distinct location.[16] Hallstein states that each person has a particular racial location, defined primarily in terms of the racial and ethnic groups to which they belong.[17] Yet, an important distinction exists between occupying a racial location and having a racial standpoint.[18] While everyone has a racial location from which they understand the world around them, not everyone chooses to actualize a racial standpoint. A racial standpoint must be achieved—"earned through critical reflections on power relations and through the creation of a political stance that exists in opposition to dominant cultural systems."[19] In short, a racial standpoint refers to more than a social location or a collection of life experiences. It is established through a concerted awareness that encompasses a critical, oppositional understanding of how one's life is shaped by historical, social, cultural, economic, and political forces.

According to Collins, the largest difference in racial standpoints exist between those racial and ethnic groups that have the least versus the most societal power.[20] In the United States, African Americans, Latina/o Americans, and Native Americans have similar racial locations, informed by having less access to societal power. In comparison, white European Americans have a racial location reflective of dominant group status, possession of and access to societal power, and systemic racial privilege. Standpoint theories thereby account for how different racial and ethnic groups can have drastically different perceptions of the same stimuli.[21] Although this foundational idea about racial locations explains how diverse perceptions emerge, it must be situated within a recognition that each individual simultaneously has multiple social locations that ultimately inform their perceptions. Consequently, categorizing perceptions simply according to racial identity is problematic because it fails to embrace an intersectional approach whereby each person is seen as a multidimensional being whose social location is informed by multiple group memberships that reflect privilege and/or marginalization.[22]

QUALITATIVE THEMATIC ANALYSIS

To facilitate an analysis of audience reactions to, and perceptions of, *Scandal*'s "The Lawn Chair," I completed a qualitative thematic analysis of comments from self-identified fans of the show. While several options exist to obtain this type of audience data, the show's Facebook fan page provided a convenient sampling of reactions that reflected organic commentary free of researcher subjective bias.[23] The *Scandal* "official" fan page posted a short video clip promoting the episode on March 5, 2015; this clip, as well as a second posting a day later, generated thousands of comments—and additional "replies" to comments— about the episode. To create a comprehensive, definitive data set, I focused on (1) comments that were posted over the two days following the airing of the episode (March 6–7, 2015) and (2) replies and exchanges prompted by the initial comments (which continued for several weeks past March 6–7, 2015). All of the comments from the Facebook fan page were copied and pasted, using Microsoft Word, into a separate document. Once this process was complete, the result was 135 single-spaced pages of narrative data.

Once the data set was created, I utilized qualitative thematic analytic processes to theorize the diverse reactions to the charged episode.[24] The process was modeled after McCracken's work and began with an initial review of data whereby relevant commentary was sorted from irrelevant comments (e.g., those that were not related to the show, episode, or episode content). Following this initial reduction of data, a reexamination was conducted to identify slices of data for logical relationships and contradictions. A third review worked to confirm or disconfirm emerging relationships and contradictions and begin the process of formulating paradigmatic themes. A final review of paradigmatic themes was then conducted whereby the large number of potential themes were synthesized—combined, separated, or deleted—into core organizing thematic structures.[25]

The qualitative analytic principles of William Owen proved invaluable in this process.[26] Specifically, I utilized three criteria to guide the reduction of data and thematization process.[27] First, I searched for frequent appearances of particular words and phrases (repetition). Second, I took note of how common meanings were communicated via various articulations (recurrence). Third, and finally, I highlighted excerpts that were emphasized through different forms (e.g., use of ALL CAPS), punctuation (e.g.,!!!! or ???), or format (e.g., **bold** or *italics*). The next section incorporates comments and exchanges[28] from the data into an explication that captures the essence of diverse fan reactions to the "The Lawn Chair."

THEMATIC ANALYSIS: FOUR POINTS OF EMPHASIS WITH CONTRASTING POINTS OF REFERENCE

The overall reactions of self-identified fans to "The Lawn Chair" episode, as documented on the show's official Facebook fan page, were immediate, intense, and full of insight. Fans[29] typically used words like *moving, intense, heartfelt,* and *brilliant* in their descriptions. The most common response described the powerful nature of the episode with hundreds of viewers describing their strong emotional reactions. Most recounted how hard it was to watch certain scenes and how they were moved to tears throughout the show. Several fans shared that the episode prompted uncontrollable emotional outbursts. The early consensus was that the closing scene of the two fathers, one white and one black, hugging in the Oval Office was the peak of the emotional rollercoaster. One fan wrote, "I just watched the episode tonight. I honestly loved it! . . . The most touching moment of the episode was when both fathers are standing in the Oval and have the moment to know the feeling of losing their son's. I started to cry, which just show's me that once again Shonda hit the mark above and beyond. At this point it isn't even about Fitz or Jake, it's about Liv becoming Olivia Pope again." Multiple replies to this and similar messages signaled a similar sentiment. Many viewers identified with the pain that both fathers felt in regard to the "senseless murder of their sons" at the hands of "corrupted systems." A substantial number of fans, however, spoke to the emotionality of the episode connected specifically to the "fear for the Black sons of my family"—a connection that for one fan resulted in "sobbing like a baby." These individuals spoke passionately about the "raw emotion" that accompanied viewing an episode that hit so close to home. For example:

> Kudos to brilliant writing & superb acting. The "Lawn Chair" episode is most deserving of an Emmy nod. I have never been so emotionally spent after viewing an episode of anything on TV & I have watched it twice since it aired leaving me in the same state of mind & emotion. Everything even down to the background music of the scenes filled you with emotions so raw & real. As a mother of a beautiful, intelligent, respectful conscientious, young Black man, this episode resonated profoundly with me. He is a college freshman living about 300 plus miles away from home & not a day goes by that I [don't] pray to God to keep him safe from "harm" which comes in so many forms in these troubling times. I am especially fearful of law enforcement on so many levels as depicted in this episode. . . . Outstanding & quite "timely" episodic TV!!!

While the earliest posts were filled with unanimous praise for the episode, fan page discourse quickly became divisive in terms of individuals either loving or hating the episode. This shift occurred after several posts described the episode as "boring." Polarized audience perceptions became so distinct that it prompted one fan to question another with, "Ummmm are you watching the same Scandal as we are?" This section explicates four thematic points of analysis that capture the essence of the data collectively while acknowledging contrasting perceptions. Taken altogether, these four themes are significant in demonstrating the complexity of diverse fan reactions to the episode.

"Not Our Usual *Scandal*"

A consistent theme was grounded in fans' recognition that "The Lawn Chair" episode departed from existing *Scandal* storylines. Some comments were general in nature such as, "This episode had nothing to do with the normal Scandal episodes," "what i saw last night was so far beyond what i have come to love about scandal," and "It was an emotional show but didn't fit for 'Scandal.'" Other reactions expressed a more specific critique in regard to how "The Lawn Chair" seemed out of context; this related to how the episode, and to some extent the entire season, lack cohesiveness. For example, a fan reported, "Confused how this tied into the previous story line-she was kidnapped, saved and no real mention of it this episode. Seems like it was a lead in to the show after Scandal last night. Getting too far from what made Scandal popular." Another fan described season 4 as "off to a shaky start," critiqued the episodes as not "fitting back-to-back," and given this, wondered "WHERE ARE WE GOING HERE?" Other comments focused on how "Scandal doesn't fit Scandal anymore. It's veered so far from where it started." Several fans articulated varying levels of "disappointment" that the show had seemed to "jump the shark."[30] One fan was especially critical:

> Just when I thought a season 4 episode couldn't get any worse. Here it is. . . . And there's bad black cops as much as there are bad white cops. Just nobody goes crazy when a black cop kills a white kid. The scene where they show the kid go for something in his pocket and the cop shoots him looked pretty justified to me regardless of race. And Kerry Washington never looked more unattractive to me than when she stood in the crowd and started protesting in this episode. This is not Scandal. Where are the Olitz scenes, OPA solving mysteries, B613 action, and the rest of Scandal.[31] Me and my girl would kill for a full on Olitz scene. Been waiting for it all season. Shonda really crossed the line in this.

At the core of the above fan's reaction is that this episode is out of context with the traditional content of the show: the romantic tensions between Olivia Pope and President Fitz Grant in the larger context of political scandal in Washington, D.C. In this frame, and in the larger context of other comments, Rhimes's portrayal of a storyline based on a real-life series of events where issues of race and racism are salient "really crossed the line." This is the fine line, in the eyes of some fans, between creating programming that is entertaining versus political in nature.

Several comments questioned a perceived shift in content and noted a lack of cohesiveness in the storyline. Commentary notably described the episode akin to "a newscast," and questioned "Why do I feel like I'm watching CNN?" One fan asserted that the content "would have made a great Law and Order episode," referencing the popular long-running crime series whose storylines parallel current news events. Such an approach, however, seemed atypical for Scandal. One fan posted, "The episode felt inappropriate for the context of the show. It was overly simplified for an issue that is much deeper than a white cop killing a black teen. It felt like a cheap rip-off of a news topic to me." In this regard, many fans commented on how the close parallel between "The Lawn Chair" and events across the United States led them to believe that the episode was inserted for political reasons. This was implied within several comments and lengthy exchanges but was captured concisely by one individual who described themselves as "Very disappointed! It was as if the storyline was put on hold while the writers made a political statement." Even fans who appreciated the courage to address important racial issues thought the focus of the episode did not fit. "While I thought it was a gutsy and awesome episode, and one that was deep and brilliant, it felt way out of context with the flow of the show. It felt like it just got stuffed in the middle of it and didn't quite fit. Especially since it came right after Liv was rescued. I think it might have been better suited had it been done after she was back for a while."

Not all *Scandal* fans felt the episode was atypical of the show's storylines. In fact, a couple of viewers argued that "most of Scandal's plots are loosely based on actual events." Another viewer responded by writing, "I love the person above who said all of the shows are 'loosely' based on actual events. Hmm, a rigged election, President who is a cheating egomaniac, a crazy Vice President, a first Lady who wants the power, assorted Senate and Congress who are ALL cheating, lying and spend all their time committing fraud and assorted crimes. YEAH, it is just like real events!!" Other fans articulated how "this episode was right in context." In their comments, they made reference to Olivia Pope's commentary in the episode referencing the terror that African Americans face on a daily basis. "The notion of 'TERROR' and living with terror EVERY day of your life. . . . Racism and Police Brutality in Washington D.C., please check the statistics. It was in context because some of privilege (black and white) cannot get past the Politics of Respectability. They don't get that you can still be a model citizen and get a bullet through the skull, AND be framed by law enforcement." A few self-identified African American viewers were quick to point out that *Scandal* fans were more accepting of some real-life events but not others. As one fan wrote, "This particular episode seems to have upset a lot of people who don't want to accept the fact that these kinds of things happen."

The Essence of Shondaland: Tensions of Reality versus Fantasy

Audience reactions to "The Lawn Chair" episode also reflected debate about the desire for realistic or fictional programming content. One of the primary articulations was how *Scandal*, like other shows, represents a much needed "escape from reality." Reflecting this, a relatively new fan wrote about her disappointment with the episode:

> Very disappointed in this WHOLE Season of Scandal. My husband and I have binged watched all previous seasons over the Christmas break and literally was glued to the drama, mystery, scandal, and twist and turns in the show. The politics, and of course the love triangle was so intriguing it was a great escape from the everyday realities of life—terrorism, racial tension, and overall stuff you see and fear in the news daily.

That is why most of us watch tv to begin with—to escape the reality. Not quite sure why it is touching on such sensitive, fearful, and controversial topics.

As explicated earlier, some viewers resisted "storylines ripped from the headlines" and instead sought fictional content where they could avoid reality. These individuals looked "to 'Scandal' for entertainment and escape, not to hold a mirror up to society."

While some viewers appreciated the fantasy of *Scandal* generally, others praised Rhimes for the reality-based content featured in "The Lawn Chair" episode. As illustrated in the comments below, the tension between reality and fantasy resisted a binary either/or preference.

> I watch these shows to escape reality. . . . And Shonda used her platform to bring reality right back in your face. . . . Stand Up! Fight Back! No More Black Man Under Attack![32] Ive never had a show give me such an array of emotion simultaneously all at once maybe because it is too close to reality? So many families had their lives played out in an episode last night. . . . I find myself having a hard time separating that episode from reality . . . and I can only imagine how it was writing, directing and acting it out.

Other fans experienced a similar tension—appreciating the storyline, with its powerful ending, but also feeling uneasy with what they characterized as "one very strong piece of fiction." One fan articulated their sentiments by writing "I'm glad it ended with the officer's arrest, that unfortunately, is fantasy." Another described the fictional portrayals on the episode as problematic: "I'm sorry I am a Scandal fanatic but last night's episode was so off base. We all know that a black man on a crime scene with a shot gun would've been shot down instantly. Not even Jessie Jackson or Al Sharpton's presence would have changed that. I understood the message but it could have been delivered better." As one person articulated, the creative license of blending reality and fiction resulted in the "Worst episode of Scandal. We all get it. You 're-enacted' an event but made up your own ending . . . EPIC FAIL!!!"

Some of the tension related to reality versus fantasy revolved around the fictitious effect that Olivia had on the unfolding of events. In terms of the episode's ending, comments from avid fans expressed happiness with the just outcome and also sadness that "justice like this doesn't happen in real life!" Several viewers described the episode as "excellent . . . like a dream" and articulated how the ending reflected "wishful thinking: IF ONLY!" In this context, this reference was explicitly clear: "If only we had #OliviaPope for Michael Brown, Tamir Rice, etc #ShondaAtHerBest." The desire to "really have a olivia pope to help all the black young men that are d[ue] justice" was seen in a wide range of comments. The effects that the lead character's presence, expertise, and activism had were evidenced throughout the episode. While fictional, this type of programming was appreciated by some viewers, including one who thanked Olivia (and interestingly, not Rhimes) for her efforts: "Thanks Liv for fixing it. Glad that the father did not go to jail or to the morgue. He got a chance to see and talk with the President."

According to some fans, this type of ending is only possible in Shondaland, a televisual reality where Rhimes and her production team make decisions about how storylines begin, progress, and end. Some viewers applauded her attempts to portray how things could be in a more just world. As one articulated, "Fiction is usually based off of reality [and] for me this episode hit home, the reality that for black people our lives are not held at the same value." Another fan wrote:

> This episode of Scandal was on point and necessary. Everyone who has a problem with how it was presented or the type of episode it was (based on what's typically aired), clearly lack vision, imagination and substance. The scandal of this particular episode is the Reality that was presented (no justice; no peace no matter how cliche it sounds). You can't only be happy and pleased with Shonda Rhimes with just the expectation that's she's giving people the fantasy storyline they want. . . . You have to also recognize that she will give the people some true reality of what they need as well. Well played Shonda Rhimes. . . . Well played#trueGladiator.

Other comments directed specifically at Rhimes were not as positive. One fan complained that "it seemed almost like a fantasy on what the writers may have wished had happened in real life." This person went on to question others' perception that the episode "showed the 'truth.'" They asserted, "It's not the truth, it's tv. Where were the looters? Where were the violent protesters? It definitely felt one sided." One highly critical viewer correlated Rhimes's storyline decision with her "liberal agenda:" "Well, since Shondaland is a fantasy land where she pushes her political agenda by re-enacting real life events and twisting them to line up with her liberal agenda. . . . I am looking forward to the following episodes: 'O. J. DIDNT DO IT' 'TUPAC LIVES' 'OBAMA DOES ANOTHER EIGHT YEARS' 'ISIS IS OUR FRIEND.'" This particular fan response speaks to a larger issue that is explicated in the next section, one that focuses on perceptions of how the episode reflected Rhimes's political and personal platforms.

Shonda Rhimes's Political and Personal Platforms

"I am SO TIRED of Hollywood and television using their positions and shows as platforms for their personal political views," wrote one fan articulating their perception that "The Lawn Chair" was more about Rhimes's political agenda and less about *Scandal*'s storyline. Several lengthy exchanges between fans involved comments regarding this issue. One fan's critique of Rhimes's "political agenda" was clear and concise: "Only episode gone from the dvr and only episode I never watched all the way thru. . . . Keep it up and will not be on my list of shows to watch. Delete!" While several fans articulated their dissatisfaction with what they described as the politicking of race-based protest and advocacy, several went as far as saying that they would never watch the show again. One wrote, "Love Scandal and KW but will never watch it again. I go to TV not for Shonda's personal political opinion. I go for an escape. Too bad she felt the need to voice her political opinion that way."

Rhimes's decision to create an episode mirroring #BlackLivesMatter is also described by some fans as "just another cheap shot by the media to produce more hate." As one person asserted, "I found the lack of creativity sad. Let's spread more racial hate by a fake scenario that mimics a real situation that spread racial hate. Very disappointed in the delivery of this personal agenda." A few fans accused Rhimes of "fanning of the flames" of "racial tension" by airing the episode when she did. One specifically wrote, "This episode was irresponsible and designed to re-ignite racial conflict as a result of what happened in Ferguson, any claim otherwise is a lie. The show is capitalizing on a national tragedy and anyone who thinks it was designed to get out a message of racial equality is in denial. It comes down to ratings and $for the show and the network. I am a huge fan of the show but last nights episode was not only irresponsible but out of context and ridiculous." Fan comments condemning the episode as political race-baiting were refuted by other fans who quickly, and on several accounts passionately, came to Rhimes's defense. Several applauded her courage for shedding "the light on the reality of being a minority in America." One fan described "the message [of the episode] as CLEAR, TIMELY and PROFOUND." Others were unapologetic in their praise of Rhimes as someone who has "the power to provide an even larger and more visable platform to showcase (for lack of a better word) the issues at hand."

One individual recognized the episode as "much needed and gutsy" and acknowledged that the topic "can't be resolved in one episode" but that "The Lawn Chair" is "a great way to begin a robust discussion." Within this vein, another fan posted the following response to earlier comments: "For those worried that this episode is 're-igniting racial tension,' please know that it never really goes away and that the only way to beat it is to face it, talk through it, etc and not avoid it. And the opportunity to do so is organic; it never comes at an ideal time. We all have our individual frustrations about race-relations, but directing blame toward the messenger serves no utility." Several fans shared how the episode stimulated discussions regarding race, racism, and police brutality, including one who disclosed "there was a dialogue at my job today and I had a conversation with my 13 year old and my 9 year old boys this morning." These individuals reaffirmed the need to "continue to have the conversation otherwise it will continue to happen over and over. It can no longer just be put aside until the next time it happens."

The idea that most television programming is informed by reality was something that many fans referenced within their responses. In this light, some fans questioned the intense criticism of the episode and its producers and writers. One self-identified African American female viewer focused her critique on the above-mentioned comment that condemned the episode as reigniting racial hate and articulated a need for programming that served as a "break" from the real world:

> I think your comment is indicative of why Shonda thought this ep[isode] was necessary. Whereas certain groups of people are able to receive the "break" that you're asking for and go home at night and not fear for their lives or their children's, others don't have that privilege. She's making a political statement and . . . pushed the issue into our faces and her statement was very clear. This is not the first statement she's made, however. If you're a consistent viewer, she's also been a HUGE advocate for gay rights by pushing the envelope in the relationships she portrays (Hello, gay elected officials with a prostitutes!) . . . but ironically enough, people don't seem to be as offended by these types of politically statements.

This set of comments, in no uncertain terms, challenges the white privilege of some viewers and identifies how Rhimes uses her mediated platform to highlight other social issues, seemingly with little to no pushback. Other African American viewers also took note of the general pattern of those who quickly condemned the episode as problematic. One conducted her own investigation and offered the following reflection:

> Out of curiosity [I] clicked on the people who liked [the critical] post to see the racial makeup. I'm not suggesting that people of color wouldn't agree but in all honesty, I wasn't surprised [that everyone was white]. We, America, need to address these issues. Putting our heads in the sand, making nice, and avoiding tough subject matter does not serve us well. We have to walk in truth even when it is ugly. I'm glad the writers of Scandal had the courage to create this episode. . . . As for fanning flames of hate, whose flames are being fanned? Should they have just created a nice warm fuzzy episode? To me that would be a coward move. Change doesn't come by just going with flow or walking on eggshells just to ensure the crazies won't get upset.

This fan was one of several who commented on the perceived racial differences in reactions to the episode, which is the focus of the final theme.

Polarizing Perceptions Based on Racial and Personal Differences

Each of the themes thus far has explicated a particular aspect of fan emphasis and illustrated how contrasting points of reference inform divergent audience perspectives. According to some, these divergent perspectives are informed by racial differences. The most intense—and at times hostile—exchanges debated the saliency of race in fan reactions to the episode. This debate began when a self-identified African American woman referenced the "fact" that each fan that hated the show appeared, based on their Facebook profile picture, to be white. Her initial comment, as seen below, prompted reactions from several other fans.

FAN#1: LOL the people who hated this episode. What do they all have in common? hmm

FAN#2: If you're implying only white people hated it you're wrong. It was a great episode and I was in tears at the end.

FAN#1: That makes both of us! I loved this episode I said: "what do all of the folks WHO HATED the episode have in common?" I am talking about a group of people who hated this particular episode.

FAN#3: Well, unfortunately thus far only "white[s]" are stating that the episode was poor, boring, etc. It's simply not "their" reality. To you thanks for understanding!

FAN#1: Exactly.

FAN#4: The commonality is people didn't like the episode-stop trying to make it about race. It is about a matter of opinion. Stop trying to make something out of it.

FAN#5: An episode about racial injustice against black people aired during a time police brutality against black lives is a hot topic (not news). Only white people have said they hate the episode. OMG DUH! How can this remotely be tied to race!?????

This exchange, and others like it, created a wedge between viewers who noted the racialization of fan reactions and others who defaulted to colorblindness to argue that liking or disliking the episode was based on personal preference. The divisiveness of comments led one fan to conclude, "Looks like this episode split the Scandal fan base down the middle. . . . I guess half relate to it, half don't." Within this thread, the discussion then moved to whether or not "The Lawn Chair" contributed to the existing racial divide in the United States or incited interracial dialogue and understanding. Some viewers expressed disappointment with the episode's divisiveness and beliefs that it would "antagonize" racially charged situations across the United States. Other viewers, many of whom self-identified as African American, argued that the episode simply acknowledged the existing state of affairs. Addressing their post to Scandal's white Facebook fans, one presumably African American fan penned, "You may live in America, but for me and so many others, it is Amerikkka. And the name is justified. FOR US. That isn't aiding in the 'racial divide' it's just stating how it is for US. There's already a divide. Us acknowledging that there is a divide, won't divide us even more. And if shining light on the problem makes you uncomfortable, you're a part of the problem." Other individuals were also hopeful that the episode could generate some important dialogue. A small but significant number interpreted the content of the show as racially and politically balanced and encouraged viewers to resist reductions of difficult topics into polarizing categories of them/us:

> I'm sorry you found this episode to be divisive. I thought that it did a great job of showing the POV [point of view] of black/brown communities as well as the police officer. While the divergent POVs were presented, I felt that the bigger focus was the humanity of us all. The teen lying in the street, a father's protection, and a father's love. Whether you related more to the father, the protesters, the police, or the govt officials . . . the show ended with two father's sharing the pain of losing a son to murder. Viewing this show as divisive falls into the narrative of what Fox News and MSNBC want us to believe. This show brought both sides of the argument together so that we all can get a glimpse of someone else's perspective. If we focus on that, we can begin the process of unification.

Comments regarding the saliency of race led to a number of contentious exchanges that also appeared to be steeped in particular racial locations and standpoints. Describing Olivia's existence on the show as reflective of "a serious disconnect from her people," several self-identified African American fans wrote passionately about how the episode signaled a "wake up moment" for Olivia in terms of her racial identity. "I'm glad Olivia's black card was finally reinstated," penned one such fan referring to the imaginary documentation of allegiance that exists among African Americans. Other viewers—self-described as white or presumed white by their profile picture—were just as passionate in arguing that race was not relevant in the discussion. None of these individuals acknowledged or responded to the comment about Olivia Pope's "black card"; instead a few critiqued the entire line of discussion as "playing the race card."[33]

DISCUSSION: "#BRINGBACKTHEREALSCANDAL"

#BlackLivesMatter has been described as critical race theory in action.[34] Extending this argument, Rhimes's decision to feature a storyline focused on this formidable sociocultural movement was interpreted as markedly political in nature. As I progressed through the thematic analysis and theorized fan commentary, the contrast in audience reactions—especially those that confronted perceived division based on race—prompted an application of standpoint theories and a nod toward embracing a dialectical perspective. Within this closing section, I utilize existing literature to further engage the four overarching themes synergistically.

Standpoint theories in general and recent research on racial locations and racial standpoints provide a useful lens to understand similar and divergent responses to "The Lawn Chair." The contrast of responses within each of the four themes appears to be reflective, to a certain extent, of a particular location that fosters a viewing lens that is personal/racial and attached/detached.[35] However, divergent perspectives were not solely steeped in racial difference. As such it is imperative that we embrace the concept of intersectionality, which allows us to recognize how multiple aspects of our identity—inclusive of but not limited solely to race—impact our perceptions.[36] Doing so provides much needed insight in explaining how fan reactions to this particular episode did not fall solely along racial lines. Understanding diverse fan reactions is contingent on avoiding arguments that race and racism are or are not a salient issue; instead, assuming a dialectical approach encourages a rejection of either/or and a preference for both/and.[37] In this regard, scholars can acknowledge the diverse reactions to the show and validate how *Scandal* is simultaneously about and not about race and racism depending on who is watching the show and how they experience the world. This line of theorizing resists polarizing viewer perceptions and instead promotes a keen understanding of how a particular media text can mean something different to different audiences. This point is best reflected in the comments of an African American viewer whose socioeconomic status informed her dislike of the show:

> Wow the ignorance is real on this thread. I was bored with the show and I'm an African American woman. I don't need to be reminded by Shonda what I experience daily. I watch television to escape reality. . . . Do you think Shonda has to worry about her children going to school in the hood . . . Guess what? She doesn't. She has money and can afford for her children to mingle with the elite. So stop blaming this on race and do something active in your actual communities, not the Facebook communities to make a change.

Standpoint theory productively highlights how social locations and standpoints inform different interpretations of *Scandal*'s "The Lawn Chair." The themes explicated within this chapter also highlight polysemy, a concept that has been used to analyze explicitly racialized media texts.[38] As demonstrated, fans' Facebook comments reflect how one episode is capable of signifying multiple meanings for different individuals. The saliency of race in this particular episode— given the show's overwhelmingly colorblind approach—fuels an awareness of the polysemic nature of media texts in light of the personal, social, and racial perspectives that individuals bring to their viewing experience.[39] Polysemic analyses can take a number of forms, including resistive readings, strategic ambiguity, hermeneutic depth, or a combination of different forms.[40] While all three forms of polysemy could function as potential lenses for "The Lawn Chair," strategic ambiguity seems the most relevant in understanding fans' reactions within the larger context of Rhimes's successful Shondaland Productions television shows. This particular form of polysemy highlights the creator's ability to intentionally craft highly polysemic texts in order to appeal to the most broad, diverse audience possible.[41] As such, polysemy can be understood as a rhetorical strategy enacted by those in power for profit with little regard for the consequences of diverse polysemic interpretations.

In the 1980s, *The Cosby Show* (NBC 1984–1992) broke new ground as the number one most watched show overall and, more specifically, in European American *and* African American homes. From racially diverse social locations and standpoints, the show was praised for its positive representation of a successful and relatable African American family.[42] Following the overwhelming success of the show, Sut Jhally and Justin Lewis conducted a comprehensive audience analysis.[43] Their findings revealed a thought-provoking (and somewhat unexpected) conclusion: white European American viewers enjoyed watching the everyday lives of a fictional family whom they perceived as typical of a U.S. American household. In contrast, African American viewers saw the Huxtables as an *African American family* with recognitions of race through language, music, art, and other cultural artifacts. While implicit references to race existed, the long-running sitcom was void of any storylines reflective of issues of racial prejudice, discrimination, or racism. This example of a parallel colorblind televisual product provides an interesting line of questioning regarding Shondaland's inclusion of "The Lawn Chair" episode in *Scandal*. Did airing the episode violate the implicit rules of achieving mainstream success through storylines that allow racially diverse audiences to enjoy the show albeit for different reasons? How will the attempt to address race and racism impact viewership? Will this type of content become the new norm in Shondaland, or will it exist as an isolated, never-to-be-referenced-again experience?

These questions reflect a central issue raised implicitly by fan reactions to "The Lawn Chair" episode: What is *Scandal* really about? Based on the data collected for this project, for many fans, the show is about "the drama [and] complex relationships in the White House" and viewers are consumed by all of the "passion and drama" between Fitz, Olivia, Jake, and others. Such sentiments prompted fans to conclude their comments with several exclamations including "#BringBackTheRealScandal," "I miss the old Scandal," "I want the juicy back!!!!," and "its time to get back to the down and dirty Scandal! #SexLies&Deceit." For others, "the main focus of the show" has always been "the intrigues, political 'scandals,' and government secrets of Washington, D.C." Still other viewers are committed fans because of the positive portrayal of an attractive, intelligent, successful, and powerful, African American woman. Clearly, like Bill Cosby and *The Cosby Show*, Shonda Rhimes has created a television program that attracts diverse viewers to the same show through different points of connection. Given this, several core questions remain as I attempt to conclude this analysis: Is *Scandal* about politics or romance? Do storylines reflective of current events fit in or distract from the legacy of the show? Is it based on reality or fantasy? Does the show work to promote or disrupt racial harmony? And finally, will Rhimes continue to create a televisual colorblind experience or use her platform to explicitly address race-related issues? Embracing the core idea of radical polysemy—that textual ambiguity fosters media interpretations that "endorse contradictory principles as both being true"—my emphatic response to each of these questions is to resist choosing one option over the other, and instead, answer with a resounding YES! In Shondaland, everything and anything is possible.[44]

NOTES

1. Kat Ward, "The Lawn Chair: Ferguson Comes to Olivia Pope's Washington," *Entertainment Weekly*, March 5, 2015, http://www.ew.com/recap/scandal-season-4-episode-14.

2. Ward.

3. Mark Orbe and Tina M. Harris, *Interracial Communication: Theory into Practice* (Thousand Oaks, Calif.: Sage, 2015), 276–277; Maryann Erigha, "Shonda Rhimes, *Scandal*, and the Politics of Crossing Over," *Black Scholar* 45, no. 1 (2015): 10–11.

4. Erigha, "Shonda Rhomes," 11.

5. Mark Orbe, "The Quest for Normalcy: Signifying Interracial Romantic Alliances in Post-Racial *Scandal*ous Times," in *Gladiators in Suits: Race, Gender, and the Politics of Representation in* Scandal, ed. Kimberly Moffitt, Simone Puff, and Ronald Jackson II (Syracuse, N.Y.: Syracuse University Press, forthcoming).

6. Black Lives Matter, "About the Black Lives Matter Network," accessed August 1, 2017, http://blacklivesmatter.com/about/.

7. "At Least 1134 Black Lives Matter Demonstrations Have Been Held in the Last 513 Days," *Elephrame*, December 7, 2015, https://elephrame.com/textbook/protests.

8. Ward, "The Lawn Chair."

9. Alicia Garza, "A Herstory of the "BlackLivesMatter Movement," *Feminist Wire*, March 8, 2014, http://thefeministwire.com/2014/10/blacklivesmatter-2/.

10. Tara-Lynne Pixley, "Trope and Associates: Olivia Pope's Scandalous Blackness," *Black Scholar* 45, no. 1 (2015): 28.

11. Brenda J. Allen, "Black Womanhood and Feminist Standpoints," *Management Communication Quarterly* 11, no. 4 (1998): 575.

12. Lynn O'Brien Hallstein, "Where Standpoint Stands Now: An Introduction and Commentary," *Women's Studies in Communication* 23 (2000): 1–15; Sandra Harding, *Whose Science? Whose Knowledge? Thinking from Women's Lives* (New York: Cornell University Press, 1991); Dorothy Smith, *The Everyday World as Problematic: A Feminist Sociology* (Boston: Northeastern University Press, 1987); Katrina Bell-Jordan, Mark Orbe, Darlene Drummond, and Sakile Camara, "Accepting the Challenge of Centralizing without Essentializing: Black Feminist Thought and African American Women's Communicative Experiences," *Women's Studies in Communication* 23, no. 1 (2000): 41–62.

13. Orbe and Harris, *Interracial Communication*, 13–16.

14. Patricia Hill Collins, "Learning from the Outsider Within: The Sociological Significance of Black Feminist Thought," *Social Problems* 33, no. 6 (1986): S14–S32.

15. Julia T. Wood, "Feminist Standpoint Theory and Muted Group Theory: Commonalities and Divergences," *Women and Language* 28 (2005): 61–64.

16. Harding, *Whose Science?*

17. Hallstein, "Where Standpoint Stands Now."

18. Hallestein, 16.

19. Wood, "Feminist Standpoint Theory," 61.

20. Collins, "Learning from the Outsider Within," S18.

21. Mark Orbe, "'Diverse Understandings of a 'Post-Racial' Society," in *Globalizing Intercultural Communication: A Reader*, ed. Kathryn Sorrells and Sachi Sekimoto (Thousand Oaks, Calif.: Sage, 2016), 23–34; Kiesha T. Warren, Mark Orbe, and Nancy Greer-Williams, "Perceiving Conflict: Similarities and Differences between and among Latino/as, African Americans, and European Americans," in *Brown and Black Communication: Latino and African American Conflict and Convergence in Mass Media*, ed. Diana I. Rios and A. N. Mohamed (Westport, Conn.: Praeger, 2003), 13–26.

22. Orbe, "Diverse Understandings," 25; Warren, Orbe, and Greer-Williams, "Perceiving Conflict," 22.

23. Facebook, "Scandal," https://www.facebook.com/ScandalABC/; Nancy Cornwell and Mark Orbe, "'Keepin' It Real' and/or 'Sellin' Out to the Man': African-American Responses to Aaron McGruder's *The Boondocks*," in *Say It Loud! African-American Audiences, Media, and Identity*, ed. Robin Means-Coleman (New York: Routledge, 2002), 27–43.

24. Grant McCracken, *The Long Interview* (Newbury Park, Calif.: Sage, 1998); William Owen, "Interpretive Themes in Relational Communication," *Quarterly Journal of Speech* 70, no. 3 (1984): 274–287.

25. McCracken, *The Long Interview*, 19.

26. Owen, "Interpretive Themes."

27. Etsuko Kinefuchi and Mark Orbe, "Situating Oneself in a Racialized World: Understanding Student Reactions to *Crash* through Standpoint Theory and Context-Positionality Frames," *Journal of International & Intercultural Communication* 25, no. 1 (2008): 70–90.

28. To maintain the authenticity of viewers' comments, I have retained the original wording, grammar, syntax, and spelling. The only exception to this guiding principle was making corrections that were deemed necessary for reader comprehension.

29. Throughout the analysis, specific comments generally will be attributed to "fans" or "one fan in particular." However, when relevant, additional descriptors will be added (e.g., "a self-identified African American fan").

30. "Jumped the shark" is a phrase used in the television industry to describe when a show reaches a point where far-fetched events are featured for novelty's sake. Referencing a *Happy Days* episode that literally had a lead character (Fonzie) jumping over a shark on water skis, such a practice typically is indicative that a show has lost its way and is declining in quality. See *Happy Days*, "Hollywood Part 3," season 5, episode 3, directed by Jerry Paris, written by Fred Fox Jr., aired on September 20, 1977, on ABC.

31. "Olitz" is a term used by fans to refer to Olivia and Fitz as a couple.

32. This is the chant that protesters in the episode used when they rallied to confront police following Brandon Parker's death.

33. "Playing the race card" is commonly used by European Americans when people of color raise issues of race within situations where it has no relevance. The implied metamessage is that African American fans brought up the issue of race to gain advantage in a discussion where race had little, if any, saliency.

34. Mark Orbe, "#AllLivesMatter."

35. Kinefuchi and Orbe, "Situating Oneself in a Racialized World."

36. Kimberlé Crenshaw, "Mapping the Margins: Intersectionality, Identity, Politics, and Violence against Women of Color," in *Critical Race Theory: The Key Writings That Formed That Movement*, ed. Kimberlé Crenshaw, Neil Gotanda, Gary Peller, and Kendall Thomas (New

York: New Press, 1995), 357–383; Warren, Orbe, and Greer-Williams, "Perceiving Conflict," 24–25.

37. Judith Martin and Tom Nakayama, "Thinking Dialectically about Culture and Communication," *Communication Theory* 9, no. 1 (1999): 1–25.

38. Lisa Glebatis Perks, "Polysemic Scaffolding: Explicating Discursive Clashes in *Chappelle's Show*," *Communication, Culture & Critique* 3, no. 2 (2010): 270–289; Robert Rowland and Robert Strain, "Social Function, Polysemy and Narrative-Dramatic Form: A Case Study of *Do the Right Thing*," *Communication Quarterly* 42, no. 3 (1994): 213–228.

39. Tara-Lynne Pixley, "Trope and Associates," 28.

40. Leah Ceccarelli, "Polysemy: Multiple Meanings in Rhetorical Criticism," *Quarterly Journal of Speech* 84, no. 4 (1998): 395–415; Lisa Glebatis Perks, "Polysemic Scaffolding," 270–289.

41. Ceccarelli, "Polysemy," 404.

42. Orbe and Harris, *Interracial Communication*, 290.

43. Sut Jhally and Justin Lewis, *Enlightened Racism: The Cosby Show, Audiences, and the Myth of the American Dream* (San Francisco: Westview Press, 1992).

44. Rowland and Strain, "Social Function, Polysemy and Narrative-Dramatic Form," 214.

10 · BLURRING PRODUCTION BOUNDARIES WITH FAN EMPOWERMENT

Scandal as Social Television

MARY INGRAM-WATERS
AND LESLIE BALDERAS

Since the debut of the political thriller *Scandal* (ABC 2012–2018), its fans have used social media to engage each other and the show's actors and producers with their thoughts, desires, and criticisms. A fast-paced melodramatic serial, the show follows Olivia Pope, played by Kerry Washington, as she orchestrates crisis interventions for Washington, D.C., elites including the president, with whom she has an on-and-off-again affair. For seven seasons, social media platforms such as Twitter, YouTube, Tumblr, and Instagram have served as sites for direct interaction between fans and *Scandal*'s cast and crew, including showrunner and coproducer Shonda Rhimes. Fans, the majority of whom are thought to be African American women, have used these social media platforms to create and maintain a vast arena for exploring every conceivable aspect of the show, from Olivia's fashion and home décor to links to real-world activism and politics such as the Black Lives Matter movement and the campaign of the first female U.S. presidential candidate.[1] At the same time, Rhimes has deliberately crafted a social media presence for *Scandal* that has, from the very beginning, gone above and beyond traditional web-based advertising. In doing so, she has set a new industry standard and, as we explore in this chapter, actively reshaped the ways that television producers and audiences interact. From a critical media studies perspective, the industry standard set by Rhimes's production company, Shondaland, is especially fruitful to examine because it has restructured power relations between producers, actors, and fans by opening up an avenue for fan empowerment.

Though fans have an array of online spaces to perform their fandom, including curatorial and image-based platforms Tumblr and Instagram, they are most
prolific on Twitter, a social media platform that allows users to post 140-character
"tweets" and to access others' real-time and archived tweets. On Twitter, fans can
tag other fans, retweet others' tweets, and use hashtags to add their tweets to an
ongoing chain discussion. Tens of thousands of fans "live-tweet" their reactions
during first-run episodes of *Scandal*. In 2012, Nielsen, a global consumer trends
firm, began collecting data from Twitter to assess televised shows' social media
impact.[2] Since 2013, *Scandal* has been in its top ten list of shows represented on
Twitter.[3] In 2015–2016, season 5 of *Scandal* averaged 133,000 tweets per episode.[4]
Though Shondaland has other popular shows including *Grey's Anatomy* (ABC
2005–present; also referred to as *Grey's*), *How to Get Away with Murder* (ABC
2014–present; also referred to as *HTGAWM*), *The Catch* (ABC 2016–2017), *Grey's*
spinoff *Station 19* (ABC 2018–present), and *For the People* (ABC 2018–present),
Scandal has had the strongest and most consistent social media presence.

Scandal's use of Twitter has been deliberate and successful. According to
Rhimes, she initially used Twitter to remind fans to watch her shows, but "it later
became a different tool" when, at Washington's suggestion, she "mobilized everyone to live tweet the episodes."[5] For journalists, entertainment analysts, bloggers, and scholars who write about *Scandal*, the cast and crew's commitment to
connecting with fans via Twitter is a key ingredient to its commercial success.[6]
Though Rhimes's other shows use similar social media strategies like live-tweeting
first-run episodes, *Scandal* is unique because its Twitter presence is dominated
by the strategic live-tweeting of its first-run episodes by cast, crew, and fans. Since
its 2012 debut, nearly all of its series regulars, including Washington, Tony Goldwyn (President Fitzgerald "Fitz" Grant), Bellamy Young (senator, former first lady,
and now president, Mellie Grant), and its producers, including Rhimes and Betsy
Beers, use Twitter to live-tweet during first-run episodes. They also tweet reminders to watch the show the day of the new episode. Fans tweet at each other, the
actors, and other industry professionals using official hashtags such as #ABC-
Scandal and #AskScandal that are always promoted in the hours before, during,
and after a first-run episode. Fans also generate their own hashtags in direct
response to an episode or storyline such as #olitz (a portmanteau of Olivia and
Fitz that represents a preference for a romantic relationship between the two
characters) and #DieJakeDie. Fans also regularly tweet their reactions to
show gossip, and actors' and producers' professional and personal tweets. For
example, Washington hosts an #AskKerry hashtag to answer fans' questions. One
fan, @WilliamGrace18, writes, "@kerrywashington have you talked to any of the
#scandal cast lately about something other than work? #AskKerry," to which
Washington replies, "Yep. Talked to @KatieQLowes a few days ago. Hung out with
@ShondaRhimes last week. #AskKerry."[7] This one exchange has 10 positive and
enthusiastic comments left by fans, 286 likes, and 68 retweets, demonstrating

that fans respond and reuse industry professionals' tweets. Fans often respond to and retweet official material, such as previews, one of which we analyze in this essay. As a final distinction of fans' Twitter use, fans are incredibly loyal, tweeting multiple times in a single episode.[8]

African American women use Twitter at a rate higher than expected given their representation in the overall population.[9] Similar to general studies on their use of Twitter, African American women tweet about *Scandal* and *How to Get Away with Murder* to build community and empower each other through callouts and shared cultural criticisms.[10] For example, Williams and Gonlin describe how black women use Twitter to respond with code switching language to *HTGAWM*'s critically acclaimed "reveal" scene in which Annalise Keating, portrayed by African American actor Viola Davis, removes her wig, revealing her natural kinky hair. They argue that the wig scene operates as a moment for shared but intimate values, recognizable for its importance as a political moment mostly to other black women.[11] Politicizing Twitter as a potential site of exploitation, scholars have also suggested that African American women—more broadly, women of color—perform massive amounts of unpaid physical, emotional, and "informational labor" to highlight social injustices and educate their Twitter peers who benefit from race- and gender-based privilege.[12] The burden that women of color carry in having to explain racism and intersectional feminism, often on their own behalf, to people occupying positions of power extends far beyond Twitter and social media platforms.[13] Thus, when African American women tweet using the hashtag #twiceasgood, a reference to a monologue delivered by Olivia's father, Rowan Pope, played by African American actor Joe Morton, in which he spells out how he raised Olivia with the expectation that she had to be "twice as good to get half as much as what they have," their tweets function as pedagogical labor with the presumed intent to expose and challenge normative viewpoints.[14] In effect, these tweets also function as a site of resistance against racism and sexism.

Scandal's Twitter presence is a nexus between its actors, producers, and fans, and thus reflects the new phenomenon of "social television" which has been ushered in via the evolution of technology and new media. Social television, also known as "Social TV" and "second screen viewing," refers to watching a televised program while simultaneously engaging with others also watching the show through social media applications or other internet media platforms.[15] Social television describes the process by which thousands of fans and *Scandal*'s actors and producers live-tweet their reactions during the show and engage in conversation enabled by social media. It also refers to accessing other related media content while watching televised programs, such as fans watching *Scandal* while also looking at the show's website or other fans' Tumblr pages. Live interactions with other fans, actors, producers, and ancillary texts, all in relation to a source text such as *Scandal*, are the primary channels of fandom participation in social television.

Scandal offers a unique case study for examining social television–based fandom dynamics because of its mass popularity at a time when new media technologies are revolutionizing communication. Scholars who study social television often explore the newly reconfigured power relationships between fans and producers that are facilitated by the convergence of televised programming and social media.[16] Scholars who study fans often investigate the content and form of fan interactions as well as the new knowledge created by those interactions around source texts.[17] Merged together, social television fandom is a fandom whose performance of fan activities and knowledge plays out across social media during the consumption of the source text in real time. Drawing on scholarly work on social television and fans, we examine how *Scandal* fans, through their social media interactions with other fans and actors and producers, utilize the new configurations of power afforded by social television to perform their fandom and generate new fan knowledge. In the following section, we bring these two fields, social television and fan studies, into conversation.

SOCIAL TELEVISION AND FAN STUDIES

Selva describes social television as the "social practice of commenting on television shows with peers, friends, and unknown people, who are all connected together through various digital devices."[18] Social television, as a manifestation of media convergence, is thus a site for the collective power of consumers as fans to directly, visibly, and rapidly, make demands on producers.[19] While early studies of fans similarly focused on their collective ability to influence producers, more recent work focuses on fan engagement with a range of industry professionals across multiple media platforms.[20] While fans theoretically could use social television to interact with producers in influential ways, research thus far shows that they do not upset existing industry power structures that privilege media producers as decision makers.[21] Further, fans perform valuable unpaid labor by marketing, advertising, and educating other consumers about the media text through social mediated fan practices.[22] When fans use Twitter hashtags, especially corporate-sponsored and promoted hashtags, to discuss televised or live events, they literally extend those events to time-shifted audiences and would-be consumers in other parts of the world.[23] Producers largely set the terms for social television–based fan practices and thus, as previously mentioned, arguably benefit more than fans do from what seems like an empowering position for fans.

Though social television practices harness fans' enthusiasm in ways that benefit industry professionals, these practices also form a liminal space for fans' engagement with each other and with media texts.[24] Whether through sharing reactions, challenging narratives, offering interpretations, or connecting through their own identities, fans create added meanings for source texts, which then circulate as ancillary texts, contributing to "collective intelligence."[25] Industry professionals who use social media can be called out, retweeted, and tagged by fans, thus getting caught up in fans' meaning-making processes.[26] Fans see themselves as cocreators of media texts, if through nothing more than voicing their opinions and attempting to harness the collective power of their desires.[27] This can be contentious because industry professionals hold institutional power over media texts, which engenders fans' resentment when it is used to shut them down. Fans can thus draw on the technological features of social media platforms like Twitter to co-opt industry professionals' voices, simultaneously blurring boundaries and creating new meanings for the text.

Even fan studies scholars who are skeptical of fans' power to influence producers and source texts recognize that fans, by virtue of their collective identity, wield a great deal of cultural power.[28] Fans' cultural power resides in their influence on how texts are interpreted, remixed, and connected to other domains of fans' lives.[29] When fans connect texts to these new domains, they extend the texts' reach to new audiences.[30] Many studies of media fans revealed them to be communities of mostly women who, through word of mouth, email listservs, and now, social media, participated in "talking story" as they challenged source texts and created fan knowledge.[31] Fans use commonly held source texts as cultural touchstones from which they can affirm or transform texts' dominant narratives.[32]

Scandal fans' cultural power manifests in tweets where they react to the text while they are watching it. In their tweets, they imagine, desire, critique, and transform the text in dialogue with other fans and, often, industry producers and actors. According to Nielsen, millions of others on Twitter are exposed to these tweets and, in a 2014 Nielsen study on the impact of television-related tweets, a whopping 90 percent of people who see television-related tweets go on to "take action to further engage with the show—whether to watch, search for, or share content about it."[33] While this is certainly evidence of fans doing unpaid labor on behalf of the multibillion dollar global media industry, it also conveys fans' tremendous cultural power to inspire and inform engagement with television. These two lines of scholarly focus prompt us to position *Scandal* as an informative case study of the dynamics of social television–based fandom. We see how industry professionals' deliberate strategies to use Twitter to simultaneously build, maintain, and expand a fan base can prompt fans to engage in voluminous unpaid fan labor that benefits the industry. Yet, we simultaneously see this fan engagement, performed in significant part by African American women, resulting in a shared fandom space to celebrate, criticize, and reimagine *Scandal*. The added significance of *Scandal* is that it is a history-making television show at the crossroads of race and gender; it was created by Rhimes as a black female showrunner and features Kerry Washington as the black female protagonist whose character is inspired by Judy Smith, a black woman who founded a Washington, D.C., crisis management firm.[34]

METHODS

We employ a qualitative case study approach to analyze how industry profession-als and fans use Twitter to interact with each other. Given the literature discussed above, we start by identifying two categories of purposes for tweeting: (1) how industry professionals use Twitter for promotion of the show and (2) how fans use Twitter to react to the show. With those two distinctions in mind, we then analyze industry professionals' and fans' tweets for both the tweet technique and content. Next, we analyze how the channel of power works between industry pro-fessionals and fans by interpreting if the tweet is an example of unpaid fan labor, fan engagement, or some combination of both.

We started by identifying two official Twitter accounts associated with *Scandal*, @Shondaland and @ScandalABC. From there, we identified two recent social media campaigns as examples of industry professionals using Twitter for promo-tion purposes: #ScandalCutOut, a game for fans, and #SaveJake?, a promoted hashtag posted with the season 5 finale trailer. We used Twitter's official search and advanced search mechanisms to identify relevant tweets. This allowed us to target specific users, both senders and recipients, by their Twitter handles, along with key words in their Tweets, hashtags, and a date range for tweets. With #ScandalCutOut, we analyzed all 60 tweeted fan responses, including the win-ning tweet of the fan competition. With #SaveJake?, we analyzed all 195 tweeted fan responses. During the season 5 finale, we noted one trending fan-generated hashtag as an example of fans using Twitter to react to the show: #DieJakeDie, which is critical of both Jake Ballard's character and his romantic relationship with Olivia Pope. For #DieJakeDie, we analyzed an estimated 200 tweets that appeared on May 12, 2016, the date of the season 5 finale. We present our data analysis of social television interactions through a discussion of each hashtag.

DATA ANALYSIS

#ScandalCutOut

The hashtag #ScandalCutOut indicates an official game sponsored by industry professionals, whose images and voices are represented by the @Shondaland Twitter account. During the hiatus between seasons 5 and 6, industry profession-als initiated #ScandalCutOut as a means to continue engagement with fans in lieu of the usual strategy of live-tweeting first-run episodes. The game was designed to tweet a caption in response to an image of life-size cardboard cutouts of series regulars Washington, Young, Goldwyn, and Katie Lowes (Quinn Perkins). In the image, the cutouts of the four actors are propped up in a tiered-floor lecture hall, reminiscent of the one used by Viola Davis's character, Annalise Keating, when she teaches her law classes in *How to Get Away with Murder*.

Everything about the tweet, from the image to the content to the hashtag to the rules of the game was clearly controlled by industry professionals. Immediately prior to tweeting the image to be captioned, @Shondaland tweeted five short rules, which specified: the length of the caption, that fans could submit unlimited captions, that the image should be retweeted with the caption, that the #ScandalCutOut hashtag should be used, and that fans should have fun. The rules, even if loosely followed, would ensure that fans' engagement would include multiple technical features that would bring other fans or potential fans into contact with *Scandal*, including the visibility and continued promotion of ABC's hashtags, conversation about two Shondaland shows, and space for unlimited fan engagement.

Underscoring the industry as the primary source of power, the content of the image brought together the most famous faces of *Scandal* with the most recognizable setting in *HTGAWM*. @Shondaland also controlled the technical aspects of the tweet, including its timing, and the creation, sponsorship, and use of the #ScandalCutOut hashtag. Presumably, @Shondaland controls the content that shows up under the hashtag as all of the visible, tweeted captions are, at the very least, positive. While the rules could have allowed fans to vote for their favorite tweeted caption, industry professionals controlled this too. @Shondaland picked the winning tweeted caption, one of five submitted by @Ana_Elle971, which reads, "We already know how to get away with murder. We just want to compare our methods." The caption brings *Scandal* and *HTGAWM* into alignment, as all of the characters pictured had literally gotten away with murder on the show: Olivia murdered former vice president Andrew Nichols, Fitz murdered Supreme Court justice Verna Thornton, Mellie facilitated the murder of sixteen grand jurors, and Quinn murders regularly through her work with Olivia's firm.[35] Therefore, each character's crimes could certainly be imagined as a "case" to be discussed by Keating with her law students.

Though Twitter has proprietary algorithms that control exactly what a user sees when they click on any given hashtag (i.e., language settings, filters for content, users' previously noted preferences for content), when we followed #ScandalCutOut, we counted sixty original tweeted captions, most of which followed the set rules. Of those sixty tweeted captions, twenty-seven were related to *Scandal*, sixteen were random, eleven referenced *HTGAWM*, and six alluded to the 2016 U.S. presidential election. The majority of the captions were about *Scandal*. Examples include @tortillatat's "When Fitz was with Olivia & Mellie but they both left him and are now BFFS and Quinn wants to desperately be in with them" and @merthantrash's "O:You bet your ass we will win this election F: go vote for my exwife O: I'll rig it if I have to . . ." With both of these captions, fans are reaffirming the source text. Moreover, in season 5, Olivia and Mellie have both separated from Fitz and are working together on Mellie's presidential campaign. Fans also submitted sixteen captions that seemed relatively unrelated to any source text, such as @bobblheadlives' "Random: college rule 101 if the teacher isn't here in 5mins class is cancelled." The winning caption was one of the eleven tweets that connected *Scandal* with *HTGAWM*. Others in this group include @basicllybellamy's "When squad rolls up in Annalise Keating's class" and @oliviakepners' "How To Get Away With Rigging A National Election." This last caption also crosses into the final category of six captions that referenced the ongoing presidential election. Others include @jelianpriscely's "fitz, liv, mellie, & quinn watching last night's debate" which references one of the U.S. presidential debates.

Capitalizing on unpaid fan labor, this contest serves the network's interests in pooling the popularity of both shows and enticing fan loyalty and crossover. Fans apply their creative energy for an opportunity to win an official contest and, in doing so, sustain interest in the show during its hiatus. This example illuminates a traditional media power dynamic: producers interact with fans on their own terms, control fan responses, and control discourses about each show. Yet, fans' creative energy also produces new ways of thinking about the source text. While @Shondaland rewards the fan who brings together *Scandal* and *HTGAWM*, fans also use the space to affirm captivating story lines from the current season. Finally, fans use the contest to link their shared source text to current political events, which offers the clearest picture of fans' empowerment as it manifests through social television's newly configured channels of power.

#SaveJake?

In this section, we look at the promoted hashtag, #SaveJake? and the overwhelm-ingly negative direct responses it generated to illustrate the tension that can arise when industry professionals and resistant fans come into conflict via social television. On May 9, 2016, @ScandalABC tweeted a trailer for season 5's finale. The trailer indicated that Jake, played by Scott Foley, would be imperiled and that only Olivia might be able to save him. The tweet read, "Can Oliva #SaveJake?" Between that tweet and the May 12 finale, there were 195 direct comments to the tweet, 161 retweets of it, and it was favorited 486 times. In our analysis of the content of the 195 direct comments in response to @ScandalABC's tweet, only nine comments voiced support for Olivia saving Jake, while three seemed to address other unrelated storylines, and 183 comments rejected the call for Olivia to save Jake, instead wanting Jake's storyline to end.

Eight of the nine comments in support of #SaveJake allude to support for Olivia and Jake's romantic relationship. Fan @enola_pc writes, "@ScandalABC I hope so. Amazing chapter 5*20" and @debsabedin writes, "Tell her I'm chasing the sun. I do love that reference to their past." @enola_pc expresses general support for the characters' pairing and references satisfaction with a recent episode where Jake renewed his commitment to being with Oliva. @debsabedin also demon-strates support by directly referencing Jake's quote, "Tell her I'm chasing the sun," which is an allusion to a romantic interlude between Olivia and Jake on a remote tropical island at the end of season 3. The one quote that shows support for the tweeted trailer and hashtag but not necessarily the character pairing is @jeneadeheayea's "And EVEYONE else has to remember SHONDA and her writers is on a journey w/THEIR. T.V.characters!" @jeneadeheayea's comment shows support for the creative process by calling out Rhimes by her first name, but also criticizes the vast majority of fans who have vocalized their disdain for Jake.

The majority of the 195 direct comments posted to @ScandalABC's tweeted season 5 trailer and promoted hashtag #SaveJake? are negative. When analyzed, the comments manifested three, sometimes overlapping, categories of meaning: general negativity toward Jake; negativity toward Jake and Olivia's relationship; and resentment toward a recycled storyline. Fans who generally dislike Jake's character tweeted responses similar to what @belladamenoir writes, "Liv gotta save his whiny ass AGAIN?! Three seasons and he still can't save himself?" The tweet includes an animated image of a celebrity saying "That's pathetic" and generates further fan attention, receiving two direct comments, thirty-three retweets, and eighty-six favorites. Implicit in @belladamenoir's critique is that Jake is not worth Olivia's attention as he should be more than capable of saving himself. Close to the general disregard for Jake is the more nuanced dislike for his relationship with Olivia and, usually, a preference for Olivia to be romantically involved with Fitz (often referred to as "Olitz"), as expressed by @sugarsugar95, "its amazing that the season you advertised as #AtLast for Olitz is ending with Olivia saving Jake. Lie much?" This fan refers to the dramatic season premiere trailer which seems to promise that Olivia and Fitz would finally be together, open and public with their relationship. Further, @sugarsugar95 indicates a feeling akin to betrayal for now seeing the season end with Oliva and Jake together.

A second notable nuance from this critique comes from three presumably African American women (as derived from their Twitter handles and their profile pictures). @Schulersistas, whose profile picture is a cartoon version of an older African American woman in a generic superhero costume, writes, "@ScandalABC We watch a black woman struggling with PTSD and we supposed to care about this crap. .#saveliv." Even though she is directly answering the tweeted trailer, @Schulersistas begins her tweet by tagging @ScandalABC. This technique allows her response to be attached to the show's official Twitter account. @Schulersistas then critiques not only the Olivia/Jake relationship but indicates that she would prefer to see Olivia engaging in self-care to heal herself. @Schulersistas finishes her tweet with a new content-based fan-generated hashtag, #saveliv. Her tweet garners five retweets and twenty-eight favorites, indicating that her specific criticism is shared and appreciated. As a Twitter user, @Schulersistas has more than 1,300 followers, one of whom is former U.S. president Barack Obama.

Addressing a third category of negativity toward the trailer and hashtag, fan @bellebailey2 writes, "This whole story including that hashtag is pathetic. Can we go one season without him needing to be saved?" Notably, her comment generates three direct comments, twenty-one retweets, and is favorited seventy-nine times, thus garnering about as much Twitter-based attention as @belladamenoir's tweet. This fan's dissatisfaction is due to what she sees as a resurrection of previous seasons' storylines, which had Jake in danger and surviving only because Olivia, in some way, rescued him.

A further distinction on this line of critique comes from @marilynprescott (whose profile picture is of former U.S. president Barack Obama), who writes, "@kendradws @ScandalABC African American women made this show popular. We watched, tweeted, and advertised." Her comment comes directly after @kendradws's tweet, which itself is a broad commentary about not feeling appreciated as a fan who has continued to express loud, sustained criticism about the Jake/Olivia relationship. By directly replying to @kendradws's tweet, @marilynprescott connects their critiques and implies her explanation: that African American women, who imagine shared ownership of *Scandal* by virtue of their fan work on Twitter, are not valued for their substantive criticisms or taken seriously. Her tweet gets one direct reply and three favorites. @griffithcleo, whose profile picture is a snowy landscape, responds with, "@MarilynPrescott @kendradws @ScandalABC Now it's catering to the young white ones who is all about Mellie and Joke. I want Fitz/Liv back s1." Like @marilynprescott, she tags sympathetic fans as a means to be in conversation with them and express like-minded support. She furthers @marilynprescott's explanation to include who she thinks does carry influence: "young white ones" who prefer "Mellie and Joke." Presumably, Joke is a deliberate misspelling of Jake. Like many other fans, she expresses her desire for a return to Olitz, even specifying season one's portrayal of their relationship.

Arguably, any Twitter-based attention, ranging from exuberantly positive to cynically negative, directed toward a season finale trailer functions in @Scandal ABC's and Shondaland's interests. Fans see that the initial tweet gets attention in the form of hundreds of responses, comments, retweets, and favorites, and are thus motivated to watch the trailer and partake in social television. Because the Twitter platform does not have a visual icon for showing "dislike," akin to an iteration of Facebook, fans' protest appears to be general fan engagement unless individual tweets are read to grasp the author's positive or negative sentiment. Furthermore, fans who retweet the initial post, sometimes with their own commentary on it, effectively send and subsequently promote the trailer to their followers. Three of the fans discussed above, @bellebailey2, @belladamenoir, and @schulersistas, each boast followers that number in the low thousands. Though it would be hard to know which of their followers see any given post, based upon earlier discussed research on Twitter users' impact, we can assume that many of them do and that many of them go on to "take action" with regard to watching the show.[36]

Yet, the collective power of the fans to resist the hashtag and the relationship it connotes cannot be ignored here. Consider @jenodomoth's tweet, ". . . Hahahah that was so hilarious . . . I'm just everyone's response," which is slang to mean that she identified with everyone's else's tweet. As a fan disgruntled by Jake's storyline, regardless of the reason, she could easily see that she was in good company. In our analysis of the 195 tweeted responses, we noted one additional trend in technique. The few fans expressing support had no direct responses, nor were they tagged by any other fans in their own tweets. However, fans expressing dissatisfaction received direct responses, retweets, favorites, and @belladamenoir, @bellebailey2, @schulersistas, and many others were tagged in responding tweets. Thus, the collective intelligence here, that Jake should not be saved, which would end their romantic relationship, drew fans together in a networked conversation enabled by the Twitter platform.

#DieJakeDie

#DieJakeDie is a fan-generated hashtag that emerged on Twitter in August 2013, shortly after Jake joined the cast of *Scandal*. As indicated in the above discussion of fans' negative responses to @ScandalABC's promoted #SaveJake?, many fans regularly criticize Jake and his relationship with Olivia. Though it rarely reaches the level of trending, #DieJakeDie is used during fans' live-tweeting of first-run episodes in response to two general themes: when Olivia is romantic with Jake rather than Fitz and when Jake is central to a plotline, regardless of his romantic involvement with Olivia.

Again, Twitter's algorithms for how hashtags trend is proprietary knowledge, meaning that Twitter does not make public exactly how many tweets in a certain amount of time it takes for a hashtag to trend "organically." However, hashtags do make its official trends list when they are promoted, meaning that the parent corporation has paid to have its hashtag appear at the top of Twitter's trends list, and when they emerge at a very quick rate across a population. During the season 5 finale, for a few brief minutes, #DieJakeDie made the list. Fans who do not like Jake, or do not like Jake with Olivia, live-tweeted their reactions to the show and included the #DieJakeDie hashtag. Their specific techniques also included tagging other sympathetic fans and sometimes, industry professionals. For example, @travelfoodfun writes, "@iMargo_CEO @kerrywashington @tonygoldwyn OK!!! Vermont was a possibility!! Barely 20 minutes and my pressure is up! #Die-JakeDie can fix it!" This fan first tags a fellow fan, @IMargo_CEO, who has more than three thousand followers and has also used the #DieJakeDie hashtag. Then she tags industry professionals Washington and Goldwyn by their Twitter handles, presumably because she supports Olivia's romantic relationship with Fitz. The content of her tweet also shows her preference as it is a recognition that Fitz alludes to his desire to end up in a house he built in Vermont for he and Olivia to settle into after his presidency. Finishing her tweet with the hashtag indicates that @IMargo_CEO sees Jake as an impediment to the actualization of Olitz's Happily Ever After.

Within a few minutes of live-tweeting, like-minded fans deliberately tried to get #DieJakeDie to trend, meaning that it would show up on Twitter's top ten trends list. Fan @ward_myla writes, "@allanhaswave Ima fall out on the floor in this shit really happens. Do u think we pull this off? #Goddamn #DieJakeDie #DieJakeDie." She goes on to write similar tweets, repeating the hashtag as many as seven times in a single tweet. In one tweet, she writes only #DieJakeDie and #Scandal. In her first tweet, @ward_myla uses the technique similar to the one described above: tag a like-minded fan and then use hashtags to indicate content. While #DieJakeDie is a hashtag with a specific function, it is also a substantive statement on the source material, indicating that fans want to influence Jake's storyline. @Ward_myla's later tweets link her hashtag critique to #Scandal which means that any fan who clicked on that hashtag would encounter #DieJakeDie too. It is difficult to assess exactly how many fans used the #DieJakeDie hashtag during the season 5 finale because Twitter does not make that data available through its own search and advanced search mechanisms; however, we estimate that about two hundred tweets show up in Twitter's archive of the hashtag on that date. While that number is low for the hashtag to reach trending status, it is possible for hashtags to emerge at such a quick rate that they make the list of top trends despite the total number of tweets. Twitter's archived tweets may change over time so that only "top" tweets from a hashtag archive remain.

#DieJakeDie offers a complex look at the fan-industry dynamics of social television. On the one hand, the fan-generated hashtag shows that fans are watching the show and live-tweeting it, thus performing fan labor alongside fan engagement. Though their tweets are negative, they are still tweets that serve the industry's interests because they assure the continued deployment of official *Scandal* hashtags, are a measure of viewership, and indicate that the source material is worth talking about. However, they convey a strong sense of dissatisfaction with a character and an entire storyline. In doing so, they form the boundaries of a community of fans who do not like aspects of the show yet do presumably value and enjoy communicating about their dislike. In other words, for some fans, we imagine that #DieJakeDie is a reflection of their love-to-hate the villain fan engagement. For others, the hashtag may be a warning shot to *Scandal*'s producers: drop the character and the storyline before fans "take action" together and leave the show. Either way, it is vital to underscore Shondaland's, and more broadly the television industry's, ability to govern fan engagement and profit from the attention that social television generates. Given that tens or even hundreds of thousands of tweets circulate, and in *Scandal*'s case, a high number of which operate as black women's "informational labor," it is important for critical media scholars to continue to examine social television and the power dynamics between fans and industry professionals.[37]

SOCIAL TELEVISION AS THE NEW NORMAL

Scandal offers a unique case study of the dynamics of the new industry standard on social television. Social television blurs the boundaries between industry professionals and audiences by allowing fans to interact across social media in ways unheard of before the advent of social media. Traditionally, these boundaries were only crossed with a great deal of effort, such as fans' letter-writing campaigns and boycotts. Prior to social media platforms, fans had to mobilize their social networks through circulated zines and word of mouth to make demands on the television industry. Famously, *Star Trek* fan Bjo Trimble started a massive letter-writing campaign that resulted in a third season of the original *Star Trek* series.[38] Social media platforms such as Twitter provide fans and industry professionals cheap, easy, and rapid access to each other. Though social television seems to promise shared influence between industry professionals and fans, it does not deliver a democratization of creative inputs. Previous scholarship and our work here confirms that industry professionals continue to benefit more than fans from social television's reconfiguration of power. Furthermore, platforms are not neutral technologies and Twitter is friendlier for industry professionals in that they can purchase promoted hashtags, have officially verified handles that confirm their "real" identities, and control some of the visibility of negative feedback. However, through Twitter, fans can exercise their collective cultural power as they access industry professionals and each other. The dynamics of social television between industry professionals and fans in Shondaland is happening elsewhere between other audiences, networks, and industry professionals. Social media platforms such as Twitter allow fans to mobilize quickly to "save" their favorite shows, for example, *Arrested Development* (FOX 2003–2006/Netflix 2013–present), *Friday Night Lights* (NBC 2006–2011), *Veronica Mars* (CW/UPN 2004–2007), and *Firefly* (FOX 2002–2003), by appealing directly to networks and showrunners or even raising money to fund a show's resurrection in a different format. Even media organizations' efforts, such as *USA Today's* "Save our Shows" polls, capitalize on social television's vast and accessible cultural space.[39]

Our analysis of three hashtag movements, #ScandalCutOut, #SaveJake?, and #DieJakeDie, demonstrates how social television allows industry professionals and fans to access each other while still privileging industry professionals, including producers and actors. With #ScandalCutOut, industry professionals tried to sustain fan engagement with the show during a hiatus and in doing so they controlled all aspects of the social media campaign. Fans who played along may have enjoyed the game but they were clearly working within the confines of ABC and Shondaland's desire to maintain audience interest and develop crossover appeal between *Scandal* and *HTGAWM*. Still, there are fans who used the game to communicate larger-scale cultural critiques, taking the opportunity to tie their shared text to national politics. With #SaveJake?, industry professionals used a promoted hashtag to control fans' narrative possibilities for the season 5 finale. They were met with an overwhelmingly negative response as the vast majority of fans who responded used the opportunity to reject Jake's storylines. But their responses gave the appearance of fan engagement and thus, ultimately operated as fan labor in support of the show. Finally, in response to #SaveJake? during their live-tweeting of the season 5 finale, some fans deliberately generated a trending hashtag of their own, #DieJakeDie. While fans used their collective cultural power to demonstrate their dissatisfaction, their work still appeared to confirm that the show has vast fan engagement, a boon for industry professionals despite the critique embedded in the tweets.

Fans' social television–based cultural power manifests in their abilities to transform the source text and extend it across their social networks. If tens of thousands of fans live-tweet an episode of *Scandal*, they have effectively declared that the episode is worth watching and talking about, regardless of what they actually say. They have, as @marilynprescott put it when describing the work of the show's African American female fans, "watched, tweeted, and advertised." However, if they are disgruntled with the show, beyond just loving to hate its antagonists, their fan labor creates a space for them to achieve collective consciousness with their dissatisfaction. Although their Twitter-based critiques give the appearance of fan engagement, they still achieve a sense of community and may find among themselves new texts that better meet their expectations.

NOTES

1. Naeemah Clark, "Connecting in the Scandalverse: The Power of Social Media and Parasocial Relationships," in *Digital Technology and the Future of Broadcasting: Global Perspectives*, ed. John V. Pavlik (New York: Routledge, 2015), 179–193.

2. "Nielsen and Twitter Establish Social TV Rating," *Nielsen*, December 12, 2012, http://www.nielsen.com/us/en/press-room/2012/nielsen-and-twitter-establish-social-tv-rating.html.

3. "Tops of 2013 TV and Social Media," *Nielsen*, December 17, 2013, http://www.nielsen.com/us/en/insights/news/2013/tops-of-2013-tv-and-social-media.html; "Tops of 2014: Social TV," *Nielsen*, December 14, 2014, http://www.nielsen.com/us/en/insights/news/2014/tops-of-2014-social-tv.html; "Tops of 2015 TV and Social Media," *Nielsen*, December 8, 2015, http://www.nielsen.com/us/en/insights/news/2015/tops-of-2015-tv-and-social-media.html.

4. "TV Season 2015–2016 in Review: The Biggest Social TV Moments," *Nielsen*, June 6, 2016, http://www.nielsen.com/us/en/insights/news/2016/tv-season-2015–2016-in-review-the-biggest-social-tv-moments.html.

5. Shelli Weinstein, "How 'Scandal' Paved the Way for ABC's Twitter-Based '#TGIT' Marketing Strategy," *Variety*, September 22, 2014, http://variety.com/2014/tv/news/scandal-twitter-shonda-rhimes-tgit-abc-shondaland-1201311282/.

6. Mary McNamara, "Scandal Has Become Must-Tweet TV," *Los Angeles Times*, May 11, 2013, http://articles.latimes.com/2013/may/11/entertainment/la-et-st-scandal-abc-social-media-20130511; Clark, "Connecting in the Scandalverse."

7. All tweets have been left in their original form as they appear on Twitter, including any misspellings. Additionally, where relevant, users' gender and race identity has been presumed by hand-coding users' avatars.

8. "The Making of Social TV: Loyal Fans and Big Moments Build Buzz," *Nielsen*, August 24, 2015, http://www.nielsen.com/us/en/insights/news/2015/the-making-of-social-tv-loyal-fans -and-big-moments-build-program-buzz.html.

9. Aaron Smith, "African Americans and Technology Use: A Demographic Portrait," PEW Research Center, January 6, 2014, http://www.pewinternet.org/2014/01/06/african-americans -and-technology-use/.

10. Clark, "Connecting in the Scandalverse"; Apryl Williams and Vanessa Gonlin, "I Got All My Sisters with Me (on Black Twitter): Second Screening of *How to Get Away with Murder* as a Discourse on Black Womanhood," *Information, Communication & Society* 20, no. 7 (2017): 984–1004.

11. Williams and Gonlin, 992–995.

12. Elizabeth Losh, "Hashtag Feminism and Twitter Activism in India," *Social Epistemology Review and Reply Collective* 3, no. 3 (2014): 12; Lisa Nakamura, "The Unwanted Labour of Social Media: Women of Colour Call Out Culture as Venture Community Management," *New Formations* 86 (2015): 106–112.

13. Cherríe Moraga and Gloria Anzuldúa, eds., *This Bridge Called My Back*, 4th ed., (Albany, N.Y.: State University of New York Press, 2014).

14. *Scandal*, "It's Handled," season 3, episode 1, directed by Tom Verica, written by Shonda Rhimes, aired on October 3, 2013, on ABC.

15. Ruth Deller, "Twittering On: Audience Research and Participation Using Twitter," *Participations* 8 (2011): 216–245; Donatella Selva, "Social Television Audience and Political Engagement," *Television & New Media* 17, no. 2 (2016): 159–173.

16. Selva, "Social Television Audience and Political Engagement"; Megan M. Wood and Linda Baughman, "*Glee* Fandom and Twitter: Something New, or More of the Same Old Thing?," *Communication Studies* 63, no. 3 (2012): 328–344.

17. Kristin M. Barton and Jonathan Malcolm Lampley, eds., *Fan CULTure: Essays on Participatory Fandom in the 21st Century* (Jefferson, N.C.: McFarland, 2013); Karen Hellekson and Kristina Busse, eds., *The Fan Fiction Studies Reader* (Iowa City: University of Iowa Press, 2014); Henry Jenkins, *Textual Poachers: Television Fans & Participatory Culture* (New York: Routledge, 1992); Michaela D. E. Meyer, "'Something Wicca This Way Comes': Audience Interpretation of a Marginalized Religious Philosophy on *Charmed*," in *Investigating Charmed: The Magic Power of TV*, ed. Stan Beeler and Karin Beeler (London: I. B. Taurus, 2007), 3–17.

18. Selva, "Social Television Audience and Political Engagement," 160.

19. Selva, "Social Television Audience and Political Engagement." See also Michaela D. E. Meyer and Megan Tucker, "Textual Poaching and Beyond: Fan Communities and Fandoms in the Age of the Internet," *Review of Communication* 7, no. 1 (2007): 103–116.

20. Jenkins, *Textual Poachers*; Henry Jenkins, *Fans, Bloggers, and Gamers: Exploring Participatory Culture*, 1st ed. (New York: New York University Press, 2006).

21. Tim Highfield, Stephen Harrington, and Axel Bruns, "Twitter as a Technology for Audiencing and Fandom," *Information, Communication & Society* 16, no. 3 (2013): 315–339; Michaela D. E. Meyer, "Slashing *Smallville*: The Interplay of Text, Audience and Production on Viewer Interpretations of Homoeroticism," *Sexuality & Culture* 17, no. 3 (2013): 476–493; Selva, "Social Television Audience and Political Engagement"; Wood and Baughman, "*Glee* Fandom and Twitter."

22. Wood and Baughman, "*Glee* Fandom and Twitter."

23. Highfield, Harrington, and Bruns, "Twitter as a Technology for Audiencing and Fandom"; Matthew Pittman and Alex C. Tefertiller, "With or Without You: Connected Viewing and

Co-viewing Twitter Activity for Traditional Appointment and Asynchronous Broadcast Television Models," *First Monday* 20, no. 7 (2015): http://journals.uic.edu/ojs/index.php/fm/article/view/5935.

24. Jenkins, *Textual Poachers*; Jenkins, *Fans, Bloggers, and Gamers*; Henry Jenkins, *Convergence Culture: Where Old and New Media Collide* (New York: New York University Press, 2006); Henry Jenkins, Sam Ford, and Joshua Green, *Spreadable Media: Creating Value and Meaning in a Networked Culture* (New York: New York University Press, 2013).

25. Melissa Gray, "From Canon to Fanon and Back Again: The Epic Journey of *Supernatural* and Its Fans," *Transformative Works and Cultures* 4 (2010): http://journal.transformativeworks.org/index.php/twc/article/view/146/149; Mary Ingram-Waters, "When Normal and Deviant Identities Collide: Methodological Considerations of the Pregnant Acafan," *Transformative Works and Cultures* 5 (2010): http://journal.transformativeworks.org/index.php/twc/article/view/207; Mary Ingram-Waters, "Writing the Pregnant Man," *Transformative Works and Cultures* 20 (2015): http://journal.transformativeworks.org/index.php/twc/article/view/651/544; Pierre Levy, "The Creative Conversation of Collective Intelligence," in *The Participatory Cultures Handbook*, ed. Aaron Alan Delwiche and Jennifer Jacobs Henderson (New York: Routledge, 2013), 99.

26. Clark, "Connecting in the Scandalverse."

27. Anna Everett, "Scandalicious: Scandal, Social Media, and Shonda Rhimes' Auteurist Juggernaut," *Black Scholar* 45, no. 1 (2015): 34–43; Kristin Warner, "If Loving Olitz Is Wrong, I Don't Wanna Be Right: ABC's *Scandal* and the Affect of Black Female Desire," *Black Scholar* 45, no. 1 (2015): 16; Lynn Zubernis and Katherine Larsen, *Fandom at the Crossroads: Celebration, Shame and Fan/Producer Relationships* (Newcastle upon Tyne, U.K.: Cambridge Scholars, 2012).

28. Nancy Baym, *Tune In, Log On: Soaps, Fandom and Online Community* (Thousand Oaks, Calif.: Sage Publications, 2000); John Fiske, "The Cultural Economy of Fandom," in *The Adoring Audience: Fan Culture and Popular Media*, ed. Lisa A. Lewis (New York: Routledge, 1992), 30–49; Matthew Hills, *Fan Cultures* (New York: Routledge, 2002); Henry Jenkins, "Interactive Audiences? The Collective Intelligence of Media Fans": https://pdfs.semanticscholar.org/9a55/ba037c0b34782baa94e8b2f0bc5aeddac4af.pdf

29. Rhiannon Bury, *Cyberspaces of Their Own: Female Fandoms Online* (New York: Peter Lang, 2005); Abigail T. Derecho, "Illegitimate Media: Race, Gender and Censorship in Digital Remix Culture" (PhD diss., Northwestern University, 2008), ProQuest (3303803).

30. Rebecca Wanzo, "African American Acafandom and Other Strangers: New Genealogies of Fan Studies," *Transformative Works and Cultures* 20 (2015): http://journal.transformativeworks.org/index.php/twc/article/view/699/538.

31. Camille Bacon-Smith, *Enterprising Women: Television Fandom and the Creation of Popular Myth* (Philadelphia: University of Pennsylvania Press, 1992), 158.

32. Linda Baughman and Michaela D. E. Meyer, "Slashing *Alias*: Viewer Appropriation of Lauren Reed as Commentary on Female/Female Desire," in *Investigating Alias: Secrets and Spies*, ed. Stacey Abbott and Simon Brown (London: I. B. Taurus, 2007), 174–185; Alexis Lothian, Kristina Busse, and Robin Anne Reid, "'Yearning Void and Infinite Potential': Online Slash Fandom as Queer Female Space," *English Language Notes* 45, no. 2 (2007): 103; Mary Ingram-Waters, "Writing the Pregnant Man."

33. April Midha, "Exposure to TV Tweets Drives Consumers to Take Action—Both on and off of Twitter," Twitter blog, May 8, 2014, https://blog.twitter.com/2014/study-exposure-to-tv-tweets-drives-consumers-to-take-action-both-on-and-off-of-twitter.

34. Rachel A. Griffin, "Olivia Pope as Problematic and Paradoxical: A Black Feminist Critique of *Scandal*'s 'Mammification,'" in *Feminist Theory and Popular Culture*, ed. Adrienne Trier-Bieniek (Rotterdam, The Netherlands: Sense, 2015), 35–48.

35. Shonda Rhimes, *Scandal* (ABC, 2012–2018).

36. Midha, "Exposure to TV Tweets."

37. Losh, "Hashtag Feminism," 12.

38. "Bjo Trimble," Wikipedia, accessed June 23, 2017, https://en.wikipedia.org/wiki/Bjo_Trimble.

39. For an example, see "'Timeless', the Save Our Shows Favorite, Canceled by NBC," *USA Today*, May 10, 2017, https://www.usatoday.com/story/life/tv/2017/05/10/timeless-nbc-save-our-shows-cancelled/101528360/.

11 · MEDIA CRITICISM AND MORALITY POLICING ON TWITTER

Fan Responses to *How to Get Away with Murder*

MELISSA AMES

In an alarmist age when tirades about society's eroding ethics are abundant, the media is often a scapegoat for those who fear that cultural values are disintegrating. For decades, from reality television's debauchery to celebrity programming's narcissism to fictional drama's excessive violence, television has been blamed for contributing to society's so-called moral decline.[1] Recently, concern has expanded from content to include twenty-first century television viewing practices. Studies argue that binge watching television leads to antisocial dispositions, depression, and immorality.[2] Likewise, social media is credited for creating a generation of narcissists and prompting increased levels of depression, jealousy, and apathy.[3] Television viewing today often entails double screening—wherein viewers are not only engaging with the content on television but are also commenting on that content through social media. Forty-three percent of tablet and smart phone owners report using their devices while watching television every day, and 95 percent of the conversation occurring on social media concerning television is taking place on Twitter, making it an ideal site to examine what viewers are doing with their double screens.[4] Reading dual-media use data alongside alarmist rhetoric about the negative impact technology has on cultural ethics, one might conclude that this tag team of Twitter and television is bound to destroy humanity as we know it. Or not. Unsurprisingly, online television fandom studies indicate that audience engagement—even with programs packed full of scandalous storylines—is much more complicated than fear-mongering implies.

When Nielson reported which television programs had the most active social media fans in 2015, it was not shocking that two of Shondaland's shows—*Scandal* (ABC 2012–2018) and *How to Get Away with Murder* (ABC 2014–present; also referred to as *HTGAWM*)—made the top ten list.[5] Media critics have analyzed how Rhimes's social media practices, as well as those of her fans, have transformed network television production and consumption.[6] While the postnetwork era has resulted in fragmented and noncollective viewing experiences, Rhimes's three-hour programming block on ABC prompted a return to live television watching—and, more importantly, live television commentary. Capitalizing on the must-see nature of her "fan-obsessed TV dramas" and the Twitter activism they inspire, Rhimes has evolved into a "savvy media mogul" who has cultivated prime-time viewing practices wherein viewers, actors, and producers engage in synchronous online dialogue on a weekly basis.[7] Eager to replicate Shondaland's success, now virtually every television program has a hashtag, and networks eagerly promote them. Given Rhimes's revolutionary impact, her shows are ideal for studying the consequences and benefits of active viewing practices. Moreover, considering Rhimes's use of fictional texts to address social justice, studying these viewing practices reveals how they interplay with Shondaland's politicized public pedagogy.

HOW TO GET AWAY WITH MURDER'S BRAND OF MORALITY

How to Get Away with Murder forefronts tenuous societal debates concerning the morality and immorality of the U.S. justice system. Mirroring recent headlines of peer-pressure incentivized murder and child abduction, the show merges real-world criminality into its fictional narratives and exposes how the legal system fails to achieve justice. This melodrama's complicated, interlocking plots showcase a slew of sudsy storylines—backstabbing, betrayal, blackmail, and adultery—that tackle morality in terms of romantic relationships, family power dynamics, educational competition, and professional aspirations. Weekly, fans storm Twitter to interact with the show by live-tweeting their viewing experiences, engaging with the fictional morality tales, and debating the real-world ethical implications of *HTGAWM*. Interrogating morality is a constant thread running throughout Shondaland—medical ethics are questioned on *Grey's Anatomy* (ABC 2005–present; also referred to as *Grey's*) and *Private Practice* (ABC 2007–2013); political ethics are challenged on *Scandal*; and testing legal morality is the heartbeat of *HTGAWM*. Collectively, Shondaland shows function as public pedagogy designed to challenge normativity and prompt social activism.[8] Contrary to alarmist rhetoric concerning the detrimental effects of screen-centric lifestyles, social media platforms and interactions are functioning pedagogically. Therefore, studying audience engagement reveals how viewers react to Shondaland's weekly morality "lessons."

How to Get Away with Murder features Annalise Keating, a middle-aged African American legal professor, and her five ambitious law students, but it is Annalise who draws increased audience attention for her peculiar scruples. Critics often note her "ambiguous" morals and "Machiavellian moral compass," which suggests that she acts in duplicitous and self-serving ways.[9] The pilot encourages such readings by underscoring the moral grey area the characters operate within. During Annalise's opening lecture to her students, she says, "The question I'm asked most often as a defense attorney is whether I can tell if my clients are innocent or guilty. And my answer is always the same: I don't care."[10]

Viola Davis plays Annalise and is often asked to comment on her character's ethics; she says, "I think we're all morally questionable . . . I think that we . . . act on nature and not on morals. I [find] her to be a realistic protagonist. I find her to be very human, as we all are, in that we have grey areas."[11] Peter Nowalk, the show's creator, argues that Annalise's personalized form of justice is a response to an unjust system: "It's not so black and white to her. . . . Justice is very complicated, and the justice system is much more corrupt than you would think it would be. . . . I think Annalise feels like she's being moral. She's standing up for people who don't get stood up for a lot."[12] These ethical critiques of the criminal justice system are unsurprising; they align with the social commentary woven throughout Shondaland that debunks the myth that we are living in a postidentity society wherein equality has been achieved.

While Rhimes is certainly not alone in combating insinuations that the United States is postidentity and, particularly, postracial, she has been garnering increased media attention amid diversity debates in Hollywood.[13] Two events that reignited this conversation were Davis's becoming the first African American to win Best Actress in 2015 for her *HTGAWM* role and the massive outcry that followed the 2016 announcement—for the second year in a row—of an all-white slate of Oscar nominees.[14] During her 2016 Producers Guild's Norman Lear Award for Achievement in Television acceptance speech, Rhimes told the audience, tongue-in-cheek, "I completely deserve this . . . I have against the odds, courageously pioneered the art of writing for people of color as if they were human beings."[15] She then more seriously explained that her practices should not be revolutionary in the twenty-first century: "I created the content that I wanted to see and I created what I know is normal . . . The respect of this award does mean the world. It just makes me a little bit sad. First of all, strong women and three-dimensional people of color is something Norman [Lear] was doing 40-something years ago. So how come it has to be done all over again?"[16] This speech underscores Rhimes's commitment to equality and her belief that representation can pedagogically function in service to greater equity.

To study how Rhimes's "lessons" are received by massive audiences, this chapter analyzes the live-tweeting practices of *HTGAWM* fans. Hosting over five hundred million users generating approximately 340 million tweets a day,

Twitter is steadily attracting academic analysis.[17] Building upon previous scholarship, this study examines how fictional programming viewers use Twitter as a medium to engage with important societal critiques and situates live-tweeting as a form of digital activism. By focusing, in part, on tweets responding to Annalise's morality, this essay also investigates to what extent live-tweets reflect larger cultural sentiments concerning gender, sexuality, and identity politics.

(S)HE DID A BAD, BAD THING: THE RISE OF THE ANTIHERO ON TELEVISION

Television scholars have long suggested that television programming reflects societal values.[18] If television acts as a cultural mirror, the rapid rise of the antihero on the small screen—a classification that Annalise belongs to—might be seen as disconcerting. Alarmists would posit that the increasing number of shows featuring dark and twisty, morally compromised antiheroes points toward a weakening ethical landscape within U.S. American culture; but this is not likely the case.

The antihero has existed as a character archetype since the early Greek comedies and tragedies, and its popularity often resurfaces at distinct points in history.[19] Hypothesizing the causes behind the recent resurgence, Michael notes, "If we consider the 21st century so far—9/11 terrorist attacks, the Iraq War, Enron, Hurricane Katrina, the economic recession, Hurricane Sandy, the Newtown shootings, the Boston Marathon attacks—there's been a steady stream of terrible events to shake our faith in humanity."[20] Counterintuitively, in dark times, audiences immerse themselves in even darker narratives. Thus, the early twenty-first century is an era of television drama filled with antiheroes like Tony Soprano (*The Sopranos*, HBO 1999–2007), Walter White (*Breaking Bad*, AMC 2008–2013), Dexter Morgan (*Dexter*, CBS 2006–2013), Jack Bauer (*24*, Fox 2001–2010), Don Draper (*Mad Men*, AMC 2007–2015), and Gregory House (*House M.D.*, Fox 2004–2012) who relieve us from real-world evils by transporting us into ethically compromised fictional worlds.[21] As this list of prominent antiheroes reveals, they often share a defining feature that fosters popularity: masculinity.[22] However, the televisual tides have been turning with female antiheros like *UnREAL*'s (Lifetime 2015–present) Rachel Goldberg, *Nurse Jackie*'s (Showtime 2009–2015) Jackie Peyton, *Weeds*'s (Showtime 2005–2012) Nancy Botwin, *The Americans*'s (FX 2013–present) Elizabeth Jennings, and *Homeland*'s (Showtime 2011–present) Carrie Mathison who suggest that women, like men, can be "morally bereft *and* relatable at the same time."[23]

Part of the appeal of watching characters who trangress morality is seeing ourselves (or our potential selves) in such characters and glimpsing a "relatable version of a good self that has gone bad."[24] The typical antihero formula includes a backstory that allows us to forgive, or at least explain, the character's transgressions, which in turn, make these characters palatable. Annalise's backstory aligns with this expectation; her past is scripted with childhood trauma and spousal abuse. Viewers also gain pleasure from the cognitive dissonance created by conflicted characters who are not purely good or evil. Steward notes this phenomenon in his analysis of *Nurse Jackie*'s antihero: "Jackie is an adulterous, drug-sniffing, domineering, devious super nurse, who at times, also displays the unwavering moral compass of a burning Catholic saint . . . [W]e see her juggle such contradictions as giving free medical care to cash strapped patients while also robbing an epileptic of their Oxy-Contin stash during a seizure."[25] Alongside internal conflicts, the antihero's sinful side also lures us in. These storylines tap into our scariest fantasies—the ones lurking, often unacknowledged, within the human psyche and "provide a sense of catharsis."[26]

The cathartic relationship between antiheroes and viewers contextualizes the large fan following of *HTGAWM*'s Frank Delfino, Annalise's assistant and ethically unbound fixer. Charlie Weber, the actor who plays Frank, calls him "a hit man with a heart of gold" but clarifies that he does not consider him an antihero, rather he's a cold-blooded killer who "enjoys it."[27] Despite drowning a student, stuffing a corpse into a suitcase, and sending someone innocent to jail, fans do not react as harshly to his immorality as they do to Annalise's. The differing reactions these two characters draw arguably stems from the double standards that exist for male versus female characters and are further complicated by the black/white racial dynamic in the Annalise/Frank pairing.[28] One might ask: would Frank be beloved as a "hit man with a heart of gold" if he was of color? The latter half of *HTGAWM*'s second season features flashbacks to explain how both characters arrived at their respective compromised ethics. Interestingly, the scenes devoted to Frank's downfall cast Annalise as the catalyst for his initial moral lapse. This narrative conjures up the female temptress trope and problematically presents a black woman as the force that corrupted a white man.[29] Although individual storylines depict Frank's immorality trumping Annalise's, their backstories highlight how moral superiority is often granted by default to white men.

While devious male characters are easily labeled as antiheroes and are often popular, similar female characters are typically described as "'off-putting' and 'obnoxious'" or, more commonly, they get tagged with the all-too-popular "unlikable."[30] Countless critics have addressed the gendered "double-standard of likability" that results in "infinitely more obstacles faced by leading ladies making morally questionable choices."[31] For example, antiheroes like *Girls*'s (HBO 2012–2017) Hannah Horvath, *Orange is the New Black*'s (Netflix 2013–present) Piper Chapman, and *Nashville*'s (ABC 2012–2018) Juliette Barnes have been criticized for being "annoying, selfish and entitled."[32] It seems that when we are faced with "women who act in a way we're used to seeing only male characters act," it's "alienating" and we unfairly brand them as "unlikable rather than well-crafted and complex."[33] Female characters—like their real-world counterparts—are punished for projecting masculine-coded traits like ambition, aggression, or strength.[34]

These gendered power dynamics are evident with female characters in leadership roles, often "portrayed as icy, heartless, manipulative, and vindictive."[35] The question is: are audiences reading these female characters as critiquing this double standard or reinforcing it? In response, I argue that Shondaland's female characters critique gendered double standards. Additionally, *Scandal*'s Olivia and *HTGAWM*'s Annalise importantly complicate the double standard as black female antiheroes; they are not deemed unlikable solely for failing to fit the traditional mold of white femininity but also because of their moral transgressions. Interestingly, media criticism suggests that Annalise is more commonly deemed unlikable and receives harsher criticisms, while Olivia is often forgiven because her determination to do good—to wear "the white hat"—usually prompts her transgressions.[36] Critics assert that the absence of the white hat trope on *HTGAWM* might account for the harsher criticism directed at Annalise.[37] Nowalk confirms that Annalise was meant to stand in contradistinction to Olivia: "Olivia believes in the White Hat, and there's no hat for Annalise; there's reality and justice. I don't think she thinks there is justice; it's kind of whoever plays the game the best."[38] Annalise "does not offer a compelling justification for her behavior . . . her job is to get her client off—not get her client off *because* she is innocent or *because* the legal system requires perfection from the defense and prosecution in order to promote the best sense of justice."[39] Due to her contentious antihero status, Annalise makes for a fascinating case study of fans' Twitter reactions to complex fictional characters embroiled in ethical dilemmas.

TWITTER AS MORALITY POLICE? AN ANALYSIS OF LIVE-TWEETING PRACTICES

To study live *HTGAWM* tweets through the lens of morality, I focus on tweets that "critiqued" the show to answer these research questions:

1. Do the majority of live-tweets focus on portrayals of the justice system or melodramatic subplots?
2. Do live-tweets reflect the research on gendered ethics, especially in terms of female antiheroes or "unlikable" characters?
3. How do live-tweets engage with Rhimes's public pedagogy and demonstrate that live-tweeting fictional television programs is a form of digital activism?

Twitter data was collected from September 24 through November 19, 2015, spanning nine weeks from the season 2 premiere of *HTGAWM* until its mid-season hiatus. Live-tweets associated with #HowToGetAwayWithMurder were scraped (i.e., collected) weekly using NodeXL—a program that gathers all tweets associated with a specific hashtag and transfers them to Excel.[40] To narrow the data pool, I focused on tweets posted from 8:00 P.M. EST to 9:01 P.M. EST during the one-hour original broadcast of the program, which aired simultaneously in the Eastern and Central time zones. The data pool was further reduced to 18,439 tweets by limiting analysis to English content and original posts (i.e., retweets and replies were not included).

The data was then coded to highlight "critiquing" tweets.[41] The critiquing tweets were sorted into two large categories based on the following criteria: (1) small scale critiques, which includes subcategories such as personal opinions and criticisms concerning characters, actors, show creators, writing, plot, and so on, and (2) large scale critiques, which includes subcategories engaging with law or justice related storylines and/or the social commentary embedded into such storylines. The tweets included in the analysis below were selected from this narrowed data set because they were representative of the posts or sentiments appearing most frequently on the feed.[42]

Do the Majority of Live-Tweets Focus on Portrayals of the Justice System or on the Melodramatic Subplots?

Since *HTGAWM* is a legal drama, I expected that many critiques would focus on its depiction of the justice system and the illegal actions of the central cast of lawyers. While this was present (see table 1), this focus was rather minimal.

I anticipated that Annalise, as the main character, would often be of interest, but expected a primary focus on her compromised professional ethics—especially since the cliffhanger between seasons 1 and 2 predicted that she would be involved in yet another murder cover-up. While Annalise was the character most often targeted, her personal rather than professional actions were commonly highlighted. Out of 18,439 tweets, Annalise was directly mentioned in 2,463 and indirectly referenced in many more, making mentions of her account for approximately 13.36 percent of #HowToGetAwayWithMurder.[43] Annalise's personal actions were critiqued in numerous tweets that framed her as a skilled liar, bully, or two-timing romantic player. By comparison, her professional ethics were mentioned only occasionally. On September 25, 2015, @dawniebgood87 wrote, "Annalise plays dirty just like the justice system" and on October 15, 2015, a dispute between Connor and Annalise over how to handle evidence that incriminated a client sparked online debate. Rachel Romanczuk (@RachelER22) wrote, after Annalise sided with protecting the client while Connor actively worked toward the client's conviction, "I'm with Connor. Annalise only cares about money and winning."

Annalise was more often the topic of superficial critiques focused on various programming aspects ranging from costuming and acting to characterization and plot (see table 2). The tweets pertaining to Annalise's appearance could be disregarded as just one-off opinions about trivial elements such as costuming. However, often these comments attended to her stylized racialization, indicating that viewers were picking up on the program's attention to race. The most frequent comments, though, critiqued Annalise's personality and actions. Many

TABLE 1   Sample Tweets Critiquing Portrayal of Justice System

Twitter User	Timestamp	Tweet
Trillmermaidxxx	9/24/2015 9:23	Crazy how they really be breaking the laws as lawyers though ☹☹☹☹ smh #HowToGetAwayWithMurder
rt1959	10/1/2015 9:01	Everybody is a criminal on this show. #howtogetawaywithmurder
pentylu	10/1/2015 9:38	If Nate is convicted just shows how fucked up the justice system is #HowToGetAwayWithMurder
Kendallkuban	10/15/2015 9:29	#HowToGetAwayWithMurder when the lawyers are worse criminals than the criminals they defend . . . OMG.

TABLE 2   Sample Media Criticism Tweets Focusing on Annalise's Costuming

Twitter Handle	Timestamp	Tweet
azsahd_	10/8/2015 9:56	I'm sick of Analeese's wigs. Just sick and tired. #HowToGetAwayWithMurder
trendingtopic_o	10/1/2015 9:59	The authenticity with the head tie lol #HowToGetAwayWithMurder
Wilgafney	11/12/2015 10:01	Shonda teaching folk how we twist our hair! Can't we have any secrets? #HowToGetAwayWithMurder #HTGAWM #DatMurda

negative tweets focused on Annalise's drinking. On October 8, 2015, Vale Váz (@valeria13201422) wrote, "she is pissy drunk." Even more tweets focused on her adulterous relationship with Nate; on October 15, 2015, Maria Nkata (@CrackHead-Jemi) posted, "'What kind of woman sleeps with a man who's wife is dying?' The Annalise kind who doesn't give a F@&$$." Some even attended to Annalise's position of privilege. On October 8, 2015, @_therealmami wrote, "Annalise walks like she owns a cotton gin," which associates Annalise with slavery but complicates her empowered, intersectional positionality by comparing her to a slave owner. Users also praised her for behavior they viewed as positive. When Annalise refused to commit euthanasia when asked to by Nate's dying wife, on October 16, 2015, Hajarah Mamman Nassi (@Hajmannas) posted, "Proud of you Annalise, really thought she was gonna help Nate's wife, glad she didn't."

The fact that tweets more often engaged with superficial aspects rather than underlying storylines suggests that *HTGAWM*'s melodramatic stylistics and over-arching plot often overshadow its episodic focus on legal cases. These findings support Rawden's critique of *HTGAWM*'s employment of legal motifs: "The actual courtroom drama is mostly . . . used as a device to show off the talents of the law school students."[44] She argues that other legal dramas, such as *The Good Wife* (CBS 2009–2016), more effectively use their legal storylines "to look at the complexities . . . politics, and moral ambiguities" involved in practicing law.[45] This suggests that *HGTAWM*'s scripting as a hybrid where legal drama meets prime-time soap opera undercuts its potential to spark reflection on legal injustice.

Do Live-Tweets Reflect the Research on Gendered Ethics, Especially in Terms of Female Antiheroes or "Unlikable" Characters?

Analyzing how Annalise figures into small scale critiques of *HTGAWM* reveals that some reactions to her characterization align with research on the reception of female antiheroes. Although not as regularly as anticipated, the dreaded buzzword of *unlikable* was associated with her character. On October 1, 2015, @laurentluvsfenty called Annalise "strangely unlikable" and, on October 17, 2015, T. J. Newton (@tnewton92) asked, "Has there ever been such an UNLIKABLE lead on television before? Annalise is a truly horrible person." Still others posted tweets critiquing Annalise alongside *Scandal*'s Olivia, labeling them both as unlikable black female characters.[46]

Consistent with aforementioned scholarship on the gendered double standard, Twitter data also revealed that viewers more willingly accept (and even embrace) Frank's unethical behavior rather than Annalise's (see table 3). Most interesting was viewers' willingness to forgive Frank's extreme transgressions simply because they found him physically attractive. This aligns with research documenting that characters with lighter skin are often perceived as being more attractive and friendly than characters with darker skin, suggesting that Frank's white male iden-tity factors heavily into why his wrongdoings are so easily forgiven.[47] Skin tone differentials also illuminate underlying dynamics of why and how light-skinned Olivia is deemed more likable than dark-skinned Annalise.[48]

In comparison, Annalise faced a range of criticisms for her moral missteps—and not one of them was forgiven based on her personal appearance or sex appeal. Although, unlike Frank, she had never committed murder, Annalise was more often called "terrible" or "evil." On September 24, 2015, Nakia Morton (@NGMBeauty) called her "the devil." Meanwhile, users celebrated Frank's immo-rality. On November 19, 2015, Marco Montalván (@desperategossip) tweeted, "Frank, you are the MVP." Reactions to these two characters signal society's forgiveness of bad behavior enacted by men rather than women and white people rather than people of color. This data also suggests that a large subset of live-tweeting viewers are heterosexual women who find white masculinity more appealing than

TABLE 3   Sample Tweets Discussing Frank's Moral Transgressions and Sex Appeal

Twitter Handle	Timestamp	Tweet
purplehearts441	9/24/2015 9:07	He's a shady, shady man. But God, Frank is hot #HowToGetAwayWithMurder #HTGAWM
jesusgarcia_90	10/8/2015 9:35	Let's all be honest with ourselves. Frank is a bad person. He does bad things. But we still love him. #HowToGetwayWithMurder #HTGAWM
ang_belita	10/15/2015 9:05	Frank is so sketchy. But ugh, so fine . . . #HowToGetAwayWithMurder #HTGAWM

black femininity. It also indicates that the harsh critiques targeted at Annalise are presumably coming from female viewers.[49]

However, contrary to female antiheroes research, Annalise's character also received audience support. Many tweets focused on the disloyalty of her law students and their lack of appreciation for her extreme efforts to save them. On October 15, 2015, B. Addison tweeted, "Like Annalise is giving her all to everybody trying to protect them all the while being called a killer." More telling are the posts which praised her transgressions, specifically those that could be interpreted as caretaking attempts. That "motherly" acts motivate forgiving a black woman's moral lapses is problematic but not surprising. Thus far on *HTGAWM*, Annalise is not a biological mother. Season 2 provides a backstory wherein she was pregnant and miscarried, a narrative inclusion that will likely help justify impending transgressions. Presently Annalise's motherly acts include mentoring and protecting adult protégés, and tweets often comment on her pseudo-parental role. On October 29, 2015, Joan Bushur (@joanbushur) posted, "Asher's back in the fold. Let momma Annalise fix everything." The following week, on November 5, 2015, two others similarly noted her protective motherly role. @alisahelene referred to her as "Mama bear Annalise" and criticized the students for not respecting her while @musicmonetradio posted, "omg! They've all been talking back to Annalise this season. I never talk back to my mom."

The inclusion of this surrogate mother plot device aligns with scholarship concerning how the mammy caricature lingers in twenty-first-century popular culture.[50] It also begs the question: would Annalise's acts be read as generously if they were done on behalf of her own biological children, or are they only forgiven because they are done in *service* to nonfamily members? This underscores that notions of nurturing are particularly troubling at the intersections of gender and race. While white women and women of color are received similarly as antiheroes, race plays a multiplicative role in how their moral slippage is framed and perceived. That viewers are more willing to accept illegality from female characters when they were viewed as "motherly" also aligns with research on gendered ethics. Gilligan theorized the social construction of gendered morality, claiming that men operate according to "an ethics of rights" whereas women operate according to "an ethics of responsibility."[51] Gilligan's concept of female morality "emphasizes attachment and the urge to care" as the driving force underlying right versus wrong decisions, while male morality aligns with traditional notions of justice including "commitment to rules, values, and principles."[52] While few *HTGAWM* characters—male or female—operate according to Gilligan's masculine definition of morality, that Annalise's behavior conforms to this feminized definition is interesting. Since many of her illegal acts are committed to protect her protégés, this contributes to her positive reception among viewers who judge her actions as justified.

Ultimately, tweets suggest that reactions to Annalise are quite idiosyncratic and, even though she is harshly criticized, many embrace her actions regardless of whether they are protective, caring acts. A subset of viewers gain pleasure from her "bad" behavior. Her most quoted lines of dialogue were almost always harsh—even shocking—comments directed at her legal team, and users celebrated these moments where she performed the role of "the bitch." At times, Annalise embraces the title for herself. In season 2's "I Want You to Die," Annalise told her adversary, prosecutor Emily Sinclair, "You're messing with the wrong bitch."[53] Twitter then erupted with a series of tweets quoting this dialogue, @pentylu quoted the phrase, adding the exclamatory approval of "yeeeeeessss" afterward.

Embracing Annalise for being a self-described bitch is quite interesting. In some ways Annalise does not actually fulfill the typical role that the bitch plays in fictional narratives. This role serves as "the embodiment of female evil: the foil for literature's icons of morality and the scourge of the male hero."[54] First, Annalise really is not a foil for anyone. Second, to varying degrees, almost all of the female characters could be classified as bitches. Further, *HTGAWM* lacks any traditional heroes, male or female, to thwart. Quite simply, Annalise is not completely evil or virtuous, moral or immoral. This suggests that Shondaland has created a more complicated, nuanced portrayal of women who are forced to (or choose to) embody the paradoxical elements of constructed caricatures like the bitch.[55]

There was, however, one particular storyline that prompted mixed reactions concerning Annalise's so-called bad behavior, specifically her use of sexuality as a means of power. In *HTGAWM*'s pilot, Annalise sleeps with Nate, a police officer, in order to win a case which sets the precedent that she is willing to use sex as a means to an end. Throughout season 2, the pilot prompted tweets about her potential motivations whenever she has sex with someone. This prior history also influenced how some viewers reacted to her mentoring Michaela Pratt to use her sex appeal to control clients. In the episode "Skanks Get Shanked," Annalise orders

Michaela to keep their murder defendant, Caleb Hapstall, in line.[56] When Michaela is at a loss, Annalise asks, "What's the matter? Don't know how to use your boobs?"[57] Like most of her hard-hitting punchlines, this line echoed across Twitter when users quoted it. On October 15, 2015, Derek St. John (@Dieter117) called it the "best line of the night." When Michaela befriends Caleb rather than seducing him, Annalise barks: "I told you to use your boobs, not your heart."[58] Again, viewers appreciated the line. On October 8, 2015, Mary Bushur (@joanbushur) quoted the line adding, "Love Mikaela and Annalise together." While multiple viewers compared Annalise to a pimp, not all did so critically as evidenced by Paris Hodges's tweet (@brownxsuga) on October 15, 2015, "lmao annalise pimping Makayla."

Weeks after this episode, some were still expressing their corrective outrage; on November 12, 2015, @msmjfan14 posted, "Michaela is MORE than her boobs Annalise." This tweet aligns with criticisms concerning sexual or romantic storylines undermining female characters, particularly strong female characters like Annalise.[59] Keating notes that storylines that involve female protagonists using their femininity and sex appeal ultimately undermine the character's intellect, ability, and success.[60] Shondaland's other black female powerhouse, Olivia, has received critiques of this nature. Many claim that the romantic story arc focused on Olivia's on-again-off-again romantic relationship with President Fitzgerald Grant undercuts her strength and respectability. Rising to her defense, Gallager writes:

> While Olivia is by no means a role model for young women, she is much more nuanced, complex, and three dimensional than most black female characters that have risen to her level of popularity. *Scandal's* success is a testament to the fact that female characters can be imperfect and still be popular. In fact, imperfect characters are much better vessels for representation. Audiences are ready for female characters that evoke contradictory emotions and encourage critical reflection.[61]

This same argument easily applies to Annalise. The ways viewers embrace her suggest that audiences desire more complicated portrayals of women who do not fit easily into outdated, unrealistic gendered archetypes.

How Do Live-Tweets Engage with Rhimes's Public Pedagogy and Demonstrate That Live-Tweeting Fictional Television Programs Is a Form of Digital Activism?

As evident so far, of the two classifications of critiques—small scale criticisms focused on the show versus large scale criticisms engaging with societal issues—the majority of the critiquing posts focused on rather trivial content. However, when particular moments pointedly drew attention to a societal issue, large scale criticisms predominantly surfaced. This commonly occurred when Rhimes's pedagogical social commentary manifested as character dialogue. In this instance, the most frequent tweeting practice was quoting, wherein the poster would tweet the line of dialogue containing the social critique. While this practice can logically be read as embracing or promoting the critique, quoting dialogue is ambiguous. While some tweets provided additional commentary along with the quote that revealed their opinion on the dialogue or their purpose for citing it, the majority simply tweeted the actual dialogue as a standalone post free of explanation. While this lack of context could stem from the character limits imposed by the medium, it could also reveal our tendency to allow quotes to stand in place of making bold, potentially controversial statements. This practice is particularly prevalent on social media where it is more acceptable to circulate a meme or quote from someone else concerning a controversial topic rather than to make a direct statement of one's own stance. Paradoxically, this allows posters to showcase their opinion from a distance.

In terms of quoting practices, the comedic undertone of many circulated quotes further complicates their reading. Since some of the quotes were delivered as punchlines, the tweets could be read as celebrating their humor *or* their cultural critique. The inability to determine authorial intent is another limitation of analyzing Twitter data, as is the difficulty in determining tone. On September 25, 2015, Dianne Carusell (@diannecarusell) wrote, "Another Black lawyer and a Black judge—I feel so empowered." This post could be read as a straightforward statement of, perhaps, an African American viewer celebrating the racially diverse cast. However, this post could also be read as a sarcastic critique of diverse representation, perhaps indicating that the user feels it is cliché or ineffective. Although my interpretation may be incorrect, Carusell's profile picture visually indicates that she is a white woman, which raises speculation concerning the intent of her tweet. This example demonstrates the difficulty of interpreting meaning from uncontextualized comments written within the constraining 140-character limit. This makes proclaiming the purpose of an *individual* tweet difficult; yet, analyzing trends within Twitter posts *collectively* provides more reliable insight into the crossroads of Shondaland's fictional morality lessons and real-world cultural values.

Quoting practices suggest that Rhimes's public pedagogy is not completely overshadowed by *HTGAWM*'s melodramatic soap opera nature. Highly quoted moments of dialogue involved season 2's critiques of white privilege. One of the most quoted lines stemmed from "It's Time to Move On": "White folks always bring up race when it suits them, never when it matters."[62] Another popularly tweeted line circulated weeks later during "Meet Bonnie": "Add your whiteness on top of that, the police are trained to believe you."[63] Both prompted supportive comments on Twitter. On October 22, 2015, @refinedsmarts tweeted, "preaching about white male privilege, yasss!" and @EDubb_41yfe tweeted, "White privilege is real y'all. I'm telling you."

Overall, often the highest volume of tweets within an episode's airing aligned with narrative moments that mirrored Rhimes's pedagogical social commentary.

Her storylines on sexuality garnered significant commentary, although analysis does not indicate that these lessons were always well received. The October 8, 2015, episode, "It's Called the Octopus," involved the legal team representing the owner of an elite sex club.[64] Many tweets posted on this date celebrated Shondaland addressing sex shaming and queer sexual practices. @kpringer tweeted, "hella sex shame-y episode tonight," Candace Nicole Werts (@candacenwerts) posted, "Sex fetish, yes!" and Monet Sutton (@MusicMonetRadio) wrote, "People shouldn't be ashamed of their sexuality. They shouldn't be ashamed of liking sex." However, others resisted the episode's message. Micah Ouroboros (@micahouroboros) tweeted, "That's not sex positive. That's f-ing trashy and dirty. There's a difference," and Inda Lauryn (@indascorner) wrote, "Sex parties tho? That's nasty." Viewers also tweeted appreciation for the attention given to topics such as sexual violence and transgender identity. On October 22, 2015, @AverageCockram tweeted, "Viola Davis dropping some real talk on America's rape culture," and on October 1, 2015, after "She's Dying" @PretentiousUSA wrote, "Wow! What a great PSA/promo at the end of episode for sexual assault." Similarly, on October 29, 2015, @EDubb_41yfe wrote, "Glad and surprised that Shonda inserted a transgender centered mini-storyline into the season."

Connor and Oliver's (i.e., Coliver's) same-sex relationship also generated numerous tweets. Their romantic relationship was well received, with most mentions of Coliver being positive, such as Ashley Graham (@Shleekins)'s September 24, 2015, post: "I <3 Conner and Oliver so much!!!" However, the storyline related to Oliver's HIV diagnosis, and Connor's decision to take PrEP (pre-exposure prophylaxis, a drug for people at high risk for being exposed to HIV) to continue their sexual relationship sparked diverse reactions (see table 4). Looking critically at the lovefest that Coliver sparks online also reveals troubling cultural values. The many tweets praising Connor for staying with Oliver after his diagnosis conjure up white savior ideology amid their interracial relationship and a man of color being scripted as the partner who contracts HIV.[65]

Although Coliver's storyline prompted much Twitter activity, it paled in comparison to the season 2 reveal that Annalise had a former female lover.[66] The scene that revealed her layered identities as a bisexual dark-skinned black woman prompted the most tweets of the entire data pool (see table 5). The six-minute scene recounting Annalise's history with fellow attorney Eve Rothlow includes a kiss that helped skyrocket #HowToGetAwayWithMurder to 1,206 tweets (accounting for 20.78 percent of the episode's tweets). These posts represent a range of reactions from explicitly homophobic to implicitly homophobic to sex positive to LGBTQA (lesbian, gay, bisexual, transgender, queer, asexual) inclusive. The tweets indicate that many embraced Annalise's backstory and applauded *HTGAWM*'s inclusivity, but others reacted negatively, revealing that Shondaland's pedagogy on sexual diversity is not always well received.

TABLE 4   Sample Tweets Focused on HIV/PrEP Storyline

Twitter Handle	Timestamp	Tweet
itslouismcduff	9/24/2015 9:16	Wait HIV isn't a big deal? #HowToGetAwayWith-Murder . . . Someone explain
chelsea_rana3	9/24/2015 9:16	Conner Awesome For Staying With Him Knowing He Has HIV. #BreakTheStigma #HTGAWM #HowToGetAwayWithMurder #TGIT 🙈 ℹ️
mandamari3	9/24/2015 9:16	Yes PrEP!!! #Awareness #HowToGetAwayWith-Murder
Itsjaniez	9/24/2015 9:17	I love the way how Connor is dealing with this whole HIV situation . . . #HTGAWM #HowToGetAwayWithMurder #TGIT
sweetcorn4	9/24/2015 9:17	I'm sorry bae got AIDS ummm relationship over #HowToGetAwayWithMurder

TABLE 5   Sample Reactions to Annalise's Bisexual Storyline

Twitter Handle	Timestamp	Tweet
callingshots_	9/24/2015 9:48	HELL YEAH BI REPRESENTATION #HTGAWM #HowToGetAwayWithMurder
Shirlzrene	9/24/2015 9:50	Lesbian kiss!!! #HowToGetAwayWithMurder
jeremy_chino13	9/24/2015 9:50	Oh ok so Annalise is bi?? Cool #HowToGetAwayWithMurder
jamie132xo	9/24/2015 9:50	This is really awkward 💀💀 lmfao #HowToGetAwayWithMurder
Glamazonianash	9/24/2015 9:50	Why is everybody gay on all these shows? #HowToGetAwayWithMurder
britt_brat62	9/24/2015 9:50	Omg please don't let Annalise sleep with that woman! #HowToGetAwayWithMurder
_popdhattunechi	9/24/2015 9:51	Yes!!! Fluid sexuality! #HowToGetAwayWithMurder

Twitter enables producers and actors to interact directly with viewers, which allows for straightforward pedagogical statements. The morning after the queer reveal, Peter Nowalk, *HTGAWM*'s creator, tweeted, "Thanks all for watching last night! And just a tip: *It's not a lesbian kiss, it's just a kiss*. Love you all" (emphasis added). Although Nowalk's tweet appears positive, it actually undermines the significance of Annalise's bisexuality by minimizing their kiss, and the storyline it crystalizes, with it is "just" a kiss. Additionally, "It's not a *lesbian kiss*" is also troubling because Annalise is portrayed as bisexual, different from Eve who is portrayed as a lesbian. Ultimately, Nowalk's "supportive" tweet functions akin to colorblind rhetoric that erases racial differences in our supposed postidentity era. As an articulation of Shondaland's production outlook that mistakes minimization and erasure of difference for inclusion, alongside casting Eve as a white woman and scripting Coliver's narrative with white savior ideology, critically considering identity politics exposes how *HTGAWM*'s creators utilize normative characterizations and pairings.

The juxtaposition of Coliver and Annalise/Eve tweets indicate that a variety of factors influence why the former was better received. Both feature interracial couples, yet the former features a white man/light-skinned man of color versus the latter's white woman/dark-skinned black woman. Further, that the relationship featuring two gay men was more popular highlights the patriarchal prevalence of gay male relationships when LGBTQA identities are represented in popular culture.[67] Equally significant is that the white male character's (Connor's) relationship is embraced more so than the black female character's (Annalise's). Illuminating the dynamics at play, Meyer argues that bisexual women of color are a common plot device, manipulated so their intersectional "'Otherness' is layered to produce a commodifiable image that is both economically profitable and exploitative through its erasure of difference, and by implication, identity."[68] Compounding multiple "discourses of 'Otherness' in one character makes it easier to 'check all the boxes' of identity politics and appease the most number of identity constituents in a given audience."[69] Meyer's analysis focuses primarily on secondary characters; therefore, Annalise's positionality as the protagonist is notable, especially when the cast contains other queer characters. Queering Annalise's character directs attention to the racial politics of representing a dark-skinned black woman and the queer politics of bisexuality. Audience responses to Shondaland's pedagogy illustrate a pervasive investment in whiteness and patriarchy.

AND THE PEDAGOGICAL MORALITY
OF SHONDALAND IS . . . ?

Obviously, Rhimes and her Shondaland team aim to "teach" audiences various lessons about diversity through casting, scripting, and consciousness-raising narratives. Rhimes is completely transparent about doing so; when she received the 2015 Ally for Equality award at the Human Rights Campaign Gala, she said, "I really hate the word 'diversity,' it suggests . . . something unusual about telling stories involving women and people of color and LGBTQ characters on TV. I have a different word: NORMALIZING . . . I am making the world of television look NORMAL."[70] Rhimes's quest to normalize television and address social inequalities is complicated by using melodramatic narratives to do so, because her lessons are often delivered through plots featuring scandal, crime, and secrecy and saturated with malfeasance. When viewers are prompted to learn moral lessons from immoral characters this creates dissonance that masks the didactic roles these storylines serve. Further, this data indicates that viewers are not live-tweeting fictional programs—or at least this fictional program—to primarily engage with social commentary. That *HTGAWM*'s live-tweets did not always align with Shondaland's pedagogical aims mirrors other research on how audiences often diverge from media texts through Twitter.[71] For *HTGAWM*, this means that live-tweeting could distract from Shondaland's social commentary. While I cannot necessarily claim this occurred, the number of tweets devoted to melodramatic commentary versus social commentary suggests that Twitter users were more preoccupied by the fictional bad behavior than the real-world bad behavior they were scripted to highlight. Consequently, this suggests that live-tweeting fictional television may not constitute an easily recognizable form of digital activism.

At a glance, *HTGAWM* presents a postidentity wonderland of equality for all; the cast reflects a diverse multicultural ensemble led by a powerful bisexual black female protagonist involved in interracial relationships. Shondaland both crafts and shatters this idealization by spinning storylines in ways palatable to normativity. Utilizing Coliver as an example, the storyline inclusively depicts a gay interracial couple productively coping with an HIV diagnosis amid real-world ignorance and bigotry (e.g., Asher's comment that *Philadelphia* is his favorite movie). Moreover, Shondaland punctuates Rhimes's pedagogical intentions with hard-hitting commentary on identity politics, power dynamics, social justice and injustice through characters that parrot Rhimes's social critiques conveyed through Twitter and public speaking appearances. The diverse reactions in response to Rhimes's and Shondaland's public pedagogy indicate that some viewers are particularly receptive and use Twitter to further reinforce or comment on these lessons (e.g., by quoting dialogue). However, other viewers resist these lessons (e.g., by ridiculing or challenging dialogue). Therefore, conflicting tweets ultimately express the warring sentiments (and different ideological camps) that still surround discussions of identity politics, including portrayals of women of color in lead roles, same-sex relationships, and interracial relationships.

Overall, this chapter suggests that Twitter discourse cannot provide declarative insight into larger cultural sentiment. Like all media, if it acts as a social mirror, it is a distorted one at best. The performative nature of Twitter posts, along with character limitations and the inability to determine authorial identity, intent, and tone make this medium an unreliable predictor of cultural values. Even if user sentiment could be determined by analyzing tweets, the population that live-tweets a television show may not accurately represent viewer sentiments more broadly. Therefore, future studies to determine how fans receive Rhimes's pedagogical lessons should partner Twitter analysis with other research methods such as interviewing to more fully gauge viewer sentiment. This project also suggests that further study is needed to identify the live-tweeting practices common among viewers of fictional television. Previous scholars claim that live-tweeting purposes are consistent across televisual genres, yet this study suggests this may not be the case.[72] Studying live-tweeting practices across televisual genres will reveal rich possibilities for the tag team of Twitter and TV to spark societal reflexivity and, perhaps someday, a consistent form of digital activism.[73]

NOTES

1. Tim Dant, *Television and the Moral Imaginary: Society through the Small Screen* (London: Palgrave, 2010).

2. Sidneyeve Matrix, "The Netflix Effect: Teens, Binge Watching, and On-Demand Digital Media Trends," *Jeunesse: Young People, Texts, Cultures* 6, no. 1 (2014): 119–138.

3. Maria Konnikova, "How Facebook Makes Us Unhappy," *New Yorker,* September 10, 2013, http://www.newyorker.com/tech/elements/how-facebook-makes-us-unhappy.

4. Fabio Giglietto and Donatella Selva, "Second Screen and Participation: A Content Analysis on a Full Season Dataset of Tweets," *Journal of Communication* 65, no. 2 (2014): 260–277.

5. *Scandal* was ranked first and *HTGAWM* was ranked fourth.

6. Anna Everett, "Scandalicious: *Scandal,* Social Media, and Shonda Rhimes's Auterist Juggernaut," *Black Scholar* 45, no. 1 (2015): 34–43.

7. Everett, 34.

8. International Centre for Public Pedagogy, "Welcome to the International Centre for Public Pedagogy (ICPUP)," April 14, 2016, https://www.uel.ac.uk/icpup/.

9. Michael Idato, "How to Get Away with Murder: Viola Davis Prefers Moral Ambiguity," *Sydney Morning Herald*, February 5, 2015, http://www.smh.com.au/entertainment/tv-and-radio/how-to-get-away-with-murder-viola-davis-prefers-moral-ambiguity-20150202–133tri.html#ixzz3xzWZ18MG; Tirdad Derakshani, "Love Is Murderous in 'How to Get Away with Murder,'" *Philly.com*, November 23, 2015, http://articles.philly.com/2015–11–23/news/68487289_1_peter-nowalk-love-shonda-rhimes.

10. *How to Get Away with Murder,* "Pilot," season 1, episode 1, directed by Michael Offer, written by Peter Nowalk, aired on September 25, 2014, on ABC.

11. Idato, "How to Get Away with Murder."

12. Idato, "How to Get Away with Murder."

13. H. Roy Kaplan, *The Myth of Post-Racial America: Searching for Equality in the Age of Materialism* (New York: Rowman & Littlefield, 2011).

14. Roxane Gay, "The Oscars and Hollywood's Race Problem," *New York Times*, January 22, 2016, https://www.nytimes.com/2016/01/24/opinion/the-oscars-and-hollywoods-race-problem.html.

15. Carita Rizzio, "Shonda Rhimes's Powerful Message on Receiving Her PGA Award: 'I Deserve This,'" *Vulture*, January 24, 2016, http://www.vulture.com/2016/01/shonda-rhimes-on-pga-award-i-deserve-this.html#.

16. Rizzio.

17. Michael Zimmer and Nicholas John Proferes, "A Topology of Twitter Research: Disciplines, Methods, and Ethics," *Aslib Journal of Information Management* 66, no. 3 (2014): 250–261.

18. Jennifer Pozner, *Reality Bites Back: The Troubling Truth about Guilty Pleasure TV* (New York: Seal, 2010).

19. Jonathan Michael, "The Rise of the Anti-Hero: Why the Characters in TV and Movies We Love Most Are the Ones with Fatal Flaws," *Relevant*, April 26, 2013, http://www.relevantmagazine.com/culture/tv/rise-anti-hero.

20. Michael.

21. Akash Nickolas, "Where Is the Female Tony Soprano," *Atlantic*, June 27, 2013, http://www
.theatlantic.com/entertainment/archive/2013/06/where-is-the-female-tony-soprano
/277270/.

22. Meghan Gallagher, "Scandal's Olivia Pope and the Rise of the Female Antihero," *Artifice*,
January 5, 2015, http://the-artifice.com/scandal-olivia-pope-female-antihero/.

23. Lauren Duca, "Anatomy of the Female Antihero," *Huffpost Entertainment*, July 13, 2015,
http://www.huffingtonpost.com/entry/anatomy-of-the-female-anti-hero_us_55a3c250
e4b0ecec71bc684a.

24. Paula Bernman, "Sisters Are Doing It for Themselves: The Female Antihero on Television,"
Broadstreet Review, May 31, 2014, http://www.broadstreetreview.com/cross-cultural/the-female
-antihero-on-television.

25. Jason Steward, "Tube Talk: TV's Female Anti-Heroes: A Trend for the 21st Century's Teen
Years," *Critic Studio*, July 20, 2011, http://criticstudio.com/tube-talk/tv%E2%80%99s-female
-anti-heroes-a-trend-for-the-21st-century%E2%80%99s-teen-years/.

26. Michael, "The Rise of the Anti-Hero"; see also Richard Keen, Monica L. McCoy, and Elizabeth Powell, "Rooting for the Bad Guy: Psychological Perspectives," *Studies in Popular Culture* 34, no. 2 (2012): 129–148.

27. Michele Corriston, "*HTGAWM*'s Charlie Weber on That Heart-Stopping Finale and Annalise's 'Crazy Little Family,'" *People Magazine*, November 20, 2015, http://www.people.com
/article/how-get-away-murder-charlie-weber-talks-season-2-fall-finale.

28. Duca, "Anatomy of the Female Antihero."

29. David Thornburn and Henry Jenkins, *Rethinking Media Change: The Aesthetics of Transi-
tion* (Cambridge, Mass.: MIT Press, 2003), 269; Clint Wilson, Felix Gutierrez, and Lena Chao,
Racism, Sexism, and the Media: Multicultural Issues in the New Communications Age (London:
Sage, 2013).

30. Michelle Juergen, "Why Critics Can't Handle the Female Anti-Hero," *Mic*, January 15, 2014,
http://mic.com/articles/79047/why-critics-can-t-handle-the-female-anti-hero#
.zUNRI4SZo; Jenefer Robinson and Stephanie Ross, "Women, Morality, and Fiction," *Hypa-
tia* 5, no. 2 (1990): 76–90.

31. Duca, "Anatomy of the Female Antihero."

32. Juergen, "Why Critics Can't Handle the Female Anti-Hero."

33. Juergen.

34. Alyssa Rosenberg, "Why We'll Never Have a Female Tony Soprano," *Slate*, June 27, 2015,
http://www.slate.com/blogs/xx_factor/2013/06/27/james_gandolfini_and_the_male
_anti_hero_why_we_11_never_have_a_female_tony.html.

35. E. Keating, "Once Upon a Time and the Villainization of Women," *Artifice*, January 7, 2015,
http://the-artifice.com/once-upon-a-time-villainization-women/.

36. Gallagher, "Scandal's Olivia Pope."

37. Lesley Goldberg, "'How to Get Away with Murder' Creator Breaks Down Shondaland's
New Drama," *Hollywood Reporter*, September 25, 2014, http://www.hollywoodreporter.com
/live-feed/how-get-away-murder-creator-730206.

38. Goldberg.

39. Brian Cantor, "'How to Get Away with Murder' Gets Away with Risky Character," *Head-
line Planet*, September 25, 2015, http://headlineplanet.com/home/2014/09/25/abc-takes
-character-risk-get-away-murder-review/.

40. #HowToGetAwayWithMurder is the second most popular hashtag associated with the program. The most frequently used hashtag associated with the show is #HTGAWM?. While
many of the tweets in my data collection utilized both hashtags, not all did. Therefore, this study

cannot claim to have collected all of the live-tweets connected to this show during the nine-week period but rather collected a subset of them.

41. This study's focus on "critiquing" posts aligns with studies determining that opinion posts dominate social media. See D. Yvette Wohn and Eun-Kyung Na, "Tweeting about TV: Sharing Television Viewing Experiences via Social Media Message Streams," *First Monday* 16, no. 3 (2011): http://journals.uic.edu/ojs/index.php/fm/article/view/3368/2779; Giglietto and Selva, "Second Screen and Participation."

42. There is much scholarly debate concerning the ethics of studying and, specifically, citing tweets (see Zimmer and Proferes, "A Topology of Twitter Research," 256). I side with scholars who argue that "publicly visible Twitter messages are guaranteed to have been published to the internet at large," and therefore they are an ethical site of study. See Steven Harrington, Tim Highfield, and Axel Bruns, "More Than a Backchannel: Twitter and Television," in *Audience Interactivity and Participation*, ed. José Manuel Noguera (Brussels: COST Action Transforming Audiences, 2012), 12.

43. These figures actually underrepresent the number of tweets that focused on Annalise as this count only includes correct spellings of her name and omits indirect references to her.

44. Jessica Rawden, "How to Get Away with Murder Review: A Frantic Pace and Viola Davis Are Reasons to Watch," *CinemaBlend*, 2015, http://www.cinemablend.com/television/How-Get-Away-With-Murder-Review-Frantic-Pace-Viola-Davis-Reasons-Watch-67487.html.

45. Rawden, "How to Get Away with Murder Review"; see also Michaela D. E. Meyer, "*The Good Wife*'s Fatalistic Feminism: Televised Feminist Failures in Work/Life Balance, Romance and Feminist Alliances," in *Women, Feminism, and Pop Politics: From "Bitch" to "Badass" and Beyond*, ed. Karrin Vasby Anderson (New York: Peter Lang, 2018), 205–222.

46. Leon Barrington (@LeaonBarrington), Twitter, February 14, 2015, http://twitter.com/LeonBarrington; Cara Cooper (@caramariecooper), Twitter, October 23, 2015, http://twitter.com/caramariecooper.

47. Alicia Edison, "The Impact of the Media on Biracial Identity Formation" (master's thesis, University of North Texas, 2007), 53.

48. Wilson, Gutierrez, and Chao, *Racism, Sexism, and the Media*.

49. This corresponds with studies that found women are as likely to be harassed online by other women as they are to be harassed by men. See "Women Troll Each Other Online: How Females Are Just as Likely to Be Abused by Their Own Sex as By Men," *Daily Mail*, May 14, 2015, http://www.dailymail.co.uk/news/article-2628755/Women-troll-online-How-females-just-likely-abused-sex-men.html.

50. Jennifer Kowalski, "Stereotypes of History: Reconstructing Truth and the Black Mammy," *Transcending Silence* (Spring 2009): http://www.albany.edu/womensstudies/journal/2009/kowalski/kowalski.html.

51. Robinon and Ross, "Women, Morality," 77.

52. Robinon and Ross, 77.

53. *How to Get Away with Murder*, "I Want You to Die," season 2, episode 7, directed by Kevin Bray, written by Warren Hsu Leonard, aired on November 5, 2015, on ABC.

54. Sarah Appleton Aguiar, *The Bitch Is Back: Wicked Women in Literature* (Carbondale: Southern Illinois University Press, 2001), 5.

55. See Karrin Vasby Anderson's collection *Women, Feminism, and Pop Politics: From "Bitch" to "Badass" and Beyond* (New York: Peter Lang, 2018) for a comprehensive analysis of this dilemma across multiple media texts.

56. *How to Get Away with Murder*, "Skanks Get Shanked," season 2, episode 4, directed by Stephen Williams, written by Peter Nowalk and Angela Robinson, aired on October 15, 2015, on ABC.

57. *How to Get Away with Murder*, "Skanks Get Shanked."

58. *How to Get Away with Murder*, "Skanks Get Shanked."

59. Melissa Ames, "Sex Undoes Her: What the Fall Premiers of *How to Get Away with Murder, Scandal, & Grey's Anatomy* Reveal about the Effects of Sexualizing Strong Female Characters," *Small Screen Scholar*, September 30, 2014, http://smallscreenscholar.blogspot.com/2014/09/sex-undoes-her-what-fall-premiers-of.html.

60. Keating, "Once Upon a Time."

61. Gallagher, "Scandal's Olivia Pope."

62. *How to Get Away with Murder*, "It's Time to Move On," season 2, episode 1, directed by Bill D'Elia, written by Peter Nowalk, aired on September 24, 2015, on ABC.

63. *How to Get Away with Murder*, "Meet Bonnie," season 2, episode 5, directed by Stephen Cragg, written by Sarah L. Thompson, aired on October 22, 2015, on ABC.

64. *How to Get Away with Murder*, "It's Called the Octopus," season 2, episode 3, directed by John Terlesky, written by Joe Fazzio, aired on October 8, 2015, on ABC.

65. Erica Chito Childs, *Fade to Black and White: Interracial Images in Popular Culture* (New York: Rowman & Littlefield, 2009).

66. *How to Get Away with Murder*, "Time to Move On."

67. Brian Moylan, "Most LGBT Characters on US TV Are White and Male, Study Finds," *Guardian*, October 27, 2015, https://www.theguardian.com/tv-and-radio/2015/oct/27/most-lgbt-characters-on-us-tv-are-white-and-male-study-finds.

68. Michaela D. E. Meyer, "The 'Other' Woman in Contemporary Television Drama: Analyzing Intersectional Representation on *Bones*," *Sexuality & Culture* 19, no. 4 (June 2015): 904.

69. Meyer, 911.

70. Brennan William, "Shonda Rhimes Says She Isn't 'Diversifying' Television, She's 'Normalizing' It—There's a Difference," *Huffington Post*, March 20, 2015, http://www.huffingtonpost.com/2015/03/16/shonda-rhimes-diversity-normalize-television_n_6878842.html.

71. Megan Wood and Linda Baughman, "*Glee* Fandom and Twitter: Something New, or More of the Same?," *Communication Studies* 63, no. 3 (July–August 2012): 340.

72. Wohn and Na, "Tweeting about TV."

73. I want to thank my research assistant T. J. Martin, who helped collect research on contemporary Twitter practices, and Sara Amato, whose work on female antiheroes influenced this project.

12 · DYING FOR THE NEXT EPISODE

Living and Working within Shondaland's Medical Universe

SEAN SWENSON

"It's just like *Grey's Anatomy!*"

It is less a comment and more an exultation. The true fruition of fandom. A culmination of rumors proven true. The words cut through the silence and snap me out of my wandering thoughts. The elated woman, the wife of my patient, beams at her husband laid out on the stretcher, asleep. It is about four in the morning and the three of us are parked outside a bank of elevators, awaiting one's arrival. I reflexively smile, perhaps due to her emotional display or in response to her television reference. I have worked as a transporter at a large community hospital since 2005, the same year *Grey's Anatomy* (also referred to as *Grey's*) premiered. It is a job few people recognize or even acknowledge because it carries little prestige in the hospital system. Additionally, our labor as transporters is often invisible in medical melodramas such as *Grey's Anatomy* (ABC 2005–present) and *ER* (NBC 1994–2009). I watch these shows as a fan, scholar, and employee of the medical industry. To explain my role, I often tell people to imagine a scene in a medical drama where the doctors are dramatically rushing a patient down the hall to some urgent destination; you hear screams, you see a blur of IV tubing, and you feel a determination to save a life. On television, viewers typically see stylish doctors and nurses leading the way and pushing the gurney. In real life, I am the one actually doing the pushing and the scene is far less glamorous.

As a patient transporter, in effect, I am the legs that nurses are not permitted to have because they are place-bound to their patients. I move patients between destinations, retrieve blood, and fetch equipment. I keep people alive when they are apart from nurses and take them away from nurses when they die. What began as a summer job out of high school has become a secondary career of sorts as well as a site of inquiry. However, I spend the majority of my time as a doctoral student of communication. As a critical media scholar, I find it difficult to explain why I continue to work in the medical industry, especially given the low prestige afforded to my bottom-of-the-ladder clinical role. When I am asked by my peers, patients, and patients' families to discuss my role in either or both contexts, I feel apprehensive about delving into the complicated nature of my relationship to health and media. That same apprehension boils up in front of the elevator when I realize that I have given myself away to my patient's wife when I reacted to her comment with a smile. She reads in my smile an acknowledgment of her love for *Grey's Anatomy*, a mutual kinship with the work of Shonda Rhimes and Shondaland. Any hope of remaining invisible to this family member is dashed.

A wide grin spreads across her face. "Do you watch the show?" she asks.

She clearly knows the answer. It is the same smile I see on my students' faces when I mention the show during lecture, a calling card that signals one has joined the fandom of Shondaland. Not wanting to get into the complexities of my relationship to media and medicine I nod "yes," but nonverbally suggest that she will only get one-word answers out of me by averting my gaze. I pretend to be aloof.

She gestures to her husband in excitement, "We love it. It's so crazy!"

In the hospital, she is every bit a tourist as much as a patient/customer. Her eyes dart around the walls anthropologically in a land she has watched on television but never gotten to witness. In my opinion, there is not much to look at. I would call the wall color parchment, but only to fancy up the fact that the walls are stark white. If this were a medical melodrama, it would suffer from poor set dressing. If she is this excited about the hallway, she must have been exuberant about having been in the ER these past few hours.

"Is there as much drama here as on the show?" she asks.

"You better hope not," I say. There is a tad more sarcasm then I would have liked in my response, but she laughs at my distaste masked as humor.

The elevator dings and slides open. I ease the stretcher over the bumpy tile and across the threshold. She takes one last look around before entering behind me and says, "Being here is just like being in the show. Except on that show everyone seems to die!"

As I push the button to launch us up to the third floor, I wonder if she fully considers the gravity of her words.

Grey's Anatomy premiered in 2005, and its spinoff *Private Practice*, in 2007, with a simple premise for each show: to follow the lives of physicians at the fictional sites of Seattle's Grey Sloan Memorial Hospital (*Grey's*) in Washington and Los Angeles's Oceanside Wellness in California (*Private Practice*). However, this simple premise is juxtaposed against the complexity of how Rhimes and her team write each show, because the particularities of doctors' and patients' lives matter in terms of representation. From a critical television studies perspective, I should be more specific: some lives matter more than others. In this chapter, I argue that medical melodramas in general, and *Grey's Anatomy* and *Private Practice* in particular, live by the dictum that for some to live meaningfully, others must die. This has layered implications because the ability to improve and extend life is fostered by death. Organ donation and the withdrawal of treatment often get most of the press for end-of-life ethics, but even something as simple as the ability to open up a bed for a new patient typically rests upon the death of another.[1] Even more problematic, but rarely considered, are how the lives and livelihoods of doctors—and to a lesser degree all medical professionals—are sustained by the deaths of patients; not just in terms of continued employment in the real world, but as a plot device on television. From an industry and production vantage point, medical melodramas require a continuous stream of sick and dying patients to be introduced each week. Quite literally, producers and writers must sit around and think: how can we move storylines along by hurting or killing someone? Shondaland's production labor to create and sustain successful medical shows is so deeply invested in power dynamics that I find it incredibly necessary to critically deconstruct the representations and implications of *Grey's Anatomy* and *Private Practice*. Because I, too, watch and love the shows, I feel an equal call to be autoethnographically self-reflexive about enjoying them *because* of the wounding, not in spite of it.

When I describe my academic work, I often use the term *interdisciplinary*, but that is just a fancy word for saying it's complicated. It is complicated because at the unique crossroads of being a Shondaland fan, media scholar, and clinical hospital worker, I'm assumed to only be one kind of vessel for what I see. Research on audience engagement with medical melodramas diverges based upon how viewers identify. Clinicians have been found to be most interested in interpreting the shows as a collection of case studies, episodic instances of how to maneuver ethical dilemmas in practice.[2] Scholars, particularly in health communication, have interpreted the shows as an opportunity, a means for educating the general public through representation.[3] The weekly audience, like my patient's wife, are expected to be consumers, sponges for taking in the information presented.[4] At the crossroads of all three social locations, I watch medical melodramas as a fan with an academic gaze and work within a hospital setting that requires connecting with real people and encountering real life and death circumstances as a patient transporter. These overlapping vantage points provide a space for autoethnographic inquiry, rendering the personal political and worthy of close examination.[5]

I suspect that much of what I experience as a *Grey's Anatomy* and *Private Practice* fan mirrors the experience of others who work in health care—a mixture of voyeuristic pleasure and unbridled conflict. However, being part of a scholarly community has provided the language and analytical skills to theorize my engagement with Shondaland shows in distinct ways that highlight how rarely society and scholarship alike simultaneously examine the social institutions of medicine and media. This approach draws concerted attention to how power is imbued through the technologies and discourses of medicine and media, both languages with which to understand the world. My experiences dealing with hospital deaths substantiate the invisible reliance upon death that permeates Shondaland's health care centers as a cultural reflection of how the U.S. American health care system privileges a narrative of medical rescue and turns away from those bodies—human beings—who cannot or choose not to endure treatment.[6] How can death be erased and forgotten when it happens every day? What are the dangers of propagating these cultural practices through the popularity of Dr. Meredith Grey, Dr. Addison Montgomery, and their fellow doctors? How am I implicated?

"You need to watch this show!"

My sister is insistent and I can tell by the excitement in her voice that she really wants to watch it, and wants me to want to watch it with her. My sister and I both work the overnight shift on the weekends at the hospital; our shifts end at 7:00 A.M. Our schedule lets her spend the weekdays with her family; for myself, it allows me to enroll in a full load of courses and teach two undergraduate classes during the week. I put down my lunch tray and walk over to the sink to wash my hands. It is 3:00 A.M., the time when leftover work from the evening tends to dry up. Patients are less likely to come into the emergency room after midnight, so our lunch breaks allow us to catch up and relax. My sister started as a patient transporter two years before I did, and now she is an ultrasound technologist. She earns more pay and her position requires less schooling, something she loves to point out to me. We spend our downtime together and stream shows on her phone during our breaks.

"You will love it!" She has been pushing for me to start watching *Grey's Anatomy* for some time now. Until tonight I resisted, but this time I give in. "Sure, why not!?!"

We quickly devour the first season over the course of the proceeding days.

From the beginning of Shonda Rhimes's trek into health care, health communication scholars have criticized the ethics of how medical issues are resolved on Shondaland shows. Debuting in proximity to *House M.D.* (Fox 2004–2012), another television show featuring criticized ethics of practice, alarm was raised concerning the interns—Meredith Grey, Cristina Yang, Izzie Stevens, George O'Malley and Alex Karev—because they were making patient care choices that were at best ethically ambiguous and at worst illegal.[7] In the early 2000s, medical melodramas were on a collision course with ethics watchdogs, sparking scholarly interest in how medical students might be interpreting these ethical scenarios.[8]

However, these same fears were not lobbied in relation to the general audience, presumably consumers of both media and health care. I argue that the general audience was considered beyond the boundaries of corruption because the show does not entice identification with the patients but rather with the physicians. On television, physicians are scripted to be the eyes through which the audience experiences the medical melodrama setting. They become medicalized superheroes because the storylines are largely conveyed from their narrative points of view. For example, there are no transporters in the show, and although there are nurses, they do less work on television than they do in real life.

The surgeons on *Grey's* and physicians on *Private Practice* do all forms of work. They draw blood, run labs, and perform very fast and diagnostically accurate ultrasound exams; a feat my sister finds both hilarious and infuriating. Medical melodramas really do seem to be prepping the physicians of today to be polymaths if physicians are absorbing as much as scholars theorize they are.[9] To me, it matters less that ethics are put in question and more that these ethical questions are played out across patient's bodies with little to no regard for the role that technologies of ethics play on and through certain bodies. If the storylines of Shondaland's medical universe more holistically reflected invisible hospital participants such as nurses, radiologists, custodians, patients, and transporters, then ethics would be more readily accounted for and fully fleshed out. As it stands, the singular focus on physicians throughout multiple seasons of *Grey's* and *Private Practice* renders patients and ancillary staff largely invisible and subsequently unknown. The considerable invisibility of everyone except the physicians is normalized in the television industry despite the fact that fictional patients represent a positionality that all people will one day occupy—the sick and dying. And ancillary staff comprise the majority of health care employees—without us, the medical industry would cease to exist.

I would be grossly negligent to assert that death is not extremely important to Shondaland's storylines and viewers. One only needs to consider audience responses to the deaths of fan favorite *Grey's* characters such as Dr. Mark Sloan ("McSteamy") in season 9 and Dr. Derek Shepherd ("McDreamy") in season 11 to know that death is taken seriously by fans.[10] However, it is significant that the lens through which we experience death is often constructed through physicians' experiences rather than patients' experiences. This is especially poignant because patients die on medical melodramas far more commonly than physicians, yet the storylines involving deaths of physicians garner far more emotional attention from the audience. On *Grey's* and *Private Practice*, we experience the loss of life repeatedly through the eyes of crossover character Dr. Addison Montgomery and not her OB-GYN patients' personal experiences because discussions of life and death are mediated through her medical expertise. Additionally, while we are subjected to countless instances of tragic fetal demise, it is the portrayal of Dr. Amelia

Shepherd's loss of her son in season 5 (as a doctor on *Grey's* and a patient on *Private Practice*) that narratively processed the loss as personal, complicated, and real.[11] Disassociating from patients' perspectives is not necessarily a nefarious plot device, rather it is a byproduct of writers and producers typically ending the patient's storyline prior to rolling the credits in preparation for the next episode. Because most doctors are series regulars, they are scripted for viewers to become attached to them week after week; this attachment solidifies our allegiance to them compared to the guest-starring patients. By bookending storylines around a protagonist-physician, it is nearly impossible to finish watching an episode thinking about anyone except the doctor-hero. In season 2 of *Grey's*, Denny Duquette, Dr. Izzie Stevens's fiancé, dies from complications after a heart transplant. We spend the rest of season 2 and beginning of season 3 empathizing with her grief and concern for her career after she unethically cut Denny's LVAD (left ventricular assist device) wire to secure his spot at the top of the transplant list. We are thoroughly centered on her grief as a fiancée and physician rather than on his death as a patient and person who suffered a stroke.[12] Moreover, Denny's character posthumously returns in season 5 for an afterlife love affair with Izzie.[13] His return functions as a plot device to prompt Izzie's storyline as a physician who becomes a patient; she has cancer and her hallucinations of Denny warn her of her illness.

Because physicians are scripted as the hub of the shows, patients never fully star in the narratives of their own lives and deaths, nor do their storylines extend beyond the reach of the physicians they seek treatment from. At best, patients function as a medical mystery to solve; at worst, patients are cast as a hurdle for doctors to deal with. Even more troublesome is that negative outcomes for patients are often depicted more as negative outcomes for doctors. We see this scripted in *Private Practice* psychologist Dr. Violet Turner's season 2 interactions with patient Katie Kent. Originally presented as a patient suffering from schizophrenia during her pregnancy, Katie later suffers a fetal demise. Shortly afterward, due to her not taking her medications, Katie becomes delusional to the point that she believes Violet has stolen her baby from her. Mentally ill and vengeful, Katie returns at the end of season 2 and literally steals Violet's unborn child by cutting the baby out of her body and leaving Violet for dead. Seasons 3 and 4 address Violet's trauma from this assault by positioning Katie as a violent challenge that must be legally dealt with in order for Violet to recover from her ordeal. While this storyline makes for great television, it does little to blur the boundaries between patients and doctors as antagonists and protagonists, respectively. This is important because very little is done to explore Katie's loss of her baby, her mental illness, or the impact this ordeal had on her. Given Shondaland's hyperattentiveness to physicians, had Katie's storyline been scripted for a doctor, it would likely have contained an emotional appeal for understanding and treating mental illness. Instead, it became an example of overcoming a terrible criminal act committed by a terrible person. Even when we know that Violet has forgiven Katie, we only feel for Violet because Shondaland's writers failed to script empathetic space for Katie as the patient.

Traveling through Shondaland's medical universe as a participant and fan, I am drawn more to the theme of death than any of the others presented, which range from friendship to loss to relationships. Watching *Grey's Anatomy* and *Private Practice*, I am specifically drawn to the invisibility of death because a small but often ignored aspect of my work as a transporter is dealing with death's inevitability. While most of my patients live, some die, and when patients die, my assigned role is to remove and erase them from sight. Drawing from my lived experiences, when I watch *Grey's* and *Private Practice*, I am troubled by the cycle of patients being quickly disposed of—like trash—and quickly replaced with new patients, often scripted with increasingly convoluted and depressingly complicated acute and chronic ailments. Within these seemingly endless cycles that are required for the show to stay on air, patients are put on display as a testament to the doctors' persevering education and medical acumen. Countless people have been wounded, diagnosed, killed off, and subsequently confined within medical narratives so the doctors of Grey Sloan Memorial and Oceanside Wellness can learn new procedures, repeat procedures they botched or failed the first time around, and experience the satisfaction of saving a patient or the distress of losing a patient. I try to imagine what that looks like enacted outside of television. It is easy to forget that I work in the same trade of bodies.

I knock softly on the glass door to the emergency room's trauma suite. The curtain whips open and the nurse smiles at me. "She's all ready to go!" she says. Another nurse stands in a corner collecting debris and cleaning the surface of the room's countertops. The trauma room is one of the largest spaces in the hospital in terms of patient care. One wall is lined with baskets of clean linens, an assortment of latex gloves, and metal chart racks. On the opposite wall, glass door cabinets are filled with procedure trays, medications, and equipment for resuscitating a coding patient. The sign on this patient's chart explains why the nurse is cleaning and lets me know that no more cabinets will need to be opened. "Comfort Measures Only" is written in bold. This means the patient is at the end of life and the patient or family has decided to withdraw care so as not to prolong suffering when death is imminent. Death on television is usually acute, fast, and chaotic, not the long drawn-out descent that often characterizes the end of life in today's real world. I begin to pump up the stretcher, my eyes are glued to her gaunt frame barely hidden by the bedding tucked in around her. I've had over a decade of experience, and it has never gotten easier or more natural for me to be so close to death. Knowing that my patient will die, I want to be extra kind by speaking softly and pushing the stretcher gently so as not to rattle her worn body, but I am not sure how much is getting through to her. She could be asleep, unaware, or something else entirely. I tend to err on the chance that the patient is fully conscious, or at least "with it" to some degree. I begin my scripted spiel.

"Hi. My name is Sean. I'm the transporter. I'm going to take you out of the emergency room, upstairs." The nurse cleaning in the corner turns around, points to the ceiling and jokes "Yeah, the 'Big' room upstairs." My patients' nurse begins to laugh uncontrollably in response. My eyes widen. I look down at the unflinching patient, there is no physical response. The two nurses descend into fits of giggling. Commandingly I point to the door, ordering them outside, my mouth agape. I am unsure if they read my response as funny or condemning. I am horrified that I find their response clever, if inappropriate. Their laughter trails off as I make my way down the hallway. I understand the turn toward humor at this awkward point near death. When you feel like you have nothing else to offer, perhaps humor is the last medicine delivered. Dark humor runs deep in hospitals, in and out of Shondaland.

Grey's Anatomy has been simultaneously praised and critiqued for its popularity, particularly with regard to the medical and nursing students who comprise a strong weekly following.[14] What has not been addressed is how power, especially power over death, is enacted on and through the bodies of patients. Whether this plays out akin to my example above as humor constructed through the body of a dying woman or as advancement of a storyline through the wounding of a fictional TV character, bodies are being commodified and used as narrative vehicles for others. They literally become the site upon which dialogue and exposition take place. What is missing on television for those who die and those who treat the dying is an integration of the entangled relationships between patient autonomy, ethics, and agency in the particular context of biopower. Michel Foucault coined *biopower* to discuss and politicize the manipulation of bodies in the pursuit of life itself.[15] Previous conceptions of the dynamic between power and death articulated control as being able to determine who would live and who would die, akin to a monarch possessing the power to order someone to die. Foucault conceptualized biopower as a new means of controlling bodies, enacted by discursively manipulating bodies in the pursuit of creating healthy populations according to dominant views, akin to people who smoke cigarettes being deemed social pariahs as a means of social control.[16]

Although biopower is quite significant to life and death representations on medical melodramas, I stop short of asserting that Shondaland is manipulating bodies and controlling viewers' behaviors through weekly doctor-hero displays. However, power undoubtedly circulates through each storyline and reestablishes itself through the interdependent discourses of bodies, medicine, and televisual narratives that comprise the arc of any given medical melodrama. This is especially important because the racial and ethnic diversity of the cast allows for specific kinds of bodies, in particular, persons of color, to serve as the sites upon which this biopower is often played out. History provides countless cases of the systemic exploitation of black bodies for the progression of medical knowledge. Black bodies have served as technological sites for medical research without consent and without acknowledgement of fault and malpractice to this day.[17]

Alongside racial politics, gendered politics in medicine are equally important to consider. Female bodies are constructed as public, open for display, and sites of societal debate and conflict. Take for example the private yet sensationalized end-of-life cases that have resulted in heated public discourse and debate such as Terri Schiavo and Nancy Cruzan.[18] Men's bodies are rarely assumed to be public in the way that women's bodies are; so, seeing a woman open on a table in a surgical suite on television draws from a common societal practice of displaying and consuming women's bodies in specific power-laden ways. This is not to imply that men's bodies are not displayed and consumed on *Grey's* and *Private Practice*; they certainly are. Rather, it is to underscore how mediated consumption is informed by identity politics. Thus, the implications for marginalized gendered bodies (e.g., cisgender, transgender, and gender queer women's bodies) differ from the implications for privileged gendered bodies (e.g., cisgender men's bodies). It also matters that the representation of women of color is strong in Shondaland given that Western medical knowledge was in part built on experimenting on the bodies of women of color.[19] Failing to acknowledge this is problematic. I worry that Shondaland's commitment to portraying marginalization and diverse identity groups—made manifest by including characters who represent, for example, transgender identity, queer love, taboo relationships, the aged, and the differently abled—draws attention away from the identity politics of death. More specifically, in Shondaland, death is essentialized across identities—even though in the real world, how you die and how people treat your dying body or dead body is impacted by your positionalities. This is especially significant on and off screen because the means to control death are as important as the ability to direct life.

Necropolitics was first introduced by Achille Mbembe to name the nation-state's role in constructing power and legitimacy through death.[20] Whereas the ability to control life has been the Foucauldian standard for biopower, necropolitics analyzes how power ascribes meaning onto death. For example, a person walking through what is constructed as the "wrong side of town" (i.e., dangerous side) at night could be branded as blameworthy for their death, similar to how death via obesity is ascribed value differently than death via breast cancer in terms of patient culpability.[21] In this example, the consideration of biopower focuses on how bodies might be willed to behave in certain ways, whereas the consideration of necropolitics focuses on how those bodies might be perceived following death. In ways that are quite invisible to the general population, death is handled ironically in hospitals as a common but secret occurrence. It gets constructed in shameful ways that convey that dying has no place in a hospital and those who chose to die, or failed to live, are at fault. The people who have the technological ability to prolong life are the heroes, even past the point of what might be considered a "good death."[22] A conceptual lens that accounts for issues of power, privacy, and body politics is necessary for critically interrogating death, especially as death does not mark an end. It is a process that plays out control through the navigation, or transport, of emotion. Shondaland could and should be a place of liberatory meaning making that holds the audience as culpable as the showrunners. When I witness a mother grieve for her child after he dies from a complication in surgery on *Grey's*, why is it that I feel sadder for Dr. Miranda Bailey as the doctor who breaks the news? Perhaps the problem is in how we construct Western medicine as a site and source of definitive knowledge rather than how the shows and their real-life counterparts play it out.

"Do you need a minute?" I pause the playback.

I look with concern at my sister shifting in her chair in obvious discomfort. She is eight months pregnant and experiencing increasing contractions from being on her feet too much at work. "No it's fine. I'm just going to try to go to the bathroom." She winces and presses down on the top of her belly in an attempt to subdue her discomfort. "You can keep playing it," she adds as she lifts herself up and heads to the restroom. Part of me is glad for a break; in less than a year we have made it through three hundred plus episodes of *Grey's* and *Private Practice* during our shared lunchbreaks at work. The show is getting remarkably dark, which is saying something for a show built around death. Though my sister has seen these episodes already, I wonder if they cause her any distress.

"Okay. You can restart." She eases herself back into her chair. I brace myself for our return to Shondaland but am surprised by the buzzing against my leg. I reach into my scrub pants pocket and retrieve the vibrating beeper that caused me to jump unexpectedly. Rather than being called directly, my hospital now uses an automated system that sends pages to a beeper. It includes the location, patient identification information, and any pertinent material such as whether or not the patient is to be isolated for infection. I flip my beeper around and my eyes focus on the name of my next patient: "Body."

My phone begins to ring. Caller ID shows it is the administrator on duty, the nurse in charge of the entire hospital facility.

"Hello?" I put on my most professional and confident voice.

"Hey Sean, it's Greg. Listen, we really need that room for a patient who has been waiting in the ER for a bed, so can you put a rush on that body?"

I smile. "Yeah, I just have to grab the key to the closet."

"Thank you sir!" He hangs up quickly.

I turn to my sister. "Have to get a body."

"Have fun!" she says with a laugh. "And wash your hands!"

Walking to my department's office, I am thinking about how death permeates Shondaland. To be sure, the audience sees bodies and body parts all the time and people die regularly, but we never get left with the mess when people die. Not just the blood or linens. I mean that *Grey's* and *Private Practice* mask that the medical industry is also in the business of death, with real bodies that once breathed and talked to and smiled at their loved ones and health care professionals. Too often, the death of a character on television is montaged away, backed by a slow and emotional soundtrack that allows a smooth transition from death to the end of a shift. Hospitals are presented as liminal spaces between life and funeral. In the real yet hidden world, I grab the key to begin the process of cleaning up my own hospital's mess.

The small storage closet is in the basement—a literal descent. If you were to disembark from the main bank of elevators you might surely miss it. The loading dock doors are only a few feet from the elevator to the right and the loud noises from the kitchen and environmental service department would lead anyone to think that anything worth seeing would be at this end of the hospital and not the cul-de-sac of unremarkable pine doors to the left. With the buzzing air growing more still as I walk, I approach the first door. It has a blue sign marked "Holding." I pull out the key looped through a broken-off broom handle. It is smooth from age and in black marker has "Holding Room Lower Level" scrawled on it.

The door opens with an audible click, revealing the five-foot-wide by eight-foot-deep closet. There is little to draw your attention away from the blue velvet draped gurney sitting in the middle of the room. The lights flicker momentarily as electricity warms the dormant florescent lighting. The light draws the eyes to the only points of interest in the room: the banana yellow linen bag in the corner, the empty metal latex glove box holder, and the draped gurney. The gurney itself was vintage in age when I first started working at the hospital about twelve years ago; now it looks more like a relic than a repository for a body. For something designed not to draw attention to the presence of a body, crushed blue velvet seems an odd choice of fabric. Its size, too, is overwhelming. It gives the odd appearance of a blue coffin perched atop a flimsy metal cart. In actuality, the blue velvet acts as a fitted slipcover, concealing a four-poster canopy that creates a rectangle of air atop the metal gurney. The blue velvet and flat canopy top must be removed to receive the body but in the interim, remains in place.

The walls of the room are just as white as the rest of the hospital, but they are dull and chipped with neglect. There is also a missing ceiling. The tiles that once resided in the checkerboard metal ceiling frame have long been removed, too stained and bloated from years of dripping water leaking from industrial pipes to remain. Evidence of this leak manifests in a water stain atop the flat surface of the blue velvet slipcover. It is a noticeable blemish, but a person would need to be looking at the gurney to see it. I doubt many have noticed it. The gurney itself is oddly light but top-heavy. It has the feel of a stagecoach in terms of its shock absorption, bouncing and teetering ever so. The door lightly catches on the carpet as I pull it shut, causing it to slam harder than intended when I pulled hard to overcome the resistance. Pushing the gurney toward the elevator, I contemplate the scenario I will be faced with when I reach the room. Familiar with this process, I anticipate the labor that I will expend to remove the patient from their current setting in preparation for the new patient the nurse called about.

As I pull the curtain behind me, I can feel the air succumb to the stillness of death. The door is already closed but I pull the curtain as an extra privacy measure. This gesture, which usually signals respect for a person's privacy in the hospital, now signals an effort to hide their death. To give someone privacy in life is to make known that a person is present and a boundary should be maintained; in death, privacy makes it as though they were never present at all. The ambient noise of equipment buzzing, shoes scuffing on linoleum, and the idle chatter at the nurses' station permeate the air throughout the rest of the unit, but in here, I can only hear my own breath. While various hospital staff bustle in and out of the spaces of the living, in here, I am the only one coming and going. The scratching of the gurney's ill-fitting metal on itself reminds me that it is less than sturdy, if it ever had been. The fluorescent lights shine brighter than normal. They reverberate around the room, waves audibly humming as their beams bounce against the white walls, blank television screen, and silver IV poles. Tellingly, the silver IV poles are piled in the corner awaiting cleaning and the next patient. My eyes make a cursory glance around the room. It is unremarkable, stripped clean of memory. It had surely once been littered with papers, photos, perhaps drawings and flowers; longer stays usually bring gifts from well-wishers. Only one marker remains that speaks to the person the previous patient had been; it was waiting for me on the bed.

The bagged patient is the whitest object in the room, whiter than the sheets which, over time, have grown thin and patchy from industrial washing. The thinness of the sheets is all the more relevant as I pace the room with my eyes to develop my strategy. I will have to rely on these sheets for support. I never look at the tan tag at the foot of the bed but I can tell a lot from the opaque bag. This is most likely a man. He is short but his arms, pinned to his sides, press hair against the bag. He is small enough that I won't need help to move him, not that any is offered. I circle the bed and unlatch the sheet corners; they spring to life and fly toward the dead patient. I press the metal gurney to the bed. It is cold and stings my belly through my scrub top. The gurney does not have a mechanism for adjusting its height so I must lower the bed to match the gurney. Because the gurney does not have a brake, I inch my feet closer to the bed and press my weight against it. I only have one chance to successfully transfer the patient to the gurney. There are no do-overs.

When I first started as a transporter, I had no idea how to accomplish moving a dead patient from their bed to a gurney. I struggled to move a patient through the hospital's process and perform my job duties because both conflicted with my intense desire not to touch the dead patient. I learned very quickly that the integrity of the bag was essential, its plastic molding to my fingers as I grabbed and pulled, mere atoms separating the exposure of the patient to the air; it is more Hefty than of heft. The nurses refer to the bag as a shroud and while that sounds ritualistic, there seems to be less religion and more efficiency in the plastic packaging. I reach across the gurney's sunken surface, calculating whether it will hold the width of this patient—it always does but it never looks sufficient and causes me to wonder each time. My eyes dart up, looking at the bag. I swear I can see the body move even though it could not have. I force myself to focus and then I gather as much of the bedding under the patient as possible. I tighten my grip. I then regather and tighten. Tighten again. I cannot rely on my weight to pull this man over. If I lean away from the gurney, I will open up a chasm between the bed and gurney. I think often about a scenario where the patient falls, hitting the floor. Would I call for help immediately? Would I stand in shock? Would I laugh? I think back to Shondaland. Hasn't a body been dropped on the show? I know Dr. Meredith Grey dropped a kidney during surgery in season 5.[23] I would get into much worse trouble than she did. She is a doctor.

I count slowly in my head as I prepare to pull on the bedsheets before I remember: the pillow. I place a pillow where the patient's head will land; past experience has taught me that no sound is more lasting in the psyche than that of a heavy human skull hitting aged industrial metal. One goes from the soft embrace of the bed in life to the cold crust of metal in death. I regather the thinned sheets and brace myself. I pull, wanting the package to move, and it gives slowly, moving over the lip of the bed, onto the gurney, resting with an audible thud. I take hold of the bag, its translucent plastic stretched over the patient's face. In some circumstances, I cannot see the contours of their facial expressions but today I can see his death mask: eyes open wide and mouth agape, as if he were surprised by death. I pull the bag up and toward me, releasing the tightened plastic and the patient's arm which had been flattened against the gurney. I look away so as not to catch a second glimpse of his face, one uneasy glimpse was enough. I can hear wheels outside the room, the housekeeping staff has arrived to finish cleaning the room for the next patient. I wonder if the floor will still be wet when I bring the new patient/tenant up from the emergency room after I drop this patient off in the "Holding Room Lower Level."

I unfurl the blue velvet tarp that covers the gurney. The tight-fitting nature of the tarp is frustrating, like attempting to put a fitted bedsheet on a differently sized mattress by yourself—only I am trying to respectfully cover a dead body that I feel nervous about touching. It adds a couple feet to the top of the gurney to the point that it is impossible to imagine that I am pushing anything other than a precariously driven and precariously covered blue velvet coffin. I roll slowly out of the room; the maid looks away, not making eye contact. Staff on the floor pretend not to notice me, I assume. The acknowledgement and greetings that normally accompany a visit to this floor are absent when I transport the dead, even though I can be heard and seen. The squeaking of the wheels is noticeable, and since the patient has just died, the staff is aware of my existence. It is an odd feeling to be very conspicuous and yet ignored by everyone I come into contact with. I feel the pressure of eyes upon me but never a direct gaze; they might stare covertly behind their computer screens or catch a fleeting glimpse as we pass. They know what I am delivering.

Family members and visitors often cock their heads in confusion. A visitor once asked me if I was headed to a meeting. I asked in confusion why she asked that, and she said that she assumed I was pushing a caterer's cart of sandwiches. Now, I keep my eyes fixated so as not to draw attention to myself any more than necessary. I stare at the water stain. I press the elevator button; it lights up and opens almost immediately. The nurse already on board sees my load, immediately understands, and ejects herself from the elevator. I roll in, careful of my top-heavy load as I cross the seam between floors. I get off in the basement. There is a soft blue light emanating from a bug trap just below the line of the ceiling. The air is louder here, warmer than I remembered when I retrieved the gurney; the humidity is slowly creeping into the basement as a result of the loading bay doors being opened frequently. Soon, the funeral home will sneak this delivery out through the loading bay, a sort of anti-ambulance inlet. I pull out the key on the worn, broken broom handle. I turn the key and its characteristic audible click opens the door. I roll the patient into the closet. Of course, the ceiling tiles are still missing from the leaking water pipe and the bag of linens still sits idly in the corner. They highlight the regard for the patient who perhaps stepped into a meticulously designed lobby and will now exit from this unkempt, understated space. I turn off the light and whisper, "Good Luck," as I close the door on this patient. The funeral home is on their way by now to retrieve their package. He will be gone by the time I need to use the gurney again.

What stings about death in the hospital is that the positions we believe exist on the spectrum of life and death are reversed in ways that prove contradictory, unscientific even. In death, a person/body is rendered dead, same and different, present and gone. Roles change too; nurses become cleaning staff, transporters become specialized clinicians, and patients who started as clients end as waste. To put it lightly, death in the hospital space desanctifies the space of healing and reveals the vulnerabilities of health, meaning that every individual will die, timely or otherwise. Death envelops, and in the case of a body on a gurney, it appropriates space. If I had an infrared death camera of sorts, I imagine I could see waves of revulsion radiating off of the gurney and myself, creating a disruptively repugnant space in the social, cultural, and public space of healing that hospitals are typically presumed and portrayed to be. In Shondaland, power emanates from death itself. It is a furnace that fuels the storylines of the show. Yet some deaths take priority, such as in season 6 of *Grey's*, when Dr. George O'Malley suffers brain death in surgery after saving a stranger's life and being hit by a bus.[24] The other physicians, his friends and colleagues, wait with bated breath for confirmation that it is, in fact, George. Their fearful anxiety subtly alerts the audience that, should the maimed man be merely a patient, rather than a doctor turned patient, we would be much happier to know the good doctor was okay despite the man's grim prognosis.

Shondaland shows us the reality of life and death; people do, in fact, die, and they become placeless, neither body, health consumer, nor leftover. Death disrupts our perceptions of hospitals as places of rescue and makes the space that we occupy at the moment of death's rupture real by virtue of death's presence. In other words, the hospital is constituted as a space of healing where death is unacknowledged and disavowed. It is not surprising that death functions as a liminal space, because hospitals thrive as timeless places, flooded with fluorescent lights and few windows to betray the actual time. Likewise, time is punctuated by staff intrusions at all hours, without regard for knowledge of the actual hour. Hospital death is the disorientation of the disoriented place. Despite the totality of what we think we know about what happens in hospitals, we give ourselves over to uncertainties of prognosis, time, and treatment. While constructed in different realities, Shondaland is in the business of death and so am I.

I feel disoriented. My mind is shifting back and forth between the hospital and Shondaland. As I walk to the emergency room to pick up a patient who has been waiting for a bed, I consider my position in the hospital, my role in the process of death, and my relationship to televisual narratives. I contemplate the use of death in my research; death bolsters my future career. Am I any less culpable than Rhimes and her team of producers, writers, and actors for trading in death as a commodity? I imagine my pregnant sister and the last few episodes we will surely binge-watch our way through. I let muscle memory guide my body in pushing my patient, accompanied by his wife, to the elevators. I think about what anchors my fascination with the control that Shondaland has over the lives and deaths of a multitude of fictionalized patients who have meaning ascribed to them primarily for the character development of the doctor-heroes imbued with medical power. How does the exploitive machination of the real-world hospital I work in differ from the exploitation of patients in Shondaland? I am both implicating and defending: myself and my sister as audience members and medical professionals, Rhimes as the showrunner, Shondaland, and others—we all profit from the movement of bodies in, through, and out of life and death experiences. She and her team cannot be held solely liable for correcting the social ills of medicine through television any more than we can hold Shondaland responsible for the U.S. American public redeeming or abandoning faith in the White House via *Scandal* (ABC 2012–2018). To me, the red flag is that most of what I see and experience watching *Grey's Anatomy* and *Private Practice* does not feel odd. My desire would be for Shondaland to become a site of provocation, where it would serve as a source and site of entertainment, education, technology, *and* analysis—personal analysis. This is why autoethnographic inquiry proves to be such a valuable tool for critique, media and otherwise. It brings the individual into focus when so often we try to hide ourselves and others to oversimplify and clean up the mess of being human.

In many cases, what the audience is exposed to on television are health care encounters that appear better than what may be typical for most of U.S. American society. In Shondaland, physicians commonly devote time and technology to curing patients without regard for cost, insurance, or access, which is an ideal rather than a reality in the real world. While I speak only for myself as a transporter, I can only imagine what nurses, radiologists, custodians, and other invisible hospital staff think and feel while watching Shondaland's medical melodramas. I wonder how I would experience these shows had I never worked in a hospital or acquired a scholarly language to deconstruct their portrayals. My mind wanders back to my sister and our streaming access to Shondaland. I am dying for the next episode. I think about how many others, real and fictitious, are too.

NOTES

1. See Margaret Lock, *Twice Dead: Organ Transplants and the Reinvention of Death* (Berkeley: University of California Press, 2002).
2. See Thalia Arawi, "Using Medical Drama to Teach Biomedical Ethics to Medical Students," *Medical Teacher* 32, no. 5 (2010): e205–e210.
3. See Brian L. Quick, "The Effects of Viewing *Grey's Anatomy* on Perceptions of Doctors and Patient Satisfaction," *Journal of Broadcasting & Electronic Media* 53, no. 1 (2009): 38–55.
4. See Heather J. Hether, Grace C. Huang, Vicki Beck, Sheila T. Murphy, and Thomas W. Valente, "Entertainment-Education in a Media-Saturated Environment: Examining the Impact of Single and Multiple Exposures to Breast Cancer Storylines on Two Popular Medical Dramas," *Journal of Health Communication* 13, no. 8 (2008): 808–823.
5. See Carolyn Ellis and Arthur Bochner, "Autoethnography, Personal Narrative, Reflexivity: Researcher as Subject," in *Handbook of Qualitative Research*, ed. Norman K. Denzin and Yvonna S. Lincoln (Thousand Oaks, Calif.: Sage, 2000), 733–768.
6. See Helen Stanton Chapple, *No Place for Dying: Hospitals and the Ideology of Rescue* (Walnut Creek, Calif.: Left Coast Press, 2010).
7. See Elena Strauman and Bethany Goodier Crandell, "Not Your Grandmother's Doctor Show: A Review of *Grey's Anatomy*, *House*, and *Nip/Tuck*," *Journal of Medical Humanities* 29, no. 2 (2008): 127–131.
8. See Matthew J. Czarny, Ruth R. Faden, and Jeremy Sugarman, "Bioethics and Professionalism in Popular Television Medical Dramas," *Journal of Medical Ethics* 36, no. 4 (2010): 203–206.

9. See Matthew J. Czarny, Ruth R. Faden, Marie T. Nolan, Edwin Bodensiek, and Jeremy Sugarman, "Medical and Nursing Students' Television Viewing Habits: Potential Implications for Bioethics," *American Journal of Bioethics* 8, no. 12 (2008): 1–8.

10. See Eliana Dockterman, "Grief Counselor Says It's OK to Mourn a Fictional Character's Death," *Time*, April 29, 2015, http://time.com/3834589/grief-counselor-mourn-fictional-character-death/.

11. *Private Practice*, "Gone, Baby, Gone," season 5, episode 22, directed by Ann Kindberg, written by Shonda Rhimes, aired on May 15, 2012, on ABC.

12. *Grey's Anatomy*, "Time Has Come Today," season 3, episode 1, directed by Daniel Minahan, written by Shonda Rhimes, aired on September 26, 2006, on ABC.

13. *Grey's Anatomy*, "These Ties That Bind," season 5, episode 8, directed by Eric Stoltz, written by Shonda Rhimes, aired on November 13, 2008, on ABC.

14. See Czarny, et al., "Medical and Nursing Students' Television Viewing Habits."

15. See Michel Foucault, *The History of Sexuality* (Harmondsworth, U.K.: Penguin Books, 1992).

16. See Monica J. Casper and Lisa Jean Moore, *Missing Bodies: The Politics of Visibility* (New York: New York University Press, 2009).

17. See Rebecca Skloot, *The Immortal Life of Henrietta Lacks* (New York: Broadway Books, 2011).

18. See Karla F. C. Holloway, *Private Bodies, Public Texts: Race, Gender, and a Cultural Bioethics* (Durham, N.C.: Duke University Press, 2011).

19. Skloot, *Immortal Life*; Holloway, *Private Bodies*.

20. See Achille Mbembe, "Necropolitics," *Public Culture* 15, no. 1 (2003): 11–40.

21. See Melissa W. Wright, "Necropolitics, Narcopolitics, and Femicide: Gendered Violence on the Mexico-U.S. Border," *Signs: Journal of Women in Culture and Society* 36, no. 3 (2011): 707–731.

22. Sharon R. Kaufman, *And a Time to Die: How American Hospitals Shape the End of Life* (Chicago, Ill.: University of Chicago Press, 2005), 70.

23. *Grey's Anatomy*, "There's No I in Team," season 5, episode 5, directed by Randy Zisk, written by Jenna Bans, aired on October 23, 2008, on ABC.

24. *Grey's Anatomy*, "Good Mourning," season 6, episode 1, directed by Edward Ornelas, written by Shonda Rhimes and Krista Vernoff, aired on September 24, 2009, on ABC.

NOTES ON CONTRIBUTORS

SHADEE ABDI, PHD, is an assistant professor of communication in the College of Integrative Sciences and Arts at Arizona State University specializing in performance studies, critical cultural communication, queer of color communication, and performances of the Iranian diaspora. Her work explores how conflicting discourses complicate and enhance our intersectional understandings of identity and power relative to sexuality, race, culture, gender, nationality, religion, ability, class, and family. Specifically, her research considers how Iranian American women negotiate the complicated intersections of sexuality, identity, culture, and family. Her work has been featured in *Critical Studies in Media Communication*, the *Journal of International and Intercultural Communication*, the *Journal of Intercultural Communication Research*, and *Liminalities: A Journal of Performance Studies*.

MELISSA AMES, PHD, is an associate professor at Eastern Illinois University specializing in media studies, television scholarship, popular culture, feminist theory, and pedagogy. Her work has been published in a variety of anthologies and journals, ranging in topic from television studies, new media, and fandom to American literature and feminist art. Her most recent and forthcoming publications include her books, *Women and Language: Gendered Communication across Media* (McFarland, 2011), *Time in Television Narrative: Exploring Temporality in 21st Century Programming* (University of Mississippi Press, 2012), and *How Popular Culture Shapes the Stages of a Woman's Life* (Palgrave, 2016); chapters in *Grace under Pressure: Grey's Anatomy Uncovered* (Cambridge Scholars, 2008), *Writing the Digital Generation* (McFarland, 2010), *Bitten by Twilight: Youth Culture, Media, and the Twilight Saga* (Peter Lang, 2010); *Manufacturing Phobias* (University of Toronto Press, 2015), and *The Vampire Diaries Collection* (Scarecrow Press, 2016); and articles in the *Journal of Dracula Studies* (2011), the *Women and Popular Culture Encyclopedia* (2012), the *High School Journal* (2013), the *Journal of Popular Culture* (2014), and *Pedagogy* (2017).

LESLIE BALDERAS graduated from Barrett, the Honors College and Arizona State University (ASU) in 2016 with a bachelor of science degree in speech and hearing science. While she is applying to graduate programs, she continues to work as a newborn hearing screener and as a researcher in the auditory computation and neurophysiology laboratory at ASU, and she continues to watch all of Shonda Rhimes's shows.

JENNIFER BILLINSON, PHD, is an assistant professor of communication at Christopher Newport University. She is an expert on media studies, social and digital media, and popular music and culture. Her primary research agenda involves the ways in which media industries leverage and promote music as part of their cultural economy. Her scholarship has been published in the *Journal of Popular Music Studies* and the *Journal of Computer-Mediated Communication*.

BERNADETTE MARIE CALAFELL, PHD, is a full professor of communication studies at the University of Denver. She is author of *Latina/o Communication Studies: Theorizing Performance* and *Monstrosity, Performance, and Race in Contemporary Culture* and is coeditor with Michelle Holling of *Latina/o Discourse in Vernacular Spaces: Somos de Una Voz?*

JESSICA L. FURGERSON, PHD, is an assistant professor in communication at the University of Cincinnati Blue Ash. She received her PhD from Ohio University in 2014 where she studied rhetoric with an emphasis on feminist rhetorical methods. Her research explores the rhetoric of women's reproductive rights from both a historical and contemporary perspective.

RACHEL ALICIA GRIFFIN, PHD, is an associate professor of race and communication in the Department of Communication at the University of Utah. As a critical cultural scholar her research interests span black feminist thought, critical race theory, popular culture, sport, education, and sexual violence. From 2012 to 2015, Dr. Griffin was awarded the Judge William Holmes Cook Professorship by the Office of the Associate Chancellor for Institutional Diversity at Southern Illinois University (SIU), and in 2013, she was awarded the College of Liberal Arts Early Career Faculty Excellence Award at SIU. She was also awarded the 2015 Scholar-Activist Award by the Critical Cultural Studies Division and the 2015 Rex Crawley Outstanding Service Award by the African American Communication Division and Black Caucus via the National Communication Association. Most recently, Dr. Griffin earned the Western States Communication Association's (WSCA) 2018 Exemplary Teacher Award and a 2018–2019 Tanner Humanities Center fellowship at the University of Utah. Currently serving as the book and media review editor for *Women's Studies in Communication,* Dr. Griffin has also published in *Women's Studies in Communication, Critical Studies in Media Communication,* the *International Journal of Qualitative Studies in Education,* the *Howard Journal of Communications,* the *Journal of International and Intercultural Communication,* and *Departures in Critical Qualitative Research.*

TINA M. HARRIS, PHD, is a full professor in the department of communication studies at the University of Georgia. Her primary interest is in the area of interracial communication. She is coauthor of the textbook *Interracial Communication: Theory into Practice* (Sage, 2015) with Mark P. Orbe. Other research interests include communication and pedagogy, diversity and media representation, and race and ethnic disparities and religious frameworks in health communication. She has published many articles and book chapters on race and communication, has served as reviewer for many top-tier communication journals, and has fulfilled many service roles within the discipline, the National Communication Association, the Southern States Communication Association, and other communication organizations. She was awarded the University of Georgia's Josiah T. Meigs Teaching Professorship (highest teaching honor) and the University System of Georgia Board of Regents' (BOR) Award for the Scholarship of Teaching and Learning for her research on pedagogy and race.

MARY INGRAM-WATERS, PHD, is an honors faculty fellow and senior lecturer at Barrett, the Honors College, Arizona State University (ASU), where she teaches courses in fan cultures and social media studies. She directs the fantasy sports working group at ASU, which maintains an active research agenda, and speaks to local and national media on all social aspects of fantasy sports fans. She has published on fan cultures in *Transformative Works and Cultures, Cultures in Conversation*, and audiences' use of social media spaces in *Sexualities*.

RICHARD G. JONES JR., PHD, is an associate professor of communication studies at Eastern Illinois University where he also serves as the director of public speaking. Dr. Jones conducts research on how people communicate and perform intersecting identities in various contexts. He is also a scholar and teacher of communication pedagogy and author of the textbook *Communication in the Real World* published by Flat World Knowledge (2013).

JOAN FABER MCALISTER, PHD, is an associate professor of rhetoric, media, and social change at Drake University. An award-winning scholar and former editor of *Women's Studies in Communication*, McAlister's research focuses on the relationship between rhetoric and social location, with particular attention to how subjects are positioned in networks of power and by markers of identity in daily life. Dr. McAlister's essays have analyzed the visual and spatial rhetoric of film, television, magazines, and architecture through many different cultural texts, and have been published in a variety of journals and edited collections in the field of communication studies.

MICHAELA D. E. MEYER, PHD, is a full professor of communication and academic director of undergraduate research and creative activity at Christopher Newport University in Virginia. She is an identity scholar primarily interested in the intersections between communication, culture, media, and interpersonal relationships. In particular, her work interrogates the complicated and complex interactions between media representation and audience reception. Dr. Meyer's scholarship has received recognition from the National Communication Association's LGBTQ Division and Ethnography Division, the Organization for the Study of Communication, Language and Gender, and the Modern Language Association. In 2013, she received the Randy Majors Memorial Award recognizing outstanding scholarly contributions to lesbian, gay, bisexual, queer, and transgender scholarship in communication. She is the author of over fifty academic publications appearing in outlets such as *Sexuality & Culture*, the *Journal of Bisexuality*, *Women's Studies: An Interdisciplinary Journal*, *Feminist Media Studies*, *Review of Communication*, *Communication Quarterly*, *Communication Studies*, and the *International and Intercultural Communication Annual*.

MARK P. ORBE, PHD, is a full professor of communication and diversity in the School of Communication at Western Michigan University where he holds a joint appointment in the gender and women's studies program. An internationally known educator, author, and consultant/trainer, his teaching and research interests center on the inextricable relationship between culture and communication as played out in a number of contexts (intrapersonal, interpersonal, intergroup, mass media). Dr. Orbe has served as the secretary-general for the World Communication Association and past editor of the *Journal of Intergroup Relations* and the *International and Intercultural Communication Annual*.

JADE PETERMON, PHD, is a visiting assistant professor in the Black World Studies department at Miami University. She received her PhD in film and media studies from the University of California–Santa Barbara in 2014. She is currently working on her book *Hyper(in)visibility: Reading Race and Representation in the Neoliberal Era*, which traces the visibility of radicalized subjectivities across several media platforms in the era of neoliberalism.

VINCENT PHAM, PHD, is an assistant professor of civic communication and media at Willamette University. He is coauthor of *Asian Americans and the Media* (Polity Press, 2009) and coeditor of the *Routledge Companion to Asian American Media* (Routledge, 2017). He specializes in critical and theoretical analysis of media representations and public discourse as they are constructed by or affect the Asian American community, specifically focusing on the intersections of race, rhetoric, and media organizations.

SEAN SWENSON is a doctoral candidate in the Department of Communication at the University of South Florida. His research interests include critical cultural studies, autoethnography, medical anthropology, and gender and sexuality in film and television. His dissertation project looks at end-of-life ethics on *Grey's Anatomy*.

EMILY VAJJALA is a doctoral student at Southern Illinois University at Carbondale. She is studying gender, sexuality, and critical pedagogy.

MYRA WASHINGTON, PHD, is an assistant professor of communication at the University of New Mexico. Her work looks primarily at the representations of mixed-race bodies in popular culture and, by extension, the interracial relationships that produce those multiracial subjects. Through critical cultural and media studies lenses which frame her analyses, she uses an intersectional approach to account for the ways race, gender, sexuality, class, and nation inform the production, reception, and representation of each other. While she mainly examines these representations on television shows and films, her research also includes digital media analyses of race and representation.

STEPHANIE L. YOUNG, PHD, is an associate professor of communication studies at the University of Southern Indiana. She received her PhD from Ohio University in 2009. She has published in a number of scholarly journals including the *Journal of International and Intercultural Communication, Women's Studies in Communication,* and *Departures in Critical Qualitative Research* and is coauthor of the textbook *Pursuing Popular Culture: Methods for Researching the Everyday.* Her research interests lie at the intersection of rhetorical studies, race/ethnic studies, and feminist scholarship, focusing primarily on how popular culture texts discursively construct race, gender, and sexuality.

INDEX

ABC (American Broadcasting Company), 25, 42, 101, 120, 158; and diversity, 103, 116, 121, 159; and hashtags, 198, 202–207; and LGBTQ, 135n38; ABC Music Lounge, 83–84, 91, 94; and Shondaland production company, 28, 75, 206, 209; and "Thank God It's Thursday" (TGIT), 23, 215

abortion, 60–75, 90–91, 138; abortion experiences, 73–74; anti-abortion, 61; anti-choice, 61; and doctors, 61, 64, 66–74, 90; National Abortion and Reproductive Rights Action League, 61; pro-abortion, 62–64, 69, 74; pro-choice, 63, 67, 69, 72, 74; pro-life, 67–72, 74. See also children; mothers; Planned Parenthood; pregnancy; reproductive rights; Roe v. Wade

abuse, 46–48, 51–52, 54–55, 67, 89, 150, 167, 218

African Americans: and Black Lives Matter, 179–181, 185; female fans, 197, 199, 201, 205–206, 210; and niche programming, 101–102, 193; representations of, 111, 134, 140, 193, 216; viewers, 185, 189–193, 195n29, 226. See also characters; stereotypes; tropes; women

agendas: liberal, 187; personal, 188; political, 62, 187–188

analog, 5

analyses: of audiences, autoethnographic, 193, 237, 250; of bisexuality, 133; class, 121; close, 28, 105, 139, 142; discursive, 105; polysemic, 192; of race, 121, 132, 139, 158–159, 167, 169–170, 181; of social television, 202, 204, 207, 209; of soundtracks, 85, 93, 102; of televised abortion, 61–62, 75; textual, 105, 139, 142; thematic, 181–183, 191, 202; of Twitter, 216–220, 230

Asian Americans, 138–140, 143, 145, 151–152. See also characters; stereotypes; tropes; women

assimilation, 105, 132–133, 142, 146

audiences, 73–74, 81–82; and acceptability, 67, 69, 219, 223; alliances, 43, 54, 62, 69, 89, 237, 239, 244–245, 249; engagement, 80–81, 197,

209, 214–216; and music, 81–82, 86, 89–90; and normativity, 120–122, 127, 132, 163; perceptions, 62, 121, 156, 183, 192, 217, 250; and race, 102–105, 112, 114, 122, 139, 141–144, 163–164, 168; reactions, 159, 168–169, 180–183, 185, 189, 191, 229, 239; segregated, 111–112; and social media, 28, 209, 216, 230; sovereignty, 3, 12–13; studies, 12. See also fans

auteurs, 25–26, 28, 61, 75, 80, 85, 91, 93–94; auteur theory, 5, 26

autonomy, 67, 130, 242

Bailey, Miranda, 38, 112, 131, 140, 244. See also *Grey's Anatomy*

Bakhtinian, 23–24, 31

Ballard, Jake, 32, 158, 162, 166, 202; Scott Foley, 204. See also *Scandal*

bamboo ceiling, 148, 155n64

Beers, Betsy, 27, 72, 198. See also Shondaland production company

bigotry, 43, 49, 51, 56–57, 230

binaries, 89, 125, 158, 186; black/white, 5, 107, 122, 149–150, 158, 218; dichotomies, 158; exception/rule, 43–44, 48; heterosexual/homosexual, 122, 124; traitor/whore, 122, 128; us/them dichotomy, 107; virgin/whore dichotomy, 122–123, 128

biopower, 242–243. See also Foucauldian

bisexuality, 52, 104, 120–127, 131–134, 227–230; biphobia, 124, 126–127, 132; pedagogy of bisexuality, 121, 126, 131, 133–134; and primitivism, 130, 133. See also sexuality

black: antiblack, 107, 166, 179–180; audiences, 104–105, 112, 114, 158; black card, 191; blackness, 105–107, 109–112, 115–116, 148, 150–151, 156, 164–166, 168, 170, 180; black-produced, 101–103, 105–106, 110–112, 114; casts, 102, 105, 111–112; characters, 52, 102, 112–113, 115; representations of, 105–106, 109, 163–164, 243; showrunners, 102–103, 112, 161, 201; shows, 102, 105, 111. See also African Americans; binaries; people of color; race; racism; women

Black Lives Matter, 49, 197; #BlackLivesMatter, 179–180, 188, 191. *See also* African Americans

bodies, 23, 34, 44, 104, 164, 241, 245, 249; and biopower, 242–244; patients', 27, 238, 239; women's, 92, 122, 164, 169

boundaries, 49, 75; blurring, 201, 209, 240; pushing, 37, 85

Burke, Preston, 29, 65, 86, 112, 139–140, 143, 148; Isaiah Washington, 112. See also *Grey's Anatomy*

Bush, George H. W., 108, 110

Bush, George W., 109–110, 114

carnival, 24–31, 33–38; and base corporeality, 25, 30–31, 33; carnival bodies, 25, 28; carousel, 29, 31, 38; crowning/uncrowning, 24, 30, 32; degeneration/regeneration cycle, 24–25, 28–38; and excess, 23–25, 27–28, 30, 33–37; non-carnival, 24; ritual spectacle, 24–25, 30, 37. *See also* Bakhtinian

casting, 26, 38, 114, 127, 139, 140–141, 158–160, 229; blind-casting, 27, 160–161. *See also* colorblindness

CBS (Columbia Broadcast System), 8, 101, 170n1, 181

characters: Asian American, 139–140, 145, 148, 151, 154n33; black, 52, 102, 112–113, 115, 121, 149, 180, 229; Chicana/o/x, 128–129; of color, 112–114, 116, 133, 139, 141–142, 160–161; complex, 38, 44, 132, 138; developed, 113, 120–121, 139, 142; flawed, 28, 52, 56; Latina/o/x, 82, 120–121, 127, 131–133; multidimensional, 120–121, 160; relatable, 26–28, 47, 193, 217; queer, 120–121, 123–125, 131, 133–134, 135n38, 229, 243; underdeveloped, 113; white, 112, 139, 145, 147, 149, 170, 229

Chicana/o/x, 122–124, 128, 135n17; machismo, 47, 130–131; marianismo, 131; *mestizaje*, 122–123

children: childbearing, 64, 66, 70, 74; childbirth, 31; childhood, 31, 218; childless, 50; childrearing, 66, 111; desire for, 51, 54, 63, 65–66; grandchildren, 129, 130. *See also* abortion; mothers; Planned Parenthood; pregnancy; reproductive rights; *Roe v. Wade*

civil rights, 55, 108–110, 115, 157, 179; post-civil rights, 113, 161

class, 93, 105–106, 110, 121, 122, 127, 133, 163, 169, 181; classism, 51; classist, 89, 169; disparity, 52, 73, 110; middle-to-upper class, 82; upper-class, 121, 133; working-class, 44; working class, 108. *See also* analyses; privilege

Clinton, William J., 108–110

colorblindness: colorblind casting, 27, 85, 102–103, 112, 114, 140–142, 159; as fairness, 107–108; multicultural colorblindness, 102, 105–107, 109, 112, 114–116; and racism, 108, 112–113, 141–144, 156, 160, 162–166, 170, 180, 190, 192–194. *See also* ideologies; multiculturalism; postracial

critical/cultural studies, 2–3, 5–9, 12

critical media studies, 62, 104, 197

critical race theory, 122, 191

critical television studies, 5, 103, 237

cultural: ambiguity, 104; commentary, 14, 85, 90, 209, 226; differences, 105, 143; memory, 87, 115; moment, 2–3, 104; norms, 42, 45, 163; power, 201, 209–210; space, 4, 85, 209; specificity, 102, 112, 116, 140; values, 46, 214, 226–227, 230. *See also* normativity

cultural studies, 5, 17n13, 93, 97n65

culture: black, 104, 115; dominant, 10, 181; of silence, 68; U.S. American, 43, 52, 62, 217

CW, The, 2, 8, 75, 81, 101–102, 105, 116, 209

death, 237–249; of characters, 45–46, 49, 155n73; death row, 48, 168; in degeneration/regeneration cycle, 29–33; end of life, 237, 241; in grotesque realism, 35–36; near-death, 31; and pregnancy, 71; and social movements, 179–180, 195n32; time-of-death, 87–88; and women's bodies, 92

decision making, 63, 69–70, 141, 150

deviance, 43–44, 55–56, 159; moral deviant, 107. *See also* exception; normativity; threatening

dialectics, 30, 106, 191–192

dialogue: absence of, 67–68, 72–73; confirmatory, 72–73; explanatory, 72; quoting (*see* fans); about race, 139, 144, 148, 151, 165, 188, 190–191; and Shondafication, 26; use of, 71, 85, 143, 242

digital activism, 217, 219, 230–231

digital media, 80, 93, 104

digital music, 82–84, 93–94

digitization, 5, 7, 12

discipline, 4, 122, 143, 147–148, 150

discourses: about abortions (*see* abortion); colorblind, 142, 157–163, 165–170; discursive analysis, 105; discursive space, 9; and end of life, 238, 242–243; and fans (*see* fans); hegemonic, 152; and Otherness, 229–230; postracial, 141–142, 144, 157–159, 161–163, 165–170; public, 103, 105, 143, 243; racial, 103, 105, 139, 141–142, 143, 147–148, 151; about sexuality, 121, 131, 133–134; transdiscursive, 37, 157–162, 167, 169–170. *See also* analysis; ideologies

discrimination, 51, 105, 110, 193; racial, 104, 109–111, 132, 167. *See also* racism

diversity: diversification, 62, 64, 75, 82, 108; in Hollywood, 161, 216; Institute for Diversity and Empowerment, 139; intentional, 26–27, 56, 85, 108, 114, 121, 160; portrayals of, 44, 53, 64, 121, 140, 154n33, 163; and sexuality, 227, 229–230; and Shondafication, 38, 114, 140–141, 148, 151–152, 159–161, 169–170, 227, 229–230, 243; on television, 85, 102–103, 112–114, 140–142, 151–152, 159, 161, 168, 229; in the television industry, 112, 141–142, 159

doctor-patient relationship, 149

Duquette, Denny, 29, 155n73, 240. See also *Grey's Anatomy*

emotion, 80–82, 146, 148, 183, 186, 225, 244; affect, 80; catharsis, 218; emotionality, 7, 31, 82, 85, 87, 90, 183; emotionlessness, 145–146; nostalgia, 82, 87, 94

equality, 44, 57, 108–109, 152, 157, 167, 188, 216, 230. *See also* inequality

erasure: of difference, 102, 140, 162, 229; of race, 106, 110, 142, 157, 229

ethics, 89, 214–216, 218–220, 222, 224, 233n42, 237–239, 242; ethically, 29, 50, 56, 215–219, 233n42, 237–239; unethical, 32, 46, 222, 240

exception: and rule, 43–44, 48; exceptionalism, 143, 145, 159–160, 163. *See also* deviance; threatening

excess. *See* carnival

expectations, 36–37, 46, 49, 65, 123, 187, 199, 210

families: blended, 52; family life, 48–50; kinship, 51, 109, 161, 236; and motherhood (*see* abortion); nonfamily, 223; portrayals of, 111, 121–124, 127–131, 133, 183, 186, 193; sisterhood, 52; values, 64–65

fans: collective intelligence/power, 200–201, 206–207, 209–210; crossover, 204; cultural power, 201, 209–210; dialogue with, 201, 215; and discourse, 183, 204, 230; empowerment, 197, 204; engagement, 197–199, 200–203, 206, 208–210; fandom, 198–201, 214, 235–236; interpretive communities, 11; knowledge, 200–201; labor, 201, 204, 208, 210; loyalty, 38, 204; and quoting practices, 224–226, 236; reactions, 125, 182–184, 190, 192–193, 195n29, 195n31, 215–216, 219, 226–227; self-identified, 180–182; studies, 3, 11, 13, 200–201; unpaid labor, 200–201, 204. *See also* audiences; labor; social television

feminism, 49, 121–122, 199; feminists, 108, 121–122, 124, 139, 165; postfeminist, 44, 56, 113, 161

foil, 46, 131, 224. *See also* mirror

formula, 93–94, 159, 162–163, 165, 167, 169–170, 217

Foucauldian, 243. *See also* biopower

Fox, 101–102, 112, 170n1, 191

friendship, 52, 66, 88, 120, 139, 142, 147–148, 241

funeral homes, 248

gender, 163, 199; bodies, 243; gendered ethics, 219, 222–225; gender neutral, 134n6, 135n17; and identity, 105–106, 115, 122, 124, 181, 211n7; and LGBTQ, 27, 121, 123–124; roles, 123, 145, 218–219; and Shondafication, 157, 163, 166, 169, 201. *See also* normativity

genres, 44, 46, 80–81, 90–93, 157, 231. *See also* melodramas; music; television

Grant, Fitzgerald, 32, 114, 158, 162, 179, 184, 198, 225; Tony Goldwyn, 198. See also *Scandal*

Grant, Mellie, 33, 38, 72, 91, 164–165, 198; Bellamy Young, 198. See also *Scandal*

Grey, Meredith, 38, 65, 79, 86, 112, 120, 138, 238, 247. See also *Grey's Anatomy*

Grey's Anatomy: and abortions, 61, 63–64; and carnival, 37–38; and excess, 23; and LGBTQ, 132; music on, 85–88; and race, 138–140, 151, 154n33; and real life, 235–238, 241–242, 250; and Shondafication, 79–80, 102, 112–114, 161, 215; and social media, 198–199. *See also* Bailey, Miranda; Burke, Preston; Duquette, Denny; Grey, Meredith;

Grey's Anatomy (cont.)
  Shepherd, Derek; Stevens, Izzie; Torres, Calliope (Callie); Yang, Cristina
grotesque, 25, 28, 30, 33–36; grotesque realism, 24–25, 28, 30–37. *See also* carnival

hashtags, 180, 198–200, 202–203, 205–210, 215, 219, 232n40; corporate-sponsored, 200; fan-generated, 202, 205, 207–208, 210; promoted, 200, 202, 204–205, 209–210. See also *Scandal*; social media; Twitter
health care, 73, 91, 237–239, 245, 250; disparity in, 151
hegemony, 49, 62, 90, 105–106, 114, 124, 130, 143, 149, 152, 156; counterhegemonic, 43, 45, 124. *See also* ideologies
Hemings, Sally, 164–165. *See also* Jefferson, Thomas
heroes, 43, 48–49, 115, 129, 224, 244; antiheroes, 44, 217–219, 222–224, 234n73; doctor-heroes, 240, 242, 249; sheroes, 28; superheroes, 205, 239. *See also* villains
heterotopias, 42–46, 50, 52, 55, 57; of compensation, 45; of illusion, 45; and temporality, 45–46; and spaciality, 45. *See also* homes
hierarchies, 24, 44–45, 148–149, 159; racial, 139–140, 143, 148, 150–151, 161, 169; social, 12, 24, 45, 56
Holocaust, 144
homes: and heterotopias, 43–46, 50–51, 53, 56; homemaking, 131; homewrecker, 164; Victorian, 44, 49
homophobia, 121, 126, 128, 130–131, 227; internalized, 126. *See also* sexuality
How to Get Away with Murder: broken fixers, 26–27, 29, 34–35, 37; and carnival, 34, 37; and excess, 27; and fan responses, 214–215; fixers, 23, 27–28, 32, 114, 162, 179, 218; and LGBTQ, 134, 157; music on, 84–85, 91–93; and Shondafication, 80, 103; and social media, 198–199, 202–204; vanity scene, 34, 54–55. *See also* foil; Keating, Annalise; Keating, Sam; mirror
hypervisibility, 86, 104, 109–110, 128; hyper(in)visibility, 104, 106, 108–110, 116. *See also* invisibility; tokenism; visibility

identity: Asian, 148, 151; collective, 44, 56, 201; hybrid, 121–122, 150; Korean, 149–150; and marginalization, 9, 107, 243; marker, 112, 159; negotiation, 55, 63, 121; public, 93; queer, 122–125, 127–128, 131, 227, 229, 243; racial, 116, 139, 141, 143–144, 159, 161, 163, 167, 170, 180–181, 191; of shows, 79, 81, 87, 93. *See also* fans; identity politics; intersectionality
identity politics, 44; of death, 243; and inequality, 167; intersectional, 104, 116, 157; and kinship, 51; and music, 85; postidentity politics, 163; racialized, 104, 163, 167, 229; and Shondafication, 26–27, 116, 157, 230. *See also* identity; intersectionality
ideologies: and the American Dream, 141; dominant, 37, 47, 62, 109, 127, 160, 162; ideological functions, 62; ideological rules, 25, 162; meritocratic, 140; multicultural, 105; neoliberal, 104, 106, 108; and race, 102, 104–105, 107–111, 115, 166, 169–170. *See also* hegemony; neoliberalism; postracial; white
inequality, 46, 141, 162, 167, 170, 229; racial, 108–109, 139–141, 160, 180; structural, 106, 160–162
injustice. *See* justice
interracial, 50, 52, 122, 152, 156, 158, 162, 168, 190, 229–230; color line, 50–51; friendships, 2; intimacies, 11, 156, 169–170; relationships, 114, 139, 141, 144, 149, 156–159, 162, 164–166, 168–170, 227, 230
intersectionality, 122, 129, 131, 133, 139, 181, 192, 199, 221, 229; hybrid, 124, 133, 150; identities, 102, 104, 116, 121, 130–132, 143, 150–151, 157, 181. *See also* identity; identity politics
invisibility, 45, 103–104, 110, 142, 159, 235–236, 238–239, 241, 243, 250. *See also* hypervisibility; tokenism; visibility

Jefferson, Thomas, 164–165. *See also* Hemings, Sally
justice, 49, 57, 151, 186–187, 215–216, 219–220, 224; criminal, 216; injustice, 44, 46, 48, 180, 190, 199, 222, 230; justice system, 43, 48–49, 55–57, 215–216, 219–221; restorative justice, 49; social justice, 215, 230; Supreme Court justice, 23, 203; U.S. Department of Justice, 179

Keating, Annalise, 44, 56, 92, 216; Davis, Viola, 36, 42, 44, 54, 56, 115, 199, 202, 216, 227; and LGBTQ, 134; and race, 38, 42, 199; and relationships, 158, 162; and students, 23, 34, 47, 202, 204. See also *How to Get Away with Murder*

Keating, Sam, 34, 45, 158, 162. See also *How to Get Away with Murder*

labor, 75, 235, 237, 246; emotional, 146; fan, 201, 204, 208, 210; informational, 199, 208; interpretative, 13; pedagogical, 199; unpaid, 14, 200–201. See also fans

Latina/o/x, 47, 82, 120–124, 127–133, 134n6, 171n1, 181; *Latinidad*, 123

Lear, Norman, 26, 60, 216

legal, 80, 83–84, 107, 131, 215; abortions, 60–63, 67, 69–70, 73, 75; illegal, 47, 50, 84, 89, 220, 224, 238; law students, 23, 27, 36, 47–48, 167, 203, 216, 223; legal melodrama, 23, 43–44, 52, 220, 222; legal system, 43, 48, 215, 219; legal team, 44, 47, 224, 227

legitimacy, 70, 72, 243

lesbianism, 52, 104, 120, 122–126, 128–130, 133, 148, 227–229. See also sexuality

LGBTQ/LGBTQA, 52, 104, 123, 125, 128, 132, 227, 229; storylines, 121, 133. See also sexuality

life: life and death, 85–86, 92, 237, 239, 242, 249; life support, 79; lived experience, 45, 66, 122–123, 133, 141, 241; pro-life (*see* abortion); real life, 35, 56, 61–62, 67, 113–114, 184–187, 235, 237, 239; work/life balance, 49–50. See also death

likability, 121, 218, 222; unlikability, 138, 218–219, 222. See also identity politics; palatability

liminal, 123, 200, 245, 249

locations, 105, 181, 191–193, 237. See also standpoints

male gaze, 88, 92. See also viewing

marginalization, 114, 124, 144, 243; challenges to, 37, 43, 85, 102, 169; and identity politics, 56–57, 107, 181. See also identity politics

markets, 81, 91, 101, 106, 112, 116, 127; cross marketing, 81, 92; marketing, 1, 200; market synergy, 81

melodramas: legal, 23, 43, 52, 197, 215, 219, 222, 226, 229–230; medical, 23, 69, 139, 143,

235–239, 242, 250; and music, 80–81, 85; political, 23, 179

military, 34, 129, 162, 166

mirror, 34, 43, 52–54, 89, 186, 217. See also foil; *How to Get Away with Murder*

misogyny, 43

modern, 25, 81, 87, 89, 141

monogamy, 132–133. See also promiscuity

morality: and ambiguity, 54, 222; amoral, 48, 89; challenges to, 43, 49, 52, 62, 215, 226; gendered, 224; immorality, 46, 50–51, 57, 63, 72, 107, 214–215, 218, 222, 224, 230; moral authority, 43, 64; moral compass, 50, 57, 89, 216, 218; moral high ground, 47, 168; morally permissible, 63, 67. See also normativity

mothers: motherhood, 31, 51, 63–67, 88, 116, 145–146, 148; mothering, 64–65; motherly, 113, 223–224; rejection of motherhood, 63, 66. See also abortion; children; Planned Parenthood; pregnancy; reproductive rights; *Roe v. Wade*

multiculturalism, 45, 102–107, 111–114, 140, 142, 150, 159, 230. See also colorblindness; postracial

multicultural programming, 111, 113

music, 34, 46, 57, 79–94, 109, 114–115, 183, 193; *Billboard* charts, 86, 89; iTunes, 83; musical, 24, 78, 80–89, 91, 94; musical signature, 81–82, 93; music industry, 83, 89; Napster, 82, 84; singer-songwriters, 87, 91, 94; soul music, 114–115; soundtrack, 79–81, 83–93, 96n35, 114–115, 245; and television industry, 85, 94

NAACP (National Association for the Advancement of Colored People), 101, 116, 120

narratives: abortion, 62–63, 68, 71, 74; of acceptability, 68; bootstraps, 103; coming out, 124, 130; conventional, 61, 201; counternarratives, 45, 71, 132, 169, 200, 229; degeneration/regeneration (*see* carnival); dramatic, 44, 49; fixed identity, 129; gay white male, 129, 133; generic, 46; and music, 80–81, 84–85, 87–90, 92–94, 95n14; progress narratives, 110, 121, 130, 133; Willie Horton, 108. See also abortion; colorblindness; plotlines; postracial; storylines

Nazi, 113, 143–144
NBC (National Broadcasting Company), 101, 111
necropolitics, 14–15, 243
neoliberalism, 103–112, 114, 116, 141; and appropriation, 104
neo-platoon, 140
network television, 25, 37, 50, 84–85, 101, 105, 110–112, 120, 138–140, 215; post-network era, 28, 215. *See also* ABC; CBS; The CW; Fox; NBC; UPN; WB; prime-time television; television
normativity: abnormal, 127, 183–184; acceptability, 24, 27, 35, 62–64, 67–69, 75, 132–133, 148, 168, 226; and audiences, 111, 121; challenges to, 61–62, 75, 132, 148, 184, 199, 215, 230, 242; and deviance, 43–44, 55, 62–63; double standards, 218–219, 222; heteronormativity, 66, 120, 124, 126, 132–133; homonormativity, 121, 126, 128, 130, 133–134; industry norms, 61, 63, 69–70, 73–75, 82, 115, 139; normalization, 116, 134, 142, 147, 216, 229; social norms, 37, 43, 45; unacceptability, 112, 168–169; and Victorian sensibilities, 89; and whiteness (*see* whiteness). *See also* palatability; sexuality; television
Nowalk, Peter, 54, 91–92, 167, 216, 228. *See also* Shondaland production company

Obama, Barack, 110, 187, 205–206
objectification, 102, 104, 169
oppression, 44, 49, 103–104, 107, 110, 123, 133, 148, 157, 165–167. *See also* justice

palatability, 103, 111, 121–122, 127, 131, 133, 217, 230. *See also* likeability
patriarchy, 61, 123, 126, 129, 131, 133–134, 148, 229
pedagogy, 85, 199, 215–216, 225–230; public pedagogy, 215, 219, 225–226, 230. *See also* bisexuality; labor
people of color, 108, 165, 222, 229; exclusion of, 101–103, 159–160, 163, 189; inclusion of, 102, 108, 112, 115–116, 140–142, 152, 161, 216; queers of color (*see* queer)
"person", 88, 139
personhood, 107. *See also* subjectivity
Planned Parenthood, 6, 61, 72–73, 91. *See also* abortion; children; mothers; reproductive rights; *Roe v. Wade*

platforms, 13, 83, 186–189, 194. *See also* social media
plotlines: abortions, 60, 62; carnival, 30–31; romantic, 32, 162, 207. *See also* narratives; storylines
pluralist, 105
politics: class, 133; colorblind, 108; as complex of relations, 45, 52, 56, 69–70, 90, 121, 148, 222, 229, 243; cultural, 106; as government, 23, 38, 89, 108, 185, 193, 197, 210; of interracial relationships, 144; likeability, 121, 218, 222; queer, 10, 121, 229; racial, 229, 243; respectability, 9, 133, 185; survivalist, 57; unlikability, 138, 218–219, 222. *See also* identity politics; queer
polysemy, 13, 192–194. *See also* radical
Pope, Olivia, 23, 28, 197; and abortions, 60; and gladiators, 34; Kerry Washington, 184, 197, 201; and LGBTQ; and race, 38, 88, 114, 179, 185–186, 191, 219, 222; and relationships, 32, 157–158, 162, 184, 202. *See also Scandal*
postidentity. *See* identity
postmodern, 5, 12
postracial: colorblindness, 103–104, 139–144, 147–148, 151, 156–159, 161, 163–166, 170; desire, 106; discourses (*see* discourses); fantasy, 44; ideologies (*see* ideologies); myths, 103, 157; post-race, 110; postracialism, 102, 107–108, 110, 116, 139, 141–142, 151, 161–162; postraciality, 110, 168–170; rhetoric, 106, 111, 151, 157; society, 106, 111, 152, 156; strategies, 139–140, 149; world, 141, 144, 148. *See also* discourses; identity
poverty, 105, 108–109
power: collective (*see* fans); disempowerment, 150, 162; dynamics, 38, 104, 152, 204, 208, 215, 219, 230, 237; empowerment, 35, 72, 88, 134, 169, 197, 199–200, 204, 226; fans' (*see* fans); positions of, 113, 199; the powerful, 24, 49; powerhouse, 23, 37, 84, 116, 225; relations, 149, 157, 181, 197, 200; speak truth to power, 9, 57; structures, 52, 158, 200; in television, 105, 209; those in/ with power, 24, 30, 37–38, 49, 113, 193. *See also* cultural; fans
pre-digitization, 94
pregnancy, 25, 31, 51, 53, 60–61, 63–66, 71–72, 74–75, 90, 240; unplanned, 60–61, 64–65,

74–75, 90, 145; false, 62, 65. *See also*
abortion; children; mothers; Planned
Parenthood; reproductive rights; *Roe v.
Wade*
prime-time television: and abortions, 60,
62, 66, 69, 75; and bisexuality, 125; and
industry practices, 75; and music, 79–80,
85; and race, 42, 101, 105, 110–112, 158, 162;
and Shondafication, 23, 26, 35, 37, 103, 115.
See also network television; television
prisons, 51, 108–109; imprisonment, 49, 109,
164; prison industrial complex, 109
Private Practice: and abortions, 63–64, 68–70,
72–73, 75; and *Grey's Anatomy*, 30, 61,
236–237, 239–241, 243–245, 250; and music,
87; and Shondafication, 102. *See also*
abortion; *Grey's Anatomy*
privilege: class, 121, 122; privileged audiences,
57, 82; privileged figures, 48–49; privileged
groups, 24, 42, 44, 181, 199, 243; racial, 122,
130, 157, 159, 181, 199; social, 46, 115, 121, 181,
185, 221. *See also* white
producers: and auteur theory, 26; and Beers,
Betsy, 72, 198; coproducer, 197; as
decision makers, 200, 237, 240; and Lear,
Norman, 60; and Nowalk, Peter, 54; and
race, 160–161, 189; and Rhimes, Shonda,
26, 140, 160, 196; and Shondaland
production company, 23, 26; and social
media, 197–201, 204, 208–209, 215, 228;
television, 60, 81–82, 197. *See also* Beers,
Betsy; Lear, Norman; Nowalk, Peter;
Rhimes, Shonda; Shondaland production
company; Twitter
progressive: depictions of abortions, 75;
modernism, 89; racial diversity as, 102, 104,
112, 116, 139, 151, 156, 165–166; representations, 133, 156; Shondaland production
company as, 159, 161, 170, 180
promiscuity, 46, 123, 132, 147–148. *See also*
monogamy
Promised Land, 103, 156, 164, 167, 170;
emancipation, 167
protests, 72, 179, 184, 188, 206; movement,
180; protestors, 73–74, 187, 191, 195n32

quality television. *See* television
queer, 27, 44, 51, 85, 121–124, 128–130, 133, 148,
227–229, 243; queerness, 121–123, 127–131,

134; queers of color, 121–122, 124, 128–129;
politics, 10, 121, 229. *See also* politics
quoting practices. *See* fans

race: minimization of, 106, 139–140, 142, 158,
191; mixed-race, 122–123; and narratives,
143, 151, 162, 164, 168, 170, 218; racebending,
160; race card, 165, 191, 195n33; raceless,
141–142; race-neutral, 141, 157; race-silenced,
139; relations, 107, 110, 112, 157, 162, 188, 194;
and television industry, 104, 107, 116, 141,
170. *See also* black
racial: barriers, 132, 141, 148; bias, 52;
discrimination, 109, 167; disparity, 107,
109–110; ethno-racial, 140–142; hierarchies,
161, 169 (*see also* hierarchies); inequality,
108, 139, 140–141, 160, 180–181, 188;
minorities, 44, 109; normativity, 159, 162,
168–170; passing, 160; profiling, 51, 180;
racialized beauty standards, 103; standpoints, 181, 191; storylines, 102–103, 114, 139,
142–143, 148–152, 167, 169. *See also*
colorblindness; postracial
racism: accusations of, 103, 114, 144, 165, 168,
188; antiracist, 150, 168, 170; critiques of,
141, 161, 165, 169, 199; denial of, 109, 113–114,
140–142, 151, 165, 170, 188; institutional, 108,
116, 151, 160, 170; reproduction of, 108, 150;
structural, 110, 115–116, 139, 141–142, 148, 157,
162. *See also* black; colorblindness;
discrimination; postracial; stereotypes
radical: reflexivity, 42–45, 49, 52–53, 57;
polysemy, 194; possibility, 123. *See also*
polysemy
Reagan, Ronald, 107–111
rejection: of authority, 25, 33, 35; of bisexuality, 124; of intolerance, 128; of motherhood
(*see* mothers). *See also* bisexuality
religion: Catholicism, 120–121, 126, 129–130,
133, 218; importance of, 122–123, 130;
Jewishness, 139, 142–144, 148–150, 155n73;
and music, 81; religious, 90, 122–123, 127,
131, 139, 150, 165, 254
representation: representational politics, 7–8,
10, 121; transformative representation, 156,
170
reproductive rights, 60, 68, 75. *See also*
abortion; children; mothers; Planned
Parenthood; pregnancy; *Roe v. Wade*

resistance, 43, 70, 88, 105, 115, 180, 182, 199, 204, 246

rhetoric, 61, 74, 105–112, 116, 122, 151, 214–215, 229; rhetorical, 62, 64, 68, 70, 142, 157, 193; rhetorical silencing, 129, 144

Rhimes, Shonda: as carnival master, 26, 37–38; influence of, 26, 157, 159; as a public figure, 115, 230; and race, 158–163, 168–170, 229–230; signature style, 23, 84–85, 93; *Year of Yes*, 2, 15, 115. *See also* Shondaland production company; showrunners

Roe v. Wade, 60–61, 73, 75. *See also* abortion; children; mothers; Planned Parenthood; pregnancy; reproductive rights

salience, 156, 159, 166–167, 180, 190–192, 195n33

Scandal: #DieJakeDie, 14, 198, 202, 207–210; #SaveJake?, 14, 202, 204–205, 207, 209–210

#ScandalCutOut, 202–203, 209; and abortions, 60–61, 63–64, 67, 70, 72–73, 75; and Black Lives Matter, 179–190; and carnival, 28, 32–34; and double standards, 219, 222, 225; and excess, 23, 26, 37; and fixers, 27; music on, 80, 84–85, 88–92, 94, 114–115; and race, 114–116, 157–159, 162–169, 192–193; and Shondafication, 28, 38, 159, 250; as social television, 197–204, 206–210; "The Lawn Chair" episode, 103, 179–188, 190–193; torture on, 27–28, 33–34. *See also* abortion; Ballard, Jake; Black Lives Matter; fans; Grant, Fitzgerald; Grant, Mellie; Pope, Olivia; Twitter

screen, 44, 62, 109, 142, 157, 215, 217, 246, 248; double screens, 214; offscreen, 70, 87, 94, 113, 125, 243; onscreen, 61, 79, 81, 85, 94, 132, 139; on screen, 81–82, 87, 125, 133, 139, 141, 158, 164, 170, 243; screenplay, 54; second screening, 13–14; second screen viewing, 199

Screen Actors Guild, 44, 120, 138

self-identified, 125, 180–182, 185, 189–191, 195n29

sexuality: bisexuality, 121–128, 130, 132–133; claustrophilia, 121; closeted, 32, 121, 128–129, 133, 244–245, 248; counternarratives of, 169, 227; heterosexuality, 49, 65, 82, 88; hypersexuality, 44, 50, 163–164; nonheterosexual, 52; overt, 73, 224; and/in

the workplace, 29, 36–37, 145, 147–148, 224. *See also* monogamy; morality; normativity; promiscuity

shame, 54–56, 93, 123, 143–144; and abortions, 63, 67–71; ashamed, 68, 71, 129, 227; and morality, 51, 148, 163, 227; and race, 165, 168; shameful, 70, 169, 244; slut-shaming, 148. *See also* morality; normativity

Shepherd, Derek, 29, 66, 79, 86, 112, 139, 239. See also *Grey's Anatomy*

Shondaland production company, 24, 26–27, 102, 104–105, 115–116, 120, 134, 152, 180, 192; and challenges to industry norms, 61, 63, 193; and copycatting, 37, 159, 215; and Disneyfication, 25–26; formula, 93–94, 159, 162–163, 165, 167, 169–170; and new industry standards, 157, 193, 197, 209; and music, 79–80, 82–85, 87–91, 93–94; production practices, 161; Shondaland team, 23, 134, 187, 229, 237, 241; Shondafication, 23, 25–29, 35, 37. *See also* Beers, Betsy; diversity; Nowalk, Peter; Rhimes, Shonda

showrunners, 116, 141, 209, 244; and race, 114, 158–159, 161, 170; and Rhimes, Shonda, 23–25, 80, 92–93, 103–104, 139, 159, 197, 201, 249; showrunning, 87, 104–105, 141. *See also* auteurs; Lear, Norman

social commentary, 216, 220, 225–226, 230

social justice. *See* justice

social media, 26, 28, 158, 180, 197–201, 209, 214–215, 226, 233n41; campaigns, 202, 209; Facebook, 13, 182, 190, 192, 206; platforms, 197–199, 201, 209, 215; presence, 23, 197–198. *See also* fans; Twitter

social television, 28, 199–202, 204, 206, 208–210; social television-based fandom, 200–201; and talking back, 14. *See also* fans; *Scandal*

soundtrack. *See* music

standpoints, 13, 52, 181, 191, 193; theories, 180–181, 191–192. *See also* locations

stereotypes: angry black woman, 150; Asian doctor, 146–147; controlling images, 54; disciplinarian, 113, 144, 148; Dragon Lady, 139–140, 143, 145, 147, 151; model minority, 139–140, 143, 145–148, 151; mammy, 113, 223; mammification, 113–114, 166; and music, 82; negative, 125; racist, 142; yellow peril, 145, 147; welfare queen, 107. *See also* tropes

Stevens, Izzie, 29, 65, 143, 238, 240. See also *Grey's Anatomy*

storylines: abortions, 60–62, 64–65, 67–68, 71–75; Black Lives Matter, 180, 183–187, 191, 193; death and rebirth cycle, 32; excess, 28; fan reactions to, 198, 204–208, 210, 214–215, 220, 224, 227, 230; familial, 124, 127; legal, 222; and music, 79–80, 86–88, 94; medical, 237, 239–240, 242; melodramatic, 28, 140. *See also* narratives; plotlines

strategic ambiguity, 9, 192

style, 24, 26–27, 51, 61, 80, 87, 93, 103, 129; stylistic, 61, 75, 80, 91–93, 222

subjectivity, 55, 57

subjects, 43–44, 54–56, 105–107, 158. *See also* personhood

surveillance, 36, 122, 166, 169

talking back. *See* social television

television: Big Five, 2; Big Four, 101, 111; cable, 102, 139; Hulu, 5; industry norms, 82, 139; licensing, 83, 90; Netflix, 1–2, 5, 75, 83, 161, 209, 218; Nielsen, 198, 201; production, 80, 115, 215; quality television, 2–4. *See also* audiences; critical television studies; melodramas; narratives; network television; plotlines; prime-time television; producers; social television; storylines

threatening, 51, 53, 64, 126, 143, 145, 147, 150, 166; nonthreatening, 103, 148. *See also* deviance; exception

tokenism, 49, 103, 112, 148–149, 151, 159. *See also* hypervisibility; invisibility; visibility

tone, 82, 86–87, 91–92, 109, 226, 230

Torres, Calliope (Callie), 120, 124, 132–133; Ramirez, Sara, 120. See also *Grey's Anatomy*

torture. See *Scandal*

transgressions, 35, 121, 132–133, 135n38, 162, 217, 219, 222–223

trauma, 29–31, 33, 43–44, 50, 56–57, 82, 146, 218, 240; posttraumatic, 64, 138

tropes, 44, 53, 151, 159; carnival tropes, 24–25, 28, 31, 33, 37; common/dominant, 62, 66, 125, 129, 132, 143; gendered, 130–131, 148, 164, 218; racial, 108, 114, 129, 139, 143–145,

147–148, 151, 164, 219; rejection of, 66. *See also* stereotypes

Trump, Donald, 15, 110

Tubman, Harriett, 42

Twitter, 28, 158, 197–203, 205–210, 214–215, 217, 219, 221–228, 230–231, 233n42; African American women's use of, 199, 201, 205–206; algorithms, 203, 207; critiquing tweets, 220; handles, 202, 205, 207, 209, 221, 223, 228; live-tweeting, 198–199, 201, 207–208, 210, 215–217, 219, 222, 230, 231, 233n40; retweets, 198–199, 201, 203–207, 220; and Rhimes, Shonda, 103, 125, 198; tagging, 205, 207; tweeting, 28, 198–199, 201–208, 210, 211n7, 216–217, 219–230, 232n40, 233nn42–43; trends, 207–208, 226. *See also* hashtags; *Scandal*; social media

unethical. *See* ethics

unlikability. *See* likability

upheaval, of social order, 24, 37, 47

UPN (United Paramount Network), 81, 101–102, 105, 111–112, 209

vanity scene. See *How to Get Away with Murder*

viewing: binge watching, 185, 214, 249; viewing experiences, 5, 81, 163, 192, 215; viewing practices, 14, 214–215. *See also* audiences; dialogue; male gaze

villains, 43, 49, 115, 208. *See also* heroes

visibility: and audiences, 203, 209, 233n42; exposure, 81, 86, 103; LGBTQ, 125, 128; of oppressed groups, 104; racial, 102–104, 106, 108–110, 122, 141–142, 152, 158, 161, 168; and Shonda Rhimes, 26. *See also* hypervisibility; invisibility; tokenism

WB (Warner Brothers), 81, 101–102, 111–112

white: all-white casting, 159–160, 216; femininity, 134, 219; honorary white status, 139; non-white, 123, 128, 131, 142; normativity, 141–142, 148, 158, 163, 166, 169; privilege, 107, 109, 129, 141, 149, 152, 160, 170, 189, 226; supremacist, 9, 148–150; supremacy, 104, 109, 150; whitewashing, 121, 142, 160. *See also* whiteness

White House, 32–33, 61, 110, 163, 166, 179, 193, 250. See also *Scandal* whiteness, 113, 130, 148, 150–151; benefit of, 116, 141, 157, 160, 163, 226; corruption of, 156, 164; ideologies of, 109, 116, 134, 142–143, 160, 229; markers of, 127; and postracial colorblindness, 141–142, 151, 161, 164, 166, 168–170; proximity to, 120–121, 124, 132–133, 160; surveillance of, 122. *See also* white

whore, 163–164, 168. *See also* binaries

wokeness, 9, 159

women: and abortions (*see* abortion); African American, 37, 55, 134, 140, 143, 190, 192–193, 197, 199, 201, 205–206; Asian American, 138–140, 143, 145, 147; of color, 27, 109, 131, 138–141, 143–144, 147, 150, 163, 180, 224, 230, 243; dark-skinned black women, 36, 227, 229; and interracial coupling, 156–158, 162–164, 166, 168–170; marginalization of, 37; and morality, 217–218, 222, 224–225, 233n49; queer women of color, 123, 128, 133–134, 229; raceless, 142; womanhood, 9, 44, 65, 168–169. *See also* families; hypervisibility; labor; stereotypes; Twitter; white

Yang, Cristina: and abortions, 61, 64, 75; and race, 138, 140, 143, 151; and relationships, 29, 86, 112, 128, 132; Sandra Oh, 87, 138, 151. See also *Grey's Anatomy*